From *Ad Hoc* to Routine

University of Pennsylvania Press

MIDDLE AGES SERIES

Edited by Edward Peters
Henry Charles Lea Professor
of Medieval History
University of Pennsylvania

A complete listing of the books in this series
appears at the back of this volume

From *Ad Hoc* to Routine

A Case Study in Medieval Bureaucracy

Ellen E. Kittell

upp

University of Pennsylvania Press

Philadelphia

Library of Congress Cataloging-in-Publication Data
Kittell, Ellen E.
     From ad hoc to routine : a case study in medieval bureaucracy /
Ellen E. Kittell.
         p.   cm. — (Middle Ages series)
     Includes bibliographical references and index.
     ISBN 0-8122-3079-5
     1. Finance, Public—Belgium—Flanders—History.   2. Bureaucracy—
Belgium—Flanders—History.   3. Belgium—History—To 1555.
I. Title.   II. Series.
HJ1199.F55K58   1991
336.493'1—dc20   90-47800
                                                       CIP

Contents

Acknowledgments

WITHOUT THE ARCHIVAL WORK made possible by a Fulbright grant to Belgium in 1980–1981 and without the expertise of such scholars as Adriaan Verhulst and Walter Prevenier of the Rijksuniversiteit at Ghent, this study would not have been possible. I would also like to express my thanks to Jean Baerten of the Vrij Universiteit van Brussel for providing me with an excellent background in medieval history and in paleography and Sheila Page Bayne of the Fulbright Commission in Brussels, Belgium, for enabling my research in Belgium to go smoothly. I owe a debt of gratitude, as well, to many archivists and librarians, notably those in the Rijksarchief of Ghent and the archives of the Département du Nord in Lille.

It gives me particular pleasure to offer my thanks to the many people who gave generously of their time to help me put this manuscript together. Lynn Campbell and Timmi Duchamp patiently read the whole manuscript and offered helpful comments and criticisms. Tom Brady and Cynthia Brokaw, both of the University of Oregon, read parts of the revision. They, too, generously offered valuable criticism. Perhaps even more important, Tom gave me the courage to stand behind my arguments and Cynthia gave me the encouragement of someone who was going through the same process at the same time. I am especially indebted to Bryce Lyon, whose expert criticism enabled me to transform a dissertation into a book. Grammatical coherence is due principally to the unflagging efforts of Kurt Queller; Ruth Kittell checked the French in the Bibliography; Walter Simons kept an eye on the Dutch and on historical facts; and Albert Scheven drew the map. If any errors or inconsistencies remain, they are entirely of my own devising. I would further like to thank Roger Cuniff of San Diego State University for his technical assistance, and Steve Balzer for the use of his computer. Finally perhaps the greatest debts of gratitude I owe are to my father, Allan Kittell, for inspiring in me a love of history, to Yvette Scheven, for providing the peace of mind necessary for completion of the work, and to Donald E. Queller, who started me on this study and who saw me through it. This book is dedicated with love and remembrance to Marilyn Queller.

Note on Place Names

FLANDERS, LIKE BELGIUM, the modern-day country which encompasses most of the medieval county, suffers from the problem of multi-lingual referents to various places. In order to avoid confusion and to provide a basis for consistency, I have chosen as a rule to use Flemish names for communities located in present-day Flemish-speaking sections and French names for communities located in present-day French-speaking sections. The exceptions to this rule are towns for which the English historical tradition has assigned English names.

Below are listed the names of the major towns of medieval Flanders as they appear in Flemish, French, and, when appropriate, English. The versions used throughout my text are marked with an asterisk.

FLEMISH	FRENCH	ENGLISH
Brugge	Bruges	*Bruges
Dowai	*Douai	
Kortrijk	Courtrai	*Courtrai
Gent	Gand	*Ghent
Ieper	Ypres	*Ypres
Rijsel	*Lille	

Below are the names of the towns and communities that appear in Vane Guy's *repertorium* of payments of the Transport of Flanders (see chapters 5 and 6). On the right are listed the names as they are currently known; most of these are in Flemish. On the left appear the names by which they appear in the *repertorium;* most of these are in French, probably because the official who drew up the list was a French-speaker. Some of these communities overlap. There is no indication why the Transport payments were apportioned to these particular communities. Some of them are no more than hamlets. (I would like to thank Walter Simons for all his help in this matter.)

REPERTORIUM VANE GUY (1336)	CURRENT
Alost	Aalst
Alost castellany	Aalst castellany
Ardembourg	Aardenburg
Audenarde	Oudenaarde
Audenarde castellany	Oudenaarde castellany
Bailleul	Bailleul
Berghes	Bergues
Berghes castellany	Bergues castellany
Grammont	Geraardsbergen
Beveren	Beveren
Beveren parish	Beveren parish
Beveren lordship	Beveren lordship
Blankenbourg	Blankenberge
Bourbourg	Bourbourg
Bourbourg territory	Bourbourg territory
Bourchete	Burcht
Bruges	Bruges
Calodam	Kallo
Cassel	Cassel
Cassel territory	Cassel territory
Coudenberg	Coudenberg
Courtrai	Courtrai
Courtrai castellany	Courtrai castellany
Crubeek	Kruibeke
Damme	Damme
Dascoot	Aarschot
Diksmuide	Dixmude
Dunquerque	Dunkirk
Ecluse	Sluis
Exarde	Eksaarde
Franc of Bruges	Franc of Bruges
Franc Métiers	(now part of Bruges)
Furnes	Veurne
Furnes territory	Veurne territory
Gand	Ghent
Ghistelles	Gistel
Gravelinghes	Gravelines

Havesdonc	Haasdonk
Houke	Hoeke
Hughesvliete	Hugevliet
Kielrecht	Kieldrecht
La Monekerede	Monnikerede
La Mue	Sint-Anna-ter-Muide
Lancardembourg	Langaardenburg
Lo	Lo
Lombardie	Lombardsijde
Mardike	Mardyck
Masumies	Massemen
Noefport	Nieuwpoort
Oostbourg	Oostburg
Ostende	Oostende
Oudenbourg	Oudenburg
Poperinghe	Poperinghe
Pombeek	Pumbeke
Quatre Métiers	Vier Ambachten
Roulers leis Ardembourg	Roeselare bij Aardenburg
Rupelmonde	Rupelmonde
Saint-Niklaas	Sint-Niklaas
Sotteghem	Zottegem
Termonde	Dendermonde
Thamise	Temse
Thourout	Torhout
Verrebrouk	Verrebroek
Waes	Land of Waas
Warneston	Warneton
Waterduinen	Waterdune
Ypres	Ypres
Ypres castellany	Ypres castellany
Ysendike	Ijzendijke

Abbreviations

ARA RK	Brussels, Algemeen Rijksarchief. Rekenkamer.
Bl. nr.	Bruges, Rijksarchief, Charters met blauw nummer.
Chron. sup.	Ghent, Rijksarchief, Chronologisch supplement.
Codex	*Codex Diplomaticus inde ab anno 1296 ad usque 1325* edited by T. Limburg-Stirum.
Gaillard	Ghent, Rijksarchief, Fonds Gaillard.
HKCG	*Handelingen van de Koninklijke Commissie voor Geschiedenis. (Bulletin de la commission royale d'histoire.)*
Nord B	Lille, Archives départementales du Nord. Série B.
Pol. chrs.	Bruges, Stadsarchief, Fonds Politiek Charters. Reeks 1.
RBPH	*Revue belge de philologie et d'histoire.*
RR	Brussels, Algemeen Rijksarchief, Rekenkamer. Rolrekeningen.
St. Baaf	Ghent, Rijksarchief, Bisdom Sint Baafsabdij.
St.-Genois	Ghent, Rijksarchief, Fonds Saint-Genois.
St. van Vl.	Ghent, Rijksarchief, Staten van Vlaandren, #1349.
Van Duyse and de Busscher	Ghent, Stadsarchief, Fonds Van Duyse et de Busscher.

CURRENCY:

g.t.	grossus denarius turonensis
l.b.	livres de blans
l.f.	libra flandrensis
l.p.	libra parisiensis
l.s.	libra esterlinga
l.t.	libra turonensis

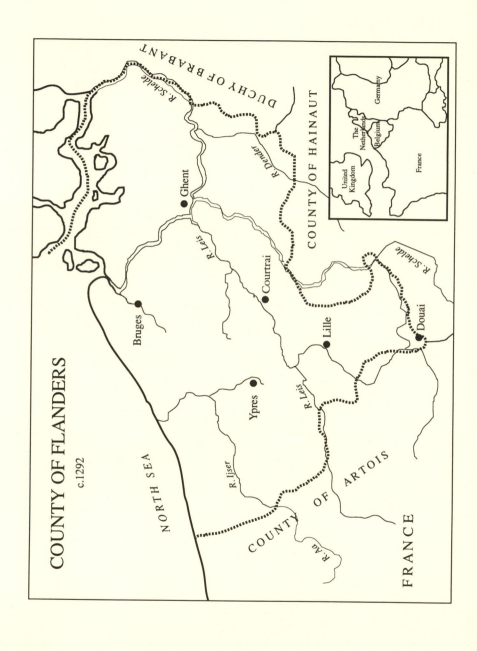

COUNTY OF FLANDERS
c.1292

NORTH SEA

Bruges

Ghent

Ypres

Courtrai

Lille

Douai

R. Schelde

R. Leis

R. Dender

R. Leis

R. Leis

R. Ijser

R. Aa

R. Schelde

DUCHY OF BRABANT

COUNTY OF HAINAUT

COUNTY OF ARTOIS

FRANCE

United Kingdom

The Netherlands

Germany

Belgium

France

1. Introduction

ONE OF THE MOST IMPORTANT developments in the High Middle Ages was the emergence of those institutions we now recognize as constitutive of the modern state. Such institutions evolved as the means by which a prince implemented the principle that his own interests superseded local ones. The household administration which characterized most European princely governments in the twelfth and thirteenth centuries was initially geared to the day-to-day management of the prince's personal needs. But as princes tightened and extended their authority over territories and peoples beyond their original domains, the household was called upon to take on a more complicated burden than it had customarily handled. Demands became more constant and increasingly complex, and princely households evolved routines out of the *ad hoc* measures that princes took to realize their political ambitions. As procedures became systematic, discrete areas of specialization, usually in the fields of finance or justice, began to take on a somewhat independent status with regard to each other and to the prince's household. In this way the bases were laid for the formation of administrative offices, such as the general receivership of Flanders.

Conventional wisdom, based primarily on the examples of the Holy Roman Empire and Italy, suggests that the foundations for the modern state would be most difficult to establish in those areas with large and numerous urban centers. (A town's economic and commercial success, after all, was frequently proportional to its ability to maintain its privilege against lordly encroachment.) In terms of such conventional thinking, the medieval county of Flanders was an anomaly. Flemish comital administration grew commensurately with the continual efforts of Flemish counts to find new ways to exploit the growing prosperity of the Flemish cities. With the commercial revolution, Flanders became one of the most urbanized and industrialized societies in the Middle Ages.[1] The county's prosperity was based chiefly, but not exclusively, on the woolen textiles which its many towns produced. The cloth of Ypres, for example, was well-known and valued as far away as Russia.[2] Moreover, Flanders's fortunate geographical location on the English Channel between England, France, Brabant, Holland, and the Holy Roman Empire, placed it at the center of many international trade routes. Items as diverse as wheat, wood, furs, spices, and alum appeared in the markets. Ghent, the second largest city in northern Europe, was particularly noted as a center of the grain trade, as well as for the quantity and quality of its cloth, while few Italian banking firms neglected to establish branch offices in Bruges.[3]

Although predominantly a commercial and urban society, Flanders successfully went through a process of state-building similar to that of other larger and less urbanized principalities, notably England and France.[4] The impetus and capacity to centralize manifested itself in the development of financial, judicial, and secretarial institutions such as the *Chambre des comptes* and *Parlement* in France, and the extension of common law machinery and Exchequer in England.[5] To what extent princes borrowed administrative strategies and practices from one another, and to what degree developments in one region influenced developments in another, is difficult to determine. It could be argued that the central location of Flanders made it particularly receptive to the influence of administrative developments taking place nearby. Equally, it can be argued that Flemish administrative advances, particularly in the financial realm, provided models which neighboring territories more or less adapted to their own needs and circumstances. It is not my intention, however, to compare Flemish financial developments with those of contiguous territories, but rather to analyze the process by which administrative developments were achieved in Flanders and what they contributed to the development of a Flemish state. By the late fourteenth century, the count's government had developed to the point where it was identifiable also as the county's government.

The significance of state-building in Flanders lies in the success of its counts' efforts to bring the county within their control, chiefly by means of an administrative apparatus. The peculiarly advanced society and economy of medieval Flanders presented unique problems and opportunities for the centralized development and management of state revenues. The early growth of towns, industry, and commerce in medieval Flanders, particularly during the thirteenth and fourteenth centuries, in certain respects foreshadowed similar developments elsewhere in Europe during the fifteenth and sixteenth centuries. Since the late twelfth century, Flemish comital government had been fiscally precocious. Indeed, the interaction of feudal institutions with bourgeois economic expansion presents modern scholarship with unparalleled material for understanding the emergence of administrative state institutions.

The General Receivership as a Central Administrative Office

Centralized government in Flanders emerged out of an increasingly complex relationship between political needs and administrative solutions. Measures taken by thirteenth- and fourteenth-century counts[6] to realize their territorial ambitions, to combat French intervention, to recover from the devastation of the Black Death and the Hundred Years War, and to extend their political control over the stubbornly independent Flemish communities resulted initially in only immediate and *ad hoc* solutions to their problems. But these solutions, combined with already existing management practices, however rudimentary, provided the basis for the establishment of administrative procedures.

The gradual evolution of the general receivership, the first central bureaucratic office in the county, provides an excellent illustration of this process. The Flemish general receivership was unlike similar offices in other medieval Western European territories in that it did not emerge as a consequence of the prior development of a general financial bureau or department. Instead, the office of general receiver gradually evolved from within the count's household as successive counts, attempting to achieve control over their finances, confided particular financial responsibilities exclusively and consistently to specific individuals. In Flanders, it was the general receivership that served as a point of departure for the development of a financial department. Previously, only officials having local jurisdiction on a permanent basis enjoyed competence in a specific sphere and were thus identifiable principally as specific officials and not as particular persons. In contrast, individuals exercising county-wide jurisdiction did so in a variety of capacities, each, however, on a one-time basis. As household members, they had no specific competence and who they were was much more important than what they did. In effect, the general receivership in the thirteenth century was an "office" of the latter sort; though its purview was county-wide, the office itself consisted of little more than a loose set of functions assigned on a discretionary basis by the count to any convenient member of his household. By the late fourteenth century, the general receiver held an office[7] that had developed into a true central administrative position with specific competence for a coherent, well-organized set of tasks, yet with jurisdiction over the entire principality.

Overview of Flemish History 1262 to 1372

The years 1262 to 1372, critical for the development of the general receivership, were turbulent ones. The two principal threads which run throughout Flemish history during these years are the tensions between the count and the Flemish communities[8] and the intervention of the French in Flemish affairs.

The thirteenth century was a period of economic success and corresponding prosperity for the Flemish communities. As they prospered, the communities experienced growing civic autonomy vis-à-vis the count as well as each other. But the thirteenth century also witnessed the development of central administrative structures by means of which the counts increased their own authority throughout the county, frequently at the expense of the Flemish communities. It was essentially the clash between these two forces that determined the shape and form of fourteenth-century Flemish history. Although the conflict ultimately ended in victory for the count—one of the few occasions where a prince succeeded in incorporating and subordinating highly developed urban communities under his or her leadership—the outcome was not inevitable. Nor was it without a price; when Louis of Male died in 1384, his county was wracked by a series of civil rebellions directed against him.

Throughout the thirteenth and fourteenth centuries, the county of Flanders retained much of the semi-autonomous status it had enjoyed since the eleventh century, despite the count's ties of vassalage to the king of France. French interference in external and internal Flemish affairs, however, added another dimension both to the shape of Flemish history and to the conflict between count and communities. French involvement for most of the thirteenth century had not been guided chiefly by imperialist principles, and the relationship between count and king remained stable and without much conflict. The accession of Philip IV in 1285, however, permanently altered the nature of Franco-Flemish relations. The attempt to absorb Flanders into the king's domain, in the same way that other territories had already been successfully incorporated into France, became the salient feature of Philip's policy toward Flanders. But the Flemish count, Guy of Dampierre, had his own ambitions. He wished not only to maintain his autonomy but also to expand the territories under his jurisdiction. The mutual incompatibility of French and Flemish ambitions led to open warfare between suzerain and vassal; in 1300, Philip overran the county. Yet although he could conquer Flanders, he could not hold it, and in 1305, after the stunning victory of the Flemish burghers over the French forces at Courtrai, the Flemish count, Guy's son, Robert of Béthune, was reinvested with the county.

Franco-Flemish relations remained troubled throughout the fourteenth century. The county retained its semi-autonomous status during Robert's reign, but the reign of Robert's grandson, Louis of Nevers (1322–1346), opened a new chapter in Flemish history. Louis was wholly and overtly on the side of the French king. The events of the late thirteenth and early fourteenth centuries, however, had impressed upon the Flemish communities the undesirability of French domination. In 1323, Louis's governmental and administrative policies, based on the French model and aimed at consolidating the count's control over his county, sparked a rebellion of the Maritime provinces. Several of the larger Flemish towns, notably Bruges, joined the revolt and even went so far as to lend their leadership to it. Although Count Louis was able, with the aid of the French king, to crush the rebellion in 1328, he remained unable to cement his personal control over the county in any permanent fashion. In 1338, the pressures associated with the worsening relations between England and France—tensions that would ultimately result in the Hundred Years War—exploded in Flanders. Politically aligned with France, at least from Count Louis's point of view, Flanders was nevertheless tied economically to England. The Flemish towns, loathing French domination, threatened with ruinous English economic policies, and angered by the intractability of their count, rose in rebellion against the latter—this time successfully. Headed by the city of Ghent, under the leadership of Jacob van Artevelde, they forced Louis and his advisors to flee the county. Louis subsequently died fighting for his suzerain at the battle of Crécy in 1346.

The assassination of van Artevelde provided Louis of Nevers's son, Louis of Male, with the opportunity to recover his county. By 1350, he had been accepted as count, and by the time he died in 1384, princely authority had effectively prevailed throughout the county. Despite several uprisings in the course of his reign, the county which Louis left to his daughter, Margaret, and to her spouse, Philip, duke of Burgundy, enjoyed a cohesion, identity, and autonomy found only rarely among the French king's vassal territories. This autonomy was in large part based on and maintained by the count's central administration. This, in effect, was the organ responsible for coordinating the count's efforts to extend and consolidate his government throughout the county. It was the apparatus of central administration which enabled the count to implement and to strengthen the principle that his own affairs and interests were tantamount to those of the county as a whole.

Flemish Household Government Before the General Receiver

Since the tenth century, the counts of Flanders had exercised a control over their dominions enjoyed by few of their contemporaries. Margaret of Constantinople succeeded her sister, Jeanne, as count in 1244.[9] Although comital authority had diminished somewhat during Jeanne's wardship and during her conflicts with the French king, Margaret inherited not only a flexible and successful system of relatively direct local control but also a tradition of comital administrative power.

At the time of Margaret's accession, the Flemish government depended principally on a set of local, chiefly secular, officials attached permanently to the person of the count. In the course of the late twelfth and early thirteenth centuries, Flemish counts had succeeded in bringing local territories, ruled by the petty nobility or by the Flemish communities, more firmly within their jurisdiction. This had been accomplished through the establishment of a new type of secular official—the bailiff.[10] Unlike earlier comital agents, bailiffs were drawn neither from locally powerful families nor from the clergy. Responsible for carrying out the count's will principally in judicial and military affairs, bailiffs answered directly to her. Margaret involved herself in their hiring and firing and presided personally over their accounting sessions. In order to preclude their becoming independent, bailiffs were not allowed to hold any land or other property rights in the territories over which they had jurisdiction. Baillivial loyalties and interests thus lay solely with the count.

The count's financial resources were managed by both bailiffs and receivers. While some receivers handled her domainal incomes, others dealt with extradomainal resources, that is, income that did not directly result from the exploitation of the comital domain. Bailiffs, meanwhile, handled judicial revenues. Domainal receivers were being held accountable as early as the late eleventh century,[11] and by the mid-thirteenth century, systems of financial accountability had developed whereby both bailiffs and receivers followed a set and routine procedure of reckoning—bailiffs three times a year and receivers (both domainal and extradomainal) once a year, in June.[12]

The sophistication of local comital administration was not reflected in Flemish comital household administration. The number of accountable officials may have risen over the course of the early thirteenth century, but the measure of their accountability does not appear to have been proportional to their numerical growth, as the disarray of financial records from this period indicates.[13] There existed no central official to coordinate and supervise the increasing number of local comital agents. Most non-local agents of the count were household members; they performed a multiplicity of tasks, principally on an *ad hoc* basis. The comital household exhibited only rudimentary departmentalization. To be sure, in the eleventh century, Count Robert II had established the provost of St. Donatian as the person responsible for domainal revenues.[14] It says a great deal for Count Robert that in 1089, when he delegated that authority to the provost, he chose not a specific person but the generic holder of a specific church office. Still, the provostship had jurisdiction only over old domainal revenues, many of which were eclipsed during the thirteenth century by new financial resources based on the county's increasing industry and commerce. Furthermore, the provostship would fall into desuetude by the thirteenth century; other administrative positions, such as chamberlain, had also declined in real authority, becoming merely honorary and heritable offices.[15] In the mid-thirteenth century, a new official, the head clerk, came routinely to exercise responsibility for the revenues managed by receivers, but he had no jurisdiction over either baillival or *ad hoc* revenues.

Thus in the mid-thirteenth century, the count personally held in her hands all the threads of princely power and policy;[16] she was directly involved in the management of her resources.[17] In the ensuing two centuries, however, the increasing variety and productivity of comital resources easily outgrew the fiscal system established in the twelfth century. During the thirteenth century, special procedures developed in an *ad hoc* fashion to handle the increasingly complex fiscal situation. It was the gradual routinization of these new procedures, and the increasing tendency for them to be performed habitually by some specific member of the comital household, which led to the development of centralized administration in Flanders. This process, as is evident in the evolution of the office of general receiver, laid the groundwork for the emergence of a bureaucratic office. At the same time, it contributed to the change from a style of management that was essentially private and personal to a form of public government that was based on impersonal administration.

By the middle of the following century, the count had ceased to oversee most aspects of the government. The shift from dependence on local officials to a preponderant reliance on a cadre of central, secular, governmental officials, representing the power of the prince but formally distinct from him, signified a crucial step in the separation of personal and private rule and authority from the exercise of abstract power. A principal consequence of such a separation was to transform the essentially private power of a prince into the public power of the state.

The Evolution of the Office of General Receiver

In the mid-thirteenth century, the general receivership, for all intents and purposes, consisted merely of an assortment of *ad hoc* functions, which might be performed by any member of the count's household. The count, then, did not set out to create a new office. Indeed, this was not even an option, for there existed as yet no concept or model of a central administrative position which, when applied to the given need, would result in the creation of a general receivership. Instead, the office emerged and gradually defined itself over time as a generic set of functions coalesced around an individual. This person's repeated performance of a particular set of tasks made them routine, and, by providing a solid and permanent foundation for administrative activity, allowed for the performance of a new and increasingly complex set of tasks. These also became routine and could accordingly be delegated to minor officials. Such officials answered not directly to the count but instead to the general receiver.

The process by which a growing number of functions came to be the routine responsibility of the office of general receiver unfolded between 1262 and 1372. It was in 1262 that Philip of Bourbourg, a member of the lesser nobility, began to perform primarily financial functions for Countess Margaret of Flanders, though not yet as the incumbent of a fully instituted office. In 1372 Count Louis of Male split the office into two by taking away judicial administration and assigning it to a newly (and consciously) created official, the sovereign bailiff. Louis's conscious act of dividing the functions which had accrued to the general receivership into two distinct official jurisdictions demonstrates not only that the general receivership had by that time evolved into an essentially bureaucratic office but also that,

with the creation of a sovereign bailiff, it had become well enough established to serve as a model that could be applied to the management of other
administrative concerns. Because the office of general receiver itself had no
such model, it is relevant to ask what had happened in the course of the
intervening century to give rise to such a centralized bureaucratic office.
That question is the focus of the present monograph.

Administrative positions had existed in Flanders before the mid-
thirteenth century, but only on the local level. Such local officials included
bailiffs, responsible for overseeing the count's military, judicial, and feudal
interests in the various Flemish castellanies and communities, and receivers,
responsible for collecting revenues from lands directly exploited by the
count. At first the general receiver, like local receivers, was charged principally with receiving the count's revenues, but only at the central level and
only insofar as they did not pertain to any existing local jurisdiction. The
predictable association of increasingly routine functions with a particular
individual, however, tended more and more to define that person implicitly
as the holder of the office of general receiver; as each individual passed on,
he left behind a set of routines, including duties and associated prerogatives, which in turn served to define more explicitly the office itself. The end
result of this process, a little more than a century after its inception, was a
recognition that the general receivership existed as a formal office with
specific duties and prerogatives continuing beyond the incumbency of any
one particular holder. By 1372, the general receiver's functions had in fact
expanded to include paying most of the count's expenses, accounting for
his finances, and even administering justice throughout the whole county;
in short, he had evolved from being "receiver of the count of Flanders" into
"receiver of Flanders."

Many administrative actions during the Middle Ages were performed
on an *ad hoc* basis. When an *ad hoc* function began to be performed over and
over again it became routine. As the performance of functions became
routine, expediency dictated that the count invest his general receiver with
the necessary authority to perform such duties on his own. Hence, the
routinization of functions often resulted in the expansion of the general
receiver's personal authority. Routinization also led to simplification (the
repeated performance of a task usually yields ways of making it less cumber-
some). Simplification of a task, in conjunction with the grant of authority
to perform it independently and on a regular basis, enabled the receiver to
delegate its performance to a subordinate. In this way, routinization also
constituted a basis for the development of a staff. Both the routinization of

functions and the development of a staff in turn increased the general receiver's administrative independence. Fixed wages, unassociated with revenues generated in the performance of official functions, further decreased the receiver's reliance on the beneficence of the count for his maintenance.

Finally, routinization led to depersonalization. When a task is habitually done in a certain way, it often comes not to matter who is doing it. The (impersonal) routine can thus become more important than the person performing it, and occasionally—as modern critics of bureaucracy are fond of pointing out—even more important than the problem the routine had evolved to handle. The depersonalization which attends the elaboration of routine methods for handling problems represents an extremely critical stage in the evolution of a bureaucratic office, a stage that culminates in the acknowledgment that the office now exists as an entity unto itself. All these phenomena—routinization, the development of a staff, and depersonalization—contributed to the evolution of the receiver from a personal servant of the count toward a more public official. Such a development in turn represents a crucial part of the more general evolution from management of private affairs to public government.

If the interposing of truly bureaucratic administrative offices between prince and subjects plays a crucial part in the evolution of a modern state, perhaps the most critical aspect of this whole development is to be found in the process by which *ad hoc* functions become routine. Such an evolutionary path toward the creation of an office, moreover, is hardly peculiar to Flanders or to the Middle Ages.[18] The evolution of the receiver of Flanders, in fact, exemplifies the pervasive importance of routine in the development of a public and bureaucratic office, but in a context where few similar exemplars had previously existed.

A word of caution is perhaps in order. Attempting to define "bureaucracy" in an abstract, universally applicable manner is at best a rather arbitrary enterprise. There exists a plethora of studies on bureaucracy, from Max Weber's construction of an ideal type[19] to Michel Crozier's discussion of bureaucracy as an essentially negative phenomenon.[20] As Martin Albrow points out,[21] so many studies and analyses of the phenomenon of bureaucracy exist as to make a single, generally applicable definition impossible. Serious problems would be raised by any attempt to apply the definitions resulting from these studies to thirteenth- and fourteenth-century institutions. Bureaucracy as a phenomenon was first described in the nineteenth century, and testing administrations of earlier periods for their bureaucratic content using data of later centuries is anachronistic.[22]

Although one cannot apply modern definitions of bureaucracy to thirteenth- and fourteenth-century institutions in Flanders, it is necessary for any analysis of bureaucracy to establish the meaning and use of terms such as "administration" and "office." In the broadest sense, "administration" means management; "to administer" means to manage, to have charge of, to be responsible for, to be accountable for. An "office," broadly speaking, is a position of authority with specific functions, transcending the tenancy of any particular incumbent. Not every manager was a bureaucrat. A manager differs from a bureaucrat in that the former is not always the holder of an office. The existence of an office implies continuity of specific, defining, functions regardless of tenant. A functional definition of a bureaucrat, therefore, may thus well be one who holds an administrative office, that is, one who carries out management functions which generally remain the same regardless of incumbent.

Conclusion

There are reasons why the Flemish central administration developed essentially around a financial focus. In England and in France, key administrative developments centered around a chancery, the department that enabled French and English princes to maintain control over the various regions and local authorities which constituted their kingdoms. The development of a Flemish chancery lagged behind that of its French and English counterparts, as indeed did that of most chanceries in the Low Countries. The Flemish counts, like the Brabantine dukes and the counts of Hainaut and Holland, were not as dependent upon chanceries as were the princes of geographically large territories. Simply because of the relative smallness of their territories, the princes of the Low Countries found personal contact much easier and more practical than did their counterparts in England and France.[23] This is not, however, to diminish the state-building achievements of the counts of Flanders. Indeed, Flemish counts faced problems similar to those of the French and English kings. Counts exercised more direct control over those areas where their officials represented the most sophisticated and immediate authority, such as the rural regions. They had, however, markedly less control over those areas where other groups or individuals exercised equally sophisticated or more immediate control, notably over the Flemish communities. Relatively unchallenged in the early thirteenth century, the Flemish communities had refined their authority within their walls, and had consolidated their control over territories immediately outside them. By the late thirteenth century, they were committed to maintaining their autonomy with regard not only to each other but particularly to the count. By the fourteenth century, the three major towns (the *drie steden*)—Ghent, Bruges, and Ypres—presented formidable obstacles to the ambitions of any prince intent upon state-building; the ultimate success of the counts was by no means assured. Keeping in mind the example of both Italy and Germany, it could be argued that the Flemish counts' triumph over the Flemish communities, the fruits of which were enjoyed and exploited by the Burgundians in the late fourteenth and fifteenth centuries, represents an achievement equal to that of any successful state-building prince, be he or she king or count. And the key to that success was the development of a central administration—a central administration initially based on the development of fiscal structures and sustained by the process by which the *ad hoc* became routine.

Notes

1. Robert Lopez, *The Commercial Revolution of the Middle Ages, 950–1350* (Englewood Cliffs, N.J., 1971), 132. See also, Michael Postan, "The Trade of Medieval Europe: The North," in *The Cambridge Economic History. Volume II: Trade and Industry in the Middle Ages,* ed. Michael Postan and E. E. Rich (Cambridge, 1952), 119–256, and Eleanora Carus-Wilson, "The Woolen Industry," in *ibid.,* 355–428. (Postan's article remains basically unchanged in the most recent edition of this volume.)

2. Henri Pirenne, "Dras d'Ypres à Novgorod au commencement du XIIe siècle," *RBPH* 9 (1930), 563–566; reprinted in O. Mus, ed., *Prisma van de Geschiedenis van Ieper* (Ypres, 1974), 356–358.

3. Raymond De Roover's *Money, Banking and Credit* (Cambridge, Mass., 1948) and Georges Bigwood's *Le régime juridique et économique du commerce de l'argent dans la Belgique du moyen âge* (Brussels, 1921) contain the most complete analysis of the Italians and Italian banks in Flanders and the Low Countries. For specific banking houses see Georges Bigwood, "Documents relatifs à une association de marchands italiens," *HKCG* 78 (1909), 205–244; *Les livres des comptes des Gallerani,* 2 vols. (Brussels, 1961); and "Les financières d'Arras," *RBPH* 3 (1924), 465–508, 769–819. For specific Italian general receivers, Georges Bigwood, "Un relevé de recettes tenu par le personnel de Thomas Fini, receveur général de Flandre," in *Mélange d'histoire offert à H. Pirenne,* 1 (Brussels, 1926), 31–42; and three articles by Paul Rogghé: "Het Florentijnse geslacht Machet in Vlaanderen," *Appeltjes van het Meetjesland* 16 (1965), 188–196; "Italianen te Gent in the XIVe eeuw. Een merkwaardig Florentijnsche hostellier- en makelaarsgeslacht: de Gualterotti," *Bijdragen voor de Geschiedenis der Nederlanden* 1 (1946), 197–225; and "Simon de Mirabello in Vlaanderen," *Appeltjes van het Meetjesland* 9 (1958), 5–55.

4. Other counties and duchies in the Low Countries did as well. For Brabant, see M. Martens, *L'administration du domaine ducal en Brabant au moyen âge (1250–1406)* (Brussels, 1954), and A. Uyttebrouck, *Le gouvernement du duché de Brabant au bas moyen âge (1355–1430)* (Brussels, 1975). For Artois, see Bernard Delmaire, ed., *Le compte général du receveur d'Artois pour 1303–1304. Edition précédée d'une introduction à l'étude des institutions financières de l'Artois aux XIIIe–XIVe siècles* (Brussels, 1977). For Namur, see D. D. Brouwers, *L'administration et les finances du comté de Namur du XIIIe au XVe siècle* (Namur, 1913–1914); J. Bovesse, "Les baillies, receveurs et châtelaines comtaux namurois aux XIIIe et XIVe siècles," *Standen en Landen* 9 (1955), 115–119; "Le comte de Namur Jean Ire et les événements du comté de Flandre en 1325–1326," *HKCG* 131 (1965), 385–454; "Notes sur l'administration du comté de Namur aux XIIIe et XIVe siècles," *Revue du Nord* 37 (1955), 71; and "Le personnel administratif du comté de Namur au bas moyen âge. Aperçu général," *Revue de l'université de Bruxelles* 1970, 432–456.

5. For French administrative institutions, see F. Lot and R. Fawtier, *Histoire des institutions françaises au moyen âge* (Paris, 1957–1962); John W. Baldwin, *The Government of Philip Augustus* (Berkeley, Los Angeles, and London, 1986); William Chester Jordan, *Louis IX and the Challenge of the Crusade: A Study in Rulership* (Princeton, 1979); J. R. Henneman, *Royal Taxation in Fourteenth Century France: The Development of War Finances, 1322–1356* (Princeton, 1971), and *Royal Taxation in Fourteenth-Century France: The Captivity and Ransom of John II, 1356–1370* (Philadelphia, 1976); R. Cazelles, *La société politique et la crise de la royauté sous Philippe de Valois* (Paris, 1958), and *Société politique, noblesse et couronne sous Jean le Bon et Charles V* (Geneva and Paris, 1982); Joseph Strayer, *The Reign of Philip the Fair* (Princeton, 1980).

There are numerous studies on English administration. Chief among them are S. B. Chrimes, *An Introduction to the Administrative History of Medieval England* (Oxford, 1959); F. L. Tout, *Chapters in Administrative History*, 6 vols. (Manchester, 1920); and J. F. Willard and William Morris, eds., *English Government at Work*, 3 vols. (Cambridge, Mass., 1940). For law, see F. Pollack and F. Maitland, *History of English Law*, 2 vols. (Cambridge, 1895).

6. For most of the thirteenth century, from 1204 to 1278, Flanders was ruled by countesses, and much of the development of the financial administration was due to the efforts of these women. Thus in order to avoid complete confusion, the generic term "count" is going to be used to mean both countesses and male counts. The reader is advised that when reference is made in this chapter to any count in the thirteenth century, a countess, and in particular, Countess Margaret, is meant. For a chronology of counts of Flanders and their general receivers, see Appendix A.

7. The idiomatic phrase "held the office" probably evolved from the feudal concept of holding or possessing an office which was actually the property of another.

8. For the relationship among the Flemish communities, the rural areas, and the count, see D. M. Nicholas, *Town and Countryside in Fourteenth-Century Flanders* (Bruges, 1971).

9. For the reign of Jeanne of Constantinople, see Theo Luykx, *Johanna van Constantinopel, gravin van Vlaanderen en Henegouwen. Haar leven (1199/1200–1244). Haar regering (1205–1244) vooral in Vlaanderen* (Antwerp, 1946).

10. The major work on Flemish bailiffs is Henri Nowé, *Les baillis comtaux de Flandre des origines à la fin du XIVe siècle* (Brussels, 1929).

11. One of the very first extant financial accounts of a prince's domain is that of the count of Flanders, contained in the Gros Brief of 1187. See A. Verhulst and M. Gysseling, eds., *Le compte général de 1187, connu sous le nom de "Gros Brief," et les institutions financières du comté de Flandre au XIIe siècle* (Brussels, 1962).

12. See herein, chapter 2.

13. Bryce Lyon and A. Verhulst, *Medieval Finance* (Providence, R.I., 1967), 65 n. 1.

14. For the provost of St. Donatian, see Verhulst and Gysseling, *passim*, as well as Lyon and Verhulst, 12–19.

15. *Ibid.,* 19.

16. This was also the case in France (Jordan, 35).

17. Under such conditions, it is not surprising that these resources were perceived to be her personal property and their management something in which other groups, notably the Flemish communities, had little or no part and no investment. Count and communities, it could be argued, each viewed the other as yet another discrete entity with whom it was necessary to compete for authority.

18. A far more recent example may serve as an illustration. In the latter half of the twentieth century, the evolution within the United States government of the office of National Security Advisor was, in many respects, a result of the process by which a prince (in this case a president) in avoiding or circumventing established political entities (in this case the State Department), resorts, in an *ad hoc* fashion, to using non-specific members of his entourage to accomplish his ends. As he continued to use a particular person for the function, such use became routine and the office of National Security Advisor was born.

19. Max Weber, "Essentials of Bureaucratic Organization: An Ideal-Type Construction," in *Reader in Bureaucracy,* Robert King Merton, ed. (Glencoe, Illinois, 1952), 18–27, and "Presuppositions and Causes of Bureaucracy," in *ibid.,* 60–68.

20. Michel Crozier, *The Bureaucratic Phenomenon* (Chicago, 1964).

21. Martin Albrow, *Bureaucracy* (New York, 1970), 13.

22. Sociologist S. N. Eisenstadt, in *The Political Systems of Empires* (New York, 1969), examined a number of historical societies in an attempt to isolate the socio-historical dynamic in the development of historical bureaucracies. Eisenstadt, unlike the majority of scholars, was more concerned with examining historical societies with bureaucracies than with defining the phenomenon. Many of his conclusions, therefore, can contribute to understanding the development of the general receivership as a bureaucratic phenomenon. Although thirteenth- and fourteenth-century Flanders was one of the major industrial urban societies of the time, Eisenstadt nonetheless omitted it from his study.

23. Edward I and III and Philip the Fair all tried the personal touch in Flanders and elsewhere in the Low Countries, but with little effect. Count Guy of Dampierre chose to throw in his lot against Philip the Fair and with Edward I more for political than for personal reasons.

2. The Reign of Margaret of Constantinople

Philip of Bourbourg and the Establishment of the Office of General Receiver

REVENUES FROM THE COUNT'S personal lands and holdings had been collected in an organized fashion since the eleventh century. By the early thirteenth century, the collection of other revenues, such as those from comital courts, had developed into a system as well. What was still lacking in the mid-thirteenth century was any single official whose job it was to take in and administer all revenues on behalf of the count. Nonetheless, the gradual consolidation at the local level of comital resources, which had characterized Flanders in the eleventh, twelfth, and early thirteenth centuries, began by the mid-thirteenth century to affect the count's court and household as well. By 1280 a single individual, Philip of Bourbourg, had come to be habitually responsible for the receipt and the accounting of all the count's revenues. The emergence of a general receiver had two highly significant effects. It brought all the count's revenues under the supervision of a single official and it brought about the fusion of the two parts of the count's financial administration—the accounting and the cashiering—represented since the late eleventh century by the provost-chancellor and the chamberlain, respectively.[1] Philip first appeared as general receiver around 1267, though he may well have been receiving the count's revenues as early as 1262.[2] He did not, however, occupy any clearly defined office. In the mid-thirteenth century the receivership still consisted of little more than an assortment of *ad hoc* functions, which might be performed by any convenient member of the count's household.

The imperatives that motivated and propelled development in the count's financial administration were threefold. First, there was the question of how the count might most expeditiously and efficaciously take advantage of the increasing wealth of her county. The county of Flanders was reaching the peak of its economic development, and Countess Margaret no doubt wished to participate in that prosperity. To that end she granted privileges to Italians—known capitalists and bankers—and to members of the Hanseatic League; she made several important concessions to the Flemish towns as well.[3] Second were considerations of how this income, as well as that from traditional resources, might be more immediately accessible to her. And third was the urgency of the count's need for money; by 1256, her financial situation was dire.

Countess Margaret's reign (1244–1278) falls roughly into two phases. The first, 1244–1256, began with her accession to the countship and the assumption of her sister Jeanne's debts, totaling about 164,000 l.f.[4] These first years were punctuated with battles between Margaret's two sets of children, the Avesnes and the Dampierres (Margaret sided with the Dampierres), and battles with the counts of Holland, primarily over Zeeland.[5] Margaret managed to achieve some settlement in both these matters, but only through expensive diplomacy and even outright pay-offs. For instance, she was obliged to pay a large indemnity to Charles of Anjou for his help against the Avesnes. Theo Luykx has calculated that between 1247 and 1256, Margaret paid out a total of 337,170 l.f.[6]

The second half of Margaret's reign (1256–1278) was relatively peaceful; nonetheless, the acquisition of the marquisate of Namur for her second son, Guy of Dampierre, and the funding of his crusade in 1270–1271 put a severe strain on her financial resources. Margaret also faced a financial burden her predecessor, her sister Jeanne, had never had to face: the maintenance and financing of numerous offspring. Margaret had eight children, three Avesnes and five Dampierres.[7] In practical terms, Margaret needed not only to augment her regular share of the increasing wealth of her county so that she could run her government and support her children, but also to gain ready access to amounts from which she could make occasional *ad hoc* payments such as that due to Charles of Anjou.

The period of relative peace which gave Margaret the respite she needed to rebuild her finances began in 1256.[8] As previously noted, however, a general receiver in the person of Philip of Bourbourg does not make his appearance as her unique agent of receipt until 1267. Moreover, the general receivership remained throughout her reign an amorphous body of functions associated almost as if by accident in the person who performed them. Such association of functions in one person—the general receivership in its most rudimentary form—was the first expression at the comital level of a process of consolidation of comital resources which had occurred essentially from the bottom up. Political events may well have provided some impetus for consolidation, but the process itself and the direction it took owed more to the local routines undergirding the system by which local revenues were collected than to any conscious policy of financial reform developed by Margaret or her advisors. Philip almost never bore the title; the habitual designation of a particular person to act as the count's "receiver" did not constitute in itself the emergence of a fully developed administrative office. At best, it was the first step of a long evolutionary process in which, with historical hindsight, the emergence of a truly administrative institution may be discerned.

Revenues

The point of departure for any investigation of the general receivership must, of course, be the count's revenues. These might conveniently be divided into those she received as proprietor of certain lands and those which she received from other sources. Initially, the most important revenues came from the count's domain—those lands of which the count was proprietor, or *dominus*. This income included products of her arable lands, manors, woods, moors, and wastelands, products such as cereals, meats, and dairy products. It also included monetary revenues which ranged from the prices the products of her domain fetched at market to *tonlieux* and *conduits*.[9] Revenues also accrued to the count in her capacities as territorial prince and as feudal lord. Such revenues constituted part of her extra-domainal income. As territorial prince, for example, she derived lucrative income from fees paid for comital confirmation of sales and other transactions and for the use of comital courts, while disturbances of the count's peace frequently resulted in the confiscation of lands or the payment of fines. From her position as feudal lord, the count enjoyed revenues from reliefs, from fees paid for the alienation of property held of her, and from fines accruing from the feudal courts, among others. In the thirteenth century, these incomes were increasingly being paid in specie.

While some of the count's resources yielded fixed income on a regular basis, others did not. The fluctuations of the market affected the income from some resources while the frequency of yield from others was influenced by contingencies such as war and death. When revenues or levies were collected on a regular basis within defined territorial boundaries, it was possible for an office to become established with such routine collection as its function. From the late eleventh century the most stable receiverships in Flanders were those collecting revenues from the count's domainal lands. Most of these revenues resulted from agricultural production and therefore could be collected on a regular basis. Domainal receivers, at first probably responsible only for the collection of revenues within a specific area, gradually assumed responsibility for repairs and for other management duties. The title "receiver" (*renneur*) thus came to mean more than simply an individual who received revenues; it meant an individual who managed domainal resources.

Over time, domainal income came to be treated in terms of a distinction between old and new. Old domainal revenues were those which had existed from the eleventh century at the latest, and perhaps earlier. The management of the old domain had become organized by the late twelfth century. Specialized territorial collection centers and warehouses had been established within the castellanies, which were the major administrative districts of eleventh- and twelfth-century Flanders. *Spicaria* were collection centers for cereals and grains and for the rents paid in such produce.[10] *Vaccaria* housed dairy products, while oils and greases were collected at *lardaria*.[11] *Brevia* were depots for revenues in specie from a particular district or fiscal circumscription (*officium*).[12] Not every district had all four specialized types of collection center; various combinations existed, depending, of course, on the productive nature of the terrain.

Throughout the twelfth century, Flanders was developing a commercial and industrial economy that by the thirteenth century had made it not only one of the major commercial centers but also the focus of the woolen textile industry in Europe. As a result, certain resources of the count's domain came to produce so much revenue as to make them too unwieldy for the system of *spicaria, brevia, lardaria*, and so forth, to handle.[13] There were also incomes which may not have existed before the twelfth century and therefore would not have been included in a *spicarium, brevium, lardarium,* or *vaccarium*, but which still accrued to the count as *dominus*.[14] In the thirteenth century these resources came to be considered as part of the new domain. They were entrusted to special receivers and not to the existing domainal, or old, receivers. A manifestation of such developments could be found in the specialization of the terms *renneur* and *recheveur* (special receiver) to refer to managers of the two specific parts of the count's domain, old and new, respectively.[15] Because of this specialization, it seems to have become necessary, oddly enough, that the term "receiver," when used in a more general sense, be qualified. Hence from the mid-thirteenth century onward, the word "receiver" is always accompanied by a description of what was received or for whom.[16]

A large majority of the count's extra-domainal incomes was collected by bailiffs. Bailiffs were responsible for maintaining the count's interests in feudal, military, and judicial affairs and were thus usually in charge of collecting the fees that pertained to such matters.[17] The bailiffs had been effectively instituted for the purpose of circumventing and thus diminishing the power of the castellans. As the count's representatives at all judicial proceedings, for example, bailiffs collected fines and confiscated goods and lands. In addition, they collected *tonlieux, conduits,* and rents from extra-domainal lands. They never collected domainal incomes.

Most of the revenues collected by *renneurs,* special receivers, and bailiffs were fixed or paid on a regular basis, or both. There were several ways in which the count's more unstable or irregular resources, domainal and extra-domainal, could be managed; many were entrusted to already existing comital officials. By the thirteenth century, however, a specific system had developed to handle such resources. Their management was frequently granted to an individual in return for an annual lump sum. This process was called "farming" the resource or making it a *cens.* The farmer, or *censier,* kept any income over the fixed yearly sum of his farm, but in cases where the annual yield was less than his fixed fee, he had to make up the difference out of his own pocket. Farming revenues guaranteed the count a fixed income paid on a regular basis from resources whose yields might otherwise have been sporadic.

Any revenues that could not be handled by the system of receivers, bailiffs, or farmers were handled on an *ad hoc* basis. Revenues of this type included income from the sale of lands, the grant of lands, the grant to a town of the right to collect and keep its own customs, and the incomes from tolls and duties. In the 1250s and 1260s, Margaret sold a large amount of land probably to pay the debts she had incurred in waging war, both militarily and diplomatically, against the Avesnes, and to provide her with ready cash. Although Philip of Bourbourg was involved in very few of these lands sales—he does not seem to have been a prominent member of Margaret's household at this time—John of Mont St. Eloi, the head clerk, was.[18] His continued participation in comital sales of land went a long way to foster the notion that a single individual was responsible for at least this type of *ad hoc* revenue. There were also revenues that were so high as to preclude collection by a minor official or that necessitated, for one reason or another, the participation of an official high in the count's favor.[19] Many incomes could be collected only once, or they might involve several different individuals or communities; consequently they could not be permanently entrusted to a local official.

The First General Receiver

By the middle of the thirteenth century, the administration of the count's incomes had become quite complex. Although bailiffs and receivers were audited on a regular basis and there already existed in the head clerk a single official who was responsible for the revenues of the special receivers, the count's revenues were not centralized (see Figure 1). Income was certainly one of the count's major interests, and it is no accident that finance was the first aspect of her government to be institutionalized. Therefore, it is also probably no accident that sometime during the mid-thirteenth century an office responsible for all of the count's income came into being.

In the late thirteenth century, the title "receiver of Flanders" appeared frequently in the records. Initially, anyone who received revenue for the count directly (rather than indirectly on the local level) might be called the count's receiver or even "receiver of Flanders." The first mention of a "receiver of Flanders," for example, is in 1246,[20] but it would be erroneous to assume that the receiver of Flanders mentioned on this occasion was anything more than an individual receiving something at the discretion of the count. It is not the case, then, that any individual receiving part of the count's revenues, even on a regular basis, was necessarily the general receiver. John of Mont St. Eloi, for example, was indeed described as "our receiver" in 1267,[21] and was later responsible for some of the domainal revenues.[22] But he probably was never general receiver, for there is no evidence that he received revenues from the comital bailiffs.[23] Henri Nowé claims that William, provost of Mons, was the first general receiver. He bases his claim on the fact that William presided over the bailiff's accounting session in 1253.[24] William's presence as presiding officer is not strong enough evidence to support Nowé's contention, for the bailiffs' audit did not include the audit of the rest of the count's financial officials. Furthermore, William never bore the title "receiver of Flanders" or even that of "our receiver."

The first general receiver of Flanders was probably Philip of Bourbourg. Luykx maintains that Philip held the office from 1267 at least, and

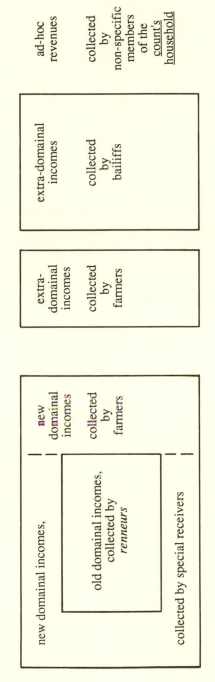

DOMAINAL REVENUES   EXTRA-DOMAINAL REVENUES

FIGURE 1. Organization of the count's finances before 1262.

perhaps from as early as 1262.[25] It was during Philip's association with the count's finances that discretionary action came to be replaced by a set of routine functions peculiar to the position. Certainly, almost all of the financial duties that Philip performed for the count would later be routinely associated with the general receivership. By the end of his tenure in 1280, Philip seems to have become the person to whom financial officials paid the net incomes from their districts.

Most important, Philip collected revenues from both the old and the new domain; it is also likely that he collected those of the bailiffs as well. In an account of the *spicarium* of Veurne for the years 1273 to 1293, Philip is clearly identified as the individual to whom this domainal payment was made in 1280, even though he does not bear the title of receiver of Flanders in this document.[26] In 1276, it was Philip who summoned the receivers of the old domain (the *renneurs*).[27] The fact that Countess Margaret apparently saw the need to stand behind her official, to "declare" that at his summons the meeting had been convened, indicates that Philip, at least in 1276, did not customarily summon the *renneurs* on his own authority. It is likely, therefore, that whereas it may not have been unusual for Philip to summon the receivers of the old domain at this time, he still may not have been able to do so solely on the authority of his position; he had not done it often enough to acquire the authority inherent in such an action's being routinely associated with him. Nevertheless, three years later, on 17 January 1279, Philip himself issued a document requiring the receivers of Flanders to convene to deliver their revenues to him.[28] He also exercised the additional power of setting the amount in currency at which wheat and hard and soft oats would be assessed in many of the count's territories,[29] which suggests that by 1279 Philip had at least informal control over these revenues.[30] The officials responsible for the new domainal incomes also paid their net receipts to Philip. A fragment of an account of incomes and expenses dated 1279 indicates that Philip received income from two farms,[31] from a fishery, and from tariffs, all of which pertained to the new domain.[32]

Direct evidence that Philip collected the bailiffs' incomes does not exist. He had, however, been bailiff of Bruges, Cassel, and Ypres—three of the most important bailiwicks in Flanders[33]—before becoming general receiver. Luykx's argument that Philip received the revenues of the count's bailiffs goes as follows: Beatrice of Brabant was to receive her thrice yearly payments for lands she had sold the count from the proceeds of the thrice yearly accounting sessions of the bailiffs;[34] she was to receive these payments at Lille.[35] Bailiffs therefore made their thrice yearly reckonings at Lille. And since Philip of Bourbourg's office was in Lille, he must have been the agent of receipt for the bailiffs' revenues. Nowé, however, maintains that bailiffs' accounts were heard wherever the count's court momentarily resided and that the count remained itinerant well into the fourteenth century.[36] A fragment of a bailiffs' reckoning, dated 1286, not long after Philip's tenure in office, indicates that the account was heard in Bruges ("facte Brugis"), not in Lille.[37] Furthermore, it is likely that the receiver went where the count went—that his position, unlike Exchequer in England, had not reached the level of development where it could "go out of court." Therefore, to talk of the general receiver's office as a physical and permanent place in Lille in the mid-thirteenth century is premature. Luykx's conclusion that Philip of Bourbourg did receive bailiffs' revenues may be correct, particularly for the last few years of Philip's tenure, but his reasoning is flawed. The count may have given Philip responsibility for her revenues in the first place because she believed that as bailiff he had obtained significant skill and experience. Thus, in view of his relationship to the incomes of the domain, and in view of the fact that he had previously been a bailiff and had drawn up an account of the bailiffs' audit, it is likely that Philip was indeed involved with the collection of the bailiffs' net receipts.[38]

Philip also received *ad hoc* income. A fragment of an account from about 1279 indicates that Philip may have been the agent of receipt for a wide variety of revenues which included gifts from the communities of Bruges and Hoec, loans, and arrears.[39] He was most often involved in the sale of comital property and in the negotiation of loans. In January 1275 Philip received 800 l. sterling for the count from Lambert le Tonnier, a burgher of Bruges, for 200 measures of polderland.[40] Philip was also mandated to receive payment for the sale of moors to the Abbey of Eename.[41] Finally, Philip was listed at least twice as a member of the group responsible for conducting land sales for the count. In April 1274, he along with the count's sons, Guy and Baldwin of Avesnes, and others, sold polderlands to Philip, a citizen of Ghent;[42] he was also a member of the group responsible for the sale of land near Hulst to the Abbey of Baudelo.[43] Philip was probably present for technical reasons; he could receive the sum and note the conditions of sale.

Philip's involvement with the count's incomes also extended to loans. Loans were an important part of comital finance, for the count was rarely able to function without going into debt. Margaret's revenues undoubtedly failed to yield enough revenues to pay for her costly familial fights, and in addition she was responsible for debts inherited from her predecessor, Countess Jeanne. The count's financial structure was geared for the routine functioning of her household and administration; unforeseen expenses of considerable amount could not usually be met either by the gross revenues of local districts or by the funds the count had on hand. Furthermore, revenues were often not immediately accessible. The count, like many of her contemporaries, was forced to borrow.[44] Philip participated in the contraction of several of Countess Margaret's loans, primarily as her go-between. Indeed, his involvement in comital loans contributed to Luykx's conclusion that Philip was general receiver.[45] Since, however, the documents which include his orders and describe his authority are lost, if indeed they ever existed, there is no indication whether he was given the power to set the terms for loans. In most cases, he appears not to have been empowered to conduct the negotiations; rather, he was the instrument by which prior arrangements were executed and he was the messenger who received the loaned money.[46]

Although collection of the count's revenues was organized and there was some system to their management, it can be argued that this system did not constitute an administration and that, in any case, it was certainly not centralized. In other words, at least in this instance, without a centralizing figure such as the general receiver, no central financial administration existed. In the thirteenth century, nobles, valets, sergeants (such as Philip of Bourbourg[47]), and clerks formed a pool surrounding the person of the count from which she could choose individuals to perform certain tasks for her.

Despite the fact that these non-specific officials, as well as bailiffs, *renneurs,* farmers, and special receivers, all handled financial matters, during Philip's tenure no other member of the count's household seems to have received *ad hoc* payments and the net receipts from local officials—that is, from domainal receivers, extra-domainal receivers, and bailiffs. Philip seems to have been the count's principal agent of receipt. Once he had become the single official responsible for the revenues of the bailiffs and receivers, it was natural for his responsibility over revenues to extend gradually over those who managed them. But it was the function of receiving which, as it became routine, formed the basis for the development of the office of general receiver. The existence of such a central agent ensured that more revenue was immediately available to the count than it had been when collection and accountability were the responsibility of a variety of officials. Thus, although the amount of the count's revenue and the sources from which it came might have changed, the nature of the general receiver's primary responsibility was not affected. This circumstance provided the basis for the further development of the office and thus of the financial administration as a whole.

Expenses

It was but a short step from receiving revenues to performing other financial functions for the count. Philip probably became more generally involved in the count's financial affairs for two reasons. First, he was an important member of the circle of people usually found around the count, and second, he was the member of the group who was most familiar with the count's income. His intimate involvement with the count's revenues logically led him to become concerned with paying comital expenses and participating in accounting sessions.

As a rule, most of the count's expenses, like her revenues, can be characterized either as regular and fixed or as irregular. They were also generated either on the local level or by the count and her household. Philip and his successors were more likely to pay the expenses of the count and her household than he was those incurred in managing local districts; these were usually paid by the local receivers without reference to the central treasury. Ordinary domainal expenses included some that were fixed, such as wages, and others that were irregular, such as the cost of maintaining horses and making repairs.[48] Ordinary payments made by bailiffs included their own wages as well as those of subordinates, prison warders, and guards of the dunes (*dunherders*); the cost of holding a court and policing an area; and payments for miscellaneous expenses such as administrative costs, repairs of public works, and the sending of messengers.[49] All these expenses were the responsibility of local officials; only rarely was the count or her household, including the general receiver, involved.

The majority of expenses did not, however, originate on the local level but were generated by the count. Some expenses, particularly pensions, money fiefs, gifts, and certain loans, could be assigned on local revenues. Others, because they needed to be dealt with only once, were too large to be met by local revenues, or were drawn on the count's treasury, were initially handled by any member of the count's household delegated to do so. Family, military, and *ad hoc* expenses were among the latter.

Members of the count's family regularly received sums from the comital treasury for their maintenance. In 1270 to 1272, Philip made at least one payment for Lotin of Bruges, the chief financial agent of Guy of Dampierre.[50] Upon several other occasions, Philip even paid John Makiel, clerk of Guy's residence, the regular sums of money from the count's treasury which Guy received for the running of his residence.[51] Philip also paid for materials such as wine and cloth,[52] discharged debts,[53] and directly met a variety of other expenses for the count.[54] These activities were largely of an *ad hoc* nature. Philip was presumably not much more involved in the affairs of the count's family than he was in those on the local level. Guy, for example, retained his own household and had his own lands and revenues. Philip, on behalf of the count, probably paid lump sums to supplement Guy's income and only occasionally paid for his specific expenses.

There were other irregular expenses that needed to be covered by the count's treasury. The count had to pay for the trips she made, the messengers she used, and the expenses of those whom she sent to handle comital matters away from the county. Payment of these expenses either was beyond the scope of local officials or involved sums beyond their financial capacities. Furthermore, with the exception of lump sums given to members of the count's family and the clerks of the count's residences, all of these payments were occasional. There is no evidence of whether Philip routinely paid these occasional expenses. If the running of Count Guy's residence is any indication, it seems that such expenses were met as they came up and that Philip paid them only as one of several members of the count's household.

Other expenses were fixed as to amount and date of payment. Of these, gifts, pensions, and money fiefs were the most important, although payments for the purchase of lands and rights, for the wages of mercenaries, and for the repayment of certain loans could, under certain conditions, also be described as fixed. It became standard practice in the late twelfth and early thirteenth centuries for regular payments to be assigned either to a local resource such as a *brevium* or, less frequently, to the count. Fixed payments assigned to the latter were often paid from the proceeds of the *renenghe* or the bailiff's accounting session. For example, a gift or pension assigned to the count, which was stipulated to be paid on St. John's Day, probably came from the gross income of the *renenghe*.[55]

The money fief, or *fief-rente*, fulfilled the same function as land in the feudal contract. In exchange for loyalty and knight service, a lord granted an annual sum of money.[56] This type of feudalism especially suited the count of Flanders, who was short on land but rich in revenues; the rapidly developing money economy and the prosperity of the region particularly encouraged the use of the money fief. Money fiefs were frequently deducted from the count's gross income (from the *renenghe* or from the bailiffs' reckoning sessions); otherwise they were paid out of the proceeds of a specific revenue, such as farms, customs, tolls.[57]

The pension, unlike the money fief, was a non-feudal payment. Many were given to servants after a long period of service, sometimes while they were still members of the count's administration.[58] In such cases, pensions functioned as salaries. Pensions were often given to ecclesiastics at the papal court, who would then, it was presumed, promote comital interests there.[59] The count's vassals and members of her family also received pensions. Some pensions were assigned upon local sources of revenues; the receiver or bailiff paid the pensioner, and the transaction became part of the receiver's or bailiff's account. Pensions to be paid by the count usually fell due on 24 June, at Christmas, or on both dates, and until the advent of the general receiver seem to have been handled *ad hoc*.

The nature of the particular expense often determined in part the agent from whom the recipient would obtain it. If a regular expense consisted of income from a specific revenue in perpetuity, it was likely that the receiver of that revenue was responsible for its payment. This was also the case if the expense consisted of a life *rente* or a rent granted for a specific period of time. Certain expenses were paid only once or occasionally, and in these cases a local receiver or any member of the count's household might be ordered to make payment.

There appears, however, to have been little relationship initially between those expenses that were paid directly by the count and those that were paid out of local revenues. Philip of Bourbourg did make at least one payment of a money fief—500 l. to the count of Bar on 1 November 1272[60]—but whether Philip made similar payments of pensions, gifts, or other money fiefs remains a matter of conjecture. Other members of the count's household certainly did so,[61] and such payments do not seem to have formed a routine part of Philip's duties, perhaps because they were not very common.

It appears that during Philip of Bourbourg's tenure, expenses paid directly by the count were not the routine responsibility of any particular official. Instead they could be paid by any member of the count's household. That Philip occasionally received such authority cannot be doubted; indeed, given his knowledge of the count's income, it would be surprising if he had not been delegated by the count for such tasks. Nonetheless, his responsibility for the payment of the count's expenses does not appear to have been as important as his responsibility for the collection of the count's revenues.

Audits

Philip's increasing responsibilities for the count's revenues had little immediate impact on existing auditing systems. Procedures for auditing bailiffs and domainal receivers had been in place by the early thirteenth century. These audits included the payment of expenses such as pensions, money fiefs, and life *rentes* assigned on the particular audit, the receiving of balances, and the adjustment of accounts. The *renenghe,* the accounting session held once a year on or around St. John's Day (24 June), included not only the accounts of the receivers of the old domain[62] but also those of farmers, almoners, and the receivers of the new domain (*rentes hors renenghe*).[63] The bailiffs' audit took place three times a year: at Epiphany (6 January), in May, and at the Feast of the Exaltation of the Cross (14 September).[64] Rarely, however, were any of these sessions or those of domainal receivers begun by the assigned dates. The Holy Cross Day session might not begin by 14 September or end before the middle or end of the month, depending upon how much business had to be transacted, how many problems arose, or how many adjustments had to be made. This problem plagued audits throughout the late thirteenth and fourteenth centuries and generated further problems, in turn. Payments of gifts, rents, pensions, and money fiefs had to wait for the completion of the session. For this reason, the bailiffs' audit, although frequently yielding large sums of revenue, was not a dependable source of ready cash.

The old and new domains were handled separately at the *renenghe.* The receivers of the old domain (the *renneurs*) were audited by receivers of the major old domainal districts (the great or *hauts renneurs*). The *hauts renneurs* also settled any irregularities, handled any complaints, and judged any disputes which occurred during the audit.[65] Although the *hauts renneurs* actually audited the accounts of the old domain, one of the count's officials usually presided over the audit. The provost of St. Donatian had been so delegated in the eleventh and twelfth centuries, but the office had declined in the late twelfth to early thirteenth century, and by the mid-thirteenth century it had become customary for the count to delegate any individual as her representative at this audit.[66]

After the audit of the old domain had been completed, the special receivers, farmers, and almoners presented their accounts to a commission.[67] If the composition of the commission of audit for the bailiffs was any indication, the group that heard the accounts of the new domain was likely to have consisted of principal members of the count's household such as important vassals or churchmen, individuals who frequently exercised major administrative functions, and the receivers of two or three of the major sources of this type of revenue, such as the receiver of the Land of Waas. Although it is unclear who made up this group, it is improbable that the *hauts renneurs* also audited the accounts of the new domain, alms, and farms.

In theory, the bailiffs accounted directly to the count, but she did not act alone. The commission which heard bailiffs' accounts consisted of knights, administrative officials apparently without definite offices, and a few bailiffs of the major towns.[68]

At first, Philip's activities at the audits may have been confined to being merely present. Because he was responsible for receiving all of the count's revenues, he had to be present at the accounting sessions themselves to receive the net proceeds after the audit had been completed. He also made payments to individuals who had some claim on the net income from these accounting sessions.[69] It was but a short step from receiving the count's revenues to being delegated by the count to supervise the *renenghe*. By 1276 Philip played an integral part in the accounting process: in 1276 and again in 1279, he summoned the *renneurs* for accounting.[70]

Philip was presumably one of the comital delegates who audited the accounts of the special receivers, farmers, and almoners as well as the accounts of the bailiffs. Since Countess Margaret seems to have used Philip as the centralizing agent for her revenues, his presence on these commissions of audit is only logical. His experience as a bailiff would have familiarized him with audit procedures. Furthermore, by 1292 the auditing commission seems to have customarily included the general receiver.[71] This may not represent definitive evidence for Philip's presence on such commissions, but it is important to note that, of the general receivers in the thirteenth century, only Philip had been a bailiff before being receiver of Flanders. This circumstance suggests that, initially, experience as bailiff was a significant qualification for handling the count's revenues, of which those of the bailiffs formed a substantial part. As the presiding officer of the audit of the old domain and as a member of the commission of audit for the rest of the count's revenues, he had the opportunity not only to carry out his duties but also to keep an eye on the count's revenues.

By 1262, the audits of accounts were characterized by routine procedure. Accounts were heard at set times and, in the case of the old domain, by specific auditors. Making Philip responsible for all of the count's revenues enabled the count to bring the various accounting systems out of their relative autonomy and isolation and into contact with the rest of the count's financial administration (see Figure 2).

Remuneration

It would be a mistake, however, to assume that the position Philip held was a fully developed administrative post. In the first place, he was not formally accountable to anyone; that is, there was neither any formal accounting procedure nor even any general account of his actions, as there were for the other financial officials. In the second place, he did not receive a set wage. Third, there is no evidence that he supervised a staff whose sole responsibility was the management of the count's finances and who were accountable to him for the performance of their jobs.

It has been suggested that Philip did indeed receive monetary remuneration for the services he rendered as general receiver. Luykx points out that Philip had received 140 l. per annum as bailiff of Cassel and Ypres and 200 l. per annum as bailiff of Bruges; approximately seventy years later, in 1335, Nicholas Guiduche received the yearly salary of 500 l. for being general receiver, while John Van der Delft received 1,000 l. in 1351. In view of these facts, Luykx argues that Philip probably received about 400 l. per annum as general receiver.[72] Luykx's argument is reasonable, but it is based on erroneous assumptions. There is no evidence suggesting that a change of position or function, such as that from bailiff to general receiver, entailed any increase in pay in the mid-thirteenth century, particularly in view of the likelihood that the receiver at this time was perceived to be chiefly a person as opposed to an official and thus still primarily a member of the count's court or household. If pay had been correlated with position within a hierarchically organized administration, then Philip's successor, Lotin of Bruges, who went from receiver of Flanders in 1281 to bailiff of Ghent in 1286, should have seen his yearly salary drop from the hypothesized 400 l. per annum to about 200 l. per annum,[73] quite a substantial reduction. To be sure, bailiffs held fully developed administrative offices, with defined districts and wages. The office of general receiver, when Philip was exercising its functions, was not yet as fully institutionalized as was that

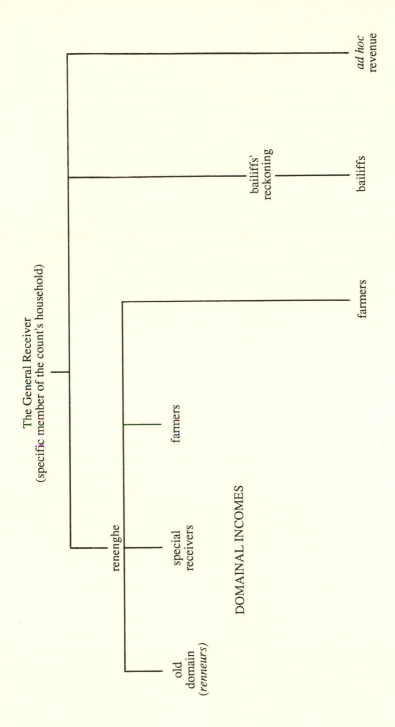

FIGURE 2. The organization of the count's finances with the establishment of a general receiver (c. 1279).

of bailiff, nor would it become so until the fourteenth century. All that can be concluded from the available evidence, therefore, is that sometime after Philip left the position of bailiff of Bruges in 1259, he became a member of the count's household and merely performed *ad hoc* duties. He probably continued in this non-specific capacity after 1262, the date when he became peculiarly associated with the functions of receiving the count's revenues. In short, Philip did not hold a fully constituted office; he only acted in the capacity of general receiver. He could not have been paid a wage, for that would have been contingent on the holding of a specific office.

There is a second problem with Luykx's theory. Domainal receivers and bailiffs received yearly amounts from the gross revenues of their circumscriptions, as reflected in their accounts. The only evidence that could be considered to reflect the circumscription of the general receiver in any comparable way is the so-called general account. The first extant general account, however, is dated 1309,[74] and it is likely that the first general account appeared no earlier than 1307.[75] Until the fourteenth century, then, there was no way of measuring the gross revenues of the general receiver's circumscription, and thus there were no gross revenues from which such a wage could be deducted. Later on, in 1335, for example, the 500 l. Nicolas Guiduche received as his wage was deducted from the gross revenues of his general account.[76] The first mention of a general receiver's wage appears, in fact, in the account of Ottelin Macet for 1334.[77] Furthermore, the first extant charter to promise a regular pecuniary remuneration to a general receiver is that of Nicholas Guiduche, dated 21 September 1335.[78] None of the three extant appointment charters of earlier receivers contains such a provision.[79] There is, then, no evidence for the existence of yearly compensation for the general receiver until well into the fourteenth century.

Philip did, however, profit from his association with the count. During his tenure as receiver of Flanders, he received from her both the fief of Verlenghem and the provostship of Lille,[80] and she probably granted him other holdings.[81] He also may have received "gifts" from a variety of people, either to encourage him to aid them or in gratitude for such aid.[82] In any case, he became wealthy enough to purchase the fief of Bambeek[83] and to loan 50 l.a. to Robert of Rumes, lord of Dossemer.[84] Most of the comital gifts consisted of revenue-producing property, which Philip received both as compensation for services rendered and to provide him with a basis for maintenance. Remuneration was not usually attached to an office or even to a specific service, but rather to a person.

Conclusion

Political and financial crises, although endemic in the first half of Margaret's reign, seem to have had little direct impact on the count's financial structure. Most of the significant administrative developments occurred in the second half of her reign, from 1260 to 1278. The chief financial officials on whom she continuously relied, with the exception of the general receiver, had been in place at least since the beginning of the century. It was thus not primarily a political dynamic that shaped and directed the development of Margaret's central financial administration.

Since the late twelfth century, the count had relied on a financial structure which was quite stable and which worked fairly efficiently under normal circumstances. This structure was based on a tri-partite system of local receivers, audits, and comital household; among these three, the local receivers bore the heaviest burden of financial activity. The count's peripatetic way of life and the relatively small size of her county lessened the necessity for developing a central depôt for ready cash. Each of these three entities generated revenues and, as such, each was an indispensable constituent of the count's theoretical "treasury." The revenue from local circumscriptions and from the periodic audits was sufficiently regular in amount and interval to permit Flemish counts to predict their financial present and future, and thus to assign fixed and regular expenses on any one of them, a customary procedure for over two centuries. Such a practice renders the concept of a "treasury" somewhat problematic. While an expense in principle might have been drawn from the count's treasury, the actual payment would have been made by the receiver of a local depôt from the revenues of that depôt. Thus, in the count's mind, these revenues were as much part of her treasury as if they had been meticulously collected and deposited altogether someplace in the count's household—say, for example, in a strong box under her bed. The count exercised the right of disbursement and assignment over all her revenues, whether in the box under her bed, in her local depôts, or collected at audits. The only distinction was that they were located in different places and were managed by different persons.

As financial burdens and responsibilities increased and as these were juxtaposed with the evolving notion of the count as head of state, a central, or primary, treasury became imperative. The increasing demand for ready cash in amounts beyond the capacity of any depôt presented difficulties. Audits offered one alternative. Unlike local circumscriptions, audits frequently produced the large amounts of money that the count found increasingly necessary to run her household and county. But the dates of reckoning, albeit theoretically fixed, were notoriously unreliable. Consequently the net receipts of audits, though comfortingly large, could not be depended upon if the count wanted them quickly.

It could be argued that the establishment of a central treasury could not be realized until the concept of a single primary depôt located in the household of the count—wherever that might be—and managed by a single official had triumphed over the tradition of semi-autonomous depôts managed by several types of officials. The emergence of Philip of Bourbourg as general receiver begins to signal that triumph. The existence of a general receiver provided the count with the opportunity to entrust all of her revenues, regardless of origin, to an individual who was always nearby. This encouraged the development of a notion of a primary treasury to which all other financial depôts would be but adjuncts. It would also explain why up until Philip's advent almost any member of the count's household could receive revenues, particularly *ad hoc* ones, in the count's name.[85]

The slowly increasing preference for one collection center (such as Exchequer in England) did not immediately result in the creation of such an institution in Flanders. Instead, the evolution of a chief financial official preceded the development of a financial department. It is the increasingly customary association of Philip with financial responsibilities that provided the foundation for the development of a central financial administration.

Notes

1. Lyon and Verhulst, 17.
2. Luykx, *De grafelijke financiële bestuurinstellingen en het grafelijk patrimonium in Vlaanderen tijdens de regering van Margareta van Constantionpel (1244–1278)* (Brussels, 1961), 65–66.
3. Raymond De Roover, *Money, Banking and Credit*, 172; Henri Pirenne, *Histoire de Belgique* (Brussels, 1929), 1:248–250.
4. Luykx, *De grafelijke bestuurinstellingen*, 98. l.f. (libra flandrensis) = l.p. (libra parisiensis) = l.a. (libra artesiensis); l.t. (libra turonensis) = 4/5 l.f. or l.p.; l.b. (livres de blans) = about 16 solidi or 4/5 l.f. = 1 l.t.; l.s. (libra esterlinga) = 4 l. 3 s. 3 d.t. or 3 l. 6 s. 2 d. Flemish or Parisian currency in 1260 or 4 l.t. = 3 l. 5 s.f. in 1270; the Gros tournois (grossus denarius turonensis [g.t.]) = 12 d.t. (*ibid.*, 23–24). For analyses of the currencies of the period see Peter Spufford, *Money and Its Use in Medieval Europe* (London, 1988); V. Gaillard, *Recherches sur les monnaies des comtes de Flandres sous les regnes de Louis de Crécy et Louis de Male* (Ghent, no date);

and J. Buntinx, *Het Memoriaal van Jehan Makiel, klerk en ontvanger van Gwijde van Dampierre* (Brussels, 1944), xxxvii–xl.

5. In 1256 Margaret also had to pay 50,000 l. ransom to the count of Holland, who had captured Guy and Jean of Dampierre (Luykx, *De grafelijke bestuurinstellingen,* 119).

6. Margaret's regular annual income (based on the income of the old and new domains and that of the bailiffs) was about 28,000 l.f. (*ibid.,* 206). Luykx breaks down Margaret's extraordinary expenses for the period 1247 to 1256 thusly:

60,000 l.t. (48,000 l.f.) for the recovery of Rupelmonde.

100,000 l.f. expenses for the years 1248–1252.

160,000 l.t. (128,000 l.f.) to Charles of Anjou.

50,000 l.f. ransom for Guy and Jean of Dampierre.

12,360 l.t. and 708 marks sterling, of which about 11,170 l.f. went to cover the expenses of Margaret's representatives at the papal curia (*ibid.,* 120).

7. She also had eighteen grandchildren, of whom her second son, Guy, produced sixteen (*ibid.,* 121).

8. *Ibid.,* 315.

9. A *tonlieu* was the fee merchants paid to be able to display their wares at market. *Conduits* were the fees paid for transporting goods along certain roads; they were like tolls.

10. Jules de St.-Genois, *Inventaire analytique des chartes des comtes de Flandre* (Ghent, 1843–1846), 568; Verhulst and Gysseling, 78; Raymond Monier, *Les institutions financières du comté de Flandre du XIe siècle à 1384* (Paris and Lille, 1948), 8.

11. St.-Genois, *Inventaire,* 570; Verhulst and Gysseling, 78–79.

12. *Ibid.,* 79; Monier, *Les institutions financières,* 8. *Officium* could also mean "domainal receipt," "domainal circumscription of a certain receipt," or "a domainal official" (Verhulst and Gysseling, 77–78 and 203). For the organization of Flemish finances before the mid-thirteenth century, see Bryce Lyon and A. E. Verhulst, *Medieval Finance* (Providence, R.I., 1967).

13. A *tonlieu,* which had been the responsibility of the receiver of a particular *brevia,* for example, might bring in so much income that it became more efficient to split it off from the *brevia* and entrust it to a special receiver.

14. Increased trade, for example, might result in the creation of a *tonlieu* where none had existed before.

15. See below, n. 63.

16. Throughout the entire period, however, the primary meaning of the word remained "one who collects" or "one who receives." Whoever was given the authority to collect or receive a payment for the count also had the authority to discharge it on her behalf. The discharge of payments was usually accompanied by written receipts or quittances.

17. Nowé divides the revenues of the bailiffs into two types: those pertaining to the bailiff in his judicial capacity (fines, settlement, and confiscations) and those pertaining to feudal and seigneurial revenues (mortmain, best cow, bastards, windfalls, derelicts, and alienations, to name a few) (Nowé, *Les baillis comtaux,* 175).

18. The head clerk supervised the special receivers. For head clerks in general,

see Theo Luykx, *De grafelijke bestuurinstellingen,* 54–62; for Giles of Breedene, one of the first head clerks, see E. Strubbe, *Egidius van Breedene (11..–1270)* (Bruges, 1942).

19. An example of this would be receiving sums from the king of England. See herein, chapter 4, pp. 65–66.

20. "Receptori autem notre generali in flandriam" (Lille, Archives départementales du Nord. Série B. 444 #816; hereafter Nord). Not all of the documents of the Archives départementales du Nord, série B were catalogued by Godefroy (#); neither do all have a piece number (n.) or a folio number (f.). Hereafter all relevant notations will be listed in the order of B number, piece number (n.), folio number (f.), and Godefroy number (#); the lack of any of these notations signifies that a document never received them.

21. "dilectus et fidelis clericus ac receptor noster, magister Iohannes de Monte Sancti Eligii, custos Montensis" (E. Strubbe, 70 n. 2).

22. In a summary of the activity of the *spicarium* of Veurne, 1273–1292, John is described as *notre recheveur* for the year 1273: "En l'annee lxxiii mesire Jehans Reifins rechut sans calenge. S'estoit maistre Jehan nostre recheveur" (Nord, B4034 #1832). Theo Luykx suggests that the second *Jehan* is perhaps John of Mont St. Eloi (Luykx, *De grafelijke bestuurinstellingen,* 467, #136 and n. 1). It is worth noting that this document was drawn up in 1293, by which time the office of general receiver had become firmly established. It is probable that the scribe was unconsciously committing an error which, after all, even the best modern practitioners of historical method, even with the greatest resolve and the best of intentions, are sometimes unable to avoid: that of projecting circumstances peculiar to the present into the past.

23. Nor had he ever been a bailiff, as had Philip of Bourbourg.

24. Nowé, *Les baillis comtaux,* 199 n. 4.

25. Luykx, *De grafelijke bestuurinstellingen,* 65–66.

26. Nord, B4032 #1832; Luykx, *De grafelijke bestuurinstellingen,* 468 #136.

27. On 25 July 1276, Countess Margaret declared that at Philip's summons, the receivers of Flanders had come together and made a judgment that those receivers who defaulted in paying their revenues three years in succession would forfeit their lands and districts to the profit of the count (Nord, B1561 n. 329 f. 96v #1922).

28. "Pretera mandamus vobis, receptoribus universis, quatinus dominica post Brandones Insulis personaliter intersitis, afferentes vobiscum que receperitis de premissis, istud nullatenus obmittentes" (Ghent, Rijksarchief, Fonds Gaillard, #758 [hereafter Gaillard]; Luykx, *De grafelijke bestuurinstellingen,* 456–457 #125).

29. Namely Veurne, Bergues, Cassel, St. Omer, Ypres, Bourbourg, Bruges, Dixmude, Ghent, Land of Waas (Gaillard, #758; Luykx, *De grafelijke bestuurinstellingen,* 456–457 #125; L. Stockman, "De brieven van Aalter," *Appeltjes van het Meetjesland* [1969], 99). Later general receivers exercised similar authority over all of the count's territories. On 11 February 1307, for instance, Thomas Fini, Count Robert of Béthune's general receiver, announced the prices at which all produce was to be converted for the term of Candlemas (Gaillard, #578).

30. It should be noted, however, that by the time of Philip of Bourbourg, the

collection of local revenues had become so systematized that the development of an office with jurisdiction over it had little direct impact. Economics had a greater immediate effect on the local districts. The *vaccaria* and *lardaria,* for example, disappeared not because the general receiver or the count ordered their abandonment, but rather because, with increased use of payment in specie instead of in produce, their reason for existence disappeared.

31. Those of the lands of Roière and of Sluis.

32. Ghent, Rijksarchief, Chronologisch gerangschikt supplement, #99 (hereafter Chron. sup.); Luykx, *De grafelijke bestuurinstellingen,* 460 #128.

33. Gaillard, #72; Nowé, *Les baillis comtaux,* 381 and 403; A. Van Lokeren, ed., *Chartes et documents de l'abbaye de St. Pierre à Gand au Mont Blandin depuis sa fondation* (Ghent, 1868–1871), 1:319 #681; Theo Luykx, "De lijst der Brugse baljuws gedurende de XIIIe eeuw," *Handelingen van het genootschap "Société d'Emulation" te Brugge* 88 (1951), 147; E. Warlop, "De baljuws van Brugge tot 1300," in *Album Albert Schouteet* (Bruges, 1973), 227.

34. Nord, B1561 n. 148 f. 47; Luykx, *De grafelijke bestuurinstellingen,* 405–406 #87.

35. "a paier a li u a sen certain commant a Lille."

36. Nowé, *Les baillis comtaux,* 196–197.

37. Gaillard, #77.

38. And probably with the audit of their accounts as well. See herein, p. 29.

39. Chron. sup., #99; Luykx, *De grafelijke bestuurinstellingen,* 460–461 #128.

40. Nord, B1561 n. 113 f. 36 #1853; Luykx, *De grafelijke bestuurinstellingen,* 415–416 #96.

41. The transaction seems to have taken almost a year to complete—from March 1275 to January 1276 (Charles Piot, ed., *Cartulaire de l'abbaye de Eename* [Bruges, 1881], 284–285 #312; 286–287 #314).

42. Nord, B1561 n. 136 f. 43–43v #1828; Luykx, *De grafelijke bestuurinstellingen,* 408–409 #90.

43. For 560 l. and an annual tax of 2 d. per measure of land. Part of the sale price of land frequently included an annual tax based on the amount of land being sold (Nord, B1561 n. 131 f. 42 #1827). Such a tax then became local revenue. It ceased to be the concern of the seller and was entrusted to a local receiver. Taxes from the lands sold to Lambert le Tonnier, for example, were paid to the *spicarium* of Bruges (Nord, B1561 n. 113 f. 36 #1853; Luykx, *De grafelijke bestuurinstellingen,* 415–416 #96). Tax from lands sold to the Abbey of Eename went to the *brevium* at Assende (Piot, 285 #312).

44. Margaret's chronic need to borrow may well have been behind the encouragement and incentives she offered Italian banking houses and families to settle in Flanders.

45. Luykx, *De grafelijke bestuurinstellingen,* 70–76.

46. "per manus . . . Philippi de Borbourgh" (13 December 1275 [Ghent, Rijksarchief, Fonds Saint-Genois, #190; hereafter St.-Genois]); "per manus . . . Philippi de Brobourgh" (14 December 1275 [Nord, B4034 #1885; Luykx, *De*

grafelijke bestuurinstellingen, 424 #102]); "Quas ducentas libras sterlingorum dictus Conradus pro se et dictis sociis suis nuper mutuo tradidit pro nobis et nomine nostro delecto et fideli nostro Philippo de Borbourgh et quas ducentas libras sterlingorum per manus dicti Philippi habuimus et integre recepimus" (September 1278 [St.-Genois, #238; Luykx, *De grafelijke bestuurinstellingen,* 443 #119]). Georges Bigwood describes Philip as the count's proxy (Bigwood, *Le régime juridique,* 1:64).

47. The *ad hoc* nature of Philip's position is reflected in the continued preference for the designation "sergeant" over "receiver" to describe him whenever he appeared in the records. Countess Margaret describes him primarily as "notre chier et foible serjante" or variations thereof (Nord, B1561 n. 113 f. 36 #1853; 1561 n. 107 f. 34 #1869). Few of the documents Philip generated remain. In the one dated 21 January 1278, he calls himself first Lord of Verlenghem and second "serviens predicte domine comtisse" (Gaillard, #758). He is described as "receiver of Flanders" once, in a document dated 28 March 1270 (St.-Genois, #147). What is interesting to note about this occasion, however, is that it is neither the count nor Philip himself who is describing him so; it is Guido de la Colti Bardi, a merchant of Florence. Since Guido is the only person to label Philip "receiver of Flanders," we conclude that appellation was merely descriptive of the function Philip was fulfilling upon this occasion and not a formal designation or title.

48. Verhulst and Gysseling, 128–129.

49. Nowé, *Les baillis comtaux,* 177–179.

50. Buntinx, *Jehan Makiel,* 61.

51. "Item ex eodem per manum Philippi de Borborg 1,000 lb. tur., per [litteras] Makelli" (*ibid.,* 8).

52. "[A Yo]bier[s Cav]er[oit bourg]ois de Laon, pour vins 212 lb; par lettres a . . . mi-Aoust l'an LXXII; paié par Fellippe de Borbourg" (*ibid.,* 89); "As Fournier d[e L]ake pour dras d'or pris a Provins par maistre Gilles de Bruges [42] lb. 6 s. torn.; paiiés par Ph[ellippe] de Bourbourg; ci en a Ph[ellippe] conté" (*ibid.,*); "A Pieron Marcheil pour les dras des chiu[s acatés, quant] on ala a Toulouse 569 l.; par lettres par Ph[ellippe] de Bourbourg; [et en] a Ph[ellippe] conté" (*ibid.,* 89–90).

53. "A Watier Reifin, baillu de 300 lb. [tur.], k'il presta contans; si les eut Jehan li Nies so[ur] se dette; paié a Phellippe de le Val[strai] par Ph[ellippe] de Borbourg" (*ibid.,* 87).

54. Although such payments were later accounted for by Makiel: "Ensi doit li cuens a Willaume de le Cort par tout 1,164 l. 4 s 8 d.; paié par Fellipe de Borbourg. S[om]é et conté a Lille les octave de le Thyfane l'an LXXIIII." (*ibid.,* 95).

55. The *renenghe* accounts were customarily audited on St. John's Day (24 June). See herein, pp. 26, 28.

56. For money fiefs see Bryce Lyon, *From Fief to Indenture* (Cambridge, Mass., 1957); Bryce Lyon, "The *Fief-rente* in the Low Countries," *RBPH* 32 (1954), 161–179; and Bryce Lyon, "The Money Fief under the English Kings," *EHR* 66 (1951), 161–193. Money fiefs were more advantageous for the count than were the usual grants of land. The contumacious vassal who broke the feudal bond had a better chance of defending and thereby keeping his land than did the contumacious vassal holding a money fief of convincing his lord to continue payment.

57. Lyon, *From Fief to Indenture,* 13.

58. Luykx, *De grafelijke bestuurinstellingen,* 115, 153.

59. Lyon, *From Fief to Indenture,* 8. Such comital interests during Margaret's reign undoubtedly included furthering the cause of the Dampierres to the disadvantage of the Avesnes.

60. Buntinx, *Jehan Makiel,* 95.

61. On 24 February 1277, for example, the count's chaplain disbursed 35 marks for a money fief (Gaillard, #172). See Jehan Makiel's account for other instances of members of the count's household making similar payments.

62. By the late twelfth century, the accounts of the receivers of the old domain were being compiled into a record known as the *gros brief.*

63. The Latin word *ratio* which begins each entry of the *gros brief* may have become *redeninghe* in Dutch by a process of loan translation (calque) and become *renenghe* in French by a process of direct borrowing from the Dutch. (The dropping of "d" between vowels in medieval French was a very general process: thus *redeninghe* became *renenghe*.) The initial *ratio* of each entry of the *gros brief* thus became the word *renenghe* which, in the record of the *renenghe,* opened each entry of the accounts of the old domain. Hence the revenues audited outside the old system became revenues *hors renenghe* even though, by 1250, the whole session itself was known as the *renenghe. Ratiocinator,* the Latin for "receiver of the old domain," may have undergone a similar process to become *renneur (ratiocinator* to *redenaar* to *renneur).* Cf. Verhulst and Gysseling, 119 f. (My thanks to Kurt Queller for bringing this point to my attention.) The *renenghe* had its origins in the meetings of the receivers of the old domain under the supervision of the provost of St. Donatian of Bruges in the late eleventh century (R. Richerbé, *Essai sur le régime financier de la Flandre avant l'institution de la chambre des comptes de Lille* [Paris, 1889], 91; Lyon and Verhulst, 27–29; Verhulst and Gysseling, 119–121). In addition to the formal audit of 24 June, the receivers of the old domain made three other payments throughout the year: on St. Martin's Day (11 November), Candlemas (2 February), and Ascension Day (fortieth day after Easter). Such sessions appear to have been informal audits. According to Verhulst, the formal audit was held "after the three payments had been made and as soon as possible after Ascension Day" (Lyon and Verhulst, 38).

As there is no record of these quarter sessions of the receivers of the old domain after 1250, it is possible that they were gradually abandoned during the early thirteenth century.

64. Nowé, *Les baillis comtaux,* 193–194.

65. Monier, *Les institutions financières,* 60–61.

66. For the organization of the count's finances before the thirteenth century see Lyon and Verhulst, 12–40.

67. Monier, *Les institutions financières,* 60–61.

68. Nowé, *Les baillis comtaux,* 186–195; Monier, *Les institutions financières,* 63–64.

69. Chron. sup., #99; Luykx, *De grafelijke bestuurinstellingen,* 460–462 #128.

70. Nord, B1561 n. 329 f. 96v #1922; Luykx, *De grafelijke bestuurinstellingen,* 456–457 #125; Gaillard, #758.

71. D. E. Queller and Ellen E. Kittell, "Jakemon of Deinze, General Receiver of Flanders, 1292–1300," *Revue belge de philologie et d'histoire* 61 (1983), 304.

72. Luykx, *De grafelijke bestuurinstellingen*, 83.

73. Nowé, *Les baillis comtaux*, 118.

74. Compte des recettes et depenses du receveur de Flandre, Thomas Fin, du 25 décembre 1308 à juin 1309, Brussels, Algemene Rijksarchief. Rekenkamer. Rolrekeningen, #1. (Hereafter RR.)

75. Comptes des arrérages de 1306 à 1309, *ibid.*, #3. See herein, pp. 119–120.

76. "Date de le recept dessus dicte: . . . Date as diverses parties: . . . Item pour les gages Nicolas recheveur pour le terme de 14 mois al avenant de 500 l. lan" (Compte du receveur Nicolas Guiduche, *ibid.*, #5).

77. "Item pour les gages Ottenin recheveur dessus dicte des le 26 jour de jenvier lan 1333 des que au 7 jour de march pro chain . . . 61 l. 10 s." (Compte du receveur, Ottenin Macet, *ibid.*, #4).

78. "Item que pour fere le dit office nous li baillerons chascun an 500 l. par. gros tournois pour 12 d. par. par cause de gages" (Nord, B1565 n. 489 f. 76v).

79. Those of Jakemon of Deinze (1292) (*ibid.*, B4050 #3382) and Thomas Fini (1306 [Gaillard, #574] and 1308 [*ibid.*, #588]).

80. He first appears as the lord of Verlenghem on 25 July 1276 (Nord, B1561 n. 329 f. 96v #1922). The provostship was later given back to the count in exchange for an annual payment of 74 l. on the great *tonlieu* of Gravelines (*ibid.*, B1564 n. 80 f. 24v #2437; Luykx, *De grafelijke bestuurinstellingen*, 83–84).

81. There is an entry in the new domainal section of the 1306 *renenghe* which begins "Contes . . . dou manoir et des terres ki fu Phelippe de Bourborch." In it is listed the *rente* of Saintesme capiele: 31 l. 14 s.; *rente* called Waltilde: 25 l. 8 s.; *rente* called Simghehem: 31 l.; the fruit of a garden (which yielded no revenue in 1306); a mill (which also yielded no revenue in 1306); cultivated lands: 51 l. 17 s.; and products from six measures of land worth 22 l. 6 s., for a total of 162 l. 5 s. for the year 1306 (Rennenghe faite par Thomas Fin à Bruges, 1306, RR, #270). Because these lands and rights were being administered by a comital official, it is likely that they did not form Philip's original patrimony, but had been granted to him by the count.

82. Luykx, *De grafelijke bestuurinstellingen*, 84.

83. On 20 October from William and Blanche Fienles (St.-Genois, #156).

84. St.-Genois, #252.

85. Nowé contends that the general receiver, because he personally received the sums handed over to the count, was the count's actual treasurer (Nowé, *Les baillis comtaux*, 199 n. 4). The office of chamberlain had fallen into decadence by the mid-twelfth century (Lyon and Verhulst, 19). His responsibilities as household treasurer devolved, in part, on the head clerk, but there is evidence that other officials in the count's household also performed cashiering functions. Until the advent of Philip of Bourbourg, it is difficult, in fact, to pinpoint any one person as the count's official treasurer. The French king's use of the Temple as treasury represents a system in advance of that in Flanders, at least until the mid-thirteenth century.

3. The First Half of the Reign of Guy of Dampierre (1278–1289)

The Transitional Period

IN 1278 COUNTESS MARGARET abdicated in favor of her son, Guy of Dampierre, and in February 1280 she died.[1] Guy's reign (1278–1305) was a troubled one. Hitherto the Flemish count's chief international enemies had been the counts of Holland and the Avesnes, counts of Hainaut.[2] But in 1285, Philip III of France was succeeded by his son, Philip IV, to whom Flanders's semi-autonomous status presented, if not an affront, at least a challenge. With Philip the Fair, French intervention in Flemish affairs lost all trace of disinterest, let alone benevolence; it also became more overt.[3] Class struggles between the "commune" and the patricians in several Flemish cities, notably Bruges and Ypres, further exacerbated the count's situation. Guy supported the communes against the patricians; the patricians responded by calling in the count's suzerain, the king of France. Relations between towns and count, which had been relatively calm for most of the thirteenth century, thus entered a period of increasing hostility—a state of affairs which the new king of France sought to turn to his advantage.

Politically the reign of Guy of Dampierre falls into four periods. Throughout the last three periods, the harsh reality of Anglo-French hostility persisted and threatened to break out in armed conflict on Flemish soil. In the first period, 1278 to 1285, French influence remained minimal. The second, 1285 to 1295, was characterized by increasing intervention on the part of Philip the Fair, first in urban and then in comital affairs. In the period 1295 to 1300, relations between king and count became more overtly confrontational; Philip confiscated the county twice, once in 1297 and again in 1300. He returned the county to Guy in 1297, but in 1300 he invaded and conquered Flanders, intending this time to incorporate it into France, the way French kings had been incorporating other counties and duchies throughout the thirteenth century. The fourth and final period, 1300 to 1305, witnessed the collapse of Philip's attempt to hold on to

Flanders. Defeated roundly in 1302 by the citizens of the various Flemish towns in the battle of Courtrai (also known as the Battle of the Golden Spurs), Philip saw fit to release the seventy-eight-year-old Flemish count (as well as his son Robert of Béthune) and to invest Robert with the county. Still hoping to bring the county to heel, Philip re-invaded Flanders in 1304 and met the Flemish in the battle of Mons-en-Pévèle, where the French won a limited victory. Both sides being unable to finance the war any further, relations between the two princes were regularized by the Treaty of Athis-sur-Orge in June 1305. By this time, however, Guy had been dead for two months.

Guy had certain personal and dynastic ambitions which contributed to these political crises. Being a Dampierre, he naturally desired to take Hainaut from the Avesnes; like most of his predecessors, he also wished to expand his territory into Zeeland. Furthermore, Guy, not oblivious to the achievements resulting from the implementation of the monarchical principle in England and France during the later thirteenth century, was keen to consolidate his position in his county and to increase his authority over the Flemish towns. He also had his sixteen children to support. Driven both by his personal ambitions and by the external political exigencies of the last two decades of the thirteenth century, Guy put increasingly heavy demands on existing procedures and routines in order to obtain the results he wanted and needed. It was under these circumstances that the general receivership began to assume a form we might recognize as that of an established office. Although this process was to culminate in an actual charter of appointment upon Jakemon of Deinze's assumption of the responsibilities of the receivership in 1292, it involved no purposeful plan of reform or consolidation on Guy's part. The impetus came instead from Guy's persistent demand that existing procedures—geared to meet the routine requirements of Margaret's reign—meet the extraordinary needs of his own reign. Formerly just a household member who had been routinely responsible for Margaret's revenues, the general receiver now became the one person responsible for the *ad hoc* financial and judicial demands of Guy's circumstances, as well as for routine management of his revenues. The result was both to broaden the purview of the general receivership and to attach its responsibilities, old and new, more firmly to the holder of the position.

From the point of view of the history of the general receivership, Guy's reign is best seen as falling roughly into two halves. In the first half, from 1280 to 1289, the receiver of Flanders continued to be chiefly a non-specific member of the count's household who performed an amorphous body of functions. In the second half, from 1289 to 1300, the receivership of Flanders became a discrete entity within the household. The informality that characterized the position in the first half of Guy's reign reflected its unstable and still somewhat inchoate nature, suggesting that the association of these functions with a single person would continue only as long as the arrangement met the count's needs. The demands Guy made on the individuals functioning as receiver in this period were relatively consistent, but in no way extraordinary. Nonetheless, toward the end of the 1280s, a period that roughly corresponds to Philip the Fair's initial involvement in Flemish affairs, Guy's increasing valuation of the office can be seen in the re-employment of Siger of Bailleul, a noble of importance who had been used by Guy in a variety of significant judicial and diplomatic capacities, as general receiver. In these early years of Guy's reign the position became more stable, lost some of its *ad hoc* character, began to be associated with judicial functions, and, perhaps most important, gained a title. Such developments provided a basis for the formalization of the position in the second half of Guy's reign, and they occurred gradually. A concept of a central administrative position had not fully formed; it came to fruition only in the second half of Guy's reign and was expressed in the formal appointment of Jakemon of Deinze as general receiver in 1292. The first eleven years of Guy's reign must therefore be regarded as a significant period of transition for the development of the office.

Revenue and Audits

By the time Countess Margaret died in 1280, Philip of Bourbourg had been performing functions which were the foundation of the office of general receiver for approximately fifteen years. During the first eleven years of Guy's reign, three different individuals continued to perform these functions and to bear the title "receiver of Flanders": Lotin of Bruges, Siger of Bailleul, and Jeffrey of Ransières. Siger was receiver at two separate times—from 1282 to 1283 and from 1286 to 1289. Unlike Philip of Bourbourg, none of these three men held the position for more than three years, and upon several occasions, two of them appeared as "receiver of Flanders" at the same time. In fact, the only firm indications that a centralizing agent of receipt continued to exist after Margaret's death consist of two receipts, several pieces of indirect evidence, and the regular use of the title "receiver of Flanders."

On 4 January 1282, Siger of Bailleul, marshal and receiver of Flanders, received 40 l.p. in partial payment for the lands of Oliver of Boulenti which the count had sold to Sohier of Erlenghem.[4] Jeffrey of Ransières, sergeant and receiver of Flanders, received the same sum for the same sale a year and a half later, on 22 August 1283.[5] Siger and Jeffrey possessed the authority to receive such sums on behalf of the count because they were receiver of Flanders, and they were receiver of Flanders because they received such sums: the action and the description mutually reinforced each other.[6] The record of Siger's transaction goes further to state that he promised to acquit Sohier of Erlenghem on behalf of the count,[7] indicating that Siger had the authority to do so without reference to Guy. Jeffrey's receipt of the following year contains no such promise, and it may be that his authority to acquit on behalf of the count was understood; by this time, it may even have been inherent in the title.

Additional evidence, albeit indirect, reinforces the contention that all three of these men functioned at one time or another as general receiver, and thus that the concept of general receiver, however vague, continued to exist. Lotin, Jeffrey, and Siger each had previous experience in a variety of financial capacities as members of Guy's household either during the reign of Margaret of Constantinople or during Guy's early years as sole count.[8] Most of this financial experience involved activities which had pertained to the office as it had been exercised under Philip of Bourbourg. Lotin and Jeffrey, for example, had both been agents of receipt.[9] Moreover, whenever Lotin appears in the records before 1280, he does so in this capacity; he received sums on Guy's behalf, a function he performed as receiver of household in 1270 to 1272 and later as receiver of Namur in 1279.[10] Jeffrey, too, had a history as a receiver: in 1281 he was receiver of the count's household at Ypres.[11] Guy may have entrusted the duties of the general receivership to Lotin and Jeffrey chiefly on the basis of these experiences.

The routine audits of the bailiffs and receivers contain similar evidence. Although scholars disagree as to what it represents, an account of the bailiffs' audit on 14 October 1286 may have in fact been drawn up for the general receiver's benefit.[12] Although Luykx agrees with Victor Gaillard that the record represents a summary of the bailiffs' activity, he disagrees with Nowé's contention that the sums therein represent receipts and expenses; Luykx claims that the larger figures signify gross revenues and the smaller signify net revenues owed to the count.[13] The absence of at least two important districts—Courtrai and Oudenaarde[14]—and the summary nature of the record indicate that the document is most likely an informal account. The question thus becomes—who would need and perhaps commission such an *ad hoc* assessment of the bailiffs' revenues? Nowé seems to have assumed that the general receiver did, while Gaillard makes no comment, and Luykx skirts the issue.[15] If, as Nowé assumes, the general receiver did indeed commission such a record to be drawn up, it is probable that the general receiver continued to be responsible for the bailiffs' audit under Guy as he had under Margaret.

During his reign, Guy seems to have assigned an increasing number of payments on these audits and only Lotin, Siger, and Jeffrey are recorded as having made them; each bore the title of "receiver of Flanders" while doing so. Moreover, common sense suggests that to disburse such sums, these individuals would have had to be present at the actual audit. They would also have had the authority to obtain access to the baillivial receipts. The position which would have automatically guaranteed their presence at these audits and empowered them to make these assigned payments was that of general receiver. And although other people paid some of the count's expenses, Lotin, Jeffrey, and Siger seem to have been the sole members of Guy's household to have the authority to do so from the receipts of the various audits.

Expenses

A larger number of records of expenses exist from the reign of Guy of Dampierre than from any previous one. The loss of records through the ravages of time, no doubt, is partially responsible for this situation, but the volume of receipts also might reflect heightened financial activity and increasing organization at the central level. (An organized system, after all, probably results in the conservation of more records than does an amorphous or *ad hoc* one.) The number of *ad hoc* expenses also rose, and it seems to have become more common for recipients of fixed payments—money fiefs, gifts, pensions, and the like—to obtain their money from the count's treasury or his audits. Two factors may have dictated that a fixed money grant, such as a pension or money fief, be drawn on these sources: the date of payment and the amount of the grant. The count most often met annual payments on 24 June (St. John's Day) and semi-annual payments on

24 June and at Christmas. June 24th was the date of the annual domainal reckoning, the *renenghe,* when farmers and domainal and special receivers paid their net revenues into the count's purse. The count's personal funds were probably at their greatest at this time of the year. Furthermore, most of the resources of the domain were agricultural and hence seasonal in nature; at Christmas, in the dead of winter, their receivers were probably not always able to make disbursements. The count's household treasury, because it was not dependent solely on agricultural produce, provided a logical alternative for fixed payments due at Christmas.[16]

The amount of a fixed expense could also dictate from which resource the count might choose to meet it. A typical local district such as the *lardarium* of Bruges may have been able to bear a regular drain of 10 l., and a particularly productive one such as the *spicarium* of Lille may have been able to meet regular payments of up to four times that much, but probably neither of them found it easy to sustain regular payments of more than about 40 l. The gross income from the *Ius Notarii* of Bruges in 1255, for example, totaled 286 l. 19 s. 8 d., and its biggest expense was 36 l. 15 s. 9 d.[17] Money fiefs, pensions, and gifts of fixed amounts could run from as little as 4 s. to as much as 500 l.; most of them ranged between 20 l. and 100 l. Only the count's purse would appear to be able to bear the heavier payments.

Although the payment of neither fixed nor occasional expenses became the exclusive responsibility of a single person or official in the count's household during the early years of the reign of Guy of Dampierre, a discernible pattern of payment associated with the evolution of the office of general receiver emerged. The count paid a large number of expenses himself in those nine years, but recipients also obtained payments, whether *ad hoc* or fixed, from a small group of household members who surrounded the count. Principal members of this group included Lotin, Siger, and Jeffrey, each of whom had functioned or borne the title of general receiver. All three had at one time or another made payments of money fiefs, pensions, and gifts.[18]

Evidence that the payment of pensions assigned on the count's purse would ultimately become the responsibility of the general receiver alone appeared as early as 1281. On 29 December of that year Brother Giles of Lermes, of the order of the Trinity, requested that the receiver, "whoever he may be," pay the pension due to the order for that year.[19] The phrase "whoever he may be" suggests that Giles assumed that the general receiver was responsible for it *ex officio*.[20] This phrase does not reappear until ten years later, indicating that the notion of a household office transcending the tenure of its incumbent was not yet fully realized in 1281.[21]

Lotin and Siger also disbursed the regular payments that went to buy lands and rights. The Flemish counts, particularly Guy of Dampierre, would contract to pay an individual a fixed annual income, usually but not always for life, in return for possession of certain lands and offices.[22] Count Guy, for example, bought the dower lands of his sister-in-law, Beatrice, by arranging to pay her a life rent for them and assigning its payment on the gross revenues of the bailiffs' accounting sessions held three times a year.[23] Lotin of Bruges made at least two such payments to Beatrice, one in 1281 and again in 1285,[24] while Siger of Bailleul made at least one, in 1282.[25]

The general receiver's responsibility for fixed expenses may have increased for two reasons. First, the count was more frequently assigning many payments of this kind, such as Beatrice's life rent, on the domainal receivers' and bailiffs' gross revenues, collectible at the particular accounting sessions. The general receiver had the responsibility for such revenues, and it was but a short step from receiving these revenues to making the payment assigned on them. Second, while many of the grants of income paid at the comital level had not been assigned on the audit of bailiffs or domainal receivers, their payment was nonetheless amenable to becoming routine because their amount, date, and frequency of payment (not to mention recipient) were fixed. Although theoretically payments were made in the count's name, in practice the count might delegate such responsibility to anyone he chose. Nonetheless, even this variable could become relatively routine. Lotin, Siger, and Jeffrey more often made fixed payments that fell due, for example, on 2 February (Candlemas) or 1 November (St. Remi)[26] than did any other member of the count's household.

Ad hoc expenses also increasingly became the responsibility of the general receiver during these first years of Guy's reign. Most of them, however, consisted of arrears of fixed payments. On 13 July 1281, Lotin of Bruges ordered Walter Loes to pay Jean Hubrecht the 1,000 l. due to Beatrice for the mid-May term of her life rent,[27] while on 3 August 1283, Jeffrey of Ransières made a payment of 30 l. of a pension in arrears to John Hérimez.[28] Such expenses by their very nature had little in common and were less amenable to becoming routine than were fixed ones. Indeed, the only thing they normally had in common was that they were met at the comital level. The payment of *ad hoc* expenses such as arrears could only encourage the development of the idea that the receiver of Flanders was the count's chief financial officer with regard not only to revenues but also to expenses.

The general receiver received and receipted incomes on his own authority without constant recourse to the count in part because he had become the only official to receive them. But he was not the only member of the household to pay expenses. Jean of Menin twice paid pensions in 1288;[29] so did Jeffrey of Ransières in 1282 when he was not general receiver.[30] In fact, the general receiver, like the others, seems to have performed this duty in a rather arbitrary fashion, and thus probably did not have authority to pay expenses commensurate with his authority to receive income.

This circumstance raises an interesting question concerning the relationship between expenses and the development of both the general receivership and the count's financial administration. Did the establishment of a central official of receipt result in more expenses being paid at the comital level, or was it the increase in expenses at the comital level that resulted in the general receiver's growing involvement with them? Over time, the count seems to have assigned more and more payments on the gross revenues of the audit of the bailiffs and domainal receivers.[31] The general receiver was responsible for the collection of these revenues, and, as we have seen, made payments out of them. The count and members of his household had, of course, been paying expenses long before the genesis of the receiver of Flanders. Yet it was inefficient for the count to permit just any member of his household to handle such matters and by the mid-1280s the number of different household members paying comital expenses had shrunk to only two: the count and the general receiver. Such a system gave the count greater control over his finances and allowed him to meet the increasing expenses generated by war, first with his traditional enemies and later with the king of France. At the same time, the very immediacy of the need for meeting such expenses militated against the institutionalization of a practice strictly limiting the number of people who could make such payments. The size of the count's household treasury and its implicit connection with the general receiver—the person who, after all, was responsible for all the revenues which supplied it—was certainly a force for such institutionalization; however, expediency dictated that any major household personage, from chamberlain to resident noble, be able to make payment. The payment of expenses at the comital level may thus well have become routine because of the existence of the general receiver. Yet although it was implicit in this routine, the institutionalization of the general receiver's exclusive prerogative to make such payments was not completed in the thirteenth or early fourteenth centuries.

The Title: Receiver of Flanders

Finally, there is the evidence of the title "receiver of Flanders" itself. In the first eleven years of Guy's reign this title, rarely used to describe Philip of Bourbourg, was commonly applied to Lotin of Bruges, Siger of Bailleul, and Jeffrey of Ransières when they performed financial functions. Implicit in the phrase "receiver of Flanders" is the concept of a single official receiving all of the revenues of Flanders, and when various members of Guy's household were so described, they probably had as their major responsibility receipt of the count's revenues. In 1279 Lotin of Bruges bore the title "receiver of Namur," Guy of Dampierre's marquisate, but became "receiver of Flanders" immediately after Margaret died in 1280 when Guy assumed sole control of Flanders. Guy therefore either borrowed the concept of general receiver from his mother or came up with it himself. Lotin of Bruges had acted as Guy's household receiver in 1270 to 1272,[32] and Guy may have generalized that position to one which had the responsibility for all of Guy's revenues as marquis of Namur. Nonetheless, as we have seen, Philip of Bourbourg had developed into a general agent of receipt of the count's revenues in Flanders before a receiver of Namur existed, which suggests that the title was a *post hoc* acknowledgment of an already existing position. By the time of Countess Margaret's death in 1280, Philip of Bourbourg had performed the functions that were the foundations of the office on a regular basis over a substantial period of time. Guy may well have seen the value of this custom and imitated his mother's practice of using a single receiver to collect all of his revenues. When he became marquis of Namur and subsequently count of Flanders, he used the title "receiver of Namur" and then "receiver of Flanders" to identify the individual in question. The functions Lotin took on in 1280 thus corresponded to an actual position, albeit a rather rudimentary one.

Lotin, unlike Philip, was almost always called "receiver of Flanders" when he performed financial functions. This circumstance encouraged the identification of such functions with a specific title. The title therefore became a label, allowing for the possibility of an individual to be defined not only by who he was but also by what he did. This step in the evolution of the office associated a recognized set of routine functions, hitherto performed by a particular person, with an impersonal label. Only then could the office exist beyond the tenancy of its incumbent.

The Association with Judicial Matters

The association of the general receiver with certain judicial functions had its origins in these early years of Guy's reign. The general receiver's responsibility for judicial matters directly resulted from the association of a particular individual, in this case Siger of Bailleul, with the office in its early stages. The assumption of jurisdiction over the count's judicial structure differentiated the development of the receiver of Flanders as an administrative office from similar offices in other principalities.[33] Two factors provided points of departure for this development. One was the general receiver's control over the count's bailiffs. Most of the revenue rendered by the bailiffs to the general receiver came from judicial fines, which bailiffs collected. The financial relationship between the general receiver and the bailiffs served as basis for the expansion of the general receiver's authority over bailiffs and hence over those aspects of the count's judicial system they customarily handled. The second factor, Siger of Bailleul's participation in the settlement of comital affairs while he was also receiver of Flanders, sprang from his personal prestige and from his close association with the count and continual presence in his household. Many disputes did not call for action to be taken by a specific official, but only by a person of sufficient prestige, authority, and, frequently, experience. Siger of Bailleul was a knight, the son of Baldwin, marshal of Flanders.[34] Baldwin had been bailiff of Bruges and Veurne and was lord of Douxlieu.[35] As Baldwin's eldest son, Siger probably inherited his father's lordship;[36] Count Guy confirmed Siger's inheritance of the position of marshal of Flanders in 1282.[37] Through his first wife, Marie of Croix, he was also lord of Plessy.[38]

Siger, a noble and a vassal of the count, could therefore claim the right to participate in comital matters. He attended the termination of at least two inquests, conducted inquests himself, and adjudicated and arbitrated disputes before, during, and after the period of time in which he appears in the records as general receiver.[39] On 14 December 1282 Siger and Gerard de la Walle conducted an inquest into a possible infraction of the rights of sanctuary.[40] In September 1286, Siger, William of Mortagne, John of Menin, and four others rendered a judgment in favor of the hospital of

Oudenaarde.[41] On 3 April 1288, Siger was among several of the count's household present when the count made his decision in the dispute between Bruges and the proprietors of certain lands (known as *remboutswerf*) over the maintenance of dikes.[42] None of these matters were trivial. The documents which report their course identify Siger variously as "lord" or "marshal of Flanders"; in none of them does he appear as general receiver. That he had become receiver of Flanders by the time he conducted the inquest of 14 December 1282 evidently did not affect his power or credibility as a comital agent of inquiry. The general receivership meant little in the matters at hand, and so mention of it was omitted. Nonetheless, the connection between the general receivership and the individual responsible for regulating disputes already existed in the form of the control which the general receiver had over judicial revenues; it became overt, and thus stronger, in the person of Siger of Bailleul. Had subsequent receivers not been involved in judicial matters, the link might have weakened and disappeared, at least for non-financial cases, but all of Siger's successors (who include Siger himself, for he succeeded his own successor, Jeffrey of Ransières in 1285) participated in such matters. Jeffrey, for example, conducted an inquiry into the jurisdictional boundaries between the community of Oudenaarde and the Abbey of Eename on 19 April 1284 while receiver of Flanders, even though the document does not call him by that title.[43] Siger himself was involved in several cases during the second period in which he had responsibility for the receipt of the count's income.[44]

Members of the Count's Household

Lotin, Siger, and Jeffrey functioned in a variety of different (non-financial) capacities before, after, and during the time that they performed duties as receiver of Flanders. Jeffrey of Ransières was even the count's chamberlain at the same time he was general receiver.[45] Lotin of Bruges spent only about two of his twenty-three years in the count's household as receiver of Flanders, from 1280 to 1282. He subsequently went on to become bailiff of Namur (1283), castellan of Namur (1283), and bailiff of Ghent (1286).[46] He also continued to perform several *ad hoc* services for the count.[47] Siger of Bailleul spent only five out of his twenty years, while Jeffrey of Ransières spent only three out of almost thirty years in the count's household as receiver of Flanders. To these men the office was little more than one among several held for short periods of time. The general receivership had, in effect, no greater administrative significance—and may well have had less—than did the office of bailiff of one of the more important towns, such as Bruges or Ghent.

Lotin of Bruges, Siger of Bailleul, and Jeffrey of Ransières, all members of the count's household at the same time, certainly knew each other, and probably Philip of Bourbourg, fairly well. Lotin of Bruges, as receiver of Guy's household, had, for example, received money from Philip of Bourbourg as Countess Margaret's receiver.[48] As an active member of the count's household when Lotin was receiver, Siger of Bailleul even performed financial duties.[49] Up to 1289, then, although the need for a general receiver of the count's revenues was probably becoming accepted, there does not appear to have been any clear-cut financial department detached from the usual activities of comital household members. Moreover, despite their relatively similar experiences in the count's household, Lotin, Siger, and Jeffrey did not come from the same social class. Like Philip of Bourbourg, Jeffrey of Ransières was a member of the lesser nobility. Lotin was a burgess from Bruges,[50] while Siger was a greater noble.

All of these individuals profited from their service to the count. Count Guy made Lotin of Bruges several grants of land,[51] while Jeffrey of Ransières received at least one fief from the count[52] and one from the count's nephew, John of Dampierre.[53] Both Lotin and Jeffrey had been valets in the household of Count Guy, which entitled them to livery each year.[54] There is, however, only one record of any actual gift the count ever made to Siger, that of thirty young swans on 2 August 1293.[55] The count made almost no grants of lands and rights to Siger, the wealthiest of these receivers.[56] The other receivers were not as well endowed as Siger and may have depended upon the count far more than did Siger. Lotin and Jeffrey accordingly derived real financial benefits from their service, while Siger received a noble gift. Therefore, although the count may have made such grants in recognition of, and maybe even in compensation for, the services these individuals rendered to him, the nature of these gifts suggests that the count made such grants for purposes of maintenance, as in the case of Jeffrey and Lotin, or honor, as in Siger's case. It should be emphasized, then, that the count gave none of these lands and rights as specific remuneration for the performance of the duties of receiver of Flanders. In point of fact, the general receiver's functions did not distinguish him from other members of the count's household who may actually have performed similar or even identical ones. Compensation suited the individual, not the job or even specific service.

The count's household by this time had not evolved into a hierarchical arrangement based on function or responsibility because few functions were the exclusive province of a single individual or a discrete group. In addition, no evidence exists that members of the household could delegate their tasks to subordinates.[57] The count seems to have assigned certain financial tasks almost arbitrarily to any member of his household and even to officials outside the comital household, such as bailiffs and domainal receivers.

Conclusion

Although the title had become associated with specific kinds of functions by the time Lotin of Bruges became receiver, it still clearly described a person and not a fully developed administrative office. The receiver of Flanders was not the only member of the count's household to perform financial tasks; other household members, even though never bearing the title, paid pensions and money fiefs. There were even several instances in which more than one individual at a time was called receiver of Flanders. Lotin of Bruges and Siger of Bailleul both appear as receiver of Flanders in early 1282. Siger also shared the title with Jeffrey of Ransières in 1285 and with Gerard Lupichimi in 1289. In addition, the count frequently assigned the payment of pensions, money fiefs, and the like on particular resources or audits, such as the *renenghe*, and not specifically to the general receiver although he had the responsibility of managing these resources. The title itself did not yet connote a particular office whose occupant took sole responsibility for the performance of specific financial functions.

That Lotin did not always bear the title receiver of Flanders when performing financial functions for the count strengthens this contention. He did not, for example, bear the title receiver of Flanders when he paid John of Harcourt's pension in 1281.[58] Lotin does not even describe himself as the count's receiver, but rather as the count's sergeant.[59] The performance of specific financial duties therefore could not become fully linked with the title during Lotin's tenure. Still, the number of times Lotin performed generic financial duties as "receiver of the count of Flanders" vastly outnumbers those when he was not so described. This circumstance encouraged the identification of the position with a certain type of responsibility. Over time, Lotin probably came to be regarded as receiver of Flanders when he executed any financial transaction, whether or not he bore the title.

It does not follow, however, that Lotin was considered to be the general receiver no matter what functions he performed for the count. Unfortunately no extant records of Lotin's activities in anything other than a financial capacity exist. His successor, Siger of Bailleul, did frequently perform non-financial tasks for the count during the same period that he performed financial ones, and he does not bear the title of receiver when acting in non-financial capacities. The office did not define the duties of its incumbent; rather, particular functions gradually defined the office and hence the officeholder. On the one hand, it could be said that Siger was receiver of Flanders only when acting in a financial capacity; otherwise he was not. The title marshal of Flanders, on the other hand, continued to describe Siger regardless of what functions he performed, in the same way that Lotin was the count's sergeant no matter what he did. The general receivership therefore had not yet developed to the point where it defined its holder regardless of his particular activities; it did not yet connote authority as did positions such as marshal or sergeant.

This circumstance reflects the rudimentary state of the office. The general receivership probably exercised authority outside his receiving capacity on a case-by-case basis as determined by the count; the position as yet had little inherent power. Furthermore, unlike other financial officials, such as bailiff and domainal or special receiver whose positions had more fully developed, the receiver of Flanders possessed neither a specific area over which he exercised jurisdiction nor any account by which his actions could be verified. Nonetheless, the continuing existence of the office of general receiver, its association with a specific title, its accretion of responsibilities in both the financial and the judicial spheres, and its identification with a figure of authority and prestige such as Siger of Bailleul, identified its incumbent, *ipso facto,* as both a customary counselor of the count and a member of his nascent household administration.

Notes

1. Although Margaret had officially abdicated in 1278, it is interesting to note that Guy made few changes in the comital administration or even in household personnel until after her death in 1280.
2. In 1299, much to the dismay of the Flemish count, Jean of Avesnes, already count of Hainaut, succeeded to the countship of Holland.
3. The history of Franco-Flemish relations in the last two decades of the thirteenth century can be found in a number of places. Although most interpreta-

tions do not differ widely, what biases do exist are usually rooted in the perspective (French or Flemish) from which the historian is retelling the story. For the Flemish perspective, see Pirenne, *Histoire de Belgique,* 1:345–403; H. Van Werveke, "Avesnes en Dampierre. Vlaanderens Vrijheidsoorlog 1244–1305," in *Algemene Geschiedenis der Nederlanden* (Antwerp, 1950), 2:315–337; Luykx, *Het grafelijke geslacht Dampierre en zijn strijd tegen Filips den Schone* (Leuven, 1952); and F. L. Ganshof, *Geschiedenis van Vlaanderen,* vol. 2 (Antwerp, 1936). For the French perspective, the classic work remains Frantz Funck-Brentano, *Philippe le Bel en Flandre* (Paris, 1897). The section on Franco-Flemish relations in J. R. Strayer's *Philip the Fair* (pp. 324–346) relies heavily on Funck-Brentano.

4. "Jou Sohier [Siger] de Bailluel, chevaliers, mareschaus et recheveurs de Flandres, fas savoir a tous ke ie ai recheu de Sohier Derlenghehem. . . . quarante l. de le monnoie de Flandre pour le tiere paiement ki eskai a ce Noel procainement passe de le dette ke li dis Soiers doit au conte de Flandres pour les biens Olivier de Boulenti kil racata et de tant je le promet a acuiter envers mon seigneur le conte devant dit. Par le tiesmoing de ces lettres saelees de men sael" (Gaillard, #430).

5. "Jou Joffrois de Ransieres, serians et recheveurs au conte de Flandre faich savoir a tous ke ie ai rechut de Sohier Derlenghehem quarante l. de par. les quel il devoit dou terme de le Saint Jehan ki passee . . . pour tiere akate et a mon signeur le conte ki fu Olivier de Bolenti des quels deniers ie me tiegn a paie par le tiemoing de ces lettres saielees de men saiel" (*ibid.,* #431).

6. There is a third receipt in which Lotin of Bruges, on 24 February 1286, quit Sohier d'Erlenghem of the same sum for the same sale, but Lotin, who bore the title receiver of Flanders in 1280–1282, does not do so in this document, and is simply referred to as the count's sergeant ("Lotin de Bruges, serians au conte de Flandre," St.-Genois, #395). Lotin had been a member of Count Guy's household from at least 1270; he was also a member of the count's household at the time he wrote this quittance. In his receipt, Lotin does not claim to be receiving this sum on behalf of the count; rather in quitting Sohier of Erlenghem, he may simply have been promising to see that the appropriate individual (probably the count or Siger of Bailleul, the receiver at the time) would receive it. Sohier may have come at an inconvenient time for either the count or Siger to receive this payment so Lotin, being available, and being a reputable member of the household, took it instead; the receipt being standing proof that the payment had been made.

7. "et de tant je le promet a acuiter envers mon seigneur le conte devant dit" (Gaillard, #430).

8. Soon after the death of her eldest son, William, in 1251, Margaret associated her second son, Guy, with her as count in order to fulfill her feudal-military obligations to the French king and to the Holy Roman Emperor (Luykx, *De grafelijke bestuurinstellingen,* 122–123). She seems to have been the dominant partner, however, for most of her reign.

9. Lotin had been in the household of Guy of Dampierre since at least 1270, Jeffrey of Ransières since 1271 (St.-Genois, #329; Gaillard, #2; Buntinx, *Jehan Makiel,* 67 and n. 2; 129–130 #3).

10. *Ibid.,* 46–69; Nord, B4035 #2054. Probably the appointment was made not long before this date, for Thierry Tempiest is also cited as general receiver of

Namur in 1279. Lotin may have held the position until appointed receiver of Flanders in early 1280 (J. Bovesse, "Le personnel administratif," 444).

11. St.-Genois, #297.

12. Nowé claims that it represents a meeting of all the bailiffs at Bruges for an audit (Nowé, *Les baillis comtaux,* 196). Luykx remarks that the account is incomplete, but suggests that smaller districts were reckoned within the accounts of larger ones, for example, Damme and Sluis with Bruges (Luykx, *De grafelijke bestuurinstellingen,* 201–202, n. 5). Gaillard inventories the document as follows: "Sommes dues par les baillis de Flandre pour arrérages échues le jour de St. Donatien 1286" (V. Gaillard, *Inventaire analytique chartes des comtes de Flandre autrefois déposées au château de Ruplemonde et récemment retrouvées aux archives de l'ancien Conseil de Flandre à Gand* [Ghent, 1857], 16 #77). He may have assumed that these sums represent payments of arrears on the basis of the fact that the bailiffs did not customarily meet on 14 October. As Luykx points out, however, audits often not only dragged on one or two weeks beyond the original date but also did not even take place until sometime after the actual audit date.

13. Luykx, *De grafelijke bestuurinstellingen,* 202.

14. Although Luykx also mentions the absence of an account for the bailiff of Douai, neither he nor Nowé notes the absence of Courtrai and Oudenaarde, both of which did exist at this time (Nowé, *Les baillis comtaux,* 395, 398).

15. *Ibid.,* 196 and n. 1.

16. As one of the two great religious feasts of the liturgical year, Christmas was the logical time for the count to make fixed payments, particularly of gifts to religious institutions.

17. Gaillard, #72bis; Luykx, *De grafelijke bestuurinstellingen,* 43.

18. Lotin paid a gift on 1 November 1280 (Gaillard, #179), a pension on 15 July 1281 (*ibid.,* #191), and a fief on 19 July of the same year (St.-Genois, #294). Siger paid, among others, a pension on 14 January 1282 (Gaillard, #193), a gift in July 1282 (*ibid.,* #202), and a fief on 6 January 1288 (*ibid.,* #280). Jeffrey made a payment, among others, of a pension on 3 August 1283 (*ibid.,* #212) and of a fief on 22 March 1285 (St.-Genois, #368).

19. Nord, B4037 #2322.

20. By 1309 pensions figured among the expenses in the general receiver's account (Compte du receveur, Thomas Fin, du 25 décembre 1308 à juin 1309, RR, #1).

21. Yet the frequency with which it appears in documents after 1291 does suggest that the concept was emerging in the last decade of the century, that is, during the tenures of Gerard Lupichimi and Jakemon of Deinze.

22. Such arrangements entailed a certain amount of risk. Should the former owner live to a great age, the total amount paid to him or her might be rather large in the end. On the other hand, there was always the possibility that the former owner would succumb to one of a variety of maladies soon after the transaction, and the counts would gain possession at little cost. In short, the counts were gambling on the life of the seller.

23. The contract was negotiated in the spring of 1273. Guy received the lands in exchange for the sum of 4,500 l. to be drawn annually from the bailiffs' audits

(Nord, B1561 n. 148 f. 47; Luykx, *De grafelijke bestuurinstellingen*, 405–406 #87).
Beatrice was married to Guy's elder brother William, who predeceased both Guy
and his mother, Countess Margaret. Beatrice died in 1288: Guy thus paid her at
least 67,000 l. For more information, see Marguerite Gastout, *Béatrice de Brabant,
landgravine de Thuringe, reine des Romains, comtesse de Flandre, dame de Courtrai
1225?–1288* (Leuven, 1943).

24. Gaillard, #190, #240.

25. St.-Genois, #303.

26. Gaillard, #179, #193, #280. Other such dates were mid-March, Ascension, and Pentecost.

27. *Ibid.*, #190.

28. *Ibid.*, #212.

29. *Ibid.*, #283, #287.

30. "je Gerars de Nevers fas savoir a tous que je ai receu de noble baron mon
signeur le conte de Flanders 15 l.t. par la main Jofroi de Rensieres, son chambellein"
(*ibid.*, #199); "par la main Gefroi chambellan" (*ibid.*, #201); "par le main Jeufroi
de Ransières, son sergent" (*ibid.*, #206).

31. Countess Margaret seems to have assigned only three payments on these
sessions, and then only later in her reign (one in 1264 [Luykx, *De grafelijke
bestuurinstellingen*, 150], one in 1273, and one in 1276 [*ibid.*, 155]). See Luykx's
tables of payment, *ibid.*, 144–156.

32. Buntinx, *Jehan Makiel*, 46–69.

33. See Delmaire, lxvi–lxvii, and Bovesse, "Les baillis, receveurs et châtelaines," 117.

34. Nord, 10 H 231 n. 3697. He is called "knight" as early as 1265 (Francis
Bayley, *The Bailleuls of Flanders* [London, 1881], 33).

35. Warlop, *The Flemish Nobility*, 2 vols. (Courtrai, 1975), 2:1:644 #17bis.

36. *Ibid.*, 2:1:644 #17bis; Bayley, 32–41. He never bears the title "lord of
Douxlieu" in the records.

37. The title was given to Baldwin and his heir in exchange for the *huisserie
héréditaire*, or hereditary bailiff (Nord, B1569 f. 13 #2404). Siger's sons do not
bear the title, and it may have reverted to the count once Siger himself died.

38. Gaillard, #208; Nord, B1561 n. 591 f. 162v #3465.

39. Siger acted as general receiver between 4/1/1282 to c.4/1/1283 and again
between 25/7/1285 and 25/6/1289. In February 1280 he acted as the count's
arbitrator in a dispute between the abbot of St. Winoksbergen and his monks (*ibid.*,
B1561 n.276 f. 81). His last case for the count seems to have been in October 1294
(St.-Genois, #738). He was alive in 1299 (J. De Smet and C. Wyffels, eds., *De
rekeningen van de Stad Brugge, 1280–1319* [Brussels, 1965], 1:770), but had clearly
died by 1301 (Rennenghe le roy, faite par Joffroi de Boi à Courtrai, 1301, RR,
#267).

40. Gaillard, #959.

41. And against the aldermen of the same community. The dispute was over a
mill. Three of the four men were bailiffs, the count's chief local judicial officers:
Thierry d'Avelghem, bailiff of Aalst; Ernoul Kelin, bailiff of Oudenaarde; and John
Sommebeek, underbailiff of Geraardsbergen (Nord, B1562 n. 47 f. 42–42v

#2756; Brussels, Algemeen Rijksarchief. Rekenkamer, #41 f. 65. Hereafter ARA RK).

42. Nord, B1561 n. 364 f. 107 #2898; L. Gilliodts-Van Severen, *Coutumes des petites villes et seigneuries enclavées* (Brussels, 1890–1893), 2:182–183 #17.

43. St.-Genois, #347; Thierry Limburg-Stirum, ed., *Coutumes de la ville d'Audenarde* (Brussels, 1882–1886), 2:19–22 #14.

44. Nord, B1562 n. 47 f. 42–42v #2756; ARA RK #41 f. 65. On 12 November 1287 he was involved in a dispute between the community of Douai and Hellin, Lord of Waziers (St.-Genois, #457), while on 3 April 1288 he was present at the resolution of a dispute over the maintenance of dikes (Nord, B1561 n. 364 f. 107 #2898; Gilliodts-Van Severen, *Petites villes*, 2:182–183 #17).

45. Jeffrey held this post from about 17 July 1282 until at least 27 June 1286 (Gaillard, #199 and 201; Nord, B4043 #2742; Ignace de Coussemaker, ed., *Documents inédits relatifs à la ville de Bailleul*, 3 vols. [Lille, 1877–1878], 1:27 #25).

46. Chron. sup. #122; L'abbé Victor Barbier, *Histoire du monastère de Géron-sart* (Namur, 1886), 295 #113; Gaillard, #77; Nowé, *Les baillis comtaux*, 378.

47. Most of which concerned disputes (I. S. Nyoff, *Gedenkwaardigheden uit de geschiedenis van Gelderland door onuitgegeven oorkonden opgehelderd en bevestigd* [Arnhem, 1830–1864], 1:17–19 #14; Nord, B1426 #3170; St.-Genois, #615; Brouwers, 4:1:258–269 #289; 4:1:263–266 #291).

48. Buntinx, *Jehan Makiel*, 46–69.

49. He made at least three disbursements, one in 1280 (Gaillard, #178) and two in 1281 (Nord, B4037 #2308; B445 #2312).

50. "recu par le main Lotin, borgois de Bruge" (St.-Genois, #294).

51. By May 1282, Lotin held a moor near Aardenberg (Nord, B1561 n. 361 f. 102v #2362). On 10 January 1283, the count granted him and his heirs four additional *bonniers* of moor near Aardenberg (*ibid.*, B1564 n. 83 and 203 f. 26 and 68 #2428). On 13 April 1294, Guy and his wife, Isabel, gave Lotin and his heirs eight additional measures of land to be held of the counts of Namur in fee simple, together with the lands and manor near Torhout which they had already given him (*ibid.*, B1561 n. 471 f. 128v #3574). Lotin became wealthy enough to stand as surety for a debt of the count of Guelders (*ibid.*, B4046 #3049).

52. On 19 September 1292, Guy and Isabella gave Jeffrey 100 *bonniers* of land near Ruddervoorde (Gaillard, #695).

53. On 7 May 1288, John gave him a fief of the rents of the forest of Bailleul (Nord, B1332 #2431bis). Jeffrey, however, also borrowed money (G. Des Marez and E. De Sagher, *Comptes de la ville d'Ypres (1267–1329)* [Brussels, 1909–1913], 1:100 #8; St.-Genois, #661), indicating that his expenditures upon at least one occasion had probably outrun his income.

54. Gaillard, #2; Buntinx, *Jehan Makiel*, 129–130 #3.

55. Nord, B1564 n. 197 f. 64v #3510.

56. Siger did purchase at least a total of ten *bonniers* of land from the count: four *bonniers* in 1286 (*ibid.*, B1561 n. 414 f. 117 #2802) and six *bonniers* on 25 January 1288 (*ibid.*, B1561 n. 218 f. 65 #3001).

57. Subordinates at this time could only mean those persons attached to an individual by reason of personal and not functional bonds, for there existed only rudimentary subordination by reason of office, responsibility, or duties.

58. "nos Jehan de Harecourt . . . avons eu et recu par le main Lotin, borgois de Bruge" (St.-Genois, #294).

59. "Jou, Lotin de Bruges, serians au conte de Flandre" (Chron. sup., #109).

4. The Second Half of the Reign of Guy of Dampierre (1289–1300)
The Office Is Realized

THE GREAT CRISIS of Guy's reign, his confrontation with Philip the Fair of France, occurred in the last decade of the thirteenth century. Earlier in the century the French kings had intervened in Flemish affairs chiefly at the behest of the Flemish count. Rarely since 1214 had they exploited such interventions with the purpose of weakening the count in her county to their own advantage. Relations between overlord and vassal had been, if not cordial, at least relatively disinterested. In response to the complaints of Ghent (1275) and Bruges (1281) concerning comital interference in urban matters, Philip III had, in fact, supported the Flemish count against the towns. When Guy of Dampierre wished to force the Flemish towns to produce a financial accounting of their affairs for his inspection, for example, he went first to Philip to obtain a royal command to that effect.[1]

Guy's early reign, then, remained uncomplicated by any costly defensive measures against the French. His expenses consisted chiefly of paying off his mother's bequests, setting up the households, and ensuring the future of his numerous children, in addition to either defending himself against the attacks of the counts of Hainaut and Holland or attacking them in turn. That Guy's reign promised to be little different from that of his mother is reflected in the relatively few changes and little extraordinary use to which Guy put his financial system in general and his general receiver in particular.

But the count had difficulty meeting all of his financial obligations even during the relatively untroubled early years of his reign, and the conflicts with France, which commenced soon after Philip IV's accession to the French throne in 1285, compounded Guy's financial difficulties. By 1289 it was clear that he needed more money. From this time forward, he stepped up his demands on his traditional resources and began to rely heavily on his general receiver to obtain additional revenues. At the same time, however, Guy's use of the general receiver as a tool to exercise what was essentially his private authority as a domainal lord in the public sphere, fostered the transformation of the general receiver into a public official. Guy's goal was to implement the notion, by use of the general receiver, that his (personal) financial problems and difficulties were those of the county as well; it is about this time that we can finally equate this "household" treasury with the primary comital treasury, supervised by the general receiver, into which, in the final analysis, all other revenue-producing entities paid their incomes. The costly political crises also worked as opportunities for Guy to pressure individuals and corporations, such as religious houses and the Flemish towns, to shoulder some of the financial burden. Any agreement, no matter how grudging on the part of the towns or religious institutions, to grant the count funds for the defense of his realm had two significant consequences. First, it implicitly acknowledged that the count's reasons for demanding such funds were valid. Having achieved this tacit acceptance, the count took the crucial first step in achieving his aim. Second, such agreement set a precedent.

The count's increasing use of his general receivers, particularly Jakemon of Deinze, in all financial affairs, contributed to the notion of the county as a political whole with the count as its prince. The generalization of the general receiver's receiving authority to include not only all of the revenues managed by previous receivers, but also amounts from the major towns, such as Bruges,[2] was the financial manifestation, albeit temporary, of Guy's political ambitions to extend his authority over them. It could be argued, then, that the series of political crises of the last decade of the thirteenth century, despite their corresponding financial expense and their ultimate outcome, aided Guy in the realization of his goal.

It was the ability of Guy's last two receivers, Gerard Lupichimi and Jakemon, to exploit the existing financial system and to go beyond it in search of funds that accounted for their relative success in meeting the count's needs. Under these two men, the general receiver's activities broadened, consolidated, and became more complex. The increase in the number of accounts suggests that financial officials were made more accountable, both in general and to the receiver of Flanders in particular. The participation of subordinates who did not work as domainal receivers or as bailiffs indicates that the count's financial apparatus had expanded to the point where additional personnel were needed to help the general receiver in the performance of his duties. As these duties became routine, the general receivership lost much of its *ad hoc* nature, and concomitantly, its personal character; this, in turn, promoted its institutional development and established the general receivership as a necessary part of the structure by which the count ruled his county. It was thus during Gerard's and Jakemon's tenures that the concept of a central financial administrator was realized.

Gerard first appears as Count Guy's general receiver in February 1289.[3] Unlike previous receivers, he does not seem to have been a member of the count's household before taking up the duties of general receiver. Gerard was a specialist, a Florentine banker, and Guy might have entrusted the general receivership to him because of his financial expertise and contacts. He may also have made Gerard his general receiver because as a banker Gerard had access to large sums of money, and, indeed, had loaned Guy a considerable sum.[4] The Florentine, for his part, may have taken the position (or perhaps even demanded it) to ensure that he would be sufficiently well-placed to safeguard his investment.

In any event, Gerard spent only three years, from 1289 to mid-1292, as general receiver. There is no indication why Guy changed receivers in 1292; his political position was perhaps stronger than it had been earlier. In the spring of 1292, Guy and Edward I of England had worked out an agreement to end the guerrilla war between Flemish and English sailors.[5] Moreover, the Flemish count had been given overlordship of Valenciennes, the major city in Hainaut.[6] Finally, a royal court of justice had ordered that financial affairs of the XXXIX of Ghent, the group who ran the city, should be open to the representatives not only of the king but of the count as well.[7] Possibly Guy felt that his finances were in sufficiently good condition that he no longer needed to rely on the Florentine banker and so appointed a Flemish cleric, Jakemon of Deinze.[8] There does not appear to have been any hostility toward Italians in the comital administration at this time—so it is unlikely that the change of receivers was motivated by political reasons. There is always, of course, the possibility that Gerard, for whatever reason, may simply have quit.

Despite the brevity of Gerard's tenure, his exercise of the office of general receiver had great impact on its subsequent evolution. This is perhaps best demonstrated by the fact that Jakemon of Deinze received a formal written appointment to the general receivership, the first of its kind.[9] The appointment charter is, for all intents and purposes, a description of the office as exercised by Gerard in 1292, at the end of his tenure. It thus provides us with evidence of the breadth of responsibility and authority Gerard had come to exercise during his three years in office. More important, the charter also functioned as a basis for the further evolution of the office.

Revenues

Jakemon's charter of 11 August 1292 clearly establishes him as the count's chief agent of receipt, as his "general receiver." It describes him as the individual to whom "all our bailiffs, receivers, and farmers of our rents and our farms of our aforesaid county . . . should pay and answer for . . . that which they owe us."[10] Receipts and accounts testify that the financial responsibilities of both Gerard and Jakemon were not limited to any specific kind of revenue; acting as general receiver, they accepted domainal and extra-domainal revenues, from regular to *ad hoc* revenues such as gifts and the income from sales. On 6 August 1292, for example, Gerard acknowledged receiving payment from the abbot of Vaucelles for the tithe of Cambrai, a resource that was part of the count's domain;[11] in that same year, he also received the fee for the farm of the sale of moor and wastelands, an extradomainal resource, from its farmer, John de Messines.[12] During his tenure as general receiver, Jakemon of Deinze receipted payments made from the sale of beer and wine by the bailiff of le Mil,[13] from the receiver of the goods of the Lady of Oudenaarde,[14] and from the receivers of the non-domainal lands and rents of Menin, the Land of Waas, and Saftingen.[15] Finally, although bailiffs had charge of the count's interest in the cities, the city of Bruges, in its accounts for 1294–1295, acknowledged that it owed Jakemon—and not the bailiff of Bruges—1,000 l. for the revenue due to the count on 28 October 1294.[16]

Other accounts present even stronger evidence of the general receiver's responsibility for comital revenues. While the general receiver's lack of involvement on the level of direct routine collection remained constant throughout the last decade of the thirteenth century, real authority manifested itself in his right to demand sums directly from the receivers of the local resources, instead of having to wait for the annual payment of net receipts during the annual audit. Such irregular payments appeared in the annual accounts. For example: "he accounted to the receiver in several pieces [receipts]: 9265 l. 15 s. 10 ½ d";[17] "Item, to Jakemon, receiver: 38 l.";[18] "to the receiver 3845 l. 3 s. 8 d., which the receiver has accounted for. . . . in three pieces";[19] and "Again by the command of the receiver to Walter de la Mer: 100 l."[20]

No complete *renenghe* accounts and only a few receipts or "pieces" exist from before 1292. We do not know if any of Jakemon's predecessors had the right he enjoyed of demanding sums directly from domainal receivers. Gerard, however, did exercise the authority to negotiate and contract loans, which included assigning their repayment to the receivers of the count's revenues.[21] It would have been but a short step from assigning payment to being able to demand actual sums from these same receivers at any time.

The assumption of similar authority was manifested in the collection of arrears. Not all of the count's debtors and officials were able to make their payments on time, and as arrears became more common, it became necessary for someone to deal with them on a routine basis. Sometime while Jakemon was receiver, and probably earlier, during Gerard's tenure, the general receiver came to assume sole responsibility for arrears, no doubt because he was the ultimate agent of receipt for other kinds of incomes, but also possibly because arrears were paid directly to the count's central treasury over which the general receiver enjoyed supervisory responsibility. On 24 July 1296, for example, the merchants of wood paid him 230 l.f. for the right to the wood in the forest of Nieppe,[22] a farm regularly due on 24 June at the *renenghe*. Late payments included not only those of regular revenue from domainal and extra-domainal resources, but also *ad hoc* payments due on a particular date. The 30,000 l. promised to the count by Bruges in 1295 is a case in point. Bruges arranged that this sum, theoretically a gift, would be paid in two installments, one on 11 November of that year and the other a year later. On 24 June 1295 the town petitioned to have the second payment put off for a year, and Jakemon had the authority to grant the delay.[23]

From the point of view of collection, little differentiated arrears and demand payments from *ad hoc* ones. Late payments, at one and the same time regular and irregular, linked regular and fixed revenues to *ad hoc* incomes. The receiver's responsibility for late payments could thus have provided the basis upon which he extended his authority over *ad hoc* ones. One such irregular payment was the fee for the right to alienate to another person or corporation lands or rights that an individual held from the count.[24] On 2 May 1293, the count of Flanders granted Roger of Gistel the right to transfer the *tonlieu* of the *tourn* of Bruges to the magistrates of that city.[25] On 13 May Bruges paid Roger for the *tonlieu*[26] and in December of the year, Jakemon of Deinze received 400 l. from Bruges as the fee for the right to buy the *tonlieu* from Roger.[27]

In so formalizing his authority over comital revenues, Jakemon's charter provided a basis upon which he, as general receiver, could demand sums from financial officials and negotiate and deal with problems of late or nonpayment. This provided Guy of Dampierre with the means whereby he could tap into his regular resources on an *ad hoc* basis, thus turning them into a source for ready cash. It allowed him to sustain and maintain his offense against the Avesnes and the Hollanders and his defense against the king of France. At the same time, it served to broaden the base of his public power. Allowing him access to his revenues on an *ad hoc* basis confirmed the notion that his needs as count, being unpredictable, transcended the system geared principally for the regular and predictable needs of a person.

Such a notion extended to demands for *ad hoc* funds from other, non-domainal sources. Individuals and corporations, such as the Flemish cities, were often pressured into giving the count gifts or loans for occasions such as war. In 1297, Jakemon received such a "gift" from the magistrate and aldermen of Bourbourg for the count's campaign in Zeeland.[28] What makes this particular case interesting, however, is Jakemon's role not only as collector of such funds but also, in the company of Roger of Gistel, as the count's enforcer of his demand for donations. The collaboration of Roger, a man of substance and a vassal of the count frequently employed upon his affairs though not an administrative official, suggests that Jakemon may have acted not only *ex officio* but also as a personal representative of the count. That Guy's financial management had developed into an apparatus strong and efficient enough to implement such a levy is in itself significant and this fact must, in no small part, be attributed to the office of general receiver as exercised by Jakemon of Deinze. It was, however, perhaps too efficient. In 1296, four of the five major Flemish towns complained against the count and the methods he used to collect the fiftieth ordered by King Philip of France.[29]

The most important *ad hoc* revenues Jakemon supervised were those collected from the English. English kings had paid a money fief to the Flemish counts since the reign of King John.[30] They may have initially made such payments directly to the counts, but an entry in Exchequer records from around 1296 records that a payment of 70,000 l. black money of Tours was delivered to Jakemon of Deinze at Bruges.[31] Jakemon received another important payment from the English in 1297 when, as part of a treaty he and two others had negotiated on behalf of the count, the English delivered to them 300,000 l. black money of Tours.[32] These were very significant revenues, and the fact that Jakemon had the responsibility for their receipt suggests that the general receiver had indeed become the chief and sole central agent of receipt for the count of Flanders.

Expenses

Jakemon's charter makes no definitive statement concerning the general receiver's responsibility for expenses. Neither Gerard nor Jakemon seems to have had the same control over expenditures that they enjoyed over revenues. But if, as is likely, Gerard wished to increase his control over the financial system in which he had invested, he would need to superintend not only the count's revenues but also his expenses. The best means of achieving this goal was to insist that certain expenses be met routinely by the household, now the central comital, treasury. Furthermore, it was undoubtedly more efficient for the central treasury to meet *ad hoc* and certain of the count's fixed expenses than to assign them on local resources, which would delay payment as well as weaken the general receiver's ability to account for and thus control such expenditures.

By the time the count appointed Jakemon of Deinze, the general receiver's responsibility for expenses had stabilized into an informal, yet fixed, pattern. In the first half of Guy's reign, as we have seen, the general receiver had come to assume responsibility for certain kinds of *ad hoc* expenses, principally arrears. During the second half of Guy's reign, the general receiver's responsibility for expenses expanded to include those assigned on the treasury or on the sessions of account, and those which for whatever reason might be called *ad hoc*. He acquired this responsibility by much the same process by which he had assumed responsibility for *ad hoc* revenues. Reimbursements, purveyance, irregular payments drawn on the count's treasury, and expenses beyond the capacity of local revenues, of the purse of the clerk of the count's residences, or of members of his family, among others, fell into this latter category.

Fixed Expenses

Since the beginning of Guy's reign, both the household treasury and the sessions of account had increasingly borne the burden of fixed expenses such as pensions, money fiefs, and life rents to pay off purchases of land. Because the general receiver usually took charge of both these resources, he logically acquired the attendant responsibility of paying fixed expenses drawn on them. Jakemon, for example, paid John le Biers of Rheims his yearly pension of 40 l. on 1 August 1294;[33] he also paid William of Mortagne's pension of 120 l., due for the term ending two weeks after 24 June 1298, the date of the *renenghe* of that year.[34]

Guy made two major purchases of lands and rights in the second half of his reign: that of the provostship of Lille from William of Mortagne, and that of the lands of Dunkirk and Wastine from Baldwin of Avesnes and his wife, Felicity.[35] Guy paid for both by granting each seller a regular, fixed, life rent, the disbursement of which was entrusted first to Gerard and then to Jakemon. On 27 November 1290, Gerard Lupichimi paid Felicity 326 l. 6 s. 3 d.[36] Jakemon of Deinze met her 24 June and Christmas payments for 1293 and the Christmas payment for 1294;[37] there are no records of anyone else doing so. Both Gerard Lupichimi and Jakemon of Deinze also made the payments of the life rent which William of Mortagne was to receive in exchange for the provostship of Lille: Gerard on 24 June 1290 and Jakemon in 1298.[38]

Regular payments for the purchase of rights and lands were not initially the exclusive responsibility of the general receiver. Lotin of Bruges, for example, although not general receiver at the time, handled at least one of Beatrice of Courtrai's payments.[39] In the early part of Guy's reign, who you were meant more than what you did; Lotin, after all, was still a significant member of the count's household. In the second half of Guy's reign, procedures changed and it was the general receiver who handled all of Felicity d'Avesnes's transactions, as well as those of William of Mortagne. That he did so as a particular official and not as a specific person is underscored by the fact that a change in incumbent occurred over the span of time in which such payments were made.[40]

By 1300 the general receiver had also become the sole agent of disbursement for money fiefs as well. Earlier, local receivers had met payments of money fiefs assigned on their circumscriptions.[41] In May 1274, for example, Countess Margaret had granted Jakemon Louchard a money fief of 200 l.f., to be drawn three times a year from the *tonlieu* of Damme.[42] John of Harecourt was to draw his money fief from the revenues of the *renenghe*, but the charter granting him the money fief in 1280 does not mention any individual or official who was to be routinely responsible for disbursing it.[43] Until about 1290, it seems that no one in particular paid money fiefs drawn on the count's purse. On 30 October 1280, for example, Siger of Bailleul paid Rasse of Vinch 20 l. for his money fief, while on

17 June 1286, Jeffrey of Ransières, the count's chamberlain, paid William, lord of Lohear, his 100 l. money fief due on 24 June.[44]

It was sometime during Gerard's tenure as general receiver that the situation changed. Most of the extant records concerning money fiefs consist of receipts;[45] four charters detailing the terms of the initial grants also still exist. Whereas prior to 1290, no effort seems to have been made to attach the responsibility of payment of these fiefs to any one person or office, after 1290, first Gerard and then Jakemon routinely appear as the specific agent from whom the recipient was to obtain his grant. The two charters of John of Harecourt illustrate the change which took place. The 1280 charter assigns John's payment to the *renenghe;* this means, of course, that he was to receive his payment around 24 June, the date of the annual domainal reckoning. Like his 1280 grant, the charter drawn up in 1296 stipulates that he receive one of his payments on 24 June; the other was to be paid on 25 December.[46] But the 1296 charter says nothing about receiving payments from the *renenghe;* instead, John was to receive payment expressly from the general receiver. Grants of other money fiefs assigned on the count's purse after 1290, such as those to John of Kuyk and William of Hornes, likewise assigned payments specifically to the general receiver and not on a particular revenue.[47] In referring to the receiver, all routinely employ the significant phrase "whoever he may be or will be for future times" when describing him. This phrase both indicates that the office was assumed to continue beyond the tenure of its incumbent, and, equally important, emphasizes that the particular responsibility in question was associated with it.

The count usually used money fiefs to procure vassals for military service. He also augmented his military forces with mercenaries; unlike payments of money fiefs, however, payments for the wages of mercenaries almost always came out of the count's central treasury and not out of local revenues. One reason for this was the relatively short length of time over which these payments were made. It was less trouble to pay wages from the central treasury than to make arrangements for wages to be paid by local receivers; furthermore, this method of payment allowed the count more control over his mercenaries.

Few actual contracts or receipts for the wages of mercenaries still exist for the late thirteenth century, and none before 1290.[48] Both Margaret and Guy had used mercenaries before 1290, but there is no indication of who paid them. In December 1288, for example, an account of military expenses incurred by the count's men-at-arms in Limburg was drawn up before Jeffrey of Ransières and Lotin of Bruges,[49] but no mention was made of who in particular was responsible for payment. The rising hostilities which marked the period 1290 to 1300 are obviously one of the reasons that records of mercenaries appear after 1290 and not before. However, the growing accountability of the count's financial system under Gerard Lupichimi and Jakemon of Deinze cannot be discounted as a determining factor in the increase in records involving mercenaries. During the tenure of Jakemon of Deinze, in fact, records indicate that mercenaries' wages came to be increasingly paid by the general receiver. Jakemon made four recorded payments to Wulfars of Berseel for his participation in the count's military action in Zeeland.[50] He also seems to have been in charge of paying mercenaries involved in the 1296–1297 conflict with France. On 24 June 1297 he made one payment to Colard d'Averey, James of Werneper, John of Cybert, knights, and John of Salewerne, squire.[51] Four months later, on 20 October 1297, he paid Gossuin of Leis and his company for the eighteen days they spent in Oudenaarde.[52] A document drawn up in 1297 makes it clear that the general receiver had also assumed the responsibility for similar expenses incurred at Ypres.[53]

War was an expense of the moment. Improved central organization of the count's finances, together with the associated increase in the immediate availability of revenues for payment of momentous and unforeseen *ad hoc* expenses, were among the principal advantages afforded to the count by the existence of a general receiver. The war with France forced the count to demand such services and, in turn, to rely heavily on his general receiver to obtain them. The ability of first Gerard and then Jakemon to exploit the existing financial system enabled that system to meet the count's needs as much as it did. An additional and unforeseen consequence was the concomitant broadening and consolidation of the general receiver's sphere of routine, and thus legitimate, activity.

Ad Hoc *Expenses*

Ad hoc expenses can be divided into three categories: those that affected more than one section of the county; those that, for whatever reason, were beyond the resources of regular officials such as domainal receivers or clerks of the count's residences; and reimbursements. Certainly by the time of

Jakemon's tenure, and probably by that of Gerard's, they were being met, chiefly by virtue of being *ad hoc,* by the count's household treasury and thus by the receiver of Flanders.

The number of expenses affecting more than one locality appears to have grown in the course of the last decade of the thirteenth century. No one particular district could logically be—nor, more important, was willing to be—charged for expenses involving other localities. They thus became the responsibility of the count's treasury. On 12 November 1301, for example, the clerks of the general receiver paid 1,500 l.f. to Baldwin, sergeant and master of the engines of the count of Flanders, for work on the fortresses of Damme and Aardenburg.[54] The count also could (and did) demand contributions from each district involved in a given enterprise. In 1294 Jakemon of Deinze and Siger of Bailleul collected a contribution from churches and religious houses which had been specifically taxed to pay for the maintenance of comital lands diked along the sea.[55]

The key figure in both these transactions is Jakemon of Deinze, the general receiver. He was a logical choice for such tasks because as general receiver he was already responsible for collecting revenues at times of audit, and as we have seen, by 1290 had acquired the additional authority to demand sums from local receivers at any time. Simple considerations of expediency may have dictated that the individuals who received such sums be responsible for paying the expense which they had been collected to cover. The general receivership, as exercised in these instances by Jakemon, had in effect become an official responsible for collecting revenues on a county-wide basis in order to pay for county-wide expenses. A reciprocal relationship probably developed whereby, on the one hand, the existence of a general receiver made it easier for the count to collect county-wide contributions for a variety of expenses; this may well have encouraged him to use the office for such purposes. On the other hand, the power and status of the general receiver were enhanced by his growing responsibility for the management of such expenses. The participation of Jakemon of Deinze and some other person—usually a noble such as Siger of Bailleul, William of Mortagne, or Roger of Gistel—in the execution of this particular aspect of the count's business is highly symbolic. Jakemon, who without his office was basically a nobody, represented the depersonalizing and bureaucratic trend of the evolution of comital government. Siger, William, and Roger, who held no specific offices but were individuals of personal prestige, represented the old traditions of personal comital government.

Another source of *ad hoc* expenses was the count's residence or household. These expenses, like local ones, were confided to the care of a single official who received money from the count's treasury to meet them. Since meeting the regular needs of the count's household was a somewhat routine task, it is to be expected at this point in the general receiver's evolution to find Jakemon of Deinze delivering various sums to, for example, Giles, clerk of the household of the countess of Flanders (Guy's wife) in 1294. Such payments do not seem to have been fixed with regard to either amount or date of payment and thus must be treated as *ad hoc* in nature. General receivers as far back as Philip of Bourbourg had handled this responsibility. In 1270–1271, for example, John Makiel, the clerk in charge of the household of Guy of Dampierre, had obtained sums from Lotin of Bruges, Guy's receiver,[56] and even occasionally directly from Philip of Bourbourg, general receiver to his mother, Countess Margaret.[57] Although no general receiver during Margaret's reign seems to have been routinely involved in the actual expenses of running a comital residence, this situation had changed somewhat by the last decade of the thirteenth century. In 1295, Jakemon of Deinze borrowed 486 l. 9 s. 4 d. from Mathew d'Arras to pay for jewels and other objects,[58] items for which Mathew himself in his official capacity was normally responsible. An account drawn up about 1296 reveals that the receiver had paid for cloth delivered to the count.[59] He was not, however, the only person to make such payments. On 1 November 1298, for example, Jeffrey of Ransières, then the count's sergeant, received forty sheep and ten large beasts, valued at 40 l.p., for the count's house.[60]

The general receiver, on behalf of the count, also paid out various sums for the maintenance of Guy's (rather large) family. Gerard Lupichimi made at least two payments, one of 560 l.f. and the second of 500 l.f., to Count Guy's son William.[61] On 19 May 1291, Gerard also advanced money to the count's son John, bishop of Liège.[62] On 26 October 1294 Jakemon of Deinze delivered 200 l.p. of the 1,000 l.p. Guy owed his son Robert.[63] Most of these sums are in round numbers, suggesting that they were not destined for specific expenses. Instead, it is likely that they were simply funds for maintenance. These sums, like those paid to residential clerks, should be considered *ad hoc* expenses, for not only were they fixed neither as to amount nor as to date of payment, they were also drawn on the count's treasury.

Occasionally local receivers, residential financial officials, and the count's family could not meet their expenses, and they called on the count to bail them out. From the time of Gerard's tenure onward, it seems to have become customary for the different creditors of the count's financial personnel and family to apply to the general receiver for reimbursement. For instance, the provost of Béthune, who had sold cloth to the count was obliged to go directly to Gerard to be reimbursed for it.[64] In September 1294, Jakemon of Deinze paid the bills of the count's sons William and John and of their people which the bailiff of Geraardsbergen had presented to him.[65] Purveyance was another form of reimbursement for which the general receiver was answerable. While not himself usually directly responsible for the count's residence, the general receiver reimbursed not only officials who purveyed items but also the individuals who had to sell them. This form of forced provisioning increased during times of war, in particular during the two years (1298–1300) when Franco-Flemish relations were at a stalemate. In April 1298, the count authorized Jakemon of Deinze to reimburse Ernoul le Dorp for the wheat and oats Ernoul had bought from citizens in Oudenaarde on behalf of the count in the name of purveyance.[66] Part of the 306 l. 2 s. 2 d. Jakemon borrowed on 30 August 1298 went to pay Herman Lindelo, a burgher of Cologne, who had sold wine to the count in the name of purveyance.[67] A large part of Flanders was occupied (either by the French or by the English), and the routine collection of comital revenues was difficult. Most of these sums, therefore, had to be paid by the treasury.

Unlike income, which was generated away from the locus of power, a majority of expenses originated with the count and his household. It was the count's domain that needed management and repairs, his household which needed maintenance, his armies that needed supplies and men, and his relationships which needed the bond and flexibility that money could provide. The choice of agents of disbursement throughout the period before 1290 was almost incidental, for it was governed by the fundamental dichotomy between payment by local revenues and payment by the household treasury. Expenses might have been either regular or irregular, but this factor had only a slight impact on the choice of person specifically responsible for payment. The development of fixed dates for payments, however, was an expression of a move toward greater supervision and centralization. In the last decade of the thirteenth century, the payment of comital expenses, like the receipt of revenues, was consolidated by entrusting responsibility for them to a single official, the general receiver. The fact that Gerard and Jakemon, throughout their respective tenures in office, increasingly took responsibility for expenses drawn on the count's treasury, exemplifies this consolidation. Being the agent of disbursement, then, ceased to be incidental and became infused with significance. In addition to bringing certain expenses more firmly under his, and, theoretically, the count's, control, an increase in business at the central level, at the expense of local receivers, would strengthen the prestige and position of the general receiver. At the same time, such consolidation of expenses and revenues, both being, as they were, more or less in the hands of a single central official, enhanced the identification of that office as a county position and not solely a comital one.

Loans

Despite increased centralization, Guy's revenues usually did not cover his expenses. He had inherited a large number of debts from his mother,[68] and incurred an almost equally large number himself. He frequently turned to the Italians for relief and gradually became to some extent dependent on them. In the mid-thirteenth century, Margaret of Constantinople had taken advantage of the migration of Italian merchants from Champagne to encourage the establishment of permanent Italian merchant and banking houses in Flanders.[69] Both she and her son, Count Guy, had favored foreign merchants.[70] In 1281, for example, Guy of Dampierre had granted Lombards licenses to settle in the three major towns, Ghent, Bruges, and Ypres, as well as in several smaller communities.[71] Such licenses were granted for a fee.[72] In return, recipients were given the privilege of residence (which enabled them to set up their businesses) and were taken into the count's protection.[73]

Gerard Lupichimi was a member of one of these Italian banking houses, and loans were a regular part of his business. Within a year after he first appears as Guy's general receiver, the count had already borrowed at least 9,000 l.p. from him.[74] Virtually from the beginning of his tenure in the count's household, then, Gerard was associated with loans.

Loans functioned both as revenue and as expenses. The task of paying off loans assigned on the comital treasury probably fell to the general receiver in the same way other expenses had; this was perhaps the basis for his connection with them. Moreover, as the individual in charge of the count's resources and revenues, the general receiver probably knew which of them could bear the burden of repaying loans. Such knowledge probably determined the involvement of early general receivers, albeit passively, in the negotiation of loans. Philip of Bourbourg had been Margaret of Constantinople's go-between in the contraction of several of her loans, but he does not seem to have had the independent authority to set their terms. In September 1281, Guy had acknowledged receiving a loan of 3000 l. from the Bonsignori at the fairs of Champagne which had been delivered to him by Lotin of Bruges, his general receiver, and Jeffrey of Ransières, the clerk of his residence at Ypres.[75] The acknowledgment does not identify either Lotin or Jeffrey with reference to their official status, which suggests that such positions had meant very little to the merchants at the fairs.

Two incidents mark a change during Gerard's tenure. First, on 21 February 1289, Gerard Lupichimi of Florence delivered to the count 1,500 l. that Guy had borrowed from Florentine merchants.[76] Although Gerard seems to have been involved only in the delivery of this loan and not its negotiation, his participation was nonetheless significant. A Florentine merchant himself, Gerard was probably known to the count's new creditors. He was also general receiver at this time, and the identification of the office with this particular individual may have lent it creditability. This identification, in turn, may even have established a basis for further ascriptions of a certain inherent creditability to holders of the office, whoever they might be.

Second, on 10 January 1291, Gerard acknowledged that he owed Ernoul le Dorp of Oudenaarde 158 l. 8 s.p. for what seems to have been a comital debt, and ordered the bailiff of Aalst to pay it to Ernoul.[77] Since Gerard claimed to owe this sum personally, he probably had negotiated the contract for its repayment himself. At the same time, however, he ordered that it be repaid from comital revenues, to wit, from those of the bailiff of Aalst. It appears that Gerard may have contracted the loan himself, but on the count's behalf. This was something entirely new. None of his predecessors exercised such authority. Furthermore, the count does not seem to have expressly given Gerard this power. At some time during his three years as general receiver, Gerard assumed the power to contract loans and concomitantly the authority to order their repayment from the count's local resources. Until 1289, no one other than the count, his wife, and eldest son seems to have contracted loans on behalf of the comital household.

The experience of subsequent receivers, particularly of Jakemon of Deinze, demonstrates that Gerard's successors in office acted with equal freedom. Jakemon contracted at least twenty-six loans for the count between 1293 and 1299, three-quarters of these falling within the first three years of his tenure as general receiver[78] (see Table 1).

Gerard's, and later Jakemon's, authority to negotiate loans grew out of the demands, largely at this time *ad hoc,* made by the count upon his finances. About two-thirds of the loans contracted by the general receiver were for the needs of the count. Most of the documents recording such loans do not describe what those specific "needs" were. As in the case of expenses, the majority of sums borrowed are in round numbers, indicating that they were probably not destined either to discharge specific debts or to pay for specific expenses; rather, the general receiver simply seems to have needed money in some form, possibly in ready cash. To be sure, the receiver does seem to have borrowed money to pay off particular debts. On 31 May 1294, for example, Jakemon of Deinze borrowed 620 l. 12 s. 5 d.f. from William de l'Espoie for unspecified, but presumably quite specific, needs of the count.[79]

Loans were discharged at a wide variety of times. For a large number of the loans which the general receiver contracted, the creditor would receive his money "on demand."[80] The particular due dates of the rest ranged from 7 March, Easter (March–April), to Pentecost (May–June), 16 June, St. Remy (1 October), All Saint's Day (1 November), and St. Martin's Day (12 November). The loans to be repaid on demand do not differ with respect to either amount or creditor from those with specific due dates. Jakemon of Deinze, for example, borrowed three times from Jakemon Vinne of Bruges: 100 l.f. on 30 December 1293, 20 l.t. on 27 April 1294, and 200 l.f. on 8 August 1294.[81] He agreed to pay back these loans on 7 March, at Pentecost, and upon Jakemon Vinne's request, respectively.

Demand loans were not the most advantageous for the general receiver to arrange. The large number of them suggest that the count's needs were pressing—which they were—and that the general receiver had to arrange loans on any terms possible. Although the records do not mention whether Gerard or Jakemon needed the count's authorization each time they contracted a loan, the frequency with which they were called upon to borrow money, when considered in relation to the broad scope of comital needs the general receiver was expected to meet, suggests that the count had given them the authority to contract and discharge loans at their discretion. In terms of efficiency, such a decision would not have been unwise. The general receiver was, after all, the center of the count's financial system. He knew the state of its finances and was responsible for its management. It would have been very inconvenient for the general receiver to have needed the count's authorization every time he wished to contract a loan.

The general receiver's exercise of the power to contract loans helped

TABLE 1. Loans Contracted by the General Receiver: 1292 to 1300

Date	Creditor	Amount	Date Due	Reason	Other Information	Source
10/1/92	Ernoul le Dorp	158 l.p.		old debt		St.-Gen., #618
29/11/92	Gerard le Nies	340 l.p.			Caution Wm. of Mortagne	St.-Gen., #655
14/10/93	Thierry de Velde	223 l.f.	on demand	Count's needs	Ready cash	St.-Gen., #699
17/6/93	Fairs of Champagne	4,000 l.t.	Fair of May 1294		at Provins	Gai., #528–30
30/12/93	Jakemon Vinne	100 l.f.	March 7	Count's needs		St.-Gen., #705
1293	Bruges	1,000 l.p.		Not yet repaid, 1298		De Smet & Wyffels, 426
13/1/94	Alisen Weytins	200 l.	on demand			Gai., #348
27/4/94	Jakemon Vinne	207 l.t.	Pentecost 1294	Count's needs		St.-Gen., #722
13/5/94	William de l'Espoie	620 l. 2 s.f.	on demand	Count's needs		Gai., #439
8/8/94	Jakemon Vinne	200 l.f.	on demand	Count's needs		St.-Gen., #732

Date	Name	Amount	Term	Purpose	Reference
8/8/94	John of Bruges	100 l.s.	on demand	Count's needs	Gai., #440
13/8/94	Pierre du Sac	500 l.p.	on demand	Count's needs	Gai., #441
26/8/94	Robert & Baldwin Crespin	253 l.	All Saint's Day (1/11/94)	Count's needs	Gai., #442
2/9/94	Lambert Louvain	100 l.p.	on demand	Count's needs	Gai., #443
1294	Gerard Bord	143 l. 2 s. 2 d.	on demand	Purveyance	St.-Gen., #181
2/2/95	Pierre du Sac	1,000 l.f.	1/2 demand, 1/2 Pntcst.	Count's needs	Gai., #446
9/3/95	Bonin, son of Gherm	200 l.p.	on demand	Count's needs	Gai., #447
16/3/95	Pierre du Sac	200 l.f.	Pentecost	Count's needs	Gai., #450
12/5/95	Pierron, son of Margaret	100 l.s.	on demand	Count's needs	Nord, B4055 #3663

TABLE 1. *Continued*

Date	Creditor	Amount	Date Due	Reason	Other Information	Source
13/5/95	John Minne	200 l.f.	on demand	wood		Gai., #453
29/6/95	Mathew of Arras	486 l. 9 s. 4 d.	on demand	Jewels & other goods		Dehaisnes *Doc.*, 1:87
30/6/95	Pierron, son of Margaret	700 l.t.	on demand	Count's needs		Nord, B4055 #3716
2/8/95	Jakemon le Couretier	300 l.p.	St. Martin (12/11/95)	Count's needs		Gai., #456
6/8/95	William de l'Espoie	1,400 l.f.	1/2 12/11, 1/2 Easter	Count's needs		Gai., #458
8/11/95	Philip Escolai	300 l.f.	on demand	Count's needs	Pucci banking house	Gai., #460
27/6/96	Philip Escolai	305 l.	Mid-July			St.-Gen., #828
12/11/96	Umberto degli Umberti	735 l.p.	St. Remi (1/10/97)		banking house	Nord, B4056 #3861

Date	Payee/Place	Amount	When	Purpose	Note	Reference
1296	Bruges	6,000 l.p.		Wages of archers		De Smet & Wyffels, 653
26/3/97	Pierre du Sac	500 l.f.	June 16	Count's needs		Nord, B4057 #3910
15/7/97	Gerard Bord	54 l.p.			For a third party	St.-Gen., #211
1297–1298	Bruges	200 l.				De Smet & Wyffels, 653
13/4/98	Ernoul le Dorp	1,326 l. 10 s. 9 d.p.			old debt	St.-Gen., #980 / Gai., #547
30/8/98	Herman Lindelo	306 l. 2 s. 2 d.	1 Sept.	expenses of castllan. Oudenaarde		St.-Gen., #989
21/1/99	William of Mortagne	174 l.p.	on demand	Count's needs, Purveyance		St.-Gen., #997
29/12/99	Henry Doeske	350 l.f.	1/2 25/12, 1/2 Parl.	various amts. and items	for Rbt. of Béthune	St.-Gen., #1023
1299	Bruges	384 l. 11 s. 8 d.				De Smet & Wyffels, 653
End of the 13th century	Gerard of Ferlin	several sums		arms & men		Ch. sup., #316

make the office itself more indispensable to the count and his financial administration. It must be stressed, however, that the relationship between the count, his general receiver, and the comital administration was still fluid. The count himself contracted many loans, in differing quantities and with differing arrangements for repayment. The amount borrowed does not seem to have dictated who did the borrowing. Many of the loans the count himself contracted were either less than or equivalent to those the general receiver contracted for him. The highest amount Jakemon of Deinze borrowed was 1,400 l.f. from William de l'Espoie on 6 August 1295.[82] The highest he guaranteed was 4,000 l.f., which the count borrowed from Lille.[83] But few of the sums borrowed by the count were demand loans, suggesting that the count may have had less direct access to his own funds than did his receiver.

The general receiver's responsibility for comital revenues, in conjunction with his responsibility for the payment of comital expenses, provided the basis upon which the general receiver's authority over comital finances came to be recognized outside Flanders. A document of 1293 illustrates this point. In June 1293, Count Guy, his eldest son Robert, and Jakemon of Deinze, as Guy's general receiver, mandated John Calvert to borrow up to 4,000 l.t. on behalf of the count at the fairs of Champagne.[84] Jakemon's separate procuration suggests that the count's personal authority might have been somehow insufficient, or that the merchants at the fairs had grown wary of the count's ability to pay. They may have wished to bind his general receiver personally to the agreement as well, in which case the procuration is in the nature of a guarantee. The most striking implication is that the office by this time had become sufficiently recognized and respected for the merchants of the fairs to accept his authorization. This recognition probably resulted from Gerard Lupichimi's tenancy of the office, for it had served to establish its creditability beyond the lands under the count's jurisdiction. It may well have been Jakemon's tenancy, on the other hand, that established its creditability within those lands.

It was not until 1295 that a general receiver whose status was based solely on his office guaranteed a comital loan. Previously, those general receivers who had guaranteed comital loans had also been individuals of some personal prestige. Neither Philip of Bourbourg, who guaranteed two loans,[85] nor Siger of Bailleul, who stood surety for at least one comital loan,[86] had been described as general receiver in the relevant transactions, although both were holding that office when the negotiations took place.[87] Earlier creditors, then, presumed that the prestige of the individual was of greater moment than his specific position in the count's household.[88] But in 1295, William of Mortagne, with Jakemon of Deinze, the count's current general receiver, guaranteed a comital loan of 4,000 l.f.[89] Jakemon was also the sole guarantor of two other comital loans.[90] He did not do so as a figure of independent status; he was, after all, only a minor cleric. He was also, however, general receiver. It is thus difficult to escape the conclusion that what creditability Jakemon had was solely due to his office.

Accounts

The marked increase in local expenses and revenues in the last decade of the thirteenth century was commensurately expressed in the growth in the number of receipts, contracts, and accounts. An increase in this kind of evidence testifies either to greater economic activity or to the institution and implementation of measures to tighten accountability for revenues and expenditures, or perhaps to both. But economic activity in Flanders was not so much greater than it had been earlier as to explain fully the sudden proliferation of these kinds of records. Not only is the amount of financial documents extant from the second half of Count Guy's reign more than triple that from the first half, but the documents record a wider variety of transactions as well; the financial records from the early years of Guy's reign chiefly concern expenses. The ravages of time cannot explain this rather abrupt rise in the number of financial documentation. Instead, the increase in both number and variety of financial records in the second half of Guy's reign seems to have resulted directly from the introduction of measures to make the financial structure more accountable to the general receiver.

On the surface, this increased accountability might seem to have resulted from the count's need for large sums of accessible money. The increased number of accounts presupposes the imposition of some kind of order—order that theoretically would have increased the predictability of the count's finances and thus allow the count to plan their use efficiently and effectively. This, in turn, would facilitate the realization of his ambitions (both offensive and defensive, and domestic as well as international). But there is no evidence that Guy involved himself personally in the organization of his finances. Although one of the richest princes in northern Europe, Guy was not a financial expert. What reforms eventuated seem to have occurred from inside the financial branch of the count's household. They most likely originated from the mind of Gerard Lupichimi. Gerard, after all, was a Florentine banker, and thus a financial expert—at least certainly more of one than Guy of Dampierre. He was the first of a series of Italians to hold the office of general receiver, and with the possible exception of Nicholas Guiduche, the most effective of them.[91]

Of equal importance is the fact that Jakemon of Deinze also possessed valuable financial expertise, gained while in the employment of Beatrice of Courtrai. It is undeniable that under Jakemon certain changes, which may have been initiated by Gerard, were realized. It would be difficult, if not impossible to determine which innovation was the brainchild of which receiver.

Before 1289, the general receiver's responsibilities for the actual auditing process had not changed markedly since Philip of Bourbourg left office in 1280. As long as general receivers continued to be responsible for the net receipts of reckoning sessions and for the payment of certain expenses drawn on them, they probably continued also to be, as Philip had been, responsible for summoning the bailiffs and domainal receivers for audit. It is no accident, however, that the first complete extant account of the *renenghe* is for the year 1296;[92] this account makes it quite clear that the audit was heard in the presence of Jakemon of Deinze, the general receiver.[93] In addition, the count, perhaps at the urging of his general receiver, had taken steps by at least 1295 to insure that his general receiver also sat on the commission that heard the *rentes hors renenghe*. In 1295 Jakemon of Deinze himself held the receivership of two of the major circumscriptions *hors renenghe*, that for the *rentes* of the Vier Ambachten of Ghent and Bruges, and that for those of the moors and lands of Aksel and Hulst. These receiverships would have entitled Jakemon to participate in the audit for this type of revenue even if he had not been general receiver. Subsequent receivers also seem always to have held these receiverships or similar ones.[94] The general receiver also probably continued to participate in the accounting of the bailiffs as a member of the auditing commission. In 1293, for example, the auditors of the bailiff's accounts, convened to conduct an inquiry into the activities of one of the bailiffs, included two former general receivers, Siger of Bailleul and Lotin of Bruges, as well as the current receiver, Jakemon of Deinze.[95] Present at the *renenghe* and the bailiff's audit and a participator in the accounting of the *rentes hors renenghe*, the general receiver by 1295 was in a position to demand not only that written evidence be produced but also that the audit itself be routinely committed to paper, and finally, that all documentation be preserved.

It should come as no surprise that the number of accounts from this period is far higher than for any earlier one. Local receivers before 1290 may have kept written accounts of their transactions, but if they did, they do not seem to have preserved them—there may not have been much incentive to do so. They may have handed them over to the count, but since there was, for all intents and purposes, no financial department, and since the general receivership was in a transitional stage, neither the motivation nor the means for conserving them may have existed. Once the general receivership was in place and its holder charged with extracting the most he could from the count's resources, a condition which certainly fits the situation from 1289 on, the count's household enjoyed a much better record for conserving financial material. We do know that local financial officials kept such records after 1289 since they did present letters and receipts at the audits in order to justify their expenses. In August 1292, for instance, Gerard Lupichimi declared in writing that he had received 7,400 l. in the name of the count from the receiver of the tithe of Cambrai, a domainal district.[96] A document dated 26 December 1295 indicates that Gilbert le Mil, bailiff of Geraardsbergen, had presented many such "pieces" at the audit of his account.[97] Extant accounts for the last decade of the thirteenth century contain a number of references to such letters, or "pieces," for example: "To the receiver 3845 l. 3 s. 8 d., which the receiver has accounted for. . . . in three pieces."[98]

Increased financial accountability may also have engendered a new kind of account, one which pertained to an individual receiver but was separate from major records of audit such as the *renenghe* or the bailiffs' account.[99] Sometime in the last decade of the thirteenth century, it became common for the transactions of certain districts to be recorded in their own separate accounts. The financial activity these separate individual accounts listed was not incorporated *in toto* into the major account as it had been in earlier records of audit, but was entered usually only in summary form. Individual bailiffs' accounts became numerous during this period.[100] Similarly, whereas *renenghes* possibly existed as early as 1250, and certainly by 1272,[101] separate records of the individual receiver's account do not appear until around 1293. By 1296, although the expenses of most of the *rentes hors renenghe* were presented in detail in the *renenghe* accounts, the receipts were not; instead only the totals are noted. Since revenues were of major importance to the count, it is likely that there existed some other account in which the receiver listed income in detail. This conclusion is borne out by the existence of specific individual accounts of the receivers of the new domain in which, after 1295, both receipts and expenses do appear in detail.

Several factors contributed to the development of separate individual accounts. They benefited the count, the general receiver, and the particular receiver. The count and the general receiver may have ordered receivers to use this form in an attempt to keep track of the details of local financial transactions. Local officials, for their part, may have had an incentive to keep a record of those of their activities which had been formally approved as proof of that approval. Separate accounts may also have developed out of a desire to minimize, or at least to cope with the growing amount of paperwork. The number of extant quittances and receipts for local transactions drops correspondingly in this period, for receipts generated by such transactions would be incorporated into the separate account of the local receiver or bailiff concerned. There may thus have been less reason to keep them.[102]

The development of separate individual accounts had repercussions for the accounts of the audits already in existence, that is, the *renenghe* and the bailiffs' general account. It appears, in fact, that an account of all of the activities of all the bailiffs, which effectively constituted a counterpart of the record of the *renenghe,* was, sometime in the last decade of the thirteenth century, jettisoned in favor of individual accounts. This would simultaneously explain why the 1255 baillivial account appears to be the last of its kind and why the number of individual separate accounts increased markedly at the end of the thirteenth century. As for the accounts of domainal receivers, they continued to be accommodated in some form in the *renenghe,* but as we have seen, the receipts in the *rentes hors renenghe* were no longer given in detail. Thus, separate individual accounts for these officials developed alongside the older form.

The common factor in all accounts, both separate and combined, was the general receiver. Without some form of centralization, as expressed by the participation of the general receiver in the audits, the development of individual accounts may never have occurred. As head of all the count's finances, in the well-being of which he seems to have had a personal investment, Gerard Lupichimi was the one individual who personally and consistently involved himself in the audits of the accounts of local officials. Regardless of any personal stake they might have had in the count's financial health, subsequent general receivers continued Gerard's practice. The general receiver received the surpluses of local officials, paid their deficits, and heard the record of their transactions. It was against his records that their activities and their records were compared. His letters or "pieces" were mentioned in the accounts as evidence of sums received or paid out. Finally, he conserved their accounts.

Accounts were not the only form of written evidence to increase in the last decade of the thirteenth century. Quittances of all kinds also multiplied. Most of these pertained to *ad hoc* transactions which were not accommodated within either of the two accounting sessions. Such transactions can be roughly characterized as financial activities which, either because they lay outside the jurisdiction of local administrators or because they arose from sources which were not local in nature, could not be dealt with by the established systems. Responsibility for these various incomes and expenses was never clearly defined. As previously indicated, certain financial affairs such as the payment of *ad hoc* expenses had become the responsibility of the general receiver on the basis of his status as the single individual in charge of the count's finances. He was the only official who had come to be directly involved in verifying a receipt for a payment drawn upon the net revenues of the *renenghe* or the bailiffs' sessions. Whereas payments of pensions, loans, and money fiefs assigned on local revenues would appear in the accounts of the local receivers, those payments the general receiver himself made, as well as those he received directly, probably went unaccounted for. The existence of these receipts and quittances indicates a lack of any accounting routine for the activities of the general receiver. There existed no system into which these *ad hoc* transactions could be fit, and consequently no general account covering all of the revenues and expenses handled by the general receiver. No group had been empowered to audit the general receiver himself; indeed, the issue may not yet have arisen. Hence, and not surprisingly, most of these receipts mention transactions which do not appear in any of the regular accounts. That is not to say that all such transactions escaped accounting. Various partial accounts of an *ad hoc* nature do exist. Gerard Lupichimi, for example, drew up a list of the count's debts on 15 September 1290;[103] another document lists the contributions assessed by Jakemon of Deinze and Siger of Bailleul which the churches and religious houses were encouraged to make in 1294 for the maintenance of lands diked along the sea.[104] Such partial accounts were probably precursors of the general account, which did, in fact, come into existence in the early fourteenth century.

Unlike the accounting systems of England and France at the end of the thirteenth century, the audit of accounts in Flanders had not, however, "gone out of court" to settle permanently in one location. Countess Jeanne and Countess Margaret's marked preference for Lille might have encouraged that tendency, but unlike his predecessors, Guy did not routinely conduct financial business in any particular place. Lille's establishment as the Flemish's count's financial center would have to wait until the late fourteenth century and the advent of the Burgundians.[105] Accounts were thus heard in a variety of places, usually in one of the major towns, and usually at the count's residence. In 1295, an audit even took place at the house of Jakemon of Deinze in Bruges.[106] But this should not be surprising; convenience undoubtedly had initially dictated that the count's accounts be heard at his own residence, and convenience probably suggested that they be heard, in this case, at Jakemon's residence. What this circumstance indicates is the degree to which the general receiver's presence had become part of the routine of the audit. Furthermore, in the physical separation of the audit of accounts from the count's residence, it is possible in retrospect to discern an important facet of the slow evolution of the treasury into a public purse. Correspondingly, the person routinely responsible for it developed from a personal servant into a public official.

During the tenures of Gerard Lupichimi and Jakemon of Deinze, the relationship of the general receiver to the task of auditing accounts was worked out. The general receiver's presence was required at the reckonings of all the count's financial officials. He participated somewhat passively as the supervisor of the old domainal session at the *renenghe,* but more actively as a member of the auditing commission for the *rentes hors renenghe;* he was also a member of a similar commission that regulated the accounts of the bailiffs. At the same time, however, he was not himself accountable for any of the *ad hoc* financial activity which had come to constitute such a large part of his day-to-day work. What was lacking was a formal audit of the general receiver's actions and a group of individuals who might have the authority to check and verify his accounts. When Philip of Bourbourg became general receiver, the count's finances still depended primarily on local resources as administered by bailiffs and domainal receivers, both of which had already developed routines of management and audit. By the end of the thirteenth century, use and custom had first established and then reinforced the general receiver's supervisory position over the accounting of bailiffs and domainal receivers. In addition, the general receiver had developed his own financial circumscription, as it were, whose main feature was the *ad hoc* nature of its revenues and expenses. It had probably taken some time before the old domain had developed the auditing system of which the *gros brief* was a manifestation, and before the audit of the old and new domains had come together to create the *renenghe* account. Similarly, it would take some time for those financial matters that the general receiver dealt with himself to become numerous enough and sufficiently routine to warrant an accounting.

Experience, Staff, and Remuneration

Financial responsibilities increased and became more complicated during Gerard's and Jakemon's tenures. Both of these men had to acquire the special and necessary skills to handle financial matters efficiently. More responsibility meant more work, but as new tasks became customary and as routine procedures evolved from discharging them, the general receiver began to delegate them to minor officials; this in turn provided the point of departure for the development of a rudimentary department or staff. All of these developments, in conjunction with the evolution of remuneration for services rendered, contributed toward the separation of the office from the comital household.

Before 1289 the lines between the functions performed by a member of the count's household and similar or even identical functions performed by the general receiver were still blurred. The office, as we have seen, was frequently one among several which a household member might hold. Those who performed its functions, although possessing some experience and skills, were in no way professionals. Remuneration was not attached to the office, and the general receiver's authority does not seem to have extended even over those members of the comital household who performed financial services. For major decisions and actions affecting his revenues as a whole, the count relied rather indiscriminately upon the different individuals who continually surrounded him and who formed his household. Until mid-century, the count rarely assigned responsibility for any specifically delimited sphere of ongoing activity to any of them; the concept that such a sphere of activity even existed at the central level had not yet developed. The major element of the count's household, of course, consisted of nobles. Members of noble families had traditionally held the major household offices of constable, chamberlain, butler, and steward.[107] Although by the mid-thirteenth century these positions had become merely honorary, nobles still continued to be found in fairly constant attendance on the count, and he continued to commission them for the performance of a wide variety of functions and duties. However, nobles usually had their own lands to manage and could not devote their whole attention to comital affairs.

The count was also attended by a variety of other servitors, variously known as valets, sergeants, *knaben,* or *familiares.* Such labels referred to any persons attached to the count's household, but without specific functions or duties.[108] Valets and sergeants included people from the towns and members of the petty nobility, such as Jeffrey of Ransières.[109] The count was also surrounded by clerics, who might be described as the ecclesiastical counterparts of valets or sergeants, and who, being literate, were usually responsible for the writing of charters. Functions a person performed defined neither position nor rank in the count's household, and few functions were reserved exclusively for a particular office. Philip, Lotin, Siger, and Jeffrey had all acquired skills from on-the-job experience in other capacities in the comital household before being made general receivers. Many of the household tasks they performed involved the management of revenues. Many, moreover, were similar to the activities associated with the general receivership, or were even among the tasks otherwise performed by the general receiver himself. Frequently, then, no great distinction separated the individual who performed functions as general receiver from one who performed them as a non-specific member of the household.

What did differentiate members of the household from each other before 1289 was their respective bases of maintenance. The nobility usually had landholdings or rights which produced the revenue and supplies that supported them, thus making them more or less independent of the count's treasury and of his goodwill. Clerics were usually maintained by means of livings, prebends, canonries, or other religious incomes. The advantage of employing nobles and clerks was obvious: their maintenance did not come out of the count's pocket. But the loyalties of nobles and clerks were correspondingly divided, in the one case between the count and personal estates, and in the other between the count and the Church. Valets and sergeants, by contrast, were more apt to identify with comital interests, precisely because they depended on him for their food, lodging, and, frequently, livery. In the thirteenth century, nobles, valets, sergeants, and clerks formed a pool from which the count could chose individuals to perform certain tasks for him. All of the general receivers up to 1289 belonged to this active pool; all continued to function in *ad hoc* capacities after relinquishing the office.[110]

The situation changed in the last decade of the thirteenth century. Before assuming the office of general receiver, both Gerard Lupichimi and Jakemon of Deinze, unlike previous receivers, had acquired specific skills outside the comital household in the performance of duties that were primarily financial in character. Little evidence still exists which would indicate precisely the nature of Gerard's activities before he became general receiver in 1289. Gerard, a banker from Florence, had established himself in Flanders with his nephew John and his brother Francis.[111] As a banker, Gerard was not only skilled in figures and in the management of money, he was also probably wealthy. Jakemon of Deinze acquired his financial expertise primarily in the household of Beatrice of Courtrai. Jakemon had functioned as Beatrice's receiver from 2 July 1280 to at least 26 July 1283.[112] Upon at least one occasion he was the agent of receipt for a life rent from Guy of Dampierre.[113] In this capacity Jakemon had thus acquired familiarity with the system of accounting and collection of revenues current at this time. Sometime after Beatrice's death in 1288,[114] Jakemon entered the service of the count of Flanders.[115]

Unlike the earlier receivers, Gerard rarely performed services for the count which were unconnected with his financial office. There is no evidence that he ever participated in land transactions, or acted as the count's agent in his disputes or on diplomatic missions. The latter circumstance is all the more remarkable in that foreigners often were used in a diplomatic capacity.[116] Gerard appears to have concerned himself solely with the collection, accounting, and disbursement of comital revenues. His position in the comital household was thus clear-cut. Consequently, anyone associated with him was probably assumed to be performing duties connected with comital finance. His nephew, John, and his brother, Francis, may also have worked for him in his capacity as general receiver.

Unlike Gerard Lupichimi, Jakemon had been a member of the count's household (albeit for only a short time) before the count appointed him general receiver. Despite the apparent promotion within the comital household, Jakemon still remained essentially the count's clerk. While Jakemon's increased obligations differentiated him from other clerks, valets, and sergeants, the distinction between being a comital clerk and being general receiver was not yet sufficiently achieved to set him wholly apart from the rest of the household, particularly as long as any of his functions remained chiefly *ad hoc* in nature.

Jakemon's jurisdiction outside the count's household was more defined. He was the acknowledged comital official to whom local financial officials were to respond. In appointing Jakemon receiver on 11 August 1292, Guy ordered bailiffs, receivers, and farmers to "obey, and answer to him [Jakemon] for that which they owe."[117] The count's order was, in fact, probably a *post hoc* acknowledgment of the general receiver's jurisdiction over them. But the general receiver's growing control over bailiffs, receivers, and farmers in no way turned them into a real staff or central financial department.

There are indications, however, that such a rudimentary department or staff was emerging. At least five officials within the comital household itself seem to have routinely executed financial duties at Jakemon's behest. Various records specifically label John of Tournai, Giles of Hertsberghe, Jakemon Louchard, John of Lille, and Pierre of Reckelines the general receiver's valet, sergeant, or clerk.[118] With the exception of John of Lille, who had been in the count's household since 1270,[119] all of these individuals first appear in the count's household as attached to Jakemon of Deinze; three of the five again show up as members of the next count's administration.[120] Under Jakemon their sphere of activity included receiving payments, giving quittance, and even supervising the *renenghe*.[121] John of Lille was also responsible for keeping the records of payments the receiver made for the count;[122] the conservation of accounts of the bailiffs and domainal receivers also seems to have become the responsibility of a clerk of the general receiver.[123] Of the five payments made to the count in 1296 from the revenues of the woods at Nieppe, Jakemon received one himself, but the other four were received by either Giles of Hertsberghe or Jakemon Louchard in their capacity as valets of the general receiver.[124] The repeated exercise of a function such as this one by a particular group of officials may have tended to encourage its identification with them.

Unfortunately, there is no way of knowing whether any of these men were associated exclusively with the general receiver. But the consistency with which they performed financial functions, always in the capacity of the general receiver's valet or clerk, strongly suggests that they formed a *de facto* financial department within the count's household.[125] Furthermore, these men appear as the "receiver's clerk" or the "receiver's valet," as opposed to the count's clerk or valet, indicating that they were answerable chiefly to the general receiver and that he determined their actions. This circumstance separated them from the rest of the clerks, sergeants, and valets in the count's household and seems to have distinguished them as a sort of "proto-staff" under the supervision of the general receiver.[126]

Underscoring this conclusion is a document of 12 November 1302. In it Baldwin, master of the count's engines, acknowledges that he received 1,500 l. for the works of the fortresses of Damme and Aardenburg from the clerks of the general receiver.[127] In the first place, the county was in French hands—hence it is unlikely that a general receiver existed in 1302.[128] Therefore the clerks of the general receiver may have been acting on their own, as a department. If the department did not dissolve with the vacancy of the office, then the office itself had taken an important step toward institutionalization. In the second place, the debt was an old one, possibly dating back to as early as 1289. Is it not more likely that a bill of that date and for that amount of money would have been paid by the general receiver if there had been one, or by someone of higher rank than mere clerk, if there had not? That the department handled this problem, therefore, indicates that the ensemble of Jakemon and his clerks had by the end of the century achieved recognition as an institution. They were no longer perceived merely as an arbitrary collection of individuals.

The office of general receiver also took the first rudimentary steps toward institutionalization in the area of remuneration. Marking a departure from previous practice, the count does not seem to have given any land to Gerard and Jakemon before, during, or after their service as general receiver. As we have seen, early general receivers received grants of revenue-producing lands and rights, both as compensation for services rendered and to provide them with a basis for maintenance. But Gerard was a banker, and it is possible that Count Guy chose him to be his receiver not only on account of Gerard's financial skills but also on account of his wealth—one of the first actions Gerard took soon after becoming receiver was to loan the count about 9,000 l.[129] It is possible that, when all else failed, Gerard may even have had to pay for comital expenses from his own resources. The general accounts and charters of appointment of the fourteenth century make it clear that when the count's resources were inadequate, the general receiver himself not infrequently made up the difference, a circumstance that may have provided Gerard with the incentive to leave the office.[130] Yet if, on the one hand, the general receiver was obliged to make up the difference when a deficit occurred, on the other hand, he may well have been entitled to any surpluses. Although this hypothesis must remain speculative for the thirteenth century, it should be noted that this practice was formalized in the mid-fourteenth. Combined with the likelihood that Gerard was personally wealthy, such an arrangement may have been why Gerard received no gifts of land or continuous income.

Jakemon of Deinze did profit directly from his tenure as general receiver. Although he was drawing a substantial living as canon of Courtrai[131] and as provost of Notre Dame of Bruges,[132] the count bestowed incomes on him as well. On 11 July 1293, the count granted Jakemon an annual income of 50 l. as the receiver of certain briefs.[133] This income was to be drawn from their gross revenues, as was the usual custom for a domainal receiver, but since the position of receiver of these briefs was a sinecure, the count's grant was more in the nature of a *gage* than remuneration for particular services rendered. A *gage* was a pledge of something of value, given as insurance that a particular action would be performed. In this case the pledge was the income from the briefs, but the actions to be performed were not those associated with that particular domainal receivership, but rather those associated with the office of general receiver. Like fiefs, *gages* could be forfeited, but only for the non-performance of the specific service. Jakemon's resources as a cleric were minimal when compared with those of his two predecessors, Gerard Lupichimi and Siger of Bailleul.[134] He was dependent upon the count for his maintenance, and, just as the count granted land and money fiefs to his vassals for purposes of maintenance and in exchange for their services, he granted Jakemon an income to be drawn from comital resources. The crucial difference between a *gage* and a money fief was in the impersonal nature of the contract. The recipient of a *gage* did not promise homage and fealty; he promised that certain actions would be taken. The *gage* regularized and impersonalized the relationship between Jakemon and the count. The "employer" (the count) was not giving a gracious gift but was contracting for services. Jakemon was granted this *gage* of 50 l. only a year after becoming general receiver, and he received it not for services rendered—as payment for actions already taken—but as insurance that certain actions would be taken. The nuance of difference between the two meanings is slight but important, and it is hard to distinguish between grants of income given as recompense for services rendered and *gages*.

Jakemon's *gage* is the first of its kind to be granted to a general receiver. Philip of Bourbourg, Lotin of Bruges, and Jeffrey of Ransières had all received grants from the count, but these had been grants of land, not of income. In December 1294, the count further granted Jakemon 100 l.t. per annum, for life, to be drawn from the gross revenues of the briefs of the Land of Waas.[135] This grant was made in recompense for his services. Since it was given for life, it was thus a gift, attached to the individual and not to the office. The juxtaposition of the grant of 50 l. as a *gage* and that of 100 l.t. as recompense may well have served to blur the distinctions between a *gage*, recompense, and a salary. In any event, a connection had been made for the first time between functions which the general receiver performed and pecuniary payments which he received from the count. It would certainly be erroneous to consider such payments as wages or as a salary, for wages were attached to the office and ceased to be paid to an individual once he no longer performed that office's functions. *Gages* were attached primarily to an individual and only secondarily to services. They ended only when one of the two contracting parties died or when, for whatever reason, the contract between them was broken or renegotiated. It was but a short step, however, from *gage* to wage.

Jakemon drew his 50 l. per annum from a domainal circumscription. A document dated 18 July 1294 indicates that Jakemon was also the receiver of the briefs from which his *gage* came.[136] It was the customary practice for all receivers and bailiffs to receive a *gage* from the circumscription for which they were responsible. The real purpose of the count's grant, however, was to provide Jakemon with an income, with maintenance; it was not a mere concomitant of the act of confiding the particular domainal district to the receiver's care. At this point there was still no conception of a circumscription which would encompass all of the revenues and all of the expenses the general receiver handled. Annual pecuniary payments of *gages* were intrinsically connected with the district on which such payments were assigned. The only payments assigned on the treasury of the count were money fiefs, pensions, and life rents, none of which entailed services in the same way as did a *gage*. Only when the count's treasury itself became identified as the general receiver's peculiar province could the basis for the conception of a general receiver's salary be formed. The arrangements by which Jakemon came to be remunerated did nonetheless prefigure the development of such a conception.

Judicial Matters

Unlike Gerard, Jakemon was involved in matters unrelated to the count's finances. Most of these matters involved regulating the count's relationship both inside the comital administration—for example, as in investigating the behavior of comital officials such as bailiffs—and outside the county— for example, in arbitrating the count's disputes with his fellow princes and even the pope. Jakemon's participation in these affairs was based on his close association with the count, an association which derived not from a personal connection but instead from his position as head of the count's finances.

Bailiffs were the count's major local judicial officers.[137] Because the judicial proceedings under their jurisdiction frequently yielded income, they were also important financial officials, and they paid their net revenues to the general receiver. Of course, he also frequently reimbursed them for expenses beyond the income of their resources. Although comital bailiffs did not have a hierarchical head,[138] the extension of the authority of the general receiver over them was implicit in the subordinate financial relationship in which they stood with respect to the receiver, and which had been developing since Philip of Bourbourg's tenure in office.[139] The bailiffs' ternary sessions not only included audits of their accounts but also provided the count or his representative with the opportunity to handle irregularities, complaints, and other problems. Since the general receiver presided over these sessions, he was thus the most constant central administrative element in bailiffs' affairs, including non-financial ones.

In the last decade of the thirteenth century, the count began to charge his general receiver, among others, with examining complaints involving bailiffs. In 1293, for example, Jakemon was among those comital counselors who acted as judges in the case against the bailiff of Veurne.[140] The fact of his participation in such actions seems to have both reflected his *de facto* power over bailiffs and contributed to its expansion. In 1296, Peter de Jumel, a former bailiff of Lille and Douai[141] who had been deprived of his office, promised specifically to present himself either to the count or to the receiver for judgment.[142] Peter's promise to present himself to the receiver implies that the receiver was in some way his superior.[143] Bailiffs were also to obey the general receiver's orders with respect to non-financial matters. On 5 September 1293, for example, Jakemon issued an order to the bailiffs to leave its bearer, who happened to be carrying 300 l.s., in peace.[144]

But the receiver's involvement went beyond judicial matters handled by bailiffs. As general receiver Jakemon was also the logical agent for the negotiation of matters concerning comital finances. Sometime between 1295 and 1299, for example, Arnold de Liederkerk, a canon of Tournai and treasurer of Leuze, wrote to Jakemon requesting his aid in the restitution of the tithe of Clemlers.[145] Such a request did not simply involve the delivery of sums due Arnold, but rather the solution of the problem which had resulted in the distraint of the tithe in the first place; Arnold obviously felt that Jakemon was in a position to help him.[146] Moreover, it was Jakemon who negotiated an agreement with Francis Lupichimi, Gerard's brother; this involved a debt the count still owed Gerard. On 10 October 1296 they agreed that the count would recognize that he owed Gerard 6,100 l. and that Gerard would deduct all that he owed the count from his own last reckoning as general receiver from this sum.[147]

Jakemon, as general receiver, also participated in inquests and arbitrations. Aroused by the suspicious actions of various citizens of Damme, Count Guy authorized Jakemon and William of Mortagne on 14 April 1298 to conduct an inquiry into these actions, and to punish those whom they judged to be guilty of disloyalty.[148] In that same year, Jakemon and William were also chosen to represent the court before arbitrators[149] appointed to settle disputes he had with the count of Gueldres.[150] No decision the arbitrators made would be accepted without William and Jakemon's concurrence.

As we have seen, a precedent for Jakemon's involvement in such matters had been established in the first years of Guy's reign. Siger of Bailleul and Jeffrey of Ransières had participated in a number of similar matters while receiver of Flanders. They, and for that matter, William of Mortagne, participated in these matters chiefly because they were individuals of some personal power and prestige. Compared with their social status, the title of general receiver was of little consequence and provided little or no basis for their involvement in such affairs; it was not even mentioned. But Jakemon had little claim to prestige or authority other than that conferred on him by his tenancy of the office. Even his status as a member of the count's household, for example, derived solely from his office. So, also, it must have been on the basis of his status as general receiver that Jakemon was assigned to conduct the inquiry at Damme, and to be the count's representative in the arbitration of the dispute with the count of Gueldres. These appointments may be said to constitute *de facto* recognition of Jakemon's status as general receiver as being comparable with that of his companion. In effect, the appellation "general receiver" functioned in the same way as did William of Mortagne's title of knight. Both titles defined the bearer in terms of his social standing and thus of his power. William's social standing did not depend on the functions he performed for the count,[151] whereas Jakemon's relied wholly on that connection. He derived creditability from his official position as William did from his birthright. Jakemon's participation in inquests and arbitration, moreover, had the effect of further promoting the association of his office with such matters, both in the count's mind and in the minds of those who lived within his jurisdiction. Coupled with the general receiver's already extant authority over the revenues of the bailiffs, Jakemon's involvement with inquests and arbitration can be seen as a small but significant step toward the later assumption by the office of jurisdiction over the whole of the count's judicial structure.

Conclusion

It is evident that the period of crisis in Franco-Flemish relations was a pivotal one in the evolution of the office, not only with respect to the specific definition of its scope and authority, but also, more fundamentally, with regard to its character as an institution. It was not until the tenures of Gerard Lupichimi and Jakemon of Deinze that a basis was established for the generalized use of the title "receiver of Flanders" to refer to the incumbent, regardless of the specific activity in which he happened momentarily to be engaged. Furthermore, under Gerard and Jakemon, functions that heretofore had been associated with the office almost as if by default developed into routines and began to take on a new coherence. Gerard had originally been brought in as a financial expert, and he never performed anything but the financial tasks associated, however loosely, with the central management of the count's revenues. This had the effect of consolidating such tasks to the point where they came to be regarded as the main responsibility of the general receiver. It was also during Gerard's tenure that the office assumed the authority to contract loans on behalf of the count and to assign their repayment on comital resources. During Gerard's three years in the count's service, then, the control of the general receiver over the count's household treasury, which had already been implicit in the establishment of Philip of Bourbourg as the agent uniquely responsible for all comital revenues, became an explicit reality; the household treasury correspondingly became the count's primary or central treasury. The increase in the number of accounts during the receivership of Jakemon of Deinze was a further reflection of such control; each account usually included the general receiver's notation of his receipt of net revenues or his payment of deficits.

Jakemon was the first general receiver for whom there is evidence of a cadre of officials, which he supervised in the performance of financial tasks. Jakemon himself had exercised various financial functions while Gerard Lupichimi held office, but nothing in the records indicates that he had been subordinate to Gerard or that he acted on Gerard's orders. Those who performed similar functions while Jakemon was receiver, however, appear to have been answerable to him. This circumstance indicates that before the end of Jakemon's tenure the office itself had acquired a measure of organizational structure and autonomy previously lacking.

Finally, Jakemon was the first general receiver for whom a charter of appointment exists. Certainly the possibility of earlier appointment charters cannot be excluded. Given that he was not a member of the household and that he performed only financial tasks while he held the position, Gerard may have been formally commissioned and the document destroyed in the course of time. But curiously enough, Gerard's tenure in office overlapped that of his predecessor, Siger of Bailleul. Gerard's possession of his office was in this way similar to that of receivers in the early part of Guy's reign. These early receivers, of which Gerard in this instance must be included, entered into the position gradually, which suggests that none of them received a formal appointment. That Jakemon's appointment charter was probably the first of its kind suggests that the office may not have achieved recognition as an entity apart from the person who performed its functions until sometime during Gerard's three years in office.

Two other circumstances support such a conclusion. First, a record drawn up during Gerard's tenure mentions him only by office and not by name. In this document, dated 26 July 1291, appears the phrase "our said receiver, whoever he will be."[152] This phrase signifies recognition of the continuance of the office beyond the tenure of its incumbent. Second, Gerard was called "former receiver" after having left the office, the first receiver to have been so described.[153] Lotin of Bruges, Siger of Bailleul, and Jeffrey of Ransières all remained in the count's service after they had ceased to be referred to as general receiver, but none of them seems ever to have been called a former receiver. Since Gerard had never held any position in the count's household other than receiver, his relationship to the position probably continued to identify him once he left the count's household. By 1293 the office had therefore developed to the point where it identified the holder in terms of his past or present position as general receiver, regardless of the particular tasks he currently performed.

During the last decade of the thirteenth century, the office came to transcend the tenancy of its incumbent, and the general receiver ceased to be strictly a personal servant of the count. Although Philip of Bourbourg became a territorial official of sorts when he assumed responsibility for all of the revenues of the count of Flanders, he remained a personal servant of the count and a member of his household. Gerard Lupichimi's and Jakemon of Deinze's status stood on the borderline between that of a personal servant to the count and that of a governmental or public official. It was the office's acquisition of an autonomous status, in part a result of the depersonalizing routinization of its functions, which constituted the crucial link between its earlier reference to a personal servant in charge of the revenues of a territorial prince and its later development in the direction of a public office.

Notes

1. Van Werveke, *Avesnes en Dampierre,* 314.
2. Bruges, Stadsarchief, Fonds Politiek charters, Reeks 1, #84 (hereafter Pol. chrs.). Bruges had promised the count 30,000 l. to be paid in two installments, the first on 11 November 1295 and the second a year later.

This payment seems to have been unrelated to the fiftieth levied on the Flemish communities, since the decision made by Philip and Guy to levy this amount was made in January of 1296. By the terms of the 1296 agreement, Guy would collect the fiftieth from the Flemish communities and have a share in it. He obviously believed that he had the necessary organization to collect this sum; he probably even welcomed the opportunity this gave him to exercise financial authority over the Flemish communities. What he did not reckon with was the opposition he encountered in attempting to collect the fiftieth from the major Flemish towns. Furious with the count, four of them lodged complaints against the count with Philip (Strayer, *Philip the Fair,* 829–830). Philip, who had commissioned the levy in the first place, sided with the towns, thus placing Guy in an unenviable position vis-à-vis not only the towns but also the French king.

3. He was repaying Renier le Flamens, a money-changer of Paris, 500 l. of the 1,339 l. 18 s. 6 d. Guy of Flanders owed him (St.-Genois, #480).

4. In a list of Guy's debts appears the entry: "A Gerart le receveur por le remanant de sen conte . . . 8,668 l. 16 s. 10 $^1/_2$ d." (Bigwood, *Le régime juridique,* 2:296 #15). Whether the 10,000 l. Guy paid (via Gerard) to John of Avesnes on 7 October 1289 for a debt had actually been borrowed from Gerard is uncertain (Nord, B4047 #3089; D. E. Queller, "Diplomatic Personnel Employed by the Counts of Flanders in the Thirteenth Century," *RBPH* 34 [1956], 395 and n. 2). It is unclear from the document exactly to whom the money originally belonged: "Nous, Jehans d'Avesnes, cuens de Haynau, faisons savoir à tous ke nous avons rechut par le main Grart de Florence, receveur de Flandres, pour noble home no treschier oncle, Guyon, conte de Flandres et marchis de Namur, dis mille livres de tornois lesquels nos dis oncle deseure dis nous devoit paier."

5. Van Werveke, *Avesnes en Dampierre,* 319–320.

6. *Ibid.,* 318.

7. *Ibid.,* 319.

8. There is no reason to suppose that Jakemon did not come from Deinze, a small town located between Courtrai and Ghent.

9. Nord, B4050 #3382.

10. "tous nos baillius, recheveurs et censisseurs de nos rentes et de nos censes de nostre devant dit contei. . . . [ke] a lui paicent et respondent de ce kil nous doient."

11. St.-Genois, #647. For the best analysis of tithes in the hands of persons or parties other than the church for whose upkeep they were paid, see Giles Constable, *Monastic Tithes* (Cambridge, 1964).

12. Luykx, *De grafelijke bestuurinstellingen,* 470 #137.

13. Gaillard, #88.

14. Also paid by a bailiff *(ibid.,* #79).

15. Domaines du bailliage de Menin. Compte de 25 juillet 1293 à 12 juillet 1294, RR, #117; Compte de 25 juillet 1294 à juillet 1295, *ibid.,* #118; Compte de 25 juillet 1295 à 15 août 1296, *ibid.,* #119; Rentes du pays de Waes. Compte du clerc Jean de Muda jusqu'au 24 juillet 1294, *ibid.,* #350; Rentes à Saftingen et vents des moeres et wastines appartenant à Madame. Compte du 24 juin 1293 au 23 juin 1294, *ibid.,* #181.

16. Wyffels and de Smet, 454.

17. Rentes à Saftingen et vents des moeres et wastines appartenant à "Monsieur," compte du 24 juin au 23 juin 1295: fragment final, RR, #518.

18. Rentes du pays de Waes. Compte du clerc Jean de Muda jusqu'au 24 juillet 1294, *ibid.*, #350.

19. Rentes à Saftingen et vents des moeres et wastines appartenant à Madame. Compte du 24 juin 1292 au 23 juin 1294, *ibid.*, #181.

20. Rentes des terres en friche et des "moeres" à Watervliet, Ardenbourg et Gorede. Compte du receveur, Barthélémy, clerc de Basssevelde 1295, *ibid.*, #535. Unfortunately there is rarely any indication why the general receiver needed these sums.

21. See herein, pp. 74–75.

22. Nord, B4056 #3834.

23. Pol. chrs., #84. Jakemon was acting in conjunction with Walter de Hamme, who had twice in the past been bailiff of Bruges (Nowé, *Les baillis comtaux*, 372). A gap in bailiffs between 14 June 1295 and 9 March 1297 exists in Nowé's list, and it is possible that Walter was again bailiff at that time. If this was the case, a grant of delay on the part of Jakemon and Walter is understandable, as they would have been the two individuals most concerned with collecting and accounting for this sum. Nonetheless, that it was Jakemon and not the count who granted this petition suggests the former had more direct control over comital finances than did the latter.

24. By the thirteenth century, the alienation of lands and rights was as much a financial matter as a political one.

25. L. A. Warnkönig, *Histoire de Flandre et de ses institutions civiles et politiques jusqu'à l'année 1305*, trans. by A. E. Gheldolf (Brussels, 1835–1864), 4:282–283 #24.

26. *Ibid.*, 4:283–284 #25.

27. Pol. chrs., #71. Roger probably passed the fee for the right to alienate the *tonlieu* on to the city of Bruges as part of his price.

28. St.-Genois, #854.

29. Strayer, *Philip the Fair*, 329–330.

30. Lyon, *From Fief to Indenture*, 202. About 1270, Countess Margaret ordered Philip of Bourbourg and others to seize English wool at Bruges in retaliation for the non-payment of this money fief (E. Varenbergh, *Histoire des relations diplomatiques entre le comte de Flandre et l'Angleterre au moyen âge* [Brussels, 1874], 138).

31. G. P. Cuttino, *English Diplomatic Administration 1259–1339* (Oxford, 1971), 225.

32. P.R.O. Dip. Doc. Exchequer E 30/33; Lyon, *From Fief to Indenture*, 290–291 #16.

33. Chron. sup., #188.

34. Nord, B1063 #41100.

35. On 7 November 1288, Baldwin and Felicity agreed to sell the lands of Dunkirk and Wastine to Guy in exchange for a life rent, which was to be paid to them annually on 24 June (*ibid.*, B1316 #2976–2977), the date of the *renenghe*.

36. *Ibid.*, B4048 #3203. On 17 August 1289, Guy had renegotiated the agreement with Felicity so that she would receive 1,705 l. 5 s. 2 d.p. twice a year, on 24 June and at Christmas (*ibid.*, B1316 #3072). Baldwin was alive on 22 July 1290, for he receipted a payment of 400 l.f. (*ibid.*, B4048 #3176), but had died by the time Gerard made his payment to Felicity on 27 November 1290. Why Guy negotiated with Felicity at this time is unclear. Perhaps Baldwin may have been seriously ill in August 1289, or perhaps the lands were held jointly. Felicity may have been his heir, for Felicity, undoubtedly wishing to guarantee that she would continue to receive this life rent in the event of Baldwin's death, had extracted a promise to that effect from the count.

37. Gaillard, #356; Nord, B4053 #3501, #3545. Since the record of this latter payment does not mention arrears, it can be assumed that she also received her 24 June payment for that year. No further records of such transactions exist after 1294, so it is possible that she died sometime between January and July 1295. By 24 June 1294, then, Felicity had received 6,826 l. 8 d. from the count. Had she lived for five more years, the total would have been 15,344 l. 6 s. 6 d.

38. *Ibid.*, B4048 #3169; B1063 #41100.

39. Gaillard, #240.

40. Gerard Lupichimi made the first recorded payment in 1290, but was no longer general receiver after August 1292. Disbursements made after that date were handled by Jakemon of Deinze.

41. For example, the receiver of the *tonlieu* of Damme and the receipts of the *renenghe* (St.-Genois, #175, #263; Lyon, *From Fief to Indenture*, 275–276 #1; 281 #5; Queller and Kittell, 301).

42. St.-Genois, #175; Lyon, *From Fief to Indenture*, 275–276 #1.

43. Dated 10 July 1280, the document reads, "ke nous dounons a noble houme mon segneur Jehan de Harecourt, le jouene, cent livres de tournois de rente a lui et a son hoir hiretaulement a paier chascun an a nostre renenghe en Flandres au mois apres le jour de la Nativitei Saint Jehan Baptiste. Et ceste rente doit il et si hoir tenir de nous et de nos hoirs . . . en fief et en houmage perpetuelment" (St.-Genois, #263; Lyon, *From Fief to Indenture*, 281 #5).

44. Gaillard, #178 (Lotin of Bruges was receiver in 1280); Nord, B4043 #2739.

45. Nord, B1562, p. 290 #3400, B4051 #3432, B4053 #3508, #3505, #3548, #3561, B4054 #3630, B4057 #4019; Gaillard, #399; De Smet and Wyffels, 653; Queller and Kittell, 302.

46. St.-Genois, #804; Lyon, *From Fief to Indenture*, 287–288 #13.

47. M. le Baron Reiffenberg, J. J. De Smet, L. Devillers, A. Borgnet, E. Gachet, and Liebrecht, eds., *Monuments pour servir à l'histoire des provinces de Namur, de Hainaut et de Luxembourg*, 10 vols. (Brussels, 1844–1874), 1:116 #23; Nord, B498 #3919; Lyon, *From Fief to Indenture*, 291–292 #17.

48. The number of money fiefs begins to grow from the mid-thirteenth century onward. The increase of this stipendiary element in military service may have prepared the way for a similar rise in the use of mercenaries (Michael Howard, *War in European History* [Oxford, 1976], 16).

49. St.-Genois, #475. The occasion was the disputed succession in the

county of Limburg; this was in essence another Flanders/Holland conflict (Van Werveke, *Avesnes en Dampierre*, 316).

50. He paid Wulfars and his men 641 l. 13 s. 4 d. for July and August 1293 (Nord, B4053 #3515; L. Van den Berghe, ed., *Gedenkstukken tot opheldering der Nederlandsche geschiedenis*, 2 vols. [Leiden, 1842–1847], 1:57; L. Van den Berghe, ed., *Oorkondenboek van Holland en Zeeland*, 2 vols. [Amsterdam, 1866–1873], 2:396), 628 l. 13 s. 4 d. for September and October 1293 (Nord, B4053 #3524), 628 l. 13 s. 4 d. for January and February 1294 (*ibid.*, B4053 #3564) and 641 l. probably for July and August 1295 (Van den Berghe, *Gedenkstukken*, 1:56; Van den Berghe, *Oorkondenboek*, 2:396).

51. Each of whom agreed to bring ten men with him (Nord, B498 #3959–3962). They received their first payment of 200 l. each on 24 June 1297 (*ibid.*, B498 #3968).

52. St.-Genois, #924.

53. "Somme toute de ceste brief ke le rechevres de Flandre doit pair" (Gaillard, #60). The record consists of a list of expenses incurred by the count's military forces defending the city of Ypres from the French.

54. Nord, B4060 #4430. The work had been ordered in 1290.

55. *Ibid.*, B1456 #3650; Ignace de Coussemaker, *Un cartulaire de l'abbaye de Notre Dame de Bourbourg (1104–1793)* (Lille, 1882–1891), 1:207 #212.

56. "Receptum ex Lotino." Buntinx, *Jehan Makiel*, xxix.

57. "Inde debet Makellus recipere ad Filippum de Borbourg: 24 l. 5 s." (*ibid.*, 61).

58. C. Dehaisnes, ed., *Documents et extraites divers concernant l'histoire de l'art dans la Flandre, l'Artois, et le Hainaut avant le XVe siècle* (Lille, 1877–1878), 1:87.

59. Compte de Jakemes de Sandmont, pour dras et pour laines livrés au comte de Flandre et au receveur, Gaillard, #58. The sums the clerk received may have been inadequate to cover the count's residential needs and it may have become easier for the general receiver to purchase the necessary extras himself. Eventually such expenses form their own section in the general receiver's accounts in the fourteenth century (RR, #1, #4, #5, #6).

60. Gaillard, #477–478.

61. On 29 September 1289 (Nord, B4047 #3087) and on 12 March 1290 (*ibid.*, B4047 #3131).

62. 276 l. 17 s. 10 d.p. for cloth and silk, 110 l.p. for a debt to Henry Bowers, a burgess of Bruges, and 290 l.p. which Gerard handed over in cash (St.-Genois, #591). The bishopric of Liège was not a poor see, and one would have expected John to be able to maintain himself on its revenues.

63. Nord, B4054 #3616.

64. Gaillard, #342.

65. St.-Genois, #734.

66. *Ibid.*, #980.

67. *Ibid.*, #989.

68. He was also responsible for implementing the generous donations she made in her will. Many of these were grants of income, which reduced the count's own revenues.

69. De Roover, *Money, Banking and Credit,* 11.

70. Pirenne, *Histoire de Belgique,* 1:164.

71. Bigwood, *Le régime juridique,* 319 and Appendix II, 2:44–46; De Roover, *Money, Banking and Credit,* 100.

72. The amount of the fee "was determined in each license and remained unchanged for the duration of the grant. In case of renewal, of course, the amount could be adjusted upward or downward" (*ibid.,* 102).

73. *Ibid.,* 102–103.

74. Bigwood, *Le régime juridique,* 2:296 #15.

75. St.-Genois, #297.

76. *Ibid.,* #481.

77. "Jou, Gérars de Florence . . . fac savoir à tous ke jou doi a Ernoul le Dorpre d'Audenarde pour li remanant dune dette . . . vies cent ciunquante et wiit livre et wiit sols de paris. Si mandons et prions au bailliu d'Alost, kikonkes le soit, ke il les dis deniers paice au devant dit Ernoul des deniers kil recevera de le baillie d'Alost. Et jou promet et ai encouvent au dit bailliu ke jou les rabaterai de sen premier conte, par le tiesmoing de ces lettres saielé des de men saiel" (*ibid.,* #618; Nowé, *Les baillis comtaux,* 192 n. 7).

78. Fewer than one-fourth were contracted between 1296 and 1299. Possible theories explaining this seemingly diminished role, while many and varied, remain speculative. It may have been that the count needed less money, an unlikely case in view of the state of war which existed between Guy and Philip of France at this time. Alternatively, the count may have been borrowing large sums to cover most of his needs, sums too large for the general receiver to take responsibility for. The count may have wanted to retain greater control over loans contracted in his name, and may have curtailed Jakemon's activities with that end in mind. Finally, those who furnished loans to Jakemon may have refused to give him credit. With the exception of the first, all of these explanations or combinations of explanations are plausible, but difficult to prove or disprove. There is some evidence to support the contention that the count wished to retain control over loans contracted in his name. Although the number of loans contracted personally by Jakemon declined over time, the number of loans he guaranteed for the count increased.

79. Gaillard, #439.

80. "a se volente."

81. St.-Genois, #705, #722, #732.

82. Gaillard, #458.

83. St.-Genois, #757.

84. Gaillard, #528, #529, #530; Bigwood, *Le régime juridique,* 2:300–303 #18.

85. One for Countess Margaret, on 11 August 1276 for 3,664 l.f. (Nord, B1561 n. 205 f. 60 #1925; Luykx, *De grafelijke bestuurinstellingen,* 429–430 #105) and one for Guy of Dampierre on 3 December 1278 for 1,300 l.t. (Nord, B4035 #2032).

86. *Ibid.,* B1491 #2796.

87. Philip is referred to as friend, sergeant, and lord of Verlenghem on 11 August 1276 (*ibid.,* B1561 n. 205 f. 60 #1295) and simply as lord of Ver-

lenghem in a record dated 3 December 1278 (*ibid.*, B4035 #2032). Siger is referred to as marshal of Flanders (*ibid.*, 1491 #2796).

88. Lotin of Bruges guaranteed one of the count's loans, but he was not the sole guarantor (St.-Genois, #615). He had also held several offices by the time he warranted this loan: clerk of Count Guy's residence, receiver of Namur, receiver of Flanders, bailiff and castellan of Namur, and bailiff of Ghent. It was probably on account of these various offices that he had become established in the minds of potential creditors as a principal and influential member of the count's household and thus not a financial risk.

89. *Ibid.*, #757.

90. For 623 l. 6 s. 8 d. loaned to the count by Treleman de Watergrave and Herman de Gluweel on 14 October 1297 (*ibid.*, #920) and 830 l. from Jakemon l'Estave, a merchant of Cologne, on 22 March 1298 (*ibid.*, #964).

91. It could be argued that Thomas Fini, who was associated with the establishment of the general account, belongs in this group. But the chaos which characterized his accounts in 1309 does not suggest efficient administration. See herein, p. 128.

92. Rennengue fait par Jean de Tournay à Bruges, 1296, RR, #266.

93. Entries such as "Ensi demeure [19 l. 8 s. 2 d.] de ce paiet a Jakemon" are ubiquitous throughout the account. Moreover, John of Tournai was Jakemon's clerk (see herein, p. 98 and n. 121).

94. Colard of Marchiennes was given the receivership of these districts the same year he became general receiver (RR, #273).

95. F. Van de Putte and C. Carton, eds., *Chronicon et cartularium abbatiae Sanctae Nicolai Furnensis* (Bruges, 1849), 174–175; Nowé, *Les baillis comtaux,* 186 n. 2. Jakemon may not necessarily have presided over this accounting, however, for the evidence suggests that the presiding officer changed from time to time.

96. St.-Genois, #647. This receipt is in the form of a procuration, in which the general receiver, who was mandated to receive the payment, declared in the same document that he has been so paid. According to Gaillard, the presence of this kind of document in the archives of the debtor signifies a quittance (V. Gaillard, *Inventaire,* 27 n. 1).

97. Gaillard, #79.

98. Rentes à Saftingen et ventes des moeres et wastines appartenant à Madame. Compte du 24 juin 1292 au 23 juin 1294, RR, #181.

99. In the late twelfth and early thirteenth centuries, accounts of each of the individual receivers were compiled into a single record. The *gros brief,* for example, consists primarily of a record of the activities of each of the domanial districts.

100. The first extant account after that of 1275 is dated 1291 (Baillis de Gand. Compte du bailli Iwan Stullart, de septembre 1291, RR, #1349).

101. The settlement in 1293 between Jan Reinfins, receiver of the *spicarium* of Veurne, and the general receiver indicates that either Jan or the general receiver referred to evidence of a *renenghe* as far back as 1273: "Ce son le fins des reneghieles puis l'an M.CC.LXXIII" (Nord, B4043 #1823; Luykx, *De grafelijke bestuurinstellingen,* 467–469 #136). Paul Thomas maintains that the *renenghe* was created around 1250, but offers no evidence to substantiate this contention (Paul Thomas,

"La renenghelle de Flandre au XIIIe et XIVe siècles," *Bulletin de la commission historique du département du Nord* 33 [1930], 169).

102. A modern analogy to this phenomenon would be the habit of keeping the bank statement and getting rid of or losing the cancelled checks.

103. Bigwood, *Le régime juridique,* 2:293–298 #15.

104. Nord, B1456 #3650; I. de Coussemaker, *Notre Dame de Bourbourg,* 1:207 #212.

105. Monier, *Les institutions financières,* 66–67.

106. Rentes à Saftingen et vents des moeres et wastines appartenant à Monsieur. Comte de 24 juin 1294 au 23 juin 1295, fragment final, RR, #518.

107. The office of butler was traditionally held by the Gavre family. The office of marshal came into the Bailleul family in 1264.

108. Nowé, *Les baillis comtaux,* 88 and n. 3.

109. St.-Genois, #329. Simon Malet, a merchant of Douai, for example bore the same title of "sergeant" that Jeffrey, a petty noble and knight, did (Buntinx, *Jehan Makiel,* 56 n. 3).

110. Philip of Bourbourg remained a member of the count's council until at least 1285 (Nord, B1562 n. 447 f. 230; B1563 n. 240 #2713) and late in 1280 was called a "bailli" of the count (Pol. chrs., #16). Lotin of Bruges continued to handle some of the count's financial matters after he left office: for example, he paid Beatrice of Courtrai her life rent in 1285 (Gaillard, #240). After Siger of Bailleul left office in 1289, Guy used him in a variety of capacities, primarily to conduct inquests (26 March 1293 [F. Van de Putte, ed., *Cronica et cartularium monasterii de Dunis* [Bruges, 1864], 1:219–221 #219 n. 374]; 21 April 1292 [Nord, B1562 n. 22 and 26 f. 24 and 30 #3339]; 10 March 1293 [Chron. sup., #174]; 1 December 1293 [Gaillard, #981]; 28 April 1294 [St.-Genois, #723]; 17 August 1294 [Nord, B1456 #3650; Coussemaker, *Notre Dame de Bourbourg,* 1:207 #212]; 14 September 1294 [Gaillard, #983], and in 1294, probably in October [St.-Genois, #738]). In November 1298 Jeffrey of Ransières was responsible for some of the expenses of the count's household (Gaillard, #477, #478, #479).

111. Nord, B4049 #3249; St.-Genois, #648.

112. *Ibid.,* #276, #279, #316, #324, #337.

113. In January 1282 (Nord, B398 #2328; St.-Genois, #303).

114. On 11 November (Luykx, *De grafelijke bestuurinstellingen,* 298).

115. Such a transition was natural. He probably had to look for employment when Beatrice died, and it was only logical that he should seek it in the count's service, which would have provided equal or even better opportunities. He was not unknown to comital officials, since there was a regular flow of financial transactions between the count and his sister-in-law.

116. D. E. Queller, *Office of the Ambassador in the Middle Ages* (Princeton, 1976), 150–152.

117. Nord, B4050 #3382.

118. John of Tournai was described as the general receiver's clerk on 19 February 1293 ("Jehan de Tournay, clerc au recheveur de Flandres" [Nord, B400 #3435]). Since he was called *clerc,* he may well have been in orders. Giles of Hertsberghe appears as the valet of the receiver upon at least four occasions in

1296–1297 (on 6 May 1296 [*ibid.*, B4055 #3803; Gaillard, #461]; 29 May 1296 [Nord, B4055 #3807]; on 17 February 1297 [Gaillard, #467]). Jakemon Louchard is described as valet of the receiver of Flanders upon two occasions in 1296 (28 September and 21 November 1296 [Nord, B4056 #3846; Bigwood, "Les financières d'Arras," 491]). John of Lille appears as the receiver's clerk on 2 February 1298 (Nord, B4058 #4021), and Pierre of Reckelines was described as the receiver's clerk on 11 January 1300 (Gaillard, #485).

119. *Ibid.*, #2; Buntinx, *Jehan Makiel*, 130 #3.

120. John of Lille was the receiver of the briefs at Lokeren (Rennengue fait par Bartélémy Fin à Ypres, 1309, RR, #271). John of Tournai was receiver of the briefs of St. Omer in 1306, 1309, and 1311 (Rennengue faite par Thomas Fin à Bruges, 1306, *ibid.*, #270; Rennengue fait par Bartélémy Fin à Ypres, 1309, *ibid.*, #271; Rennengue fait par Gilles de Hertsberghe à Bruges, 1311, *ibid.*, #282); he heard a bailiff's account in 1307 (Baillis d'Ypres. Compte du bailli, Jean le Pisson, du 30 septembre 1306 au 21 janvier 1307, *ibid.*, #1701; Monier, *Les institutions financières*, 64), and the general receiver's account in 1309 (Compte du receveur, Thomas Fin, du 25 décembre 1308 à juin 1309, RR, #1). In 1324 he was bailiff of Courtrai and in 1326 bailiff of Veurne (Nowé, *Les baillis comtaux*, 396, 389). Giles of Hertsberghe, who may have handled the *gros brief* in 1303 (Compte de gros brief, rendu par Gilles du 24 juin 1302 au 23 juin 1303, RR, #268), eventually became general receiver in 1311.

121. Nord, B400 #3435; B4055 #3803; B4056 #3846, #3863; Gaillard, #461; #467, #485; Rennengue faite par Jean de Tournay à Bruges, 1296, RR, #266.

122. Nord, B4059 #4199ter; Bigwood, *Le régime juridique*, 94.

123. Nowé points out that by the beginning of the fourteenth century, the general receiver's clerk had come to be customarily in charge of such accounts (Nowé, *Les baillis comtaux*, 199–200 n. 4).

124. Nord, B4056 #3834. Giles received 300 l. on 6 May 1296 (*ibid.*, B4055 #3803; Gaillard, #461) and 180 l. on 29 May 1296 (Nord, B4055 #3807); Jakemon Louchard received 110 l. on 28 September (*ibid.*, B4056 #3846) and 113 l. on 21 November 1296 (*ibid.*, B4056 #3863).

125. These officials may also have performed functions for other members. of the count's household or for the count. Scribes, clerks, and valets, like the general receiver himself, were fundamentally comital officials, but just as the function of the general receiver showed increasing tendencies toward specialization, so correspondingly did those of the individuals surrounding him.

126. Other members of the count's household, particularly nobles, did not cease to participate in the count's financial affairs. William of Mortagne, for example, witnessed a sale of land in October 1289 (C. Callewart, ed., *Chartes anciennes de l'abbaye de Zonnebeke* [Bruges, 1928], 136–137 #125), and, on behalf of the count, granted Lille the right to levy its own *maletote* (St.-Genois, #757). These latter continued to serve the count on an *ad hoc* basis, but the general receiver had little control over them.

127. They had been performed when Gerard Lupichimi had been general receiver (Nord, B4060 #4430).

128. Jakemon's last recorded action was to contract a loan for Robert of Béthune on 29 December 1299 (St.-Genois, #1023; Queller and Kittell, 318).

129. Bigwood, *Le régime juridique*, 2:296 #15.

130. The count might have increasingly relied on Gerard to pay off comital debts and expenses either by making special arrangements or out of his—Gerard's—own pocket. This would be convenient for Guy, but expensive for Gerard.

131. St.-Genois, #473. This living had probably been procured for him by Beatrice of Courtrai.

132. *Ibid.*, #839. Jakemon was not allowed to enjoy his canonry undisturbed. Sometime in the latter part of 1297 he was summoned by the bishop of Tournai to answer accusations of extortion. Jakemon responded by taking his case to Pope Boniface VIII, complaining that the journey to Tournai would be hazardous, and accusing the bishop and his officials of interfering in the collection of revenues due to him as provost. On 13 December 1297, the pope responded by issuing two bulls: one ordered an investigation of the bishop of Tournai's allegations, and the other an investigation of Jakemon's counteraccusations (St.-Genois, #948, #949, #950; Queller and Kittell, 317). Jakemon had been granted the provostship on 27 September 1295 (St.-Genois, #785), and on 5 January of the next year had received the right to collect the revenues of his provostship for three years, despite non-residence (*ibid.*, #795). Jakemon's right to collect those revenues without residence would not have lapsed until January 1299, and it seems on the surface that Jakemon may have been in the right. On the other hand, the offenses of which the bishop accused him may have been connected not with Jakemon's non-residency, but with something else. It is not impossible that he was taking more than that to which he was entitled. Jakemon, a significant figure in the county, may have used his prestige to abuse his position as provost. He must also have had substantial assets to initiate the costly business of a papal appeal. The *curia* received many such requests and it was not uncommon for bribery to be used to expedite a case.

There also may well have been a political component to the accusations against him. Hostile Flemish townspeople or French partisans may have lodged complaints against him in order to weaken Guy. Tournai, after all, is in Hainaut, and the bishop's action against Jakemon may have been taken at the behest of the Avesnes ruler of that county. This, of course, remains speculation.

In any case, on 27 February 1298, the pope declared in Jakemon's favor, and he was left in peace (Nord, B4058 #4029; the manuscript no longer exists, but both Godefroy and St.-Genois [Joseph de Saint-Genois, ed., *Monuments anciens essentiellement utile à la France et aux provinces de Hainaut, Flandre, Brabant, Namur, Artois, Liège, Hollande, Zélande, Frise, Cologne, et autres pays limitrophes de l'Europe*, 2 vols. (Lille and Brussels, 1806–1812), 1:871; Queller and Kittell, 317] give adequate summaries of it). Jakemon's position as a cleric placed him under the jurisdiction of the Church for religious matters, even though he occupied a lay office. On the other hand, since he was a cleric, it is unlikely that the count could do much to him if he had been found guilty of malfeasance in his capacity of general receiver. For the malfeasance of Thomas Fini, see chapter 5, pp. 128–129.

133. Nord, B1564 n. 147. These briefs are identified in the record only with reference to their former owners, Dierkin of Assenede and Henry Talluyans.

134. This is not to argue that ecclesiastical livings were not at least as solid a form of wealth as were, for example, wardships. The crucial difference between grants of ecclesiastical livings, on the one hand, and secular resources such as fiefs and grants of incomes, on the other, was that livings were not heritable.

135. Nord, B1561 n. 230.

136. *Ibid.*, B5321 #147.919.

137. Bailiffs were responsible to the count for criminal justice within their districts, except for cases involving vagabonds and the banished; burgesses, who were under the jurisdiction of urban tribunals; and the clergy, who were under the jurisdiction of the Church (J. J. Proost, "Recherches historiques sur le souverain bailliage de Flandre," *Message des sciences historiques, des arts et de la bibliographie de Belgique* [1876], 273). Bailiffs had the power to arrest suspicious persons; they also had the responsibility for holding them, arranging their trial, and executing their sentences. Initially bailiffs had authority primarily over particular castellanies and over the major communities in the castellanies, but from the middle of the thirteenth century onward, certain large and prosperous communities acquired their own bailiffs; these included Aalst, Oudenaarde, Bergues, Bourbourg, Bruges, Cassel, Courtrai, Douai, Veurne, Ghent, Lille, and Ypres (F. L. Ganshof, "La Flandre," in *Histoire des institutions françaises au moyen âge,* F. Lot and R. Fawtier, eds. [Paris, 1957], 1:404).

138. Inquests into bailiffs' management, for example, were conducted by commissions of the count's household (*ibid.,* 1:403).

139. The best discussion of the general receiver's control over bailiffs is H. Nowé, "L'intervention du receveur de Flandre dans l'administration de la justice au XVIe siècle," *Handelingen der Maatschaapij van Geschiedenis en Oudheidkunde te Gent* 32 (1924), 78–93.

140. Nowé, *Les baillis comtaux,* 186 n. 2.

141. *Ibid.,* 408.

142. "je venrois en la ville de Bruges, denviers monseigneur le conte de Flandres u denviers sen recheveur" (H. Nowé, "Fonctionnaires flamands passés au service royal durant la guerre de Flandres (fin du XIIIe siècle)," *Revue du Nord* 10 [1924], 285–286; H. Nowé, "Plaintes et enquêtes relative à la gestion des baillis comtaux de Flandre au XIIIe et XIVe siècles," *RBPH* 3 [1924], 78).

143. Nowé, "L'intervention," 79.

144. Chron. sup., #177.

145. Chron. sup., #257; Thierry Limburg-Stirum, *Les bouteillers héréditaires de Flandres. Preuves* (Bruges, undated), 117.

146. There is no evidence as to whether Jakemon complied with Arnold's request.

147. The count then borrowed another 3,000 l. from him (St.-Genois, #839; Bigwood, *Le régime juridique,* 1:201).

148. Warnkönig and Gheldolf, 2:2:28.

149. The actual arbitration was conducted by John, duke of Brabant, Gerard, count of Juliers, Everhard, count of le March, Walerans, lord of Monjoie, and John, lord of Kuyk.

150. Van den Berghe, *Gedenkstukken,* 1:92–93 #55.

151. For the best discussion of knighthood, its heritability, and the social position and prestige it represented in Flanders, see E. Warlop, *The Flemish Nobility*, 2 vols. (Courtrai, 1975).

152. "nostre dit recheveur, kiconques le serra." The document consists of a pension granted to a canon of St. Pharhaut of Ghent. The pension is to be paid by the receiver ("nostre recheveur") (Nord, B1561 n. 226 f. 67; Paul Thomas, ed., *Textes historiques sur Lille et le Nord de la France* [Paris and Lille, 1930], 2:219 #68).

153. "Gerart de Florenche jadis recheveures de Flandres," in January 1293 (St.-Genois, #665).

5. The Reign of Robert of Béthune
The General Receiver Becomes Accountable

BY THE TIME THE FORCES OF the king of France overran the county in 1300, the general receivership had become an integral component of the count's household administration. Philip the Fair did not continue the office, but in 1304, two years after the battle of Courtrai, Robert of Béthune delegated Bonsignor de Bonsignori to act as his general receiver.[1] The re-establishment of the office of general receiver may have signaled the re-establishment of the county as a semi-autonomous entity under its count, but it did not signal the end of the Franco-Flemish conflict. In 1305, Philip met the Flemish in battle at Mons-en-Pévèle, where he won a limited victory. Too financially and militarily drained to take advantage of his victory, the French king negotiated a treaty with the Flemish. The treaty of Athis-sur-Orge, promulgated in June 1305, left the county relatively intact, but exacted a heavy price.[2] The Flemish were to provide the French king with an annual payment (*rente*) of 20,000 l. to be drawn from the county of Rethel. They were to pay him an additional 400,000 l. in four years (the *taille du roi*), furnish him with a host of 600 equipped knights, and destroy the fortresses of the large towns. Bruges was further ordered to send 3,000 citizens on pilgrimage, of whom 1,000 were to go overseas.

Many of the terms of the treaty of Athis-sur-Orge were impossible to implement. Count Robert of Béthune (1305–1322) thus spent the rest of his reign trying to placate the French kings[3] without arousing the hostility of the Flemish communities, provoked by the collection of sums demanded by the French. This balancing act was almost upset by French threats to confiscate the county (1311); by the marshalling of French forces on Flemish borders (1313, 1314, 1315, and 1319); by Robert's own attempts to retake Lille, Douai, or Béthune; and by revolts, such as that of the Land of Waas in 1309. Robert, however, maintained equilibrium by negotiating and renegotiating the terms of Franco-Flemish relations, as evidenced first in the Treaty of Pontoise (1312),[4] again at a conference at Arras (1313), in the Conventions of Marquette (1314),[5] and finally in the Treaty of Paris (1320).

What success Robert enjoyed he owed in part to the ability of his household to raise at least part of the funds exacted by the French. The financial department of his household had to handle not only the management of ordinary incomes and expenses but the collection and payment of the French indemnities as well. Under these circumstances the re-establishment of the office of general receiver, particularly in the hands of Bonsignor de Bonsignori, a member of a wealthy Sienese banking family,[6] was not unexpected.

Under Robert of Béthune and his receivers the office continued to develop into a department increasingly distinct from the household. Many of Robert's receivers had served as members of the rudimentary staff which had surrounded Jakemon of Deinze in the last decade of the thirteenth century. This circumstance served at the same time to consolidate that staff into a department and to separate it from the count's household. Concomitantly a new account came into being in 1306 which comprised the financial activities involving the direct participation of the general receiver. The audit of this general account required the general receiver, for the first time, to give a comprehensive accounting of the financial activity of his circumscription. Since the circumscription of the receiver of Flanders consisted of the revenues of Flanders, this audit provided the count with the first coherent statement of the financial resources of his county.

Robert chose six receivers in the course of his reign: Bonsignor de Bonsignori, Thomas Fini, Giles of Hertsberghe, Colard of Marchiennes, Guiduche Baldechon, and Simon Vastin. Of these, Thomas Fini exercised the greatest control over the count's finances. He received not one but two appointment charters and was associated with the genesis of a general account. Accused of malfeasance, Thomas fled Flanders in 1309. Count Robert never again entrusted so much power to a general receiver.

Revenues

Thomas Fini's appointment charter, dated 18 April 1306, succinctly outlines the authority his predecessors, Jakemon of Deinze and Bonsignor de Bonsignori, had to carry out their responsibility for the count's revenues. From this and other evidence, it is apparent that Robert's receivers had the same duties and exercised the same authority as had the receivers of Guy of Dampierre. The phrase "to Thomas Fini, receiver," for example, appears as frequently throughout the *renenghe* as had "to Jakemon, receiver" a decade earlier.[7] Giles of Hertsberghe received all of the revenues from the *renenghe* of 1311.[8] But, underscoring the evolutionary character of the office, Thomas's charter also included formal acknowledgment of authority Jakemon had only informally exercised at the end of his tenure as general receiver. In particular, the count explicitly ordered his local financial officials "to pay and deliver to our said receiver or *at his certain command*, but to no other, what they will have received and will receive," authority Jakemon had exercised since at least 1295[9] but without explicit comital delegation.

Indeed, Thomas Fini took the responsibility for the count's revenues even further. As the count's agent, he (and to a lesser degree, his successors) tried to implement the principle that because the count's business was the county's business, the county should help pay for it. This concept had roots in the count's responsibility for the maintenance of his county. The count had in the thirteenth century levied specific sums to meet the needs of overlapping areas.[10] If the count could implement special levies for such things as the maintenance of dikes, which cut across several districts, he could, in principle, demand levies from the whole county for the purpose of paying for expenses only loosely connected with the theoretical welfare of the county.

One such expense was that incurred by the count when he traveled outside the country. Robert did call upon the Flemish communities to defray the expenses of several of his journeys. In 1307, the French king summoned Robert to Poitiers to renew his feudal vows before the pope. Bartholomew Fini, Thomas's brother, was deputized to collect sums from the county to pay for this journey. On 22 August 1307, Bartholomew collected 60 l. 15 s. from the mayor of Blankenberge, and on 18 October he received 25 l. 12 d. from the town of Gistel.[11] Sixteen months later, in February 1309, when Robert proposed a return trip to France, Thomas Fini collected 2,154 l. 15 s. of the 2,444 l.f. which Bruges had promised to contribute for his expenses.[12] In 1308, Robert went to Zeeland, and the town of Gistel helped defray the cost.[13] Both Bruges and Gistel contributed toward the expenses of Robert's trip to France in 1309,[14] and both payments were made to valets of Thomas Fini.

Not all of the Flemish communities may have actually contributed to defray Robert's traveling expenses in 1307, but it is doubtful that only Bruges and Gistel were encouraged to do so. The general receipt of 1309, for instance, shows that Robert received a total of 5,726 l. 18 d. from the communes of Flanders for just such expenses.[15] Although one or two communities might be asked to pay part or the whole of an expense, the nature of traveling expenses and their very size made it likely that contributions toward defraying them were demanded of and received from most of the county; they could be most efficiently managed if confided to the care of a specific individual. Furthermore, payments usually did not come in at the same time and it was probably necessary that a single individual keep track of them and be able to make them immediately available to the count. The general receiver and his department filled both of these requirements.

But the count only partly succeeded in getting the county to help defray his traveling expenses. In 1309 he had to borrow 3,456 l. 8 s. 11 d. from various individuals and corporations for a trip he took to Germany for the coronation of Henry VII of Luxembourg as King of Germany;[16] there is no record of the Flemish communities making any contributions toward the expenses of this trip. The reason why the county was willing to pay for the count's trips to France but not to Germany may lie in the purpose of each journey. The count went to France in 1307 and 1308 to negotiate and confirm the peace treaty between Flanders and France.[17] This issue concerned the whole county and as a result the count seems to have succeeded in obtaining grants of money for his trips to France.[18] The coronation of a fellow prince in Germany, however, may have been viewed as a personal matter, for the count, apparently unable to obtain voluntary grants, had to borrow.[19] Later records contain no references to any grants made to the count for such trips. If the count traveled much after 1309, and there is no reason to suppose that he did not, he must have paid for such travels from existing funds or borrowed, "faire les besoignes mon seigneur," for his needs. Trips may have come to be considered strictly the count's personal affairs, and for this reason the general account may not have included them. The absence more than the inclusion of such personal expenses from the general receiver's account, then, is testimony to the growing perception of the general receiver as a public official.

Such county-wide expenses, however, pale next to the Transport of Flanders. Begun as an indemnity to the king of France in 1305, the Transport subsequently became the principal element in the count's resources. It developed into a regular tax-system fifty years before the evolution of any such system in France.[20] The terms of the treaty of Athis-sur-Orge in 1305 stipulated that in addition to other sums, the Flemish communities were to make an annual payment of 10,000 l.p. to the king of France. Table 2 shows that from the first Thomas Fini, in his capacity as general receiver, and Bartholomew Fini, as an associate of that office, became the only individuals to take responsibility for this tax, called, from 1305 to 1312, the *taille du roi*.

Because implementing the terms of the treaty of Athis-sur-Orge of 1305 proved impossible, Count Robert in 1312 signed another treaty with Philip the Fair, the treaty of Pontoise. By the terms of this treaty, the king of France gave over (or "transported") to the count his right to the annual 10,000 l.p. from the Flemish communities in exchange for the castellanies of Lille, Douai, and Béthune.[21] In 1332, an account of what the communities had already paid and of what they owed up to that date was drawn up, possibly for Vane Guy, the general receiver at the time; it was updated in 1335.[22] It is evident that whoever drew up the *repertorium* had access to previous accounts and records. The clerk listed entries from accounts first and then those from other records, such as receipts or quittances. In the account of the castellany of Oudenaarde for instance, entries are for 1313, 1326, 1327, 1329, and then for 1323. The latter entry states "ont il payet par une lettre de Conte Gualterot, recheveur, donné à Audenarde le mardi après le Brandons lan 23."[23]

On the basis of this evidence we assume that an agent, probably a local official, would hand over to the general receiver an amount collected from a particular district. The general receiver would write out a quittance. The amount rendered would then be entered into his own records, to be reported when his account was reckoned. From Vane Guy's *repertorium* we can see that the general receiver was the primary financial representative of the count with whom the Flemish communities came into contact. The *repertorium* also indicates that Robert's receivers had some success in obtaining these payments (see Table 3).

No matter who delivered these sums, obtaining them would have been impossible if the counties had not had some experience with such levies and if the count had not had an apparatus sufficiently organized to collect them. As we have seen, such conditions developed interdependently in the last decade of the thirteenth century. The events of the early fourteenth century, particularly the imposition of the Transport of Flanders, gave Robert and his receivers the opportunity to establish more firmly the concept that the count's expenses were the county's responsibility, while the general receivership gave him the means to implement this principle.

The General Account

The audit of local financial officials had developed into a routine process by the end of the reign of Guy of Dampierre; from then on, there was little variation in the procedure. The major innovation of Robert's reign in-

TABLE 2.   The General Receiver and the *taille du roi*

Community	1306	1307	1308	1309	Sources
Aalst		TF	TF		Gaillard, #133; *Codex*, #242
Aalst castellany			BF		Gaillard, #133
					Codex, #243
Aardenburg	TF				Gaillard, #133; *Codex*, #242
Aarschot					
Bailleul					
Bergues					
Bergues castellany					
Beveren					
Beveren parish					
Beveren lordship					
Blankenberge		BF			Gaillard, #491
Bourbourg					
Bourbourg territory					
Bruges		TF			Gaillard, #582; *Codex*, #309
Burcht					
Cassel					
Cassel territory					
Coudenburg					
Courtrai					
Courtrai castellany		TF	BF		*Codex*, #219
					Codex, #246
Damme	TF				Gaillard, #137
Dendermonde	BF		BF		Gaillard, #133; *Codex*, #242
					Gaillard, #144; *Codex*, #242
Diksmuide	TF				Gaillard, #137
Dunkirk					
Eksaarde					
Franc of Bruges	TF				Gaillard, #137, #487
Franc Métier					
Ghent					
Gistel	TF	BF			Gaillard, #137, #494
Geraardsbergen		TF	TF		Gaillard, #133; *Codex*, #242
					Gaillard, #143; *Codex*, #243
Gravelines					
Haasdonk					
Hoeke	TF				Gaillard, #137
Hugevliet					
Ijzendijke	TF				Gaillard, #137
Kallo					

TABLE 2.   *Continued*

Community	1306	1307	1308	1309	Sources
Kieldrecht					
Kruibeke					
Land of Waas			BF		Gaillard, #133; *Codex,* #242
Langaardenburg					
Lo					
Lombardsijde					
Mardyck					
Massemen					
Monnikerede	TF				Gaillard, #137
Nieuwpoort					
Oostburg					
Oostende	TF				Gaillard, #137
Oudenaarde			BF		Gaillard, #133; *Codex,* #242
Oudenaarde			BF		Gaillard, #133; *Codex,* #242
castellany					
Oudenburg	TF		BF		Gaillard, #133; *Codex,* #242 Gaillard, #137
Poperinghe					
Pumbeke					
Roeselare bij					
Aardenburg					
Rupelmonde					
Sint-Anna-ter-	TF				Gaillard, #137
Muide					
Sint-Niklaas					
Sluis					
Temse					
Torhout					
Verrebroek					
Veurne					
Veurne territory					
Vier Ambachten			TF		Gaillard, #133; *Codex,* #242 Gaillard, #144; *Codex,* #244
Warneton					
Waterduinen	TF				Gaillard, #137
Ypres					
Ypres castellany	TF				Gaillard, #137
Zottegem					

BF = Bartholomew Fini; TF = Thomas Fini.

TABLE 3. The Flemish Communities and the Transport of Flanders, Payments Made to Robert of Béthune, 1312 to 1321[24]

Community	1312	1313	1314	1315	1316	1317	1318	1319	1320	1321	Sources
Aalst											
Aalst castellany											
Aardenburg											
Aarschot											
Bailleul									SV	SV	St. VI., f. 45
Bergues	CM	CM								SV	St. VI., f. 27
Bergues castellany	CM	CM	JP	G	GB	SV	SV		SV	SV	St. VI., f. 29
Beveren											
Beveren parish											
Beveren lordship											
Blankenberge											
Bourbourg											
Bourbourg territory					GB			SV	SV	SV	St. VI., f. 39
Bruges											
Burcht											
Cassel									SV	SV	St. VI., f. 43
Cassel territory											
Courtrai											
Courtrai castellany					GB						St. VI., f. 51
Coudenburg											
Damme											
Dendermonde											
Diksmuide											
Dunkirk											

Eksaarde									
Franc of Bruges									
Franc Métier	CM	JP CM	JP	GB	GB	JM	JofP		St. VL, f. 9
Ghent									St. VL, f. 5
Gistel									
Geraardsbergen									
Gravelines									
Haasdonk									
Hoeke									
Hugevliet									
Ijzendijke									
Kallo									
Kieldrecht									
Kruibeke									
Land of Waas		CM							St. VL, f. 92
Langaardenburg									
Lo									
Lombardsijde	CM								St. VL, f. 21
Mardyck									
Massemen									
Monnikerede									
Nieuwpoort			JP						St. VL, f. 19
Oostburg									
Oostende									
Oudenaarde									
Oudenaarde castellany	CM								St. VL, f. 55
Oudenburg									
Poperinghe									
Pumbeke									

TABLE 3. *Continued*

Community	1312	1313	1314	1315	1316	1317	1318	1319	1320	1321	Sources
Roesclare bij Aardenburg											
Rupelmonde											
Sint-Anna-ter-Muide											
Sint-Niklaas											
Sluis											
Temse											
Torhout											
Verrebroek											
Veurne	CM	CM	JP	GB		JM	JM	SV	SV	SV	St. VI., f. 17
Veurne territory											
Vier Ambachten		CM									St. VI., f. 4
Warneton			JP						SV	SV	St. VI., f. 47
Waterduinen											
Ypres									SV		St. VI., f. 12
Ypres castellany			JP						SV	SV	St. VI., f. 13
Zottegem											

CM = Colard of Marchiennes; G = Gheruim (Guiduche Baldechon?); GB = Guiduche Baldechon; JM = John of Menin; JofP = John de la Pierre; JP = John Preudomme; St. VI. = Staten van Vlaanderen, #1349; SV = Simon Vastin.

volved not procedure but the institution of a new account attached to the person of the general receiver. This general account, or receipt, included not only the net incomes of the bailiffs and domainal receivers but also all *ad hoc* transactions, as well as the lump sums given to the clerks of the count's residences. Bailiffs and domainal receivers had already become accountable to the general receiver by the late thirteenth century. With the advent of the general account, the general receiver himself became accountable for the revenues he managed, a logical development implicit in the establishment of a central financial official. That a single general account came to incorporate all these financial activities testifies to the efficacy of the office.

The general account may have resulted from the convergence of two circumstances: Count Robert's pressing political and financial concerns, and the appointment of a new, Italian, general receiver, Thomas Fini. Upon assumption of the countship in 1305 and throughout his reign, Count Robert of Béthune had two priorities—to restore order after the long and expensive war with France from 1297 to 1304 and to meet his financial obligations to the French, as outlined in the various treaties concluded during his reign. The count could ascertain the state of his local finances by means of the annual *renenghe* and the ternary audits of the bailiffs, but there existed no such system for incomes and expenses outside the jurisdiction of these local officials. In the general receiver there did exist a single, central official whose responsibility it had become to manage all these finances; Robert may have thus taken the opportunity afforded by the appointment of a new receiver to institute a general audit of his accounts.

This new receiver, Thomas Fini, may have had his own reasons for encouraging the establishment of a general audit. Thomas, a banker, undoubtedly had a great deal of experience with accounts. Furthermore, Thomas, like Gerard Lupichimi before him, had an interest in the count's finances even prior to becoming his general receiver. On 23 February 1306, Robert and his family and vassals recognized that they had borrowed a total of 17,414 l. 16 s. from the Society of the Gallerani and Thomas Fini.[25] Having lent the count this money, the Gallerani were in a position to influence the count's choice of receiver; they may even have gone so far as to force Thomas upon Count Robert. A general account, for its part, would furnish Thomas as well as the count with a useful assessment of the count's overall financial condition.

There exists only a single reference to Thomas Fini's first account, which appears to have covered the period from about 14 March 1306 to 24 June 1307.[26] The count formally appointed Thomas general receiver on

18 April 1306,[27] but the fact that his account begins earlier, when he "entered into the receipt of Flanders," strongly suggests that for at least a month before his formal appointment Thomas had been informally acting in that capacity. Interestingly, Thomas's 1306 charter of appointment does not address the issue of accounts at all; not until two years later, in a charter dated 7 November 1308, did the count explicitly grant Thomas the authority to settle accounts of officials whose financial transactions were outside the jurisdiction of bailiffs and domanial receivers.[28] Yet, at no point in this document is there any mention of a general receiver's account. That Thomas's first account ended on 24 June 1307 indicates that the 1308 extension of his authority was actually a formal, though *post hoc,* acknowledgment of an already existing practice. Moreover, when Count Robert formally empowered Thomas to make final account, he also gave Thomas the authority to do so without any special comital mandate.[29] Since neither formal appointment charter nor general account exists for Thomas's predecessor, Bonsignor de Bonsignori, Thomas's account of 24 June 1307 was probably in fact his first account; it may even have been the first account of its kind.

Thomas may have presented four general accounts, but only one of them still exists.[30] It opens, "Account of Thomas Fini, receiver of Flanders, of what he has received and delivered for my lord of Flanders since the day of Christmas, 1308." V. Gaillard, in his inventory, mentions the existence of two other accounts associated with Thomas, one probably dated 1307 and the other 1308.[31] Since the former is missing and the other consists merely of a short list of sums, the evidence that Thomas rendered a general account four times remains inconclusive.

The count may have intended that an audit of the general receipt should be an annual event. The day of reckoning for Thomas's first account, 24 June, was the day of reckoning for all accounts audited on an annual basis. If this had been Robert's intention, it was not fulfilled during the course of his reign. Nothing indicates that the count called for another general account after 1307. The charters of 1306 and 1308 both lack any mention of a general receiver's account, although at least two such audits may already have taken place by 7 November 1308, the date of the second charter.

The first account of a general receiver to be mentioned in the extant documentation for the period after 1309 was the third account of Colard of Marchiennes (c. 1311–1315).[32] Colard assumed the duties of the office of general receiver sometime in 1311, and by 1313 may well have faced audit three times, although that would have meant an audit on the average of about every eight months, an unlikely occurrence. The evidence for Colard's accounts and for those of Robert's other general receivers is found chiefly in the *repertorium* of payments of the Transport of Flanders and the Peace of Arques, drawn up by Count Louis of Nevers's receiver, Vane Guy, in 1332.[33] Unfortunately, this is not an easy source to decipher. The phrase "paid by the third account of Colard of Marchiennes for the year twelve [1312] in reduction of what he owes . . . 36 l." is ambiguous. The 36 l. is clearly arrears, but is the third account of which this entry speaks the third time Colard of Marchiennes was audited in 1312? Was the 36 l. paid to the third account of Colard of Marchiennes, audited at an unspecified time? Furthermore, phrases such as "paiet par le premier compte pour lan" could signify payment either in advance or in arrears. The problem lies with the phrase "the third [or first, second, etc] account of." The third account of Colard of Marchiennes may well have been different from the third occasion on which Colard was audited. The former implies a particular account (perhaps the general account?) audited at a particular time. The latter is far more vague; it could merely refer to the third time any account of Colard of Marchiennes was audited.

The hypothesis that the account mentioned the *repertorium* is not necessarily the account of a general receiver is supported by references throughout the same document to accounts of persons such as John Preudomme and John de le Pierre,[34] who, as far as we know, were never general receivers. It is possible that the *repertorium* is referring to specific accounts which recorded only Transport payments. Thus the "third account of Colard of Marchiennes" may mean not the third general account of Colard of Marchiennes, but rather the third time any account of Transport payments was drawn up under Colard's auspices. On the other hand, accounts of Transport payments were probably not drawn up on a regular basis. It seems from the *repertorium,* in fact, that Transport payments occurred irregularly, although they were supposed to be paid annually. Thus accounts of the Transport may have been drawn up on an *ad hoc* basis— sometimes by the general receiver and sometimes by some other official. Contemporaries themselves probably made no particular distinctions in this regard. This lack of clarity suggests that a general reckoning had not yet become routine or even accepted custom and that reckonings which took place during Robert's reign probably did so on an *ad hoc* basis.

The general account was not without form. Its organization is similar to that of bailiffs' accounts. Like theirs, Thomas's extant account is divided into a receipt, which was totaled, and a list of expenses, the *date,* which was also totaled. The *date* was then subtracted from the total income, and a balance was noted.[35] Both the receipt and the *date* were grouped into subsections, for example, *rentes hors renenghe* and gifts from the communities, as against expenditures for the count's residences and for pensions and money fiefs. Although some of the entries were summarized, others appear quite detailed. Those that were summarized represent the resources audited previously, such as those of the old domain. The other entries consist of little more than lists of quittances. This somewhat primitive practice of listing receipts may explain why the number of extant quittances for *ad hoc* matters declined dramatically after the appearance of a general account: there was less need for conserving receipts once the transactions they represented had been incorporated into the general account.[36] Noted at the end of the document were the place, date, and names of the commissioners who had heard the account.

Thirteen commissioners, including the count, the general receiver (Thomas himself), and Thomas's brother, Bartholomew, heard Thomas's account.[37] The mere presence of this commission set an important precedent; it implied the existence of a body to which the general receiver could be made accountable. Who made up the rest of this commission? Bailiffs and domainal receivers are known to have made their reckoning before a group that included several of their peers, that is, other bailiffs or domainal receivers. But because information about the early general accounts is scanty, one can make no such assumptions about who usually heard them. Indeed, there existed few officials at this time who could rightly be called the peers of the general receiver, and most of the members of the 1309 commission were taken from the comital household, that amorphous body of people who surrounded the count and helped manage his affairs. Perhaps their sole distinguishing feature was that they had all functioned in some administrative capacity within the two years prior to this audit. What is striking about this particular commission is the absence of any of the count's major vassals, members of such families as the Halewins and Gavres. It is conceivable that the nobility was intentionally shut out of this commission. It is quite possible, on the other hand, that the general receipt at this time was not of sufficient importance to members of these groups to warrant their participation.

The appearance of the general receipt not long after Thomas Fini's appointment as general receiver strongly suggests that its institution was primarily his doing. An important employee of the Gallerani Society—he was a factor[38]—Thomas undoubtedly had a great deal of experience, and thus, one would assume, expertise in a variety of financial affairs. Moreover, Siena, whence both Thomas and the Gallerani came, had become "the principal banking center of Western Europe."[39] At first glance, it is hard not to conclude that it was the marriage of Robert's desperate financial situation to Thomas's experience that produced the general account.

That Thomas had influence on the genesis of the account cannot be doubted, but the precise nature and degree of that influence is somewhat questionable. The accounts of the Gallerani, as well as those of other Tuscan companies, do not appear to have been notably more sophisticated than those of the Flemish counts. The two great accounting innovations associated with the Italians—double-entry bookkeeping and bilateral tabulation—were as yet undeveloped in the early fourteenth century; according to De Roover, the bilateral form did not prevail in Tuscany until 1350.[40] The first example of bilateral tabulation occurred in Northern Italy, not in Tuscany, in 1313; it is particularly associated with the Genoese, who had little influence either in the Flemish court or on Thomas Fini. Even if, as Federigo Melis contends,[41] the Gallerani used double-entry form, no such innovation appears in any of the Flemish accounts, including the general receipt. Obviously, Thomas could not have introduced it.

Instead, the organization of the general account follows that of the bailiffs' accounts. For all types of accounts, this form had been the form of choice in Flanders for almost twenty-five years prior to the appearance of the first general receipt. Moreover, the paragraph form of entry is characteristic of the Flemish bailiffs' accounts just as much as it is of the extant accounts of the Gallerani; similarly, both customarily list receipts at the front and expenditures at the end of the account.[42] The organization of the general receipt must therefore have derived from pre-existing Flemish forms—it was certainly no innovation. In addition, unlike any of the Gallerani accounts, or those of any other Italian company, the Flemish general account was presented to a commission. The use of commissioners to hear and verify accounts had been standard accounting procedure in Flanders since the middle of the previous century. Finally, like the accounts of all Flemish financial officials, the general account covered a specific, albeit frequently arbitrary, period of time, and the account was evidently not assumed to be part of an ongoing record. Most of the Italian companies did keep running totals. A general statement, such as that represented by the general receipt, was unusual in Italian businesses and customarily occurred only upon liquidation and termination of the partnership contract.[43] If the accounts of the Gallerani are any indication, Thomas may indeed have been familiar with running-total accounting, but he would have had little or no experience with the type of general statement reckoning characteristic of both the *renenghe* and the Flemish bailiffs' accounts.

Although Thomas may have had a great deal of experience with financial matters such as loans, investments, interest, and credit, his expertise apparently did not extend to bookkeeping; his accounts as Robert's general receiver, in fact, belie De Roover's contention that the Italians "kept books with the utmost care."[44] Extant records and testimony presented during Count Robert's quarrel with Thomas from 1312 to 1314 indicate that when Thomas fled Flanders in 1309, he left the office and its records in chaos.[45] Regardless of the reputation Thomas and the Gallerani enjoyed in 1306, and that which the Italian companies would enjoy in the later fourteenth century, Thomas did Count Robert and his financial administration no favors as his general receiver.

In point of fact, the general receipt differs little from pre-existing and contemporary Flemish accounts in form and accounting procedure. Its novelty lay elsewhere, in the conceptual domain. The account, after all, comprised all of the count's financial activities, irrespective of kind or permanence. The form of the account and the procedure of its reckoning indicate that the general account was a logical step in the ongoing evolutionary process which shaped the office.[46] All of the count's financial officials presented accounts encompassing all their activities for reckoning and verification, and it was arguably only a matter of time before the general receiver was made answerable in the same way. Given the financial conditions of the county in 1306, the state of Italian accounting techniques, particularly those associated with the Sienese, and the history of the office and of accounting procedures in Flanders, Thomas's actual input in the creation and realization of the general receipt may have been quite limited. Indeed, it is more likely that the general account was an indigenous Flemish development which owed little to innovative Italian accounting techniques and even less to Thomas Fini's expertise.

The fact that nothing more complex was instituted also illustrates the probable *ad hoc* and informal nature of the enterprise. The count may have believed that this reckoning was merely a one-time undertaking, dictated by a collection of adventitious circumstances. Most of the evidence seems to suggest that neither the count nor Thomas assumed that the reckoning of a general account was to be a regular feature of financial routine. All of Thomas's general accounts appear to have occurred on an *ad hoc* basis. They did occur, however, and when they did, they all seem to have followed similar patterns and procedures. Each successive occurrence lessened the *ad hoc* nature of the account and encouraged its development into a routine practice.

Furthermore, the use of a general account encouraged the delineation of the general receiver's jurisdiction and increased the receiver's accountability to the count. The general account made his activities public knowledge; the receiver became increasingly accountable also to those who figured in his account. Besides indicating the degree to which the general receivership had become a public office, the public nature of this audit further encouraged its future development in that direction. Like the count's activities, but unlike those of the bailiffs and household officials, the activities of the general receiver transcended social, economic, and political boundaries, giving him effective jurisdiction over the county as a whole. His general account truly functions as a financial account of Flanders.

Staff and Maintenance

When Thomas Fini took over the general receivership he brought with him his brother and several of his valets and clerks to help him in the routine performance of the office.[47] These clerks and valets undoubtedly answered chiefly, if not only, to Thomas. Piero Reynieri, for example, was Thomas's clerk more than he was the clerk of the general receiver, and the count may not have had any real authority over him. Although a financial department had come into existence in the last decade of the thirteenth century, the position of those who staffed it had been somewhat ambiguous with regard to the rest of the count's household and even to the count himself. The separation between the count and the office, represented by Thomas's relationship with his clerks, clearly fostered the separation of that office from the household. At the same time, however, the specialization of the office represented by the functioning of such individuals in solely financial capacities suggests that the identification of valet or clerk with an individual officer-holder was giving way to an identification with the department. Giles of Hertsberghe, Colard of Marchiennes, Guiduche Baldechon, and Simon Vastin followed Thomas as general receiver. All four of these individuals were promoted to the position of general receiver from within the financial department,[48] a circumstance that could not fail to encourage the development of the concept of a hierarchy within the department and thus concomitant to it. Finally, such consolidation gave it cohesion uncharacteristic of the count's household.

But the general receiver still depended on the count, at least in theory, for maintenance. The twin concepts of maintenance and of the office as revenue-producing governed income associated with the office. Thomas Fini's expenses for trips to Paris and to the fairs of Champagne—where he was probably trying to contract loans on the count's behalf—came out of the gross revenues of his receipt. He also received 170 l. for livery, not only for himself but for his people as well.[49] Although the existence of the general account suggests that the general receiver's responsibilities extended over a defined geographical area, Thomas does not seem to have drawn a *gage* from the gross revenues of that area. He might instead have been entitled to part of any surpluses his management of the general receivership produced, an incentive that may have resulted in his taking on the position in the first place. Unfortunately, Thomas's account reveals there were no surpluses at the end of at least the 1309 auditing session. Instead Robert of Béthune appears to have been in debt to his general receiver: whereas the revenues of Flanders yielded 26,288 l. 10 s. 4 d., Thomas paid out 31,913 l. 9 d. on behalf of the count. The count thus owed Thomas 5,562 l. 14 s. 5 d.,[50] and nothing indicates that this was an extraordinary occurrence. It logically follows that if he paid the count's expenses he was probably entitled to any surpluses. The general receivership thus fell well within the definition of a revenue-producing office.

Judicial and Other Affairs

Under Robert of Béthune, the office of general receiver acquired identifiable boundaries and functions, but had not fully gone out of court. The combination of these two circumstances provided a basis for the extension of the prestige of the receiver of Flanders in general during the course of the fourteenth century. Colard of Marchiennes's appeal to the pope, on behalf of the count, best illustrates this phenomenon. On 26 June 1314, Colard sent a formal protest to Pope John XXII concerning the hostile actions of the French king toward Flanders.[51] Prior to being sent, his letter was read out before a notary in a convocation of Flemish ecclesiastics in Ghent. Although currently holding the office, Colard did not call himself general receiver in his appeal. Instead, he referred to himself simply as a cleric and as the count's procurator. Jakemon of Deinze had sent a similar protest to

Boniface VIII in 1297.[52] Both Jakemon and Colard protested to the pope primarily as members of the religious community, for as clerics, they had the right to appeal to him as their ecclesiastical superior and to seek his protection. The two appeals differ, however. First, Jakemon made his as simply one cleric among many; Colard's appeal stood on its own. Second, unlike Jakemon, Colard does not seem to have held any important preferments; therefore he had little standing in the religious community beyond his clerical status. As general receiver, however, he was one of the count's most important officials, and it was this position that gave his protest whatever prestige and authority it had.

Colard's involvement in this type of affair was not unique. Most of Robert's general receivers did not confine their activities exclusively to financial matters. In 1308, Robert of Béthune gave Thomas Fini the right to choose and remove bailiffs and underbailiffs.[53] Moreover, the count commanded bailiffs to obey the receiver.[54] For all intents and purposes, the count formally subordinated bailiffs to the receiver, and during Robert's reign, the receiver frequently ordered bailiffs to make payments from their revenues. He does not actually seem to have appointed or removed any bailiff solely on his own authority. Rather, the general receiver's authority in this matter was confined to his presence on the comital council which hired and fired bailiffs; not until 1320 did a general receiver handle affairs as a bailiff's superior.[55] Furthermore, despite the receiver's control over bailiffs as financial officials, and despite Count Robert's grant to Thomas Fini, the general receiver did not actually exercise power over them as judicial officers until 1336.[56]

Not an innovation, Count Robert's grant to Thomas in 1308 instead formally recognized the authority Jakemon of Deinze had assumed and informally exercised. Although Jakemon had never received such authority in explicit terms, he had participated in disciplinary action against bailiffs from as early as 1293. The practice continued under Robert's general receivers. On 23 March 1314, for instance, Colard of Marchiennes and the bailiff of Ghent conducted an inquest into the reported assault on the bailiff of Oudenaarde by Jean Rogier of Oudenaarde.[57] Inquests took time, however, and the general receiver probably had more responsibility for and thus spent more time hearing their results and in passing judgment and sentence than in conducting the actual inquiries.

Nonetheless, following the precedent established by Siger of Bailleul in the late thirteenth century, Robert commissioned his receivers to take part in inquests which had nothing to do with his financial officials. Giles of

Hertsberghe, for example, participated in two inquests into illegal sales of rabbits at Bergues.[58] He took part in an inquest into the possession of certain tithes,[59] and he was involved in the settlement of disputes. On 2 February 1311, for example, he and several others from Robert's household heard the complaints of the people of Dunkirk and Bergues over certain laws.[60] Although the general receiver's participation in judicial affairs during Robert's reign did not become common, it was also not perceived as unusual; it was, in fact, well on its way to becoming routine. By the time it had become routine, about the mid-fourteenth century, such participation expressed the degree to which the association of the general receiver with the count's affairs in general and with his judicial matters in particular had become an integral part of the system by which the count governed his county.

Malfeasance

By 1309 the office had become so institutionalized that even malfeasance on the part of the general receiver could not destroy it. Sometime in the summer of 1309, Count Robert arrested Thomas and Bartholomew Fini for serious crimes; Thomas subsequently fled to France.[61] Bartholomew, unable or unwilling to flee, was executed in the latter part of 1309.[62] Thomas and Bartholomew may have been guilty of harsh exactions and perhaps even of theft.[63] Victor Fris draws a connection between the heavy exactions of the general receiver—no doubt the French levies—and a revolt which broke out in the Land of Waas.[64] In 1309, Count Robert had two accounts drawn up of the arrears of domainal revenues for the years 1306 to 1309;[65] the count was trying to put order into a financial administration which, if the records for those years are any indication, was inefficient and disorganized. That the records for these years are so chaotic, then, suggests either that Thomas did not have tight control over the collection and audition of such revenues or that he allowed them to back up.

Count Robert made several attempts to contact Fini and to force him to render account. On 3 June 1314, he consulted a lawyer, Gerard de Tillet, about possible legal proceedings against Fini.[66] On 31 January 1315, the count commissioned Colard of Marchiennes, Guiduche Baldechon, Simon Vastin, and three others, all members of the count's financial department, to find Thomas, in order to hear his account and perhaps to obtain a balance from him.[67] Once they had all agreed to meet, Robert's representatives demanded that Thomas render an account immediately, but Thomas claimed that the accounts he had rendered while general receiver were valid. Nonetheless, the count's arbitrators seem to have prevailed, for on 8 February, Thomas drew up an account from memory; he also reserved the right to modify it. The count's representatives found it unacceptable. On 10 February, Thomas declared that he could not modify his account without records, and since the records were in Flanders, the onus of proof shifted to the count.[68] Here the case rested until 25 February 1315, when Robert again empowered Guiduche and Simon as his procurators.[69] He instructed them to negotiate a compromise with Thomas in order to obtain an accounting from him. On 2 March 1315, again at Tournai, the comital procurators met with Thomas.[70] At this meeting, Simon and Guiduche, on behalf of the count, read out a list of claims against Thomas.[71] The count demanded that Thomas make restitution of not only comital letters of debt but also the sums which represented the balance of the general receiver's accounts. Thomas applied to the king of France for records with which to rebut comital accusations. He received documentation on 2 June and 10 July 1315, but we do not know how the count's representatives reacted to the introduction of such material to the case; there is, in fact, no indication of how the case in general turned out.[72]

The count's dispute with Fini reveals much about the process by which recalcitrant members of the count's administration might be dealt with. Thomas was not Robert's vassal, nor had his financial position depended upon his office.[73] There existed no *audientie* (the count's central judicial body in the late fourteenth century) or other formal or informal group constituted from the count's council to hear cases of this nature. For these reasons, Count Robert could not take disciplinary action. Instead, he had to arbitrate with Thomas. The general receiver, as a member of the count's administration, might become judgeable by a council of his administrative peers, presided over by his administrative superior (the count). In the early fourteenth century, however, the individual's position outside his office still dictated to some extent the method by which accusations could be handled. The count's lack not only of real authority, but also of an administrative body competent to handle such matters, enabled Thomas to compel the count to arbitrate with him. If, of course, Thomas had not escaped and established his credibility with the king of France, the story might have ended differently.

Depersonalization

Although the case of Thomas Fini illustrates some of the weaknesses of the count's financial administration, it also indicates the degree to which the office of general receiver had become depersonalized. Thomas Fini's actions did not bring about the abolition of the office itself. By 1309, a clear distinction existed between the person of the general receiver and the office of general receiver. Such a distinction also implied the degree to which the general receiver had ceased to be perceived as simply a personal servant of the count or as just another member of the count's household. By 1309, the count could and did dismiss his personal servant, the officeholder, at will, but in so doing could not dismiss the office. What Count Robert did do, however, was to ensure that no individual held the position for longer than a few years. He did this at the cost of entrusting the office to other Italians, the group most associated with finance and banking, for any length of time. Guiduche Baldechon, for example, filled the office for only about a year, from late 1315 to 1317. Only Simon Vastin held the office for more than three years; he held it for five, the longest of any individual during Robert's reign.[74]

Of more significance was the phrase "whoever he will be," which, during the last decade of the thirteenth century, routinely appeared directly after the term "receiver of Flanders." Its first appearance in 1291 and continued use throughout the decade signified that the office had become distinct from the individual who performed its functions. Of equal importance, however, was the disappearance from the records of the same phrase; this seems to have occurred sometime before 1314.[75] After 1314 "receiver of Flanders" seems to have sufficed to indicate who was meant. From this time on, moreover, documents rarely mention the specific individual who held the office without also mentioning the title. The disappearance of the phrase "whoever he will be" suggests that, by 1314, the permanence of the office had achieved general acceptance to such an extent that it no longer needed reiteration.

The existence of charters of appointment, for which Jakemon of Deinze's commission in 1292 had set a precedent, reflected a similar kind of permanence. Since only eight other commissions of appointment still exist, one cannot say with certainty that all of Jakemon's successors received formal commissions. One of the extant commissions of appointment, however, is that of Thomas Fini, and it stands as irrefutable evidence that Robert of Béthune chose Thomas to fill a specific office. The re-establishment of the office gave Robert the opportunity to change it substantially. He did not avail himself of this opportunity, and the essential concepts embodied in Jakemon's charter continued to define the general receivership as exercised by Thomas Fini in 1306. At the same time, extensions of the general receiver's power, such as that granted Thomas Fini in 1308[76] and the acquisition of a general account, served to solidify the perception of the office as a public permanent administrative entity.

Notes

1. Bonsignor paid fixed expenses such as pensions ("rechut de Bonsignor de Bonsignori, recheveur de Flandres" [Gaillard, #415bis, #418, #419, #420]) and attended audits (Baillis de Nieuport. Compte de la recette du bailli Eustache de le Spriete, octobre, 1304 à janvier, 1305, RR, #1521).

2. Pirenne calls this treaty more a condemnation than an agreement (Pirenne, *Histoire de Belgique,* 1:397). For the complete text of the treaty of Athis-sur-Orge, see L. Gilliodts-Van Severen, ed., *Inventaire des archives de la ville de Bruges (1228–1497)* (Bruges, 1871–1878), 1:276–289. For a more detailed description and interpretation, see H. Van Werveke, "Les clauses financières issues du traité d'Athis," *Revue du Nord* 32 (1950), and Pirenne, *Histoire de Belgique,* 1:397–398.

3. Philip the Fair does not seem to have given up trying to reacquire the county. He attempted through overt and covert means—such as alienating Robert of Béthune from his son Louis of Nevers—to force Robert into a situation similar to that in which his father, Guy, had found himself in 1297. Philip's sons continued their father's policies toward Flanders. In 1315, Louis X assembled an army to invade Flanders but died before any invasion could take place. In 1319 Philip V, in his turn, gathered another army of invasion but came to terms with Robert before any military confrontation took place.

4. Where Robert "transported" the communities of Lille, Béthune, and Douai (French-speaking Flanders) into French hands in exchange for the French king's right to the annual 10,000 l.p. dictated by the terms of the treaty of Athis-sur-Orge.

5. Where Robert ratified the Transport of Lille, Béthune, and Douai, and where his son Louis received back the counties of Rethel and Nevers.

6. The Bonsignori had been doing business with the counts of Flanders since 1287, when they made Guy of Dampierre a loan at the fairs of Champagne (Bigwood, *Le régime juridique,* 1:201).

7. Rennengue faite par Thomas Fin à Bruges, 1306, RR, #270; Rennengue faite part Bartelemy Fin à Ypres, 1309, *ibid.,* #271. The count had given Bartholomew special authority to receive payments and net receipts, and to supervise the *renenghe* in the same way the general receiver customarily did. The general receiver in 1309 was Thomas Fini, Bartholomew's brother, who may have requested that Bartholomew be given such authority.

8. Rennengue faite part Gilles de Hertsberghe à Bruges, 1311, *ibid.*, #272.

9. "paechent et delivrechent a no devant dit recheveur ou *a son certain comand* tout ce qu'il auront rechuit et rechevront" (emphasis added) (Gaillard, #574).

10. The count had in fact taken such action earlier in 1294 when he demanded a contribution from the churches and religious houses for the maintenance of comital lands diked along the sea (Nord, B1456 #3650).

11. Gaillard, #491, #494.

12. Pol. chrs., #226.

13. Gaillard, #497. The amount is illegible.

14. Bruges donated 2,444 l., the same amount it had promised in 1308 (Gilliodts-Van Severen, ed., *Inventaire*, #226; Thierry de Limburg-Stirum, ed., *Codex diplomaticus inde ab anno 1296 ad usque 1325 ou Recueil des documents relatifs aux guerres et dissensions suscitées par Philippe-le-Bel, roi de France contre Gui de Dampierre, comte de Flandre* [hereafter *Codex*] [Bruges, 1879, 1889], 2:145 #255). Gistel paid 16 l. 4 s. (Gaillard, #504).

15. Compte du receveur, Thomas Fin, du 25 décembre 1308 à juin 1309, RR, #1.

16. "Somme del emprunt fait pour le voiage fait au courounement le roi dalemaigne . . . : 3,456 l. 8 s. 11 d.," *ibid.*

17. "Item receut dou don fait a monsigneur de Flandre a la daerraine alei de son daerrain voiage de France de le confremance de pais le candeleur lan 1308" (*ibid.*).

18. Courtrai gave 369 l. 12 d., Bruges 2,404 l. 15 s., and Ghent 2,202 l. 7 s. 6 d.; smaller communities gave much smaller amounts. The community of Mardyck, for example, gave 11 l. 10 s. (*ibid.*).

19. He borrowed 300 l. from Bruges, for example, and 253 l. 6 s. 8 d. from the Abbey of Drongen (*ibid.*).

20. Adriaan Verhulst, "L'organisation financière du comté de Flandre, du duché de Normandie et du domaine royal français du XIe au XIIIe siècle. Des finances domaniales aux finances d'état," in *L'impôt dans le cadre de la ville et de l'état—De belasting in het raam van stad en staat. Colloque International Spa 6–9 IX 1964. Actes* (Ghent, 1966) 41.

21. Monier, *Les institutions financières*, 24–27; J. Foucart, *Une institution baillivale en Flandre. La gouvernance du souverain-bailliage de Lille, Douai, Orchies-Mortagne et Tournaisis* (Lille, 1937), 27–28; for the Transport of Flanders and the communities involved in paying it, see Willy Buntinx, "De enquête van Oudenburg. Hervorming van de repartitie van de beden in het graafschap Vlaanderen, 1408," *HKCG* 139 (1968), 75–137.

22. Entitled "Repertorium van Vane Guy," the document opens "En cel livre sont escript tout le compte des villes et chastellanies de Flandre de tout ce quil doivent à monsieur de Flandre pour raison des 10,000 l. tournois dou transport de Lille, de Douay et de Béthune commenchant au noel lan 1308 jusques au march lan 1331 et sunt li compte fait tout . . . parisis. Et aussi y sont li compte de tout che que on doit à mon dit singneur pour le pais de Saint Andrieu et de le pais d'Arque et en commencherons à rechevoir au noel lan 26 compte faite jusques au noel lan 1331 et

celui noel compte dedans" (Rijksarchief, Gent, Fonds Staten van Vlaanderen, #1349, f. 2. Hereafter St. van Vl.).

23. *Ibid.,* f. 55.

24. It is difficult to explain the gaps in this table. On the one hand, what lacunae exist could be attributed to a loss of records; on the other hand, certain communities may simply not have been required to pay the Transport.

25. Gaillard, #557.

26. "ke Thomas compta en son premier compte kil fist dou mis-quaresme lan 1305 kil entre en recepte de Flandre dusque au 25 juin 1307" (Comptes des arrérages de 1306 à 1309, RR, #3).

27. Gaillard, #574.

28. "Encore lui donnons nous plain pooir, pour nous et en en luy de nous, de conter et de demander et faire compte final à tous eschevins, queries, burghemeestres, asseurs, ceulleur et recheveurs par tout nostre contey et pooir" (*ibid.,* #588; *Codex,* 2:97 #238).

29. "Si mandons et requerons à tous eschevins, queries . . . pointeurs et recheveurs des dictes [tailles à] qui il poeut appartenir, que il à Thumas Fin, nostre dit recheveur de Flandres . . . final, et lui paicent et délivrecent *sans aultre commandement atendre de nous*" (emphasis added) (Gaillard, #588; *Codex,* 2:98 #238. The charter becomes somewhat illegible after this section).

30. Compte du receveur, Thomas Fin, du 25 décembre 1308 à juin 1309, RR, #1.

31. Gaillard, *Inventaire,* 21, 22; Gaillard, #126, #138.

32. St. van Vl., #1349, f. 5. It is possible that the third account of Colard of Marchiennes was indeed a general account, since a general account was the principal account to be associated with the general receiver.

33. Guiduche Baldechon acted as receiver from 1315 to 1317, and the *repertorium* mentions that his accounts were heard three times "paiiet par le tierche compte Guiduche Baldechon pour lan quinze" (*ibid.,* f. 5). The *repertorium* mentions five accounts for Simon Vastin (*ibid.,* f. 17, 43). On 6 August 1322, Robert of Béthune received and approved seven accounts rendered by Simon Vastin (Nord, B4063 #5472). It is unfortunately unclear what was involved in any of these accounts, but what is apparent is that they were rendered at the same time. The most likely explanation is that Simon presented seven contemporary reckonings. If the seven accounts together did make up a general account, however, then the general account at this time consisted essentially of a collection of separate accounts, which, given the organization of Thomas Fini's extant account, does not seem to have been the case.

34. St. van Vl. #1349, f. 5, 9, 13, 17, 19, 29, and 47.

35. For the period 25 December 1308 to June 1309 this balance totaled 5,562 l. 14 s. 5 d. (Compte du receveur, Thomas Fin, du 25 décembre 1308 à juin 1309, RR, #1).

36. Quittances and *ad hoc* accounts did not disappear altogether with the advent of a general account. Records such as these were used not only for the construction of the general account, but also as evidence of financial transactions.

On 26 February 1315, for example, the burgesses and aldermen of Bruges were able to produce receipts for sums they had paid to Thomas Fini in the period 1306–1309 (Gaillard, #592bis; *Codex,* 2:280–281 #309).

37. One of the other commissioners, Giles le Clerc, was a former bailiff of Ghent (Nowé, *Les baillis comtaux,* 378). Giles le Clerc, John of Tournai, and William Vische had all been commissioners at the audit of the account of the bailiff of Ypres in 1306 (Baillis de Ypres. Compte du bailli, Jean de Menin, du 22 janvier 1306 au 14 mai 1306, RR, #1699; Monier, *Les institutions financières,* 64). John of Tournai had also had the experience of supervising the *renenghe* in 1296 (Rennengue faite par Jean de Tournay à Bruges, 1296, RR, #266). Of the four clerks who were present, one, Wicard, was Thomas Fini's clerk, and a second, Christian, appears in no other comital records before and after this date. John de le Mer and James Rollars make their first appearance in this document; they both appear in records of subsequent years (Nord, B6949 f. 74, f. 32; *Codex,* 2:253). Two other commissioners, William Ackre and Nicolas Fisennes, do not figure in other records pertaining to the general receiver. Finally, Colard of Marchiennes was clerk of the count's residence and was to become general receiver in 1311.

38. A factor was a "salaried clerk or employee" (Raymond De Roover, "The Development of Accounting Prior to Luca Pacioli According to the Account Books of Medieval Merchants," in *Business, Banking, and Economic Thought in Late Medieval and Early Modern Europe: Selected Studies of Raymond De Roover,* ed. Julius Kirshner [Chicago, 1974], 129 n. 10).

39. *Ibid.,* 126.

40. *Ibid.,* 136.

41. Federigo Melis, *Storia della Ragioneria* (Bologna, 1950), 474–475, 479; De Roover, "The Development of Accounting," 128.

42. See Bigwood, *Les livres des comptes des Gallerani,* 2 vols. (Brussels, 1961); De Roover, "The Development of Accounting," 127.

43. *Ibid.,* 126.

44. De Roover, *Money, Banking and Credit,* 21.

45. Nord, B3231 #4994, B4062 #14524; ARA RK #4994; Compte des arrérages du même [Thomas Fini], rendu à la Rennenghe de 1308, RR, #2; Compte des arrérages de 1306 à 1309, *ibid.,* #3; St.-Genois, #1306; Dehaisnes, *Documents,* 1:212–213; Gaillard, *Inventaire,* 77; Bigwood, *Le régime juridique,* 1:205–207.

46. If, as De Roover claims, by 1300 the Florentine and Sienese companies "had reached a high degree of technical proficiency" ("The Development of Accounting," 128), the same can be said, given the similarity as well as the independence of their development, of Flemish financial accounts—testimony perhaps to the efforts of Gerard Lupichimi of Florence, but credit must also be given to Jakemon of Deinze. De Roover contends that Tuscan proficiency is manifest in their use of Italian instead of Latin (*ibid.,* 143), and by 1400, in their use of accounting as a tool of management and control (*ibid.,* 123). Flemish accounts had been in French since at least 1275, and implicit in the evolving public nature of the office of general receiver and thus the account associated with him, is the use of that account as a

mechanism of management; indeed, it is hard to escape the conclusion that the accounts of financial officials such as domainal receivers and bailiffs had served the same purpose as early as the twelfth century.

47. These were such people as Piero di Iacoppo da Gorzano, Piero Reynieri, Bartalotto Marchis, and a clerk named Wicard; they all functioned as subordinates to Thomas in his capacity of general receiver (Compte du receveur, Thomas Fin, du 25 décembre 1308 à juin 1309, RR, #1; Rennengue faite part Bartelemy Fin à Ypres, 1309, *ibid.*, #270; Gaillard, #497, #498, #499, #502, #507; Bigwood, *Les livres des comptes,* 2:134; Bigwood, "Un relevé des recettes," 1:9–10).

48. Gilles of Hertsberghe had been Jakemon of Deinze's valet. He had also managed the *gros brief* of 1302 (RR, #268) and was a domainal receiver in 1309 (Rennengue faite par Bartelemy Fin à Ypres, 1309, *ibid.*, #271). Colard of Marchiennes was one of Thomas Fini's principal agents of receipt (Rennengue faite par Thomas Fin à Bruges, 1306, *ibid.*, #270; Rennengue faite par Bartelemy Fin à Ypres, 1309, *ibid.*, #271; Julius Vuylsteke, ed., *Gentsche stads- en baljuwsrekeningen* [Ghent, 1900], 26, 100), and may also have been clerk of the count's household (Baillis de Furnes. Compte du Sohier de Ham jusqu'au mois de septembre 1306, RR, #1310). Guiduche Baldechon was also one of Thomas Fini's agents of receipt (Rennengue faite par Thomas Fin à Ypres, 1306, *ibid.*, #270). Simon Vastin was one of the minor officials responsible for carrying out routine tasks of receipt and disbursement (Nord, B6949 f. 44, 57), and one of the count's procurators in the arbitration with Thomas Fini in 1315 (*ibid.*, B4062 #14524).

49. "Item pour les despens dou recheveur . . . pour 24 jours quil furent ensamble a Paris et es foires de Champagne pour le besoignes monsigneur." "Item pour les dras dou recheveur et de ses gens dou termes de paskes: 170 l." (Compte du receveur, Thomas Fin, du 25 décembre 1308 à juin 1309, RR, #1). The latter entry seems to indicate that he probably received livery regularly.

50. *Ibid.*

51. St.-Genois, #1292; *Codex,* 2:264–278 #307. Colard is called Nicolas in this document.

52. *Ibid.*, 1:201–204 #59; I. de Coussemaker, *Bailleul,* 1:51–55 #41.

53. "ke nous avons mis et establis, mettons et establisons . . . nostre amey, foible Thumas Fin, nostre recheveur de Flandres, pour oster et pour mettre baillius, sous-baillius dans toute nostre conté et pooir de Flandres" (Gaillard, #588; *Codex,* 2:97 #238).

54. "si mandons et commandons . . . à tous nostre baillis, sous baillis, serians . . . quyconques le soit our sera . . . que il à nostre dit recheveur et à ses commans obbéissent et soiient obbéissant, toutes les fois ke il leur en requerra pour nostre besoignes et nostre droit maintenir" (*ibid.*).

55. In that year the issue involving an individual accused of interfering with the authority of a bailiff was handled by Simon Vastin (A. van Lokeren, 2:25; Nowé, "L'intervention," 79).

56. During the tenure of Nicholas Guiduche. See herein, p. 150.

57. St.-Genois, #1283; Nowé, *Les baillis comtaux,* 524–527 #75.

58. The first, which Gilles and the bailiff of Bruges conducted, opened on

22 February 1310 (St.-Genois, #1209). The second, which Gilles, the bailiff of Aalst, John of Tournai, and John Preudomme conducted, concerned the district of Veurne (*ibid.*, #1210).

59. On 17 February 1310 (*ibid.*, #1207).

60. Nord, B1312 #4752.

61. *Ibid.*, B3231 #4994; Bigwood, *Le régime juridique,* 1:204–205.

62. His testament is discussed briefly by V. Fris, "Le testament olographe de Barthélémy Fin, frère du receveur de Flandre (+ 1309)," *Bulletin de la société d'histoire et d'archéologie de Gand* 15 (1907), 193–194.

63. On 7 March 1314, Robert indemnified his eldest son, Louis, for 2,800 l. for plate and jewels which had been entrusted to Thomas when he was general receiver. The objects were never recovered (Nord, B3231 #4994; Dehaisnes, *Documents,* 1:212–213; ARA RK #4994).

64. Victor Fris, "Note sur Thomas Fin," *HKCG* 5th series, 10 (1900), 10. Fris argues that Thomas's last act as general receiver, dated 28 July 1309, preceded the revolt. The rebels did indeed complain of heavy exactions imposed by tax collectors, but they seem to have named no names.

65. Compte des arrérages du même [Thomas Fini], rendu à la rennenghe de 1308, RR, #2; Compte des arrérages de 1306 à 1309, *ibid.,* #3.

66. Bigwood, *Le régime juridique,* 1:205 n. 3.

67. The arbitration between the counts and Thomas's procurators took place at Tournai in the presence of the notary of Tournai, Jean de Rolenghien (*ibid.*, 205–206).

68. Bigwood, *Le régime juridique,* 1:206–207. There exist a large number of documents in the state archives at Ghent (Gaillard, #593–673) which concern Thomas, but which do not concern the count's financial business. Robert probably had these documents collected in preparation for his case against the Sienese (Gaillard, *Inventaire,* 77).

69. St.-Genois, #1306; Bigwood, *Le régime juridique,* 207.

70. Bigwood, *Le régime juridique,* 1:206–207, 2:234–300, #34. The first order of business seems to have been an argument over whether or not the parties would accept each other's procurators. Eventually they agreed on the replacement of Francesco de Hospitali by Reynieri Philippi Pistoia and Piero Reynieri of Siena, who had been Thomas's clerk.

71. Nord, B4062 #14524.

72. A more detailed description and analysis of this case can be found in Bigwood, *Le régime juridique,* 1:206–213. Thomas last appears in 1321. On 29 April of that year, the king of France pronounced Thomas in judicial default against the count of Flanders (Boutaric, #6391, #6393).

73. Thomas remained a member of the Gallerani society for most of his tenure as general receiver, although he appears to have ended his association with them sometime after 21 July 1308 (Bigwood, *Les livres des comptes,* 2:102). This is not to say that he did not rejoin the firm or some other after he left. Modern parallels in the late twentieth century abound, and there is no reason that Thomas Fini would have

remained any more unemployed than a former member of a presidential administration.

74. Simon Vastin filled the office from 1317 to 1322, the year of Count Robert's death. He does not, however, seem to have enjoyed the degree of authority which either of the Finis did.

75. Documents such as records of grants of money fiefs, in which it is recorded that the recipient was to be paid by the receiver, no longer include the phrase when ordering the receiver to make such payments.

76. Gaillard, #588; *Codex,* 2:97–98 #238.

6. The Reign of Louis of Nevers
The Office Becomes Political

ACCORDING TO HENRI PIRENNE, Flemish nationalism was born out of the Franco-Flemish conflicts of the late thirteenth and early fourteenth centuries. Throughout the thirteenth century, Flemish towns attempted to maintain and extend their semi-autonomous status particularly vis-à-vis the counts. The counts, for their part, set up financial and judicial systems, represented by the bailiffs in the early thirteenth century and then by the general receiver in the late thirteenth century, in an attempt to establish their suzerainty over the county. These goals were ultimately incompatible, and the resulting hostility between count and towns gave Philip the Fair the opportunity to extend his authority over the county to the ultimate disadvantage of both count and towns. The events of the early fourteenth century brought home to the Flemish communities the fact that their future might be better secured if they and the count worked together—at least to the point of ensuring that the French would never again obtain the upper hand. The French king dominated his lands, and this included towns, more than any Flemish count had been able to, a circumstance which fourteenth century counts no doubt envied. However, the political reality of Flanders in both the thirteenth and the fourteenth centuries dictated that the count could not govern without the Flemish towns, particularly Ghent, Bruges, and Ypres.[1]

Robert of Béthune understood the need to balance the French and the very real power of the Flemish communities. Only under these circumstances would he be able to fulfill his own ambitions both to extend comital authority more generally throughout the county and to weaken the Avesnes when the opportunity to do so presented itself, all the while keeping the French at bay.

With the accession of Robert's grandson, Louis of Nevers, in September 1322, the political traditions of the Dampierres came to an end.[2] Unlike the previous two Flemish counts, Louis entertained relatively few suspicions toward the French; he showed equally little interest in the actions and intentions of the Avesnes, now counts of both Hainaut and Holland. Louis had been raised at the French court in Paris and had little experience with the Flemish language or people. Unexposed to the traditions of his house and the political realities of his county, Louis's notion of his position as count of Flanders was based on assumptions colored by his experience at the French court and influenced by the advice of his pro-French counselors. His identification with the French court was completed by his marriage to Marguerite, daughter of Philip V, the king of France who had once threatened Flanders with invasion in 1319. Louis began his rule with little or no understanding of Flanders's semi-autonomous status relative to France and no understanding of the role the Flemish communities had in maintaining that status. He acquired little during his reign. In the late thirteenth century, the communities had turned to the French king against the Flemish count. In the early fourteenth century, count and communities had rallied together against the French. In the reign of Louis of Nevers, the Flemish communities would stand against both count and king.

Louis was welcomed into his county at his accession in 1322. But tensions between count and communities erupted into rebellion twice in Louis's reign, first in the Maritime Rebellion of 1323 to 1328 and again in 1338.[3] The Maritime Rebellion originated in Bruges, but soon spread to much of the rest of the county. Of the three major towns, only Ghent remained on the count's side.[4] Despite a formal peace treaty between the combatants on 19 April 1325, the Peace of Arques, fighting soon broke out again. Louis, it was clear, could not suppress the rebellion alone, and he called on the French king for help. Between them, the French king, Philip VI, and the Flemish count put an end to the rebellion at the battle of Cassel in 1328. Louis exacted heavy retribution on the rebel communities. So effective were his exactions that Bruges later hesitated to join Ghent and the rest of the county in the rebellion of 1338.

The issue over which county and count could find no common ground in the 1338 rebellion was the Hundred Years War. Louis, a true vassal, sided with his French lord upon the outbreak of war between England and France. The county, not prepared to antagonize the English who supplied the wool upon which much of the Flemish economy was based, was not willing to follow its count. Pressed by both sides, the Flemish, led by Jacob Van Artevelde of Ghent, rose against their count in 1338, and he fled to France. He died fighting for the French in the battle of Crécy in 1346.

Louis relied on foreigners throughout his reign. This was not only true of his close personal companions, but of his general receivers as well. Out of the eight individuals who functioned as general receiver during his reign, six were Italians and only two were Flemish. To be sure, there had been precedent for the appointment of Italians to this post; furthermore Conte Gualterotti and Simon Mirabello, two of Louis of Nevers's receivers, were also distinguished citizens of Ghent. Nonetheless, the appointment of these two does not indicate that Louis recognized the peculiar position and power which the Flemish communities, particularly the *drie steden,* exercised in his county. For in fact, in 1332, not long after the tenure of Simon Mirabello, Louis went so far as to appoint as receiver Vane Guy, who had been the French king's agent for the collection of punitive fines. Given the fact the French king also employed Italians, particularly in financial positions, it is more likely that Louis appointed the Italians he did in imitation of French practice than in continuation of his grandfather's.

These general receivers, both Italian and Flemish, served, as they had under earlier counts, as the chief agents for the execution of the count's financial policy. But during Louis's reign the persons who filled this office would become identified with the exorbitant punitive fines and disastrous economic policies seemingly exacted and executed solely for the benefit of the count and the French king. It was therefore no accident that in 1338 the rebels banished not only the count but also several of his general receivers, both current and previous. They even carried out retaliation against some of them. From the point of view of the institutional historian, there is some irony here that Louis of Nevers made no major innovations. Rather, developments during his reign are best understood in terms of a process of consolidation, flowing logically from the institutionalization of routine functions which had occurred cumulatively over the course of the previous seventy-five years. The institution of a fixed wage, of an auditing commission for the general receiver's account, and of set reckoning forms characterized the development of the general receivership under Louis of Nevers. Punishing the communities as well as augmenting his treasury motivated the count to attempt all this consolidation; increased administrative efficiency was more a by-product than an end unto itself.

Louis's policies of consolidation particularly affected the Flemish towns. The count had been sporadically represented at the auditing of the accounts of several Flemish towns since the late thirteenth century. In the early fourteenth century, Robert of Béthune had authorized Thomas Fini to hear urban accounts, but this did not become routine. In the reign of Louis of Nevers, however, the general receiver became a constant member of urban audits; the office thus developed into a device by which the count could insinuate and extend his authority over the towns. Thus although the apparatus remained essentially the same, Louis's policies yielded an appearance of drastic discontinuity to the townspeople. The precipitous increase in fines exacted from the towns and the burghers' concomitant feelings of impotence vis-à-vis the count's discretionary powers ultimately provoked them to rebellion.

Institution of a Fixed Wage

Louis of Nevers does not seem to have succeeded in making an annual audit of the general receiver's account customary. He may well have had that intention, for the account of his first receiver, Conte Gualterotti, covers exactly a year,[5] and in 1335 the count stated that he would hear the accounts of receiver Nicholas Guiduche annually.[6] This was not to be, for throughout Louis's reign accounts were audited on what seems to have been an *ad hoc* basis. Conte's next account, for example, covered a period of fifteen months and four days, from the date of his last account, 21 November 1323, to 25 February 1325.[7] Donato Peruzzi appears to have rendered only a single account,[8] although he executed the duties of the receivership for approximately two and a half years.[9] Jaquemard of Tournai, receiver for three years, probably rendered four accounts,[10] whereas Nicholas Guiduche, who held the office for about four years, may have had his accounts heard only once.[11]

Nonetheless, these references to a general account demonstrate that the general receiver continued to be responsible for the performance of specific functions within a defined geographical territory, Flanders, much like bailiffs and domainal receivers were responsible for their circumscriptions. But no receiver during Robert of Béthune's reign had drawn a *gage* from its gross revenues; as has been mentioned, the general receiver's case differed from that of bailiffs and domainal receivers in this respect. Robert's receivers do appear to have received livery and to have been reimbursed for certain expenses entailed in their exercise of the office, which was customary practice for most of the count's household. Louis of Nevers's receivers did as well. Although Ottelin Machet's account of 1334 does not include an entry for payment of any benefits such as livery,[12] the appointment charter of his successor, Nicholas Guiduche, dated 21 September 1335, includes a list of specific benefits to which Nicholas was entitled.[13] Among these were an annual grant of five horses, eight candles, and other items which the general receiver customarily received. Nicholas's 1336 account reveals, for example, that expenses incurred in holding the *audientie* and the audit of the accounts of the bailiffs and domainal receivers came not out of his own pocket, but were paid from the gross revenues of the general receiver's account.[14]

Instead of granting his receivers land, the revenues of which could maintain them, Louis of Nevers appears increasingly to have relied on wages.[15] Sometime after 1322 the general receiver began customarily drawing a fixed sum from the gross revenues of his receipt. The first indication of a general receiver obtaining such a sum is at the end of Ottelin Machet's general account; the account makes it clear that the amount had been calculated on a daily basis.[16] This means that Ottelin received remuneration for services actually rendered and not for services to be rendered; his *gage* had evolved into a wage. Since no appointment charters exist for any of Louis's early receivers, we have no way of knowing whether the count consciously instituted the general receiver's wage or whether it had only gradually come into being, or, again, whether one of the Italian receivers, such as Ottelin, might have convinced Louis of Nevers to pay him a wage. The first extant charter to include special provision for an annual fixed sum, 500 l.,[17] is that of Nicholas Guiduche, dated 21 September 1335, a year and a half after the appearance of Ottelin's account. Unfortunately, this charter does not indicate whether Nicholas was to receive this sum as a salary for services rendered as general receiver or if he was to receive it on account of services to be rendered, as a *gage;* his charter does not even mention the specific resource from which he was to draw it.[18] The general account of 7 November 1336 makes it clear that the 583 l. 6 s. 8 d. received by Nicholas at the time of the account's reckoning did indeed come out of the gross revenues of his receipt;[19] it is further evident that this sum was calculated on the basis of an annual wage of 500 l. The combination of evidence from Nicholas's appointment charter and his general account clearly reveals that Nicholas was entitled to (and actually received) a fixed annual wage of 500 l. for services he rendered as general receiver.

It is impossible to determine whether Italian receivers such as Ottelin and Nicholas were primarily responsible for the institution of the general receiver's wage. The concept of salaried officials was certainly not unknown in Flanders; bailiffs had been receiving wages from at least the late thirteenth century and perhaps even earlier.[20] Given the development of the practice of remunerating a general receiver, particularly the direction it took during the tenure of Jakemon of Deinze,[21] it is likely that the Italians of Louis of Nevers's reign may have done no more than to suggest extending pre-existing practices to this particular office. The routine aspects which the remuneration of the officeholder had developed up to 1336 rendered the concept of a general receiver's wage less than a novelty and facilitated the implementation of the practice.

Unlike bailiffs and domainal receivers, Nicholas could not count on receiving a regular sum every year. Despite the promises Louis made to Nicholas in his appointment charter, it is clear that the general receiver obtained his salary, dependent as it was on the gross revenues of his receipt, only when his account was reckoned.[22] Thus Ottelin received 61 l. 10 s. for the forty-one days his account covered, whereas Nicholas received 583 l. 6 s. 8 d. for the fourteen months his covered. Although his salary was fixed as to amount per year, the general receiver appears to have been audited on an *ad hoc* basis, and thus the payment of his wage could have not yet become a routine occurrence. In view of the latter circumstance, it cannot be said that his wage was wholly unconnected with his account, as it would have been if the office had been thoroughly bureaucratized.[23]

The institution of fixed *gages* for bailiffs in the early thirteenth century had achieved the break with past practices of payment according to the amounts received.[24] The establishment of fixed periods of audit guaranteed that these *gages* would be paid at fixed times as well. Amount and time of remuneration, firmly associated, came to be separated from the office itself, and the offices of bailiff and domainal receiver lost many of their intrinsic revenue-producing properties. The general receiver's circumscription was the county of Flanders. Although representing primarily the expenses and revenues of the count as a person, the general account was simultaneously evolving into the expression of the financial situation of the county. The increasing identification of the general receiver's account with the actions of the count as head of the Flemish government served to encourage the identification of the general receiver as a governing official not on the count's personal and private payroll. In addition, the general receiver was the first official to draw his salary from the general revenues of the county. The precedent thus set had consequential significance. When other officials, such as the chancellor and sovereign bailiff, who had no financial circumscriptions, were given salaries, it would only be logical that they should receive such payments from the central treasury as had the general receiver.

One particular aspect of the general receiver's wage paved the way for the application of this principle to the remuneration of other central officials. Although the receiver's wage was intrinsically connected to his account, its amount was not fixed and did not depend on how much gross revenue, as detailed by the account, the general receiver brought in. This signified the loss of much of the office's revenue-producing quality. The institution of a set wage encouraged the separation of the office from the personal service of the count in the same way as did the continuing existence of the office, regardless of the tenancy of its incumbent. The acquisition of a wage, tied as it was to the general account, completed the development of the general receivership as an administrative office.

The two extant accounts[25] of Louis of Nevers's reign, as well as the numerous documents approving and quitting the receiver of his account, testify that although auditing had not become an annual event, the general account had nonetheless become integral to the office. Ottelin Machet's account of 1334 probably was not a formal one, but by 1335 the concept of the general receiver's account had been accepted to the point that the appointment charter of Nicholas Guiduche specifically states that Louis of Nevers would hear Nicholas's accounts annually.[26] On 21 September 1335, the date on which he formally appointed Nicholas Guiduche as receiver, Louis of Nevers quit Nicholas Guiduche of all the receipt of Flanders which covered a period that ended on 7 September 1335.[27] Since this account began on either 1 October or 20 November 1334, it covered approximately a year,[28] indicating that Louis may have used the appointment of a new receiver to try, yet again, to have the account heard on an annual basis. But Nicholas's next account covered a period of fourteen months, from 7 September 1335 to 7 November 1336.[29]

Soon after completing the audit of 1336, Louis of Nevers replaced Nicholas in the office of general receiver with Gerard de la Moor, for whom neither an account nor evidence of one exists. It may have been impossible for Gerard to render any account, for not long after he took over the office rebels banished him, along with several other of Louis of Nevers's officials, and he fled to France.

The Commission of Audit

Other aspects of the audit of the general receiver's account were becoming routine. Since the mid-thirteenth century the count had relied principally on a commission to verify his accounts. Commissions had heard the accounts of bailiffs and receivers, and in 1309, a commission had verified the general account of Thomas Fini. The number of commissioners who heard both of Nicholas's accounts—that of 1335 and that of 1336—was smaller than the number who had heard the 1309 account of Thomas Fini. The numbers of auditors might differ—six and eight auditors instead of thirteen—but their background and experience were similar. The count was present at all three of these audits, and the general receiver (Thomas Fini in 1309 and Nicholas Guiduche in 1336) was present at two.[30] Of the other commissioners, only Roger de Thonis attended both of Nicholas's audits. Two auditors, the abbot of Dunes and the bishop-elect of Cambrai, do not appear in other records concerning the general receiver. The castellan of Diksmuide, Thierry de Belseel, Henry de Meetkerk, Thierry Noothaec, Roger Bristeste, Simon Mirabello, Josse de Hemsrode, Peter de Douai, and Roger de Thonis all had previous experience in the count's administration.[31] In addition, four of these men had been bailiffs.[32] Their skill and experience thus made them the general receiver's peers.[33] By the reign of Louis of Male, Louis of Nevers's successor, the number and composition of this commission had become essentially fixed. Most of the members had functioned at one time or another in an administrative capacity for the count, though few had official positions.

The Institution of Set Forms of Account

The form of the general account itself also changed little since it first appeared during the tenure of Thomas Fini. Thomas's account of 1309 had a number of categories that were not as clearly defined as they were in subsequent general accounts,[34] but a comparison with the three other extant general accounts indicates that the pattern established during Thomas's tenure was maintained. The types of revenues and expenses vary little from account to account. Accounts differ, of course, not in the type of revenues or expenses for which the general receiver was accountable, but rather in the particular incomes and expenses themselves. A few revenues, notably those from the domain, those from the resources under the jurisdiction of the bailiffs,[35] and, after 1335, those from the Transport of Flanders, are common to almost all of the general accounts.[36] Cloth, horses, the count's residence, and repairs formed the bulk of the count's expenses. Occasional receipts and expenses, such as arrears, fines for riots, and payments for wars, loans, dikes, falcons, and comital travels, appear irregularly, which is only logical given their intrinsic *ad hoc* nature. With the exception of the Transport, none of these incomes or expenses was new to the general receiver. All fall either into the category of resources which a local official could handle or into that of financial affairs handled by the general receiver.

The order in which each category of income or expense appears follows a similar pattern in all four of the extant accounts. Differences among them can be attributed, for the most part, to the inclusion of irregular incomes and expenses in a particular record. Those incomes and expenses common to all the accounts appeared roughly in the following order: first came the receipts from the old domain, then were listed the receipts from the *rentes hors renenghe,* the farmers, the bailiffs, and miscellany. Expenses for the count's residence, cloth, jewels, horses, and miscellany followed. Variations in this order did occur. In the account of Gilles de le Walle, for example, miscellaneous receipts preceded receipts from the farms.[37]

More fundamental differences do exist, however, among the four extant accounts. The accounts of Ottelin Machet and Gilles de le Walle do not include all the above-mentioned common incomes and expenses.[38] Both accounts covered a period of less than three months, and neither of them seems to have been audited by anyone. The account of Nicholas Guiduche ends with the details of where, when, and before whom the account took place, but Gilles's and Ottelin's end only with a simple balance. Furthermore, the latter two are considerably shorter in length than the former. These discrepancies are comprehensible if the accounts of Ottelin and Gilles are understood to represent not formal audits but informal reckonings, much like the early quarter sessions of the old domain. This would explain why the receipts of the *rentes hors renenghe,* for example, do not appear in either Gilles's or Ottelin's accounts. The receipts of the *rentes hors renenghe* were audited annually and would therefore figure into the general receiver's account only if it covered the whole span of a year or if it covered the period around 24 June, the date of the annual audit. The same holds true for the payments of yearly pensions and money fiefs. This is not to suggest that audits of the general account took place annually; as already shown, formal audits do not seem to have developed into an annual feature of the count's financial administration. Nonetheless, if both formal audits and informal reckonings did exist, formal ones probably covered a period of about a year and maybe more. Perhaps the count's financial department saw so much activity that it became expedient to draw up these informal accountings in order to keep track of it. They would then provide the basis for the formal account.

The General Receiver and the Accounts of the Flemish Towns

The general receiver's position as a major official in the household of the count and his experience in financial matters made him the natural choice to hear the accounts of the towns, for which he was neither directly responsible nor accountable.[39] The general receiver had attended the rendering of town accounts since at least 1288, usually as one of two or three comital representatives.[40] On 7 November 1308, Count Robert of Béthune had granted Thomas Fini the power to make final reckoning with, among others, all aldermen and mayors.[41] This grant implies that the general receiver had the authority to demand an accounting of a town's finances from the community's officials, but neither Thomas nor any of Robert of Béthune's other receivers seem to have exercised any actual authority over the Flemish towns. Robert's grant to Thomas Fini was a prescription rather than a description. Neither mayors nor aldermen were among those ordered to make accounting to the general receiver in the charters appointing Nicholas Guiduche or any of his successors, as they had been in the charter of Thomas Fini.

The earlier comital commissions and the 1307 grant of power to Thomas Fini nonetheless provided Louis of Nevers with valuable precedents for extending his real authority. Not long after the Maritime Rebellion, Louis of Nevers imposed commissions of audit on the Flemish communities. These commissions were staffed not by local officials but by members of his household, headed by the general receiver. Louis's policy was in direct imitation of the French king's traditional policy of allowing localities to run things as they had been accustomed, but supervised by his agents. On 14 June 1332, Louis commissioned Vane Guy (the general receiver), Peter of Douai (a clerk), and Thierry de Belseel (the bailiff of Bruges) to hear the accounts of Bruges covering the period 22 January 1331 to 21 January 1332.[42] On 19 June 1333, Peter of Douai and Thierry de Belseel heard the accounts of Bruges in the company of Nicholas Guiduche, who held the position of general receiver informally.[43] On 11 August 1333, Nicholas sat in on the reckoning of the treasurers of Bruges, Gilles de le Walle and John Bauen.[44] Three months later, on 10 October 1333, Louis of Nevers commissioned Nicholas, Thierry de Belseel, Peter of Douai, John of Bruges (a doctor of law), Henry de Meetkerk, and Josse de Hemsrode to hear the accounts of all towns and castellanies.[45] The next day Nicholas and John of Bruges received specific instructions to hear the accounts of Diksmuide.[46] Nicholas, Peter, and Josse heard the accounts of Bruges for 1333 on 9 August 1334;[47] the same three officials heard them the next year as well.[48] The pattern did not alter after Nicholas received formal appointment to the general receivership on 21 September 1335— he and Peter heard the accounts of Bruges in 1336 and 1337.[49] Except for the presence of the master of accounts (Peter of Douai), the elements of a regular comital commission for the audit of town accounts had been present since 1288. Not until Louis of Nevers brought these elements together on a regular basis did a commission, as such, come into existence.

Generally speaking, it was in the count's interest to be represented at the audit of a community's accounts, and the count's representative may have attended such reckonings from the time that towns first began drawing up accounts with balances. The most logical official to hear such accounts was the community's bailiff, for his responsibilities included protecting the count's interests and carrying out his wishes on the local level. In the last fifteen years of the thirteenth century, when towns first began to draw up accounts, the count probably chose who would hear these audits for him as much on the basis of an individual's prestige as on his technical skill and official position. In at least one case it appears that the prestige of a particular individual influenced the count more than did the office held by another. Both Siger of Bailleul and the general receiver had attended the audit of the account of Bruges three times;[50] nonetheless, Siger subsequently attended an audit of Bruges's accounts—he held no particular office—at which the general receiver was not present.

But by the end of the reign of Louis of Nevers, the situation had changed. What is significant is that Louis began to commission his financial officials to hear these accounts after the successful conclusion of the Maritime Rebellion and about the time when Vane Guy, former receiver for the king of France in Flanders, occupied the office of general receiver. Equally significant is the absence of commissions to hear the audit of the accounts of Ghent and the preponderance of evidence of commissions to audit the accounts of Bruges. Ghent had sided with the count in the Maritime Rebellion, while Bruges had been its instigator. Louis was obviously using these commissions as a form of social control. Although the count still chose individuals with some personal prestige but no particular position in his administration to be members of the commission who heard town accounts, the presence of such individuals ceased to follow a consistent pattern. Instead, the count began routinely to commission particular officials, notably the general receiver and the master of accounts, to audit town accounts. Occasionally they were joined by a bailiff, frequently the bailiff of the town in question. H. Nowé maintains, however, that the bailiff attended primarily on the basis of his status as comital commissioner and not on account of his position as bailiff of the particular town.[51] The same probably held true for the general receiver and the master of accounts, since neither of them was responsible or accountable for town accounts; the master of accounts at this time did not even exist as a formally commissioned official. Still, during the reign of Louis of Nevers, the presence of the general receiver and the master of accounts, regardless of incumbent, gradually came to be routinely required at the reckoning of a town's accounts,[52] and thus the significance of being "general receiver" or "master of accounts" eventually superseded the importance of being a comital commissioner. What this signifies is that the basis for the prestige and importance of the office of general receiver (vis-à-vis town accounts at least) changed from the personal prestige to the relationship of the office holder with the count, and finally to the office itself, regardless of who held it or who empowered it. Consistent use of the general receiver in this capacity worked as a device enabling the count to extend his authority over these towns. It concomitantly extended the authority of those of his other administrators who heard town accounts. At the same time, since they had little or no direct responsibility for town accounts, the involvement of the general receiver and the master of accounts served to identify these officials and the government they represented as public rather than personal.

Judicial Affairs

Sometime during the reign of Louis of Nevers, the general receiver assumed the authority to set the amount of fines levied in the courts of the Flemish bailiffs. His interference was probably based on the obligation on the part of the bailiff to obtain the general receiver's assent when excusing a fine of 60 l. or more. An account of Daniel de Neuve-Eglise, bailiff of the castellany of Courtrai, reveals that by January 1336 the general receiver had the authority to reduce a fine already set by the bailiff.[53] Nonetheless, although such authority had existed as early as 1336, it did not receive formal acknowledgment until 1349, in the appointment charter of Andrew le Russe.[54] Certainly, the abuses that resulted from allowing the bailiffs to set fines provided a motive for subordinating bailiffs to the general receiver.[55]

The general account of Nicholas Guiduche for 1335 to 1336 indicates that the general receiver had also acquired authority over those judicial matters which transcended the jurisdiction of local judicial officers. He received forfeits resulting from wars, convictions of conspiracy, and riots; fines from *kalenges* (cases in which the decision of a local official was challenged); pecuniary commutations of sentences and banishments; and fines for readmission to the count's peace after riots.[56] Forfeits had already figured among the general receiver's revenues as early as 1334.[57] The successful suppression of the Maritime Rebellion no doubt offered Louis the opportunity to confide this type of revenue routinely to the general receiver, but the collection of these revenues could only antagonize the Flemish communities and associate the general receiver more firmly with the policies of Louis of Nevers. By the reign of Louis's successor, the general receiver, then, had come to perform the functions of a bailiff with regard to outlaws and vagabonds, both of whom by definition had no fixed residence and who thus did not fall under the jurisdiction of any local official. The general receiver also performed similar functions with regard to individuals involved in riots, wars, and conspiracies because they trans-gressed the count's peace. Ultimately, these policies were efficient, logical, and rooted in traditional feudal practice. It was only Louis of Nevers's increased and consistent application of them which made them obnoxious in Flemish eyes.

The Revolt of the Towns

All these developments consolidated the office of general receiver and allowed the count to use it as an instrument of his policy. By the late 1330s Louis's financial administration seemed to many in his county to have been geared primarily toward implementing punitive financial damages and providing him with large sums of money. The increasing effectiveness of the general receivership, based on a staff and system that allowed the count to exploit the resources of the county without recourse to partnership with either the nobility or town patriciates, also insulated Louis from his county and protected him from confrontations with his populace. In the course of his reign Louis appointed six Italians and two Flemings to the position of general receiver. On the surface, none of these appointments was unusual; they followed the pattern which had been established with the assumption of the office by Gerard Lupichimi sometime in 1289. With the exception of

Gerard de la Moor, all of Louis's general receivers were either Italians with financial experience[58] or officials who had acquired financial experience in the comital[59] or in the French royal household.[60] But other than Conte Gualterotti and Simon Mirabello, the Italians had no local loyalties, and Jaquemard of Tournai's loyalty was undoubtedly to the count who had consistently employed him. Louis of Nevers may well have appointed these individuals as general receiver more for his benefit than for the benefit of his county. This, of course, was not a crime, but it does indicate the degree to which Louis of Nevers was unable to assess administrative developments and political realities. The Italians were in the business of managing finances and may have had little concern for the feelings and prerogatives of other important sectors in the county. Of the general receivers who had experience, most of them had acquired it in the count's household itself. They were dependent upon him, and they naturally identified their interests with his.

In the thirteenth century, non-specific members of the count's household had performed financial tasks under the direction of the count, but in the fourteenth century, minor officials subordinate to the general receiver performed most of the routine financial functions. When Italians (who were usually associated with Italian business interests), or an official with skills acquired in the comital household (who thus had limited outside contacts), held the office, it was unavoidable that the views of these individuals would influence the count's view of the economic situation in his county. The isolation that resulted from these conditions hindered the interplay between the political and other spheres which should have been facilitated, at least in financial matters, by the financial administration.[61]

Furthermore, the only skilled official who had not acquired his experience in the comital household, Vane Guy, was in the service of the French king. Vane had the responsibility of receiving the indemnity payments which the Flemish communities owed to the French king,[62] and nothing suggests that Count Louis did anything to obstruct the activities of the French king's agents in Flanders. Louis went so far as to make Vane his general receiver even though Vane was still functioning as the French king's agent.[63] Obviously, the interests of the king of France were well-represented at the Flemish court.

Compared with their predecessors in the reign of Robert of Béthune, most of Louis's receivers were startlingly more proficient in extracting payments of the Transport of Flanders from the Flemish communities (see Tables 4 and 5). Both Conte Gualterotti, Louis's first general receiver, and

TABLE 4. Collection of the Transport of Flanders in the Reign of Louis of Nevers, 1322 to 1331

Community	1322	1323	1324	1325	1326	1327	1328	1329	1330	1331	Sources
Aalst											
Aalst castellany											
Aardenburg		CG			DP				JT		St. VI. f. 66
Aarschot			CG	CG	CG	CG*	CG*	CG*	CG*	CG*	St. VI. f. 93
Bailleul											
Bergues											
Bergues castellany											
Beveren			CG	CG	CG	CG*	CG*	CG*	CG*	CG*	St. VI. f. 94v
Beveren parish			CG	CG	CG	CG*	CG*	CG*	CG*	CG*	St. VI. f. 95
Beveren lordship					CG	CG*	CG*	CG*	CG*	CG*	St. VI. f. 95v
Blankenberge			CG	CG	DP				JT		St. VI. f. 79
Bourbourg											
Bourbourg territory											Pol. chrs. #337
Bruges							JT	JT			St. VI. f. 93v
Burcht			CG	CG	CG	CG*	CG*	CG*	CG*	CG*	
Cassel											
Cassel territory											
Coudenburg			CG	CG	CG	CG*	CG*	CG*	CG*	CG*	St. VI. f. 92
Courtrai	CG	CG	CG			DP	JT	JT		JT	St. VI. f. 49
Courtrai castellany		CG				SM	JT	JT	JT		St. VI. f. 51
Damme	CG		CG	CG		JT	JT	JT	JT	JT	St. VI. f. 77
Dendermonde											
Diksmuide		CG	CG		CG	JT	JT	JT	JT	JT	St. VI. f. 89
Dunkirk											
Eksaarde			CG		CG	CG*	CG*	CG*	CG*	CG*	St. VI. f. 93v

								Reference
Franc of Bruges	SV	CG						St. Vl. f. 11
Franc Métier	CG	CG						St. Vl. f. 9
Ghent	CG	CG	CG					St. Vl. f. 5
Gistel	CG	CG	DP	DP*		JT	JT	St. Vl. f. 85
Geraardsbergen						JT	JT	St. Vl. f. 91
Gravelines								
Haasdonk	CG	CG		CG*	CG*	CG*	CG*	St. Vl. f. 95
Hoeke	CG	CG	DP	DP*	DP*	JT	JT	St. Vl. f. 73
Hugevliet	CG		DP	CG*		JT		St. Vl. f. 56
Ijzendijke			DP	CG*		JT		
Kallo	CG	CG		CG*	CG*	CG*	CG*	St. Vl. f. 94
Kieldrecht		CG		CG*	CG*	CG*	CG*	St. Vl. f. 95v
Kruibeke	CG	CG		CG*	CG*	CG*	CG*	St. Vl. f. 93
Land of Waas	CG	CG		CG*	CG*	CG*	CG*	St. Vl. f. 92
Langaardenburg	CG	CG	DP			JT		St. Vl. f. 60
Lo	CG							St. Vl. f. 23
Lombardsijde	CG							St. Vl. f. 21
Mardyck								
Massemen	CG	CG		CG*	CG*	CG*	CG*	St. Vl. f. 94
Monnikerede	CG		DP	DP*	DP*	JT		St. Vl. f. 75
Nieuwpoort	CG							
Oostburg	CG			DP	DP	JT		St. Vl. f. 64
Oostende	CG		DP	DP*	DP*	JT		St. Vl. f. 81
Oudenaarde	CG		DP	DP		JT		St. Vl. f. 54
Oudenaarde castellany	CG	CG	CG					St. Vl. f. 55
Oudenburg			DP	DP		JT		St. Vl. f. 83
Poperinge	CG		DP					St. Vl. f. 26
Pumbeke	CG	CG	CG	CG*	CG*	CG*	CG*	St. Vl. f. 93
Roeselare bij Aardenburg	CG		DP	CG*	CG*	CG*		St. Vl. f. 62

TABLE 4. *Continued*

Community	1322	1323	1324	1325	1326	1327	1328	1329	1330	1331	Sources
Rupelmonde			CG	CG	CG	CG*	CG*	CG*	CG*	CG*	St. VI. f. 94v
Sint-Anna-ter-Muide		CG			DP	DP*	DP*	DP*	JT		St. VI. f. 71
Sint-Niklaas			CG	CG	CG	CG*	CG*	CG*	CG*	CG*	St. VI. f. 95v
Sluis		CG	CG	CG	CG	JT	DP	JT	JT		St. VI. f. 68
Temse			CG	CG	CG	CG*	CG*	CG*	CG*	CG*	St. VI. f. 92v
Torhout	CG							JT			St. VI. f. 87
Verrebroek			CG	CG	CG	CG*	CG*	CG*	CG*	CG*	St. VI. f. 94
Veurne											
Veurne territory											
Vier Ambachten											
Warneton											
Waterduinen											
Ypres		CG	CG			SM	DP	JT	JT	JT	St. VI. f. 12, 12v
Ypres castellany	CG	CG					SM	JT	JT	JT	St. VI. f. 13
Zottegem			CG	CG	CG	CG*	CG*	CG*	CG*	CG*	St. VI. f. 92v

*Payment in advance; CG = Conte Gualterotti; DP = Donato Peruzzi; JT = Jaquemard of Tournai; SM = Simon Mirabello; St. Vl. = Staten van Vlaanderen, #1349; SV = Simon Vastin.

TABLE 5.   Collection of the Transport of Flanders and the Peace of Arques by Nicholas Guiduche and Vane Guy, 1331 to 1335

Community	1331	1332	1333	1334	1335	Sources
Aalst						
Aalst castellany						
Aardenburg	VG†					St. Vl. f. 66
Aarschot	VG†					St. Vl. f. 93
Bailleul	VG†					St. Vl. f. 45
Bergues	VG†	NG				St. Vl. f. 27
Bergues castellany	VG†	NG†				St. Vl. f. 30
Beveren	VG†					St. Vl. f. 94v
Beveren parish	VG†					St. Vl. f. 95
Beveren lordship						
Blankenberge	VG†	NG	NG*			St. Vl. f. 79–80
Bourbourg	VG†	NG				St. Vl. f. 37–38
Bourbourg territory	VG†	NG	NG*			
Bruges	VG†					St. Vl. f. 6v
Burcht	VG†					St. Vl. f. 93v
Cassel	VG†					St. Vl. f. 41
Cassel territory	VG†	NG	NG*			St. Vl. f. 43–44
Coudenburg	VG†					St. Vl. f. 93
Courtrai						
Courtrai castellany	NG†					St. Vl. f. 51v
Damme	VG†	NG	NG*			St. Vl. f. 77–78
Dendermonde						
Diksmuide	NG†	VG†				St. Vl. f. 89–90
Dunkirk	VG†	NG				St. Vl. f. 31–32
Eksaarde	VG†					St. Vl. f. 93v
Franc of Bruges		NG		NG† pd 1336	NG	St. Vl. f. 9
Franc Métier						
Ghent						
Gistel	VG†	NG	NG*			St. Vl. f. 85–86
Geraardsbergen						
Gravelines	VG†	NG				St. Vl. f. 33–34
Haasdonk	VG†					St. Vl. f. 95
Hoeke	VG†	NG				St. Vl. f. 74
Hugevliet	VG†	NG	NG*			St. Vl. f. 56–57
Ijzendijke	VG†	NG	NG*			St. Vl. f. 59
Kallo	VG†					St. Vl. f. 94
Kieldrecht	VG†					St. Vl. f. 95v
Kruibeke	VG†					St. Vl. f. 93v
Land of Waas	VG†					St. Vl. f. 92
Langaardenburg	VG†	NG	NG*			St. Vl. f. 61
Lo	VG†					St. Vl. f. 23

TABLE 5.   *Continued*

Community	1331	1332	1333	1334	1335	Sources
Lombardsijde	VG†					St. Vl. f. 21
Mardyck	VG†	NG				St. Vl. f. 35–36
Massemen	VG†					St. Vl. f. 94
Monnikerede	VG†	NG	NG*			St. Vl. f. 76
Niewupoort	VG†	NG	NG			St. Vl. f. 19–20
Oostburg	VG†	NG				St. Vl. f. 65
Oostende	VG†	NG	NG*			St. Vl. f. 81–82
Oudenaarde	VG†					St. Vl. f. 54
Oudenaarde castellany		NG†				St. Vl. f. 55
Oudenburg	VG†	NG	NG*			St. Vl. f. 83–84
Poperinghe	VG†	NG	NG*			St. Vl. f. 25–26
Pumbeke						
Roeselare bij Aardenburg	VG†	NG	NG*			St. Vl. f. 62–63
Rupelmonde	VG†					St. Vl. f. 94
Sint-Anna-ter-Muide	VG†	NG	NG*			St. Vl. f. 71–72
Sint-Niklaas	VG†					St. Vl. f. 95v
Sluis	VG†					St. Vl. f. 68
Temse	VG†					St. Vl. f. 92v
Torhout	VG†	NG	NG*			St. Vl. f. 88
Verrebroek	VG†					St. Vl. f. 95
Veurne	VG†					St. Vl. f. 15
Veurne territory	VG†					St. Vl. f. 17
Vier Ambachten	VG†					St. Vl. f. 5
Warneton	VG†	NG	NG*			St. Vl. f. 47–48
Waterduinen	VG†	NG				St. Vl. f. 70–70v
Ypres						
Ypres castellany	VG†					St. Vl. f. 13
Zottegem	VG†					St. Vl. f. 92v

*Payment in advance; †back payment; NG = Nicholas Guiduche; St. Vl. = Staten van Vlaanderen, #1349; VG = Vane Guy.

Donato Peruzzi had remarkable success in this matter; they even obtained payment in advance from many of the smaller communities.

But regardless of the success of his financial administration, Louis had squandered so much of his income by 1332 that his finances were in chaos. It was about this time that he chose Vane Guy as his general receiver.[64] After the annual audit of the *renenghe* in June, Vane and two of the count's councilors, William d'Auxonne, chancellor, and Peter of Douai, master of accounts, investigated the count's finances.[65] Vane probably drew up the *repertorium* as part of this investigation and to provide a basis upon which to demand arrears and to calculate future payments. The count's faith in Vane Guy was not misplaced. Vane and his lieutenant, Nicholas Guiduche, vigorously pursued the collection of the Transport of Flanders and the Peace of Arques (see Table 5).

To be sure, Louis of Nevers did not wholly ignore the bourgeoisie when making administrative appointments; both Conte Gualterotti and Simon Mirabello were prominent citizens of Ghent, even though they were Italians.[66] Although the appointment of Conte Gualterotti may not have been politically motivated,[67] there is every indication that the appointment of Simon Mirabello was. For Louis of Nevers, Simon's appointment had much to recommend it. Simon was Louis's brother-in-law, a rich banker, and a powerful citizen of Ghent.[68] Simon received the office of receiver sometime in 1329, the year after the battle of Cassel, a battle in which Ghent did not take part. Louis of Nevers severely punished both Ypres and Bruges for their participation in this battle. Ghent saw Simon, one of its most prominent citizens, appointed to one of the most prestigious and important positions within the count's administration. Furthermore, he appears to have done very little of the work associated with the office; his lieutenant, Jaquemard of Tournai, performed most of the general receiver's functions.[69] The count, then, probably did not appoint Simon receiver primarily on account of his administrative ability; the appointment was clearly a reward for Ghent's loyalty.

Nevertheless, appointments such as that of Simon Mirabello and other Italians may have hindered accessibility to Louis of Nevers in financial matters. Because of the nature of their business, the Italians had formed a somewhat closed network; Italian receivers may well have been each other's business associates. Both Conte Gualterotti and Vane Guy, for instance, had been connected to the Guidi. Conte and Vane Guy were at least once also simultaneously involved in Ghent's finances.[70] As important citizens of Ghent, Simon Mirabello and Conte Gualterotti were probably well acquainted with each other. Ottelin Machet had actually been a member of the Peruzzi society;[71] Donato Peruzzi may have been instrumental in bringing Ottelin to the count's attention. Finally, Donato, as a member of the largest banking concern in Bruges, was undoubtedly familiar with most of the receivers involved in commerce.

A similar network may have included the receivers who had acquired their skill within the comital household. Jaquemard of Tournai and Ottelin

Machet were members of the count's financial administration at the same time. In addition, Jaquemard had been Simon Mirabello's lieutenant, just as Nicholas Guiduche had been the lieutenant of Vane Guy. These members of the central financial administration worked together before they were appointed to the office, during their incumbency, and, in a few cases, even after they left office. Because of this familiarity, they may have formed something of a closed corporation. Few of them had outside local ties. They may have wished to preserve their positions by increasing the count's autonomy with regard to his county while at the same time encouraging his dependence upon them. The probable close relationship between Louis of Nevers's receivers may have encouraged and contributed to their desire for and achievement of such autonomy.

The county had many reasons for associating Louis of Nevers's receivers with the more oppressive actions of his reign. After the battle of Cassel in 1328, Vane Guy drew up the inventory of forfeits for the Flemish count and the French king.[72] The count levied an indemnity, called the Peace of Arques, on those communities that had participated in the rebellion; the Peace of Arques forms a large part of Vane Guy's *repertorium*. Vane also collected Bruges's and Ypres's parts of this indemnity.[73] By the time he assumed the duties of general receiver in 1332, Vane could hardly have escaped identification as a French agent whose primary occupation seemed to be collecting onerous fines. His association with Louis of Nevers could not have improved relations between the count and the Flemish communities.

Donato Peruzzi, Ottelin Machet, and Nicholas Guiduche, all Italians and all Louis's receivers in the 1330s, also collected punitive payments. Donato Peruzzi, for example, seems to have lent the count money to pay for the army that crushed the rebels at Cassel. In return, the count assigned Donato, who was his receiver at the time, the penalty which Bruges was forced to pay for its involvement in the rebellion.[74] In 1329 Ottelin Machet received forfeits resulting from the Maritime Rebellion for the count.[75] Ottelin, unlike Vane Guy, was still in the count's service when van Artevelde's rebellion broke out in 1336. The rebels then exacted their revenge. In 1338, they banished Ottelin, along with most of the count's other advisors,[76] and in 1340 they burned his possessions in Eekloo.[77] Nicholas Guiduche, another of Count Louis's general receivers banished in 1338, had been, as noted earlier, Vane Guy's lieutenant,[78] and between 1332 and 1337, had made several attempts to collect the Transport and the payments for the Peace of Arques.[79] He, too, was a foreigner, but unlike Simon Mirabello, did not hold citizenship in any Flemish town.

Nonetheless, the situation did not become dangerous until the beginning of the Hundred Years War. In 1336 Louis of Nevers proclaimed the cessation of all commerce with England; he probably made this proclamation at the behest of the French king.[80] The English retaliated by arresting Flemish merchants in England, forbidding the export of wool, and prohibiting the importation of foreign cloth.[81] This embargo wreaked economic havoc on the Flemish towns, and their leaders attempted to pressure Louis to come to some sort of agreement with the English in order to restore trade. Louis refused.[82] In early 1338, Jacob Van Artevelde, a prominent citizen of Ghent, led the town into rebellion and established a revolutionary government in Ghent;[83] by early spring Van Artevelde had rallied most of the county to his cause. The French responded by having an interdict laid on the county. Ineffective, it was retracted on 5 May.[84]

Sometime within the year preceding the Van Artevelde rebellion, Count Louis had changed general receivers. He replaced Nicholas Guiduche with Gerard de la Moor, a Flemish noble and descendant of one of Count Robert of Béthune's representatives at the negotiations of the treaty of Athis-sur-Orge in 1304.[85] Although bailiff for a brief period of time shortly before becoming general receiver in 1337,[86] Gerard does not seem to have served the count in any capacity, administrative or otherwise, before his appointment. In fact, he appears to have had little financial or administrative experience. Why did Louis replace Nicholas, a highly skilled administrator, with Gerard, a relative novice? The answer may lie in the worsening relations between count and county. Despite the lack of any extant evidence of complaints against the count's general receiver or Italians in particular, it is possible that the relationship between count and county had reached a point where the count, in an attempt to placate his county, removed Nicholas from office and replaced him with a Flemish noble. Such an action suggests either that complaints against Nicholas had indeed been made or that Louis was aware of the disfavor in which officials such as Nicholas were held. Louis, however, did not completely rid himself of Nicholas or any of the other Italians who managed his affairs; Nicholas still actively participated in the management of the count's finances after giving up his formal position.[87]

Louis's substitution of Gerard for Nicholas is a clear indication of how public an official the general receiver had become. It further demonstrates that the general receiver had ceased to function in a purely comital management position. Gerard's appointment implies that the office served as such an integral part of the county's government that the choice of incumbent and the exercise of the office's functions affected the county as a whole; the office was no longer responsible simply for the count's personal finances. The general account makes it clear that the general receiver had become accountable for what could be described as the county's finances; the general receivership had thus developed into a public office and therefore a political one. The banishment in 1338 of not only Nicholas Guiduche and Ottelin Machet, but Gerard de la Moor as well, substantiates this argument.[88] In the spring of 1338, the rebellious county reduced Louis of Nevers to compliance with their demands, demands that may well have included the banishment of those of his advisors whom the rebels felt to be detrimental to their interests and efforts. The functions these advisors performed, however, were still vital to the running of the county. On 17 November 1338, seven of the count's banished advisors were given safe-conducts to return to Bruges in order to organize the county's accounts.[89]

The rebels suppressed the office of general receiver, though, and it was not re-instated until 1349 and the re-establishment of comital power in Flanders under Louis of Male.

Conclusion

A fundamental change had taken place by the end of the reign of Louis of Nevers. Two of his receivers, Nicolas Guiduche and Jaquemard of Tournai, had performed the duties of the office without formally holding the position. Thus, the performance of functions associated with the office no longer defined either the office itself or the individual carrying out its functions. Instead, a person became general receiver only by formal appointment of the count. Such a circumstance indicates that the office existed as a conceptual entity within the domain of the count's governance. Changes that occurred now resulted less from the personality or prestige of its holder and more from the interaction of its routine functioning with the demands of the count's government, itself increasingly routinized.

By 1322, the general receivership had developed into an office responsible for the resources of the county. Few of its incumbents had authority beyond that vested in the position they held. They depended on the count for their maintenance, financial support, or other favors. They owed their loyalty only to the count. They identified with his interests and in executing their duties may have provided him with the opportunity of securing a measure of independence from the nobility and from the urban patriciates particularly for either financial personnel or financial management. Since the beginning of his reign, Louis of Nevers had pursued a policy of almost single-minded support of the French king, in direct contrast to previous comital policy, and perhaps a rejection of it. This in itself probably would have eventually brought him into conflict with the Flemish communities, but Louis also staffed his household and administration, notably his financial administration, with non-Flemings or with individuals whose interests and background were clearly identified with his own. The count seems to have made little attempt to integrate the nobles or urban patriciates into his government. Instead, he appears to have used the office chiefly to increase his autonomy with regard to his county, if not with regard to his lord, the French king. The office, in these circumstances, could no longer sufficiently facilitate the smooth and relatively equitable transactions of business between count and county. Nonetheless, the isolation of the count by his financial administration from the economic realities of the period might have meant little had an economic crisis not befallen Flanders. Louis's refusal to come to an understanding with the English focused dissatisfaction on him, but it is evident from the events of 1338 that most of that dissatisfaction was directed toward his advisors. Throughout most of the period 1338 to 1346, actions taken by the rebels were done in the count's name, even though he himself had fled his county.

Notes

1. Nicholas, *Town and Countryside*, 152–155. These three towns were often referred to collectively as the *drie steden*.

2. Pirenne, *Histoire de Belgique*, 2:7.

3. For a more complete description and analysis of the Maritime Rebellion, see Pirenne, *Histoire de Belgique*, 2:74–99, and H. Van Werveke, "De Nederlanden tegenover Frankrijk, 1305–1346," in *Algemene Geschiedenis der Nederlanden*, vol. 3 (Antwerp, 1951), 16–62. For Flanders and the Hundred Years War, see Pirenne, *Histoire de Belgique*, 2:100–134, and Henry S. Lucas, *The Low Countries and the Hundred Years War, 1326–1347* (Ann Arbor, 1929).

4. "indeed the years 1320–1332 were the longest single period of cooperation between the count and the Gentenaren in the fourteenth century" (Nicholas, *Town and Countryside*, 162).

5. Nord, B4064 #5642; Conte's account covers the period 21 November 1322 to 21 November 1323 (*ibid.*, B1568 n. 176 f. 119v); Louis became count on 17 September 1322. This account is therefore probably Conte's first.

6. "Item, que nous orrions ou ferons oir ses comptes une fois chascun an sans faute" (*ibid.*, B1565 n. 489 f. 76v).

7. Nord, B1568 n. 174–175 f. 119–119v. (Whoever numbered these documents assumed that n. 174 ended at the bottom of page 119, and that the record at the top of page 119v was a new one, hence n. 175. The record at the top of page 119v, however, is the continuation of n. 174.)

8. The *repertorium* mentions only "the first account of Donato Peruzzi" or "the account of Donato Peruzzi," which was probably drawn up sometime in 1326: "paiiet par le premier compte Donat de Perruches" (St. van Vl., #1349, f. 7, 9, 24, 50, 51, 56); "paiet par le compte Donat des Perruches" (*ibid.*, #1349 f. 26, 55, 57–61, 63–69, 70v–76, 79–80, 82–86, 90). Since the accounts themselves are not internally labeled first, second, or third, perhaps the clerk who drew up the *repertorium* anticipated that Donato would have more than one account.

9. *Ibid.*, f. 71, 73, 75, 81, 85. Donato seems to have assumed the position sometime in 1326. Both Donato and Simon bear the title of receiver in the account of Oliver de la Mote, receiver of the toll of Damme, which covers the period from 18 September 1328 to 16 September 1329 (RR, #622). On 9 August 1329, Simon was called the receiver of Flanders (Pol. chrs., #334). Thus it is likely that sometime between 18 September 1328 and 9 August 1329 Simon replaced Donato.

10. Staten van Vl., #1349 f. 7v. Jaquemard, however, appears to have performed the functions of receiver as Simon Mirabello's lieutenant.

11. Nicholas formally held the office from 7 September to sometime in 1337. During this time, Louis apparently heard Nicholas's accounts only once (Compte du Nicolas Guiduche, du 7 septembre 1335 au novembre 1336, RR, #5). On the day that he formally appointed Nicholas general receiver (21 September 1335), Louis also quit him of the accounts he had handled merely as a member of the count's household (Nord, B1565 p. 819 f. 158).

12. The account covers only three months (Compte du receveur Othon Macet du 26 janvier 1334 [n.s.] rendu en 1335, RR, #4), and livery was usually granted only once a year. Hence, such an omission is not unwarranted; Ottelin may, in fact, have received his annual livery at another time.

13. Nord, B1565 n. 489 f. 76v.

14. Compte du receveur Nicolas Guiduche, du 7 septembre 1335 au novembre 1336, RR, #5.

15. Louis does not seem to have given any of his receivers grants of land, with the possible exception of Jaquemard of Tournai. On 18 August 1331, Jaquemard received land in Menin (Nord, B1562 n. 301 f. 183 #6335), four *bonniers* of land (*ibid.*, B1562 n. 302 f. 183 #6336), and the lands of Josse de le Val and Rogier de le Wastine (*ibid.*, B1562 n. 303 f. 183–183v #6337). On 19 November 1331, he received a *rente* of 100 l. from the great *tonlieu* at Bruges (St.-Genois, #1654).

16. "Item pour les gages Ottenin recheveur dessus dicte des le 26 jour de janvier lan 33 dusques au 7 jour de march prochain apres ensuivant que est pour 41 jours, 30 s. le jour, montent: 61 l. 10 s." (Compte du receveur Othon Macet du 26 janvier 1334 [n.s.] rendu en 1335, RR, #4). If he had been receiver for a whole year, he would have received approximately 500 l.

17. "Item, que pour fere le dit office nous li baillerons chascun an 500 l.p. gros tournois pour 12 d. par. par cause de gages" (Nord, B1565 n. 489 f. 76v).

18. Charters appointing general receivers during the reign of Louis of Male

treat the issue of a wage in a similar fashion. John Van der Delft was granted "gages de mil livres par. par an" (Thierry de Limburg-Stirum, *Cartulaire de Louis de Male* [Bruges, 1898–1901], 2:121 #848). John and Peter de la Fauchille and Gossuin le Wilde were to receive "gaiges de mil livres tournois par an" (Nord, B1596 f. 100v #8146; B1596 f. 107v #8705; B1566 n. 252 f. 67 #9471. The only difference among the charters of the three latter receivers is in the placement of the word "de"). In none of these documents is it mentioned whence these wages were to be paid or at what time.

19. "Date de le recepte dessus dicte: . . . . Date as diverses parties: . . . . Item pour les gages de Nicolas recheveur pour le terme de 14 mois al avenant de 500 l. lan, monte pour le terme: 583 l. 6 s. 8 d." (Compte du receveur Nicolas Guiduche, du 7 septembre 1335 au 7 novembre 1336, RR, #5). Nicholas Guiduche's wage was not the only income he received from the count. Although he received maintenance in the form of livery, candles, and horses, his 1336 account reveals that he also received the hefty sum of 1,600 l. as *courtoisie* for his services ("Encore lui doit on lez quels monsieur lui donne en courtoisie pour le bon service que il lui a fait: 1,600 l." [*ibid.*]). *Courtoisie* is a term with many meanings, from gift to bribery. In this case it probably signifies interest for loans made to the count, for it is evident throughout Nicholas's account that he loaned Louis of Nevers several sums. Two entries above this one, for example, it is noted, "Encore lui doit on les quels il preste a monsieur pour les despens de l'ostel. . . . 2,400 l." "Despens de l'ostel" could cover virtually anything. Unfortunately there are no other accounts from this period, and so it is difficult to ascertain whether other general receivers received similar payments of *courtoisie*.

20. Nowé, *Les baillis comtaux*, 117.

21. See herein, pp. 91–93.

22. Compte du receveur Othon Macet du 26 janvier 1334 (n.s.) rendu en 1335, *ibid.*, #4; Compte du receveur Nicolas Guiduche, du 7 septembre 1335 au 7 novembre 1336, *ibid.*, #5.

23. Reinhard Bendex, "Bureaucracy and the Problem of Power," in *Reader in Bureaucracy*, Robert K. Merton, ed. (Glencoe, Illinois, 1960), 117.

24. Nowé, *Les baillis comtaux*, 115.

25. Compte du receveur Othon Macet du 26 janvier 1334 (n.s.), rendu en 1335, RR, #4; Compte du receveur Nicolas Guiduche, du 7 septembre 1335 au 7 novembre 1336, *ibid.*, #5; Compte du receveur Gilles de le Walle du 28 september 1348 au 13 décembre 1348, *ibid.*, #6.

26. "Item, que nous orrions ou ferons oir ses comptes une fois chascun an sans faute" (Nord, B1565 n. 489 f. 76v).

27. "Quittance fait a Nicolas Guiduce de toute la recepte de Flandres" (*ibid.*, B1565 n. 819 f. 158); the account itself has been lost. It is difficult to ascertain whether the "recepte de Flandres" was the actual title of the account at this time. Charters and accounts subsequent to this one, however, do not employ the term in any formal sense and it is likely that the general receiver's account remained chiefly associated with him rather than with the county. The unspecified date with which Nicholas's account began may have been 3 March 1334, the date at which Ottelin's account ended, for although a period of twenty months was a long time for any account to cover, at least one later account covered a longer period: from 25 April

1 3 5 1 to 16 October 1 3 5 3 (Limburg-Stirum, *Louis de Male*, 2:414–415 #1333), a total of two and a half years.

28. There was no receiver between 14 June and 1 October 1 3 3 4. Furthermore, although Nicholas had been acknowledged by Louis of Nevers as the receiver of "many of our rents, revenues, and other manner of goods and exploits of our county of Flanders" since 20 November 1 3 3 4 (*ibid.*, B1 5 6 5 n. 5 1 3 f. 8ov), he had not been given the title of general receiver.

29. It included receipts for the arrears of the *renenghes* of 1 3 3 5 and 1 3 3 6, for the *renenghe* of 1 3 3 6, and for the future *renenghe* of 1 3 3 7, thus indicating not only that his previous account had included the *renenghe* of 1 3 3 5, but also that the income from the domain was stable enough to permit payments to be made in advance.

30. Nicholas was not in the office of general receiver before 2 1 September 1 3 3 5, and so his absence from his first audit is not striking.

3 1. Simon Mirabello, of course, was a former general receiver. In addition, he, along with Nicholas Guiduche, Philip of Aaksel, Roger Bristeste, Henry de Meetkerk, Josse de Hemsrode, and Roger Thonis were entrusted with the government of the county during the count's absence in 1 3 3 5 (Nord, B1 5 6 5 n. 492 f. 77). Roger Bristeste also was a member of the count's council, which appointed a bailiff (*ibid.*, B1 5 6 5 n. 490 f. 77; Nowé, *Les baillis comtaux,* 5 80 #89) and supported Simon Mirabello in his attempt to regain his lands in Brabant (St.-Genois, #1672). Roger was regent of Bruges in 1 3 2 9 (Pol. chrs., #3 3 4) and receiver of the *bailliage* and farm of the *tonlieu* of Hugevliet (Compte du receveur Nicolas Guiduche, du 7 septembre 1 3 3 5 au 7 novembre 1 3 3 6, RR, #5). Thierry Noothaec, a knight, participated in an inquest around 1 3 2 3 (St.-Genois, #1431); he was a member of the count's council which rendered judgment (Nord, B1 5 6 5 n. 84 f. 1 5) and made a grant (*ibid.*, B1 5 6 5 n. 496 f. 77v). Roger Thonis witnessed a charter (Pol. chrs., #283), gave quittance (ARA RK #46 f. 5), and was a member of the count's council which rendered sentence (Nord, B1 5 6 5 n. 84 f. 1 5), ordered delivery of goods (*ibid.*, B1 5 6 5 n. 191 f. 32), and commissioned an inquest (*ibid.*, B1 5 6 5 n. 482 f. 76). Henry de Meetkerk received Transport payments for the general receiver (St. van Vl., #1349 f. 11), witnessed an accord (Nord, B1 3 5 2 #6164), heard submissions to the count after the battle of Cassel in 1 3 2 9 (*ibid.*, B1 5 6 2 p. 5 0 5 f. 2 5 5 #6049), and participated in a judicial case (*ibid.*, B1 3 1 2 #47 5 2). Thierry de Belseel witnessed a record (St.-Genois, #16 5 3), heard Bruges's account on 19 June 1 3 3 3 (F. Blockmans, "Le contrôle par le prince des comptes urbains en Flandre et en Brabant au moyen âge," in *Finances et comptabilité urbaines du XIII au XIVe siècle. Internationale Colloquium Blankenberge 6–9 IX–1962. Actes* [Ghent, 1968], 3 10) and 10 October 1 3 3 3 (Nord, B1 5 6 5 n. 3 8 1 f. 6ov), and witnessed a sale (St.-Genois, #1677). Peter of Douai was a member of Louis of Nevers's council (*ibid.*, B1 5 6 5 n. 490 f. 77), heard the accounts of Bruges on 10 October 1 3 3 3 (*ibid.*, B1 5 6 5 n. 3 8 1 f. 6ov), in August 1 3 3 4, and on 2 1 January 1 3 3 6 (F. Blockmans, 3 10). He is far better known, however, as the first, albeit never formally appointed, master of accounts. Josse de Hemsrode was a member of the powerful Halewin family. He participated in a grant of a safe conduct (ARA RK #46 f. 2v), witnessed a judgment (A. Schouteet, ed., *Regesten op de oorkonden van het Stadsbestuur van Brugge* [Brussels,

1978], 1:200–201 #530), received Transport payments in 1327 and 1330 (St. van Vl., #1349 f. 8v, 77), heard the accounts of Bruges on 9 August 1334, 21 January 1335 (F. Blockmans, 310), and 17 December 1335 (ARA RK #46 f. 2), and was master of the count's residence from at least 11 April to 31 December 1333 (Pol. chrs., #392, #397, #408). For a discussion of these commissioners and the decision-making process in general during the reign of Louis of Nevers, see Maurice Vandermaesen, *De besluitvorming in het graafschap Vlaanderen tijdens de XIVde eeuw. Bijdragen tot een politiek sociologie van de Raad en van de raadsheren achter de figuur van Lodewijk II van Nevers (1322–1346)*, unpublished dissertation, Rijksuniversiteit te Gent, 1977.

32. Henry de Meetkerk was bailiff of Ghent on 14 September 1310 (Nowé, *Les baillis comtaux*, 379) and bailiff of Bergues from May 1309 to 2 February 1311 (*ibid.*, 402); Thierry de Belseel was bailiff of Bruges 14 March 1330 to 27 August 1334 (*ibid.*, 374); Josse de Hemsrode was bailiff of Veurne from 17 September to 7 November 1328 (*ibid.*, 389), and Roger de Thonis was bailiff of Bruges on 17 June 1314 and from 20 August 1317 to 2 February 1318 (*ibid.*, 373).

33. Earlier in 1325 Peter of Douai, William d'Auxonne, Colard of Marchiennes, and Nicholas de la Pierre had undertaken a more thorough examination of the general receiver's records on the count's orders. On 10 March 1325, after examining and verifying Conte's written records, they gave his general account a favorable report (Nord, B1568 n. 174–175 f. 119–119v).

34. Receipts and expenses are itemized in the accounts of 1309, for example: "Item receut de cens de paiments escheu a noel et à le Saint Jehan" (Compte du receveur, Thomas Fin, du 25 décembre 1308 à juin 1309, RR, #1). In subsequent records, entries are also divided into categories, but they have their own headings: "Recepte des cens de Flandres" (Compte du receveur Othon Macet du 26 janvier 1334 [n.s.], rendu en 1335, *ibid.*, #4; Compte du receveur Nicolas Guiduche, du 7 septembre 1335 au 7 novembre 1336, *ibid.*, #5; Compte du receveur Gilles de le Walle du 28 septembre 1348 au 13 décembre 1348, *ibid.*, #6).

35. There is no receipt of the bailiffs in the account of Gilles de le Walle in 1348.

36. This includes the account of the receiver of the Westland, Casin de Waghenare (du 17 avril 1374 au 17 septembre 1374, RR, #849), and the accounts of Henry Lippin, receiver of Flanders to 1383 (Nord, B4069 to B4072).

37. Compte du receveur Gilles de le Walle du 28 septembre 1348 au 13 décembre 1348, RR, #6.

38. Ottelin's account includes receipts from the bailiffs, whereas Gilles's account does not.

39. The general receiver in at least one instance managed the accounts of another major institution, the monastery of St. Baaf's in Ghent. In 1314, the count sent Guiduche Baldechon and John de Muda to St. Baaf's to put order into the monastery's chaotic finances. The count had only indirect interest in the finances of St. Baaf. If they lacked order, the monastery might find it difficult to pay what it owed him. Guiduche was receiver at this time; he is called "receptorem" in St. Baaf's accounts (Rijksarchief, Gent, Bisdom St. Baafsabdij, R78 f. 1; hereafter St. Baaf). John de Muda had had some experience in the count's financial administration as

the receiver of the briefs and *rentes* of the Land of Waas (Rentes du pays de Waes. Compte du clerk, Jean de Muda, jusque 24 juillet 1294, RR, #350; *idem* du 6 août 1295, *ibid.*, #351; *idem* du 20 septembre 1296, *ibid.*, #352; Rennengue faite par Jean de Tournay à Bruges, 1296, *ibid.*, #266), but he was primarily a clerk and had probably been sent to help Guiduche with the technical aspects of the task. Guiduche and John drew up two accounts, one for 25 February to 24 June 1313 and the other for 24 June 1313 to 16 February 1314 (St. Baaf, f. 1–5, 6–15); they received first 5 l. 18 s. and then 66 l. 7 s. for the expenses they incurred (*ibid.*, f. 5v). The general receiver was neither responsible nor accountable for the monastery's finances. Nonetheless, territorial princes had felt it to be their responsibility to protect religious houses long before the fourteenth century. Furthermore, as we have seen, the count's financial administration had developed to a point where it employed skilled and experienced officials. It may thus have been logical and expedient for the monks of St. Baaf's to turn to the count for assistance. Guiduche was successful in at least one respect: upon two occasions he received sums for the count from the monastery (*ibid.*, f. 9, 10).

40. In 1288, Siger of Bailleul and Simon Lauwart, bailiff of Bruges, heard Bruges's account (de Smet and Wyffels, 142). Although Siger was general receiver at this time, he is not so entitled in the record. Two years later, on 19 November 1290, Bruges's accounts were again heard by Siger, by Gerard Lupichimi (Siger's successor as general receiver), and by Walter of Ham, bailiff of Bruges (*ibid.*, 188). In this document Gerard is called "receptore." Jakemon of Deinze and Walter of Ham heard Bruges's account on 23 December 1292, but the general receiver was not present at the accounts of 1294 and 1298 (*ibid.*, 322, 428, 509), possibly as a concession to the Brugeois. The general receiver may have heard the accounts of other towns once such audits were made mandatory after 1297 (Walter Prevenier, *Financiële geschiedenis en geschiedenis der boekhouding in de middeleeuwen en de nieuwe tijden,* unpublished manuscript [Ghent, 1971], 20), but there is no evidence to confirm or deny their presence. The count, however, needed the support of the Flemish towns in the period 1296 to 1300, and might instead have found it prudent to grant them the privilege of hearing their own accounts unencumbered by a comital representative.

41. Gaillard, #588; *Codex,* 2:97 #238.

42. Nord, B1595 f. 108; J. Buntinx, *De Audientie van de graven van Vlaanderen. Studie over het centraal grafelijke gerecht, c. 1330–1409* (Brussels, 1949), 27. They did not complete the task until 5 September 1332 (F. Blockmans, 309).

43. *Ibid.*, 310. Nicholas, a Sienese held the office between 13 May 1333 (Pol. chrs., #394) and 17 January 1334 (Nord, B1565 n. 191 f. 32), and between 21 September 1335 (*ibid.*, B1565 n. 489 f. 76v), and 25 April 1337 (Comptes de Monnaie de Gand. Compte du Jean Parcheval du Proche, dit Ops, de Lucques, maître de la monnaie de Gand du 13 septembre 1334 au 25 avril 1337, RR, #788). He was the last Italian up to the late fourteenth century to do so.

Nicholas first appears as receiver on 22 February 1333, about three months after he was given the position of "garde de la recheverie de Flandre" (Pol. chrs., #389), and is repeatedly referred to as receiver from that date until January 1334 (*ibid.*, #394; 15 May 1333 "ontfanger mins heren van vlaenderen" [St.-Genois,

#1674]; 19 June 1333 "in presentien van Nicholause Ghydouche, tien tiden ontfanghere van Vlaenderen" [F. Blockmans, 310]; 24 June 1333 [Pol. chrs., #398]; 10 October 1333 "Nicolas Guyduche, recheveur" [Nord, B1565 n. 381 f. 60v]; 11 October 1333 "Nicolas Guyduche recheveur de Flandre" ["recheveur de flandre" is crossed out in this text: *ibid.*, B1565 n. 354 f. 57]; 5 November 1333 "Nycholaie Guidouchen ontfangere van Vlaendre te dien tiden" [St.-Genois, #1677]; 23 November 1333 "Nicholas Guydouche notre ame recheveur de Flandre" [Nord, B1565 n. 154 f. 27]). There is no indication that he was formally appointed. Ottelin Machet was audited as general receiver for the period 26 January to 3 March 1334; after Ottelin became receiver in 1334, Nicholas is referred to simply as "valet" (19 March 1334 [*ibid.*, B1565 n. 226 f. 37v]). He did not regain the office until 21 September 1335, but there is evidence that he continued to carry out its functions before that date even though he was still considered only a comital valet; he probably filled the position informally. On 20 November 1334 (*ibid.*, B1565 n. 513 f. 80v), Louis of Nevers stated that there had been no formal general receiver between 14 June and 1 October. Since October, and even perhaps as early as June, Nicholas had probably been acting as general receiver on an informal basis. On the same date, 20 November, Louis commissioned Nicholas to receive comital revenues (*ibid.*). While Louis may have confirmed Nicholas's position in November, he does not seem to have formally appointed Nicholas receiver at that time. Nicholas appears in several subsequent documents performing the functions of the office, but without its title. Only on 21 September 1335 was he formally commissioned as general receiver (*ibid.*, B1565 n. 489 f. 76v). Both Nicholas and Gerard de la Moor bear the appellation general receiver in the account of Jean Parcheval du Porche, master of the mint in Ghent, which covers the period 13 September 1336 to 25 April 1337 (RR, #788). Since Nicholas last appears as general receiver on 8 November 1336 (Compte du receveur Nicolas Guiduche, du 7 septembre 1335 au 7 novembre 1336, *ibid.*, #5), it is probable that Gerard de la Moor replaced him sometime between 8 November 1336 and 25 April 1337.

44. Gilliodts-Van Severen, *Inventaire*, 3:147 #711.

45. Nord, B1565 n. 381 f. 60v.

46. *Ibid.*, B1565 n. 354 f. 57.

47. F. Blockmans, 310. Thierry de Belseel and not Josse de Hemsrode was still bailiff of Bruges at this time (Nowé, *Les baillis comtaux*, 374).

48. ARA RK #46 f. 2; F. Blockmans, 310.

49. *Ibid.*

50. In one case, Siger and the general receiver were one and the same.

51. Nowé, *Les baillis comtaux*, 209.

52. F. Blockmans, 311.

53. RR, #1054.

54. "Item, que nuls de nos baillius de nostre dicte conte ne puist quiter ne lessier appaisir a lui nulle amende de LX lib. ne deseure, et que en ce no dit bailli ne puissent allegier, ne proposer nulle costume anchienne en contraire. . . . sans le conseil dou dit Andrieu et par lui" (Limburg-Stirum, *Louis de Male*, 1:128 #126). Henri Nowé notes that the receiver's intervention in such matters, although frequent in the period 1336 to 1350, tapered off after 1350 (Nowé, *Les baillis comtaux*,

315); Louis of Male may have curtailed his use of the general receiver in town affairs as a concession to the Flemish communities.

55. Nowé, "L'intervention," 81.

56. "Recepte des rentes heritaules acquises pour cause des esmuetez," "Receptes des kalenges, tiestes rachatees, et bannis rappelles," "Recepte des fourfaitures et des receveurs de fourfaitures de Flandres de leur compte," "Recepte des pais et accors fais pour cause des esmuetes" (Compte du receveur Nicolas Guiduche, du 7 septembre 1335 au 7 novembre 1336, RR, #5).

57. "Recept des fourfaitures de Flandre pour cause des esmuetes," "Recepte des fourfaitures de Brabant pour le cause dele guerre" (Compte du receveur Othon Macet du 26 janvier 1334 [n.s.], rendu en 1335 [*ibid.*, #4]).

58. Conte Gualterotti was connected to the Guidi banking interests; Donato, Simon, and Ottelin with the Peruzzi.

59. Jaquemard of Tournai, Ottelin Machet, and Nicolas Guiduche.

60. Vane Guy.

61. Eisenstadt, 362.

62. He seems to have been somewhat successful. In the period from 16 March 1323 to 20 February 1327, Ghent made at least seven payments to him for a total of 4,108 l. 17 s. (Gent, Stadsarchief, Fonds Van Duyse et de Busscher, #321, #323, #324, #325, #328, #340 [hereafter Van Duyse and de Busscher]; Vuylsteke, 523). These payments are not to be confused with those made to the Flemish count for the Transport of Flanders.

63. Vane appears as the French king's agent in a record dated 7 January 1332 (Van Duyse and de Busscher, #370), as the Flemish count's receiver in a document dated 17 February 1332 (Pol. chrs., #429), and again as the French king's agent in a document dated 1 June 1332 (Van Duyse and de Busscher, #374). This circumstance strongly suggests that he was functioning in both capacities at the same time.

64. Monier, *Les institutions financières,* 29–30.

65. Perhaps at the suggestion (or insistence?) of the French king.

66. Although both Conte and Simon were Italians and were connected with Italian banking interests, they were also respected citizens of Ghent. Nonetheless, it is interesting to note that Ghent made no more Transport payments after 1326, the date when Conte left office.

67. He may have been appointed in order to curry favor with the citizens of Ghent.

68. He married Isabel, Louis's natural sister, on 13 May 1324. Louis's faith in Simon was somewhat misplaced. Simon supported Ghent in the 1338 uprising. He even went so far as to lend the English king a large sum of money. See J. E. Ziegler, "Edward III and Low Countries Finances: 1338–1340, with Particular Emphasis on the Dominant Position of Brabant," *RBPH* 61 (1983), 802–817. For Simon Mirabello, see P. Rogghé, "Simon de Mirabello in Vlaanderen," *Appeltjes van het Meetjesland* 9 (1958), 5–55. For a short overview, see N. De Pauw, "Les Mirabellos, dits van Halen," *Biographie Nationale* (Brussels, 1897), 14:870–882.

69. St. van Vl., #1349 f. 51v. Jaquemard was described as the general receiver's lieutenant on more than one occasion.

70. Vuylsteke, 708, 713.

71. Compte du receveur, Thomas Fin, du 25 décembre 1308 à juin 1309, RR, #1; P. Rogghé, "Machet," 191.

72. Henri Pirenne, *Le soulèvement de la Flandre maritime de 1323–1328* (Brussels, 1900), 1.

73. From 24 February 1329 to at least 26 February 1331 (Pol. chrs., #328, #342,#348, #350, #352A, #352B, #354; Bruges, Rijksarchief, Charters met blau nummer, #24, #38 [herafter Bl. nr.]).

74. Pol. chrs., #322, #327; De Roover, *Money, Banking and Credit*, 84.

75. Nord, B1562 n. 505 f. 255 #6049.

76. Pol. chrs., #442; Rogghé, "Machet," 192; F. Blockmans, 307–308. Ottelin was one of Ghent's major creditors (Vuylsteke, 65; Bigwood, *Le régime juridique*, 1:114).

77. Rogghé, "Machet," 192–193. For the customary right of the community to take vengeance, see André Delcourt, *La vengeance de la commune. L'arsin et l'abattis de maison en Flandre et en Hainaut* (Lille, 1930).

78. St. van Vl. #1349, f. 9, 51v.

79. See Table 4.

80. Pirenne, *Histoire de Belgique*, 2:106.

81. *Ibid.*, 2:106–107.

82. *Ibid.*, 2:109.

83. The most recent work on Van Artevelde is David Nicholas, *The Van Arteveldes of Ghent: The Varieties of Vendetta and the Hero in History* (Ithaca, 1988).

84. Pirenne, *Histoire de Belgique*, 2:116–117.

85. *Annales Gandenses*, trans. by Hilda Johnston (New York, 1951), 76, 85, 89.

86. He was bailiff of Veurne from about 4 July to about 7 November 1336 (Compte du receveur Nicolas Guiduche, du 7 septembre 1335 du 7 novembre 1336, RR, #5; Nowé, *Les baillis comtaux*, 389).

87. On 22 June 1337 he was present, with Gerard de la Moor and others, at the audit of the account of the mintmaster of Ghent (Monnaie de Gand. Compte de Jean Parcheval du Porche, dit Ops, de Lucques, maître de la monnaie de Gand, du 13 septembre 1334 au 25 avril 1337, RR, #788).

88. Pol. chrs., #442; F. Blockmans, 307–308.

89. Pol. chrs., #442.

7. The Reign of Louis of Male
The General Receiver and the Sovereign Bailiff

DESPITE THE UPHEAVAL of the years 1338 to 1346, Louis of Male, son of Louis of Nevers, was able to claim his inheritance as count not long after his father's death. The assassination of van Artevelde in 1345 created a power vacuum, and by 1349 Louis had restored order to most of the county and was exercising effective, if not formal, authority. The majority of the Flemish communities had accepted him by 1347, and in early 1349, Ghent, the last major holdout, finally capitulated.[1] Compared with the actions taken by his father after the battle of Cassel in 1328, the new count's measures were, with the possible exception of his treatment of the Flemish weavers, only mildly repressive.[2] Louis's principal aim was not to punish the rebels but to stabilize the county—and concomitantly, his own position. To that end he had brought about a reconciliation with England that restored trade and established good relations between the two principalities.[3] By 1350, Louis had also established fairly good relations with the upper classes of the urban population.[4]

In the ensuing years of his reign (1349–1384), Louis's intentions seem to have remained essentially twofold: to accommodate various powerful groups[5] and to extend and generalize his authority as prince throughout the county. Louis's reign represents the triumph of comital government over the autonomy of the three Flemish towns.[6] Increasingly throughout his reign it would become Louis's administration and his government that would have the final word.[7] David Nicholas has pointed out that the decline in industrial prosperity based on the textile industry encouraged the development of "reciprocal interaction" between town and countryside.[8] Louis diminished the economic power of Ghent, Bruges, and Ypres by encouraging the industrial and commercial enterprises of smaller towns such as Aksel, Menen, Beveren, and Dendermonde.[9] The blurring of economic distinctions between urban and rural areas undoubtedly made the task of the count much easier. Although the power of his natural allies, the rural nobility, had waned, the administration inherited from his father provided the means whereby comital authority might increasingly gain in scope and extent.

The terms upon which Louis acceded to his county may have been dictated by political circumstances. Although in no condition to oppose Louis's accession, the *drie steden* remained a force to be reckoned with. The reconstitution of Louis of Nevers's administration provided both Louis of Male and the Flemish communities the opportunity to keep an eye on one another. In addition to appointing a religious leader (Bernard de Castre) and two members of the nobility (John Van der Delft and Gossuin le Wilde), Louis appointed four burghers from the major Flemish towns to the general receivership: Gilles de le Walle came from Bruges, Andrew le Russe was from Ypres,[10] while John and Peter de la Fauchille were from Ghent. Unlike his father, Louis appointed no Italians to the office. Louis may have involved members of the major communities in his administration in order to accommodate their political power. The Flemish communities, in their turn, may have seen participation in the count's administration as an opportunity to direct policy.

The selection of Andrew le Russe in 1349 is a case in point. Louis made Andrew his receiver a mere eight months after pardoning him for taking part in the recent rebellion.[11] According to Andrew's charter of appointment, Louis chose him to be general receiver at the request of Ghent, Bruges, and Ypres.[12] The charter continues in an equally conciliatory tone: Louis promised to make no donations, grant any commissions, or renew bailiffs or any other officers without Andrew's counsel and advice.[13] But Andrew remained in office for only thirteen months. The next extant appointment charter, that of John Van der Delft, dated 25 April 1351, contains few such promises.[14] Indeed, from 1359 onward, Louis, wary of the undiminished aspirations of the county's elites, incorporated into appointment charters the demand that his general receiver, be he burgher or noble, not use his liberties against the count in the exercise of his office.[15]

It is unsurprising that Louis did not immediately take advantage of the re-establishment of the office of general receiver to alter any of its functions or capacities. Over the course of his reign, the scope of the general receiver's office and a few of its attendant procedures did indeed change. By 1372, a new official, the master of accounts, was verifying the general receiver's account. Mintmasters, heretofore the most independent of the count's financial officials, were subordinated to the general receiver. But perhaps the greatest change affected the general receiver's judicial capacity. In the course of the thirteenth and fourteenth centuries, the count's central judicial administration had emerged as a major aspect of the general receiver's office. By 1349, the general receiver was not only the count's principal fiscal officer but the chief judicial functionary as well. In 1372, the general receiver lost most of his judicial powers and responsibilities when the count separated the receiver's judicial from his financial capacity and confided it to a newly created administrative official, the sovereign bailiff.

None of these alterations was unprecedented. Such changes as occurred during Louis of Male's reign grew out of the routine performance of the duties assumed to be inherent in the office. They therefore did not interfere in any significant way with the essential capacity and responsibilities of the office of general receiver.

Accounts

One of Louis's first orders of business as count was to call for a general accounting. The appointment of Gilles de le Walle as Louis's first general receiver was thus not only political but practical: Gilles had been a former treasurer of Bruges from at least 1329 to probably 1337,[16] and as such undoubtedly had experienced numerous audits. Gilles's account covers only two and a half months. It includes few receipts and few expenses, and does not seem to have been formally heard by anyone. The lack of financial activity may be explained by the brevity of the period covered, but the account also mirrors the state of the Flemish economy after the turbulent years of the hostility between France and England and the revolt of Jacob Van Artevelde. Indeed, Gilles's account may well have served chiefly as a general assessment of the county's overall condition—an assessment which Louis of Male undoubtedly found useful. The ordering of such an account may have both convinced Louis's subjects that he meant business and reestablished the procedure itself in his mind and in the minds of his subjects. It is likely that the account's informality and the fact that its reckoning was entrusted to a staunch citizen of Bruges may have succeeded in calming the fears of those of Louis's subjects suspicious of any untoward comital activity.

That Louis hoped to require periodic audits of the general receiver's account is evident from the commission of Louis's third receiver, Andrew le Russe. This document, dated 6 August 1349, states that such an account would be heard without delay when the count required an audit.[17] Andrew, however, does not seem to have achieved the level of efficiency and organization which Louis desired from his financial administration. On 25 April 1351, when Louis appointed John Van der Delft to be receiver, he did so "to restore in healthy estate and good governance our rents, revenues, farms, forfeits, and lordships of our county and land of Flanders, which for a long time were managed outside the rule of reason, as much through war and past disasters, as through changes of receivers and the renewal of officers."[18] Louis was evidently serious about his finances, for John's accounts were checked at least five times. His first account covered two and a half years, from the date of his appointment in April 1351 to 16 October 1353, and was accepted on 15 December 1353.[19] His other accounts cover shorter periods: from 16 October 1353 to 4 November 1354 (12½ months);[20] from 4 November 1354 to 17 May 1356 (1½ years);[21] from 17 May 1356 to 26 March 1357 (10½ months);[22] and from 26 March 1357 to 18 October 1358 (19½ months).[23] The last account in the period for which there is evidence, that of John de la Fauchille, covered the period from 11 October 1359 (the date of John's appointment) to 20 March 1361 (17 months).[24]

But Louis of Male did not succeed, any more than Louis of Nevers had, in making the audit of the general receiver's account an annual event. Instead, the audit of the general receiver's account seems to have occurred almost arbitrarily. John Van der Delft's charter of appointment merely states that accounts of the general receiver would be heard when other receivers required the count to hear the general account in order to know the state of his finances, or to clarify and discharge it.[25] The burden of calling for an accounting was thus ostensibly laid on the shoulders of the other receivers, but it is likely that this arrangement was little more than a polite fiction, perhaps calculated to encourage the townspeople and petty rural nobility who held such positions to believe that they were participating in Louis's good governance. The charters of appointment for subsequent receivers contain almost the same wording.[26] In view of Louis of Male's expressed desire to restore his finances "to healthy estate and good governance," it is surprising that he did not ordain that audits be held at regular intervals. In contrast, one of the major responsibilities of the general receiver, outlined in all of the appointment charters since 1351, had been to see that the *renenghe* and the accounts of the bailiffs were heard at regular intervals.[27] Although these accounting sessions had long been routine, the audit of the general receiver's account still took place on an *ad hoc* basis: it had not yet become habitual. Less routine resulted in less accountability, which may have motivated Philip the Bold to establish first, in 1385, a *chambre de conseil* in which were handled judicial and financial affairs, and then, in 1405, a *chambre des comptes,* which met at a fixed location (Lille).[28]

By 1335, as we have seen, the form the accounts took had become standardized, and the fundamental make-up of the commission that heard them had become institutionalized.[29] The next step was the establishment of a routine procedure by which they would be presented and verified. As early as 1335, the count had ordered his financial officers to pay what they owed only to his general receiver and to no other;[30] almost all of the entries in the 1336 account ended with the phrase "by letters of Nicholas."[31] The appointment charters of Louis of Male's receivers also include another provision—that the master of accounts was to accept no letters of quittance other than those of the general receiver.[32] The master of accounts was a new office. In the 1330s, Peter of Douai had come to be almost as conspicuous at audits as was the general receiver himself. Peter's responsibilities culminated in the creation of the office of master of accounts, expressly established by Louis of Male on 4 January 1350; Peter himself never bore the title. The first actual appointment of a master of accounts, that of John le Clerc, was essentially a *post hoc* acknowledgment of an already existing position; the formal appointment of Jakemon of Deinze to the receivership in 1292 exemplifies the same phenomenon. The master of accounts's initial mandate was to conserve the general receiver's records. Because he was not involved in the activities recorded in the accounts, he had no personal investment in them. This made him the logical choice, either alone or together with two other individuals of the count's choosing, to verify them. The office, it could be argued, emerged as a logical consequence of the creation of the general account. When Thomas Fini was first audited in 1306, there existed no official who could check his receipts and no officials who could truly be considered his peers. A commission performed part of this function and had, as we have seen, become a part of the audit of the general receiver by the end of Louis of Nevers's reign. Although in the reign of Louis of Male a commission still heard the general receiver's accounts, their findings became secondary to the subsequent verification of his accounts by the master of accounts and his colleagues.

By 1356, a formal and consistent procedure had developed for the audit of the general receiver's account. The proceedings began with the general receiver's oral rendition of his account before the count's council.[33] The general receiver then presented his written records to the master of accounts (and occasionally to others) for scrutiny. John le Clerc, master of accounts at least until 1361, was the sole verifier of the first two accounts of John Van der Delft.[34] John le Clerc, Testard de Wastine (a jurist and one of Louis of Male's principal councilors[35]), and a third official, who varied, examined subsequent accounts.[36] It is worth noting that in only one instance, the audit of the account for 4 November 1354 to 17 May 1356, did those who verified and examined the general receiver's account sit on the council that approved and quit the general receiver.[37] The master of accounts and his colleagues, if not acting alone, probably then presented their findings to the count in his council. If the latter found in the general receiver's favor, which for John Van der Delft seems to have always been the case, the count in his council ratified and approved the general account.

The whole process usually took some time. The count in his council approved John's first account, which covered the period 25 April 1351 to 10 October 1353, on 15 December of that same year;[38] the account that ended 26 March 1357 was only approved on 16 May 1357, almost two months later,[39] and the account that ended 10 October 1358 was not approved until seven months later.[40] Such increasing delays may explain why the count promised John de la Fauchille that he would approve or reject the general account within fifteen days after he had presented it.[41] The count may not have been able to keep his promise, for the subsequent charters of Peter de la Fauchille and Gossuin le Wilde omit it.[42]

The account was settled after the master of accounts and his colleagues presented their findings. Surpluses and deficits were not carried over to the next account for both theoretical and practical reasons. Accounts were viewed as belonging to the person and not the office. Periods of accounting were integral and finite, ending when they were reckoned. At the same time that he settled the account, the count also granted the general receiver quittance,[43] emphasizing the attachment of the account to the person and not to the office.

Expenses almost always exceeded the receipts, leaving the count in debt to his general receiver. Between 1322 and 1361, the count owed his general receiver as much as 11,333 l. 18 s. 8 d.[44] and as little as 570 l. 16 s. 9 ½ d.[45] In a letter quitting Conte Gualterotti of his account on 10 March 1325, Louis of Nevers had assigned Conte certain revenues from which he was to recover his outlay.[46] Subsequent letters of ratification contain similar provisions.[47] Although the general receiver seems rarely to have taken in more than he paid out, the charter of John Van der Delft and those of his successors did provide for cases of surplus as well as for deficit (in the former case, the general receiver was to be paid a part of the surplus when he left office).[48] Louis of Nevers also had promised Nicholas Guiduche in 1335 that he and his heirs would be quit of what he had done on behalf of the count in the execution of his office.[49] Louis of Male did not change this practice, indicating that despite a growing distinction between the public and private purse, the general receivership still functioned as a revenue-producing resource. As such, it was treated as property. That is probably why, as Thomas Fini's first account suggests, a general receiver's account usually began on the day of his appointment and not on the day of the last account.[50] The charters of John Van der Delft, John and Peter de la Fauchille, and Gossuin le Wilde make this explicit, for in each of them the count ordered his new general receiver, upon his appointment, to draw up an account of the financial condition of the count's resources.[51]

By 1366, only the audits of the general receiver and of mintmasters necessitated the presence of the count. The accounts of other financial officials could thus, in principle, be held in a specific and fixed place—they could, in essence, "go out of court." That this did not happen until the next reign is less a reflection of the rudimentary state of the count's financial department than a reflection of political realities. The logical place for a permanent financial department would be a town. But relations between count and communities were never such during Louis's reign that he could be entirely satisfied with the security of any part of his administration located on a permanent basis within a Flemish town. Better that he entrust the auditing of these accounts to an individual still attached to him personally than run the risk of having his finances held hostage by a rebellious community.

Mintmasters

Since the mid-thirteenth century, the personal participation of the count at sessions audit had been decreasing as that of the general receiver increased. From the beginning of the fourteenth century onward the count appears to have taken part only in the audits of the general receiver and of the mintmasters. He presided over the audit of the latter probably out of necessity: the general receiver's jurisdiction does not seem to have extended over them. Mintmasters, in fact, are conspicuously absent from the list of officials who were ordered to pay their receipt directly to the general receiver in 1306, 1308, and 1335.[52] To be sure, the general receiver usually heard the accounts of mintmasters but only as one of the comital commissioners before whom the masters of the mints presented their accounts. Until 1348, the mintmasters' revenues are the only ones not to appear in the general accounts. The earliest extant quittance of a mintmaster is that of 15 June 1336 when Count Louis of Nevers quit Flacon Lampage of Pistoia for his account in the presence of his council, which included Nicholas Guiduche.[53] The earliest extant account of a mintmaster is that of Perceval du Porche, mintmaster of Ghent, for the period 13 September 1334 to 16 April 1337.[54] This account makes it clear that the count and seven councilors, among them the old receiver, Nicholas Guiduche, and the new one, Gerard de la Moor, had indeed been present at the audit and had verified Perceval's account.[55] Unlike other financial officials, mintmasters until 1351 seemed to have answered only to the count. At the same time, the lack of extant records of mint accounts before 1348 suggests that one of two situations obtained: either the accounts were wholly oral—an unlikely situation—or mintmasters, for whatever reason, did not do as good a job of conserving their records as did the comital administration under the general receiver.

Louis of Male changed this situation early in his reign. While the 1349 charter appointing Andrew le Russe receiver is regrettably illegible at the point where it lists the specific financial personnel to be subject to Andrew's will, a comparison with John Van der Delft's appointment of 1351 suggests that this list may have indeed included mintmasters.[56] In addition, an account of the mints of Ghent, dated 1350, was heard by a portion of the count's council which included the general receiver but not the count.[57] Nonetheless, because no general accounts exist after that of Gilles de le Walle in 1348, we do not know whether the receipts of the mints formed a part of the general account or not. The appointment charters subsequent to 1348 include mintmasters among those financial officials the count ordered to respond, obey, and deliver their receipt to the general receiver.[58] Furthermore, the accounts of the mintmasters after 1350 make it clear that mintmasters did indeed pay their receipts to the general receiver. The account of Bernard Priem in 1353 ends with the phrase "paid to John Van der Delft, receiver, and accounted";[59] the account of Pieter Platvoet on 8 February 1363 for the newly acquired mint of Mechelen reads "paid to Peter, son of John, receiver of Flanders, accounted";[60] and in 1365, Aldrighe Enterminelly paid his receipt to Gossuin le Wilde.[61] Whereas the accounts of the mints followed their own form before 1350, after 1350 their internal organization had been standardized to conform to that found in accounts of the bailiffs and of the separate individual accounts of the

receivers of the new domain. These two circumstances—a common superior and a standardized account form—brought mints and mintmasters,
the last independent resources and officials, into the count's financial administration.[62]

The general receiver did not enjoy complete authority over the mintmasters. Their accounts were heard by a commission of several of the
count's councilors, which usually include the master of accounts and a
legist;[63] furthermore, the count quit them himself.[64] The example of the
mintmasters clearly suggests, then, that although the count had delegated
much of his power to the general receiver for the practical management of
his finances, the last word undoubtedly remained his own.

Judicial Affairs

The one major change in the general account during Louis of Male's reign
concerned judicial revenues. These revenues were listed in the general
accounts up to and including Nicholas Guiduche's account of 1336, but by
1369, they had grown so numerous that it became imperative that they be
handled in a separate account.[65] This separation does not seem to have
diminished the general receiver's authority over judicial affairs. Indeed by
the middle of the reign of Louis of Male, the general receiver had come to
assume informal primacy in such matters, the logical result of the general
receiver's involvement in judicial matters since the late thirteenth century.
In the course of the first half of the fourteenth century, certain members of
the count's council, the general receiver among them, had come to be
routinely present when the council sat as a court of justice. By the reign of
Louis of Male, these councilors, when so sitting with the count, had come
to be known as the *audientie*.[66] The general receiver's presence in the
audientie was associated with his close connection with the judicial structure and later with his position as count's chief official for the administration of justice. The general receiver's assumption of control over local
judicial officers was encouraged by two circumstances. First, as head of the
count's revenues, the general receiver had acquired the responsibility to see
that judicial revenues did not diminish through negligence on the part of
bailiffs. His office had initially functioned as a centralizing link between the
count's revenues from the domain and those from resources under the
jurisdiction of the bailiffs. This circumstance served as the basis for the
extension of his authority over bailiffs themselves and thus over aspects of

the count's judicial system which they customarily handled. Second, as a member of the count's council, the general receiver also frequently took part in inquests, arbitration, and the settlement of disputes; he remained responsible for the receipt of *ad hoc* revenues resulting from such activity. These two factors formed the basis for the gradual creation of the general receiver's judicial sphere, and for his primacy within the count's judicial structure.

Consistently employed in a judicial capacity since the mid-thirteenth century, the general receiver, by the middle of Louis of Male's reign, had gradually come to exercise jurisdiction over almost all facets of the count's judicial administration. By 1336 he had acquired the authority to institute inquests[67] and to set the penalty to be exacted by comital officers against prisoners of urban tribunals.[68] By 1349 bailiffs had come to be obligated formally to obtain the general receiver's approval when excusing fines of 60 l. or more. This marked the turning point in the emergence of the general receiver as the count's major judicial officer, for 60 l. distinguished high justice[69] from low justice, and high justice was the prerogative of the territorial prince. In 1349, the count ordained that no bailiff could attempt to contravene the general receiver's authority by appeal to custom.[70] By 1352, the general receiver had acquired the significant discretionary power to halt a case taking place in a seigneurial court.[71] By 1353, he had become the agent who advised the disputants or the accused that the count in his council would render judgment.[72] By 1360, he was executing sentences passed by the count.[73] An account of the bailiff of Courtrai, dated 13 January 1365, indicates that the general receiver also had the power to order a search of those who hid outlaws,[74] while an account of the bailiff of Cassel, dated 4 May 1367, shows that the general receiver could order arrests.[75] He ordered the execution of criminals,[76] and by 1370 could order the release of prisoners.[77]

The Settlement of Disputes and the Development of an Instrument of Public Justice

The general receiver also participated in the resolution of comital matters regardless of whether they involved comital finances or not; the subject of the dispute evidently did not determine the nature or degree of the general receiver's involvement. He was, for example, a member of the count's council which settled the dispute between the brokers of Bruges and the

Spaengaerts.[78] He was present when the count ordered the bailiff of Cour-trai to set up a court to judge citizens of Courtrai who were being held at Rupelmonde.[79] Gossuin le Wilde was among the count's councilors who, with the count, renewed the laws of the city of Bruges.[80] He also partici-pated in the adjudication of disputes which did not involve comital rights (see Table 6).

Rarely did the general receiver decide cases and pass sentence, but when he did, he never did so on his sole authority—he never acted alone. On 27 August 1358, for example, Louis of Male confirmed a judgment rendered by his receiver and the chancellor, neither of whom appear in this document by name.[81] On 27 December 1353, John Van der Delft, together with John of Zantford and Maylin de la Niepe, the count's chancellor, granted a special judicial privilege to aldermen of Ghent without reference to the count.[82] While it was by virtue of his office that the general receiver sat on the count's council handling these cases, the office's particular at-tributes often had little to do with the matters discussed therein. The general receivership, therefore, had to develop a credibility and an author-ity of its own in these matters. But although by this time the office had transcended its incumbent and had become an integral part of the comital administration, the officeholder, as a customary member of the count's council, did not usually act individually, as he had in the thirteenth cen-tury.[83] It was more convenient and efficient to present cases for arbitration before a definable, experienced, and powerful body such as the count's council than to arrange arbitration between two disputants on an *ad hoc* basis, as was the usual practice in the late thirteenth century. The fact that cases were now brought up before a commission constituted by the count and consisting in large part of important members of his administration reflected the centralization of the count's government and the consolida-tion of his authority which underpinned it. The formalization of the office of general receiver and the identification of its incumbent as a comital councilor contributed greatly to the development of the comital council not only as a formal body with its own purview but also as an instrument of the count's (public) governmental apparatus.

As the century progressed, the count increasingly absented himself from the *audientie,* and authority in that body may have devolved on the general receiver.[84] Despite comital absences, the *audientie* was still essen-tially his court; the general receiver might have taken precedence in the case of the count's absence, but such precedence would have been informal, if it existed at all.[85]

The Sovereign Bailiff

Louis, as we have seen, formalized the general receiver's role with regard to judicial matters. Thus what Robert of Béthune had hoped to accomplish in 1308 was realized in 1349. Why did Louis succeed where Robert had failed? Robert had tried to institute something new, something which by 1308 had not gradually evolved out of the routine execution of the office of general receiver. By 1349, such an evolution had been achieved and what Louis did could not be considered new. His charters of appointment did little more than describe the authority that a general receiver had already been routinely exercising.

By the late fourteenth century the general receiver had assumed the position of head of both the judicial and the financial administration of the count of Flanders. He was in charge of bailiffs and receivers of the count's revenues. He could intervene in the management of both judicial and financial affairs. By 1369, judicial revenues directly obtained by the general receiver had grown so numerous that they were given their own account.[86] Given the enormity of the task set before the general receiver,[87] it is hardly surprising that sometime in June 1372 the count created the office of sovereign bailiff of Flanders.[88]

A comparison of the rights and responsibilities of the general receiver before 1372 and those of the sovereign bailiff after 1372 indicates that the latter did little more than take over all of the former's judicial functions. Both the general receiver and the sovereign bailiff could arrest, execute, or release a person accused of wrongdoing, even though they rarely did so.[89] Both were responsible for vagabonds and outlaws, both had the power to mediate disputes among the count's subjects, both supervised local judicial personnel and had the right to suspend them for abuses, and both had the power to issue safe-conducts and institute inquests. The general receiver lost to the sovereign bailiff even his most fundamental function with regard to judicial matters, that is, the responsibility for *ad hoc* judicial revenue. From 1372 onward the general receiver collected only the net income from this revenue, and he did so from the sovereign bailiff. Finally, the fact that the first sovereign bailiff was Gossuin le Wilde, who had held the office of general receiver until made sovereign bailiff in 1372, shows that the new office had, in effect, been split off from the old. Nonetheless, although the sovereign bailiff, rather than the general receiver, was the count's chief judicial officer after 1372, he did not replace the general receiver on the count's council.[90]

TABLE 6. The General Receiver and Disputes

Date of Document or of Issue	Disputants	Subject	Receiver Appears by Name or Office, or Both	Other Information	Source
12/5/49	John Arden & citizens of St. Venant	mill	name	Dutch, Courtrai	L-S, *Cart.*, #215
20/5/49	Bruges & Damme	right of Brugeois to pass through Damme	both	French, Male	Pol. chrs., #467
8/49	Beatrix Vanden Broucke & Rolf & Wm. Sannem	land	both	Dutch, Ghent	L-S, *Cart.*, #219
2/10/49	Merchants of dyed cloth and Aemaengen	new laws detrimental to dyers	office	Dutch, Ghent	L-S, *Cart.*, #83
20/12/50	Siger Cortewille & Andrew Hondertmarc	sale of wine	both	Dutch, Male	L-S, *Cart.*, #1219
22/6/50	Veurne ambacht & certain persons	tax on the *vausserie*	both	Dutch, Courtrai	L-S, *Cart.*, #240
4/6/51	Heir of Rininge & John Baroud	payment of arrears	both	Dutch, Male	L-S, *Cart.*, #1214
7/12/51	Robert of Namur & Geraardsbergen	land	both	Dutch, Bruges	L-S, *Cart.*, #1226
12/12/51	Lady of Davaing & Lord of Veichte	debt	both	French, Courtrai	L-S, *Cart.*, #1225

Date	Parties	Subject		Language, Place	Reference
4/3/52	Land of Waas and convent of Drongen	cost of emptying river	both	Dutch, Bruges	L-S, *Cart.*, #1227
18/4/52	Abbess of Groningen and parish priest of Vroendike	tithe	both	*audientie* Dutch, Male	L-S *Cart.* #1231
11/52	Ypres & the Countess of Namur	legal jurisdiction	both	French, Ghent	L-S, *Cart.*, #1239
13/2/53	Menin and Courtrai	land	office	Dutch, Ghent	L-S, *Cart.*, #474
25/7/53	Aalst & Geraardsbergen	law of residence	both	Dutch	L-S, *Cart.*, #562
3/2/54	Jacob Van de Leene & Siger's children	death of Jacob's brother	both	Dutch, Bruges	L-S, *Cart.*, #1253
19/5/54	Ghent vs Henry Alin & his brother	assault	both	Dutch, Ghent	L-S, *Cart.*, #461
30/6/54	Oudenaarde & Geraardsbergen	death of Peter of Heilbrook	both	Dutch, Male	L-S, *Cart.*, #125
6/6/55	Bishop of Tournai & John Bernage	expenses for job which Bernage did for bishop	both	French, Male	L-S, *Cart.*, #539
15/10/55	Land of Waas and Rupelmonde	fine	both	*audientie* Dutch, Ghent	L-S, *Cart.*, #1212
24/3/56	Vryen & Oudenburg	banned citizens	both	Dutch, Bruges	L-S, *Cart.*, #599

TABLE 6. *Continued*

Date of Document or of Issue	Disputants	Subject	Receiver Appears by Name or Office, or Both	Other Information	Source
4/1/57	Castellan of Courtrai & Hellekin	land	both	*audientie* Dutch, Bruges	L-S, *Cart.*, #1265
5/57	Heeren Wenselen & Duchess of Luxembourg		both	Dutch, Bruges	Mieris, 3:21
14/6/57	Lord of Diksmuide & Veurne Ambacht	toll of Diksmuide	office	Dutch, Bruges	L-S, *Cart.*, #1267
25/3/58	Roland & lord of Poukes vs John of Gistel	land	both	French, Male	L-S, *Cart.*, #1463
28/5/58	Curé of Oudenaarde & Aubert Coucy	*rentes* of cheese	both	*audientie* Dutch, Bruges	L-S, *Cart.*, #1280
26/9/58	Ecloo and Lembeek	manufacture of cloth	both	Dutch, Bruges	L-S, *Cart.*, #1277
9/8/64	Florent Vande Maelstede vs Wm. Bonds	feud	office	Dutch, Bruges	Nord, B1566 #9231
1/12/64	Audendye & Ghenredye vs Behoosten	customs	office	Dutch	Nord, B1566 #9302

Date	Parties	Subject	Type	Location	Reference
13/1/66	Parents of Jean Strommelin vs R. Vutendolre	death of Jean Strommelin	both		Nord, B1567 #9909
18/10/66	Kin of Jean de Busere vs Pierre de Langhe	death of Jean de Busere	both		Nord, B1566 #9822
1/5/67	Aalst, Geraardsbergen & land of Aalst vs Robert of Namur	privileges	both		Nord, B1567 #9969
6/6/67	Jacques de Ram & Rike de Ansane	death of François de Ram	both		Nord, B1567 #10013
7/10/67	Diksmuide & Bruges	jurisdiction	both		Nord, B1567 #10119
4/12/67	Dean & chapter ND Courtrai vs Sobe Steenard, G. de Dankaert & brothers	tithes	both		Nord, B1567 #10115
7/12/67	Bruges & Damme vs Sluys	toll	both	Bruges	Pol. chrs., #568
4/2/68	Frank de Moerkerk and Pierre Bondeenson	feud	both		Nord, B1567 #10178
26/3/68	Hannekin Van der Capelle and Michel van Cathen	feud	office		Nord, B1567 #10198
13/8/68	Verghertrudens & den Grotens	death of Jean Verghertruden	both		Nord, B1567 #10038

L-S, *Cart.* = Limburg-Stirum, *Louis de Male.*

Conclusion

The duties of the receivers of Louis of Male, as described in their appointment charters, do not differ from each other to any great degree. The office, its functions, authority, account, and wages had therefore achieved definition by the beginning of Louis of Male's reign. The acquisition both of a general account and of remuneration independent of the revenues of the office earlier, during the reign of Louis of Nevers, had solidified the concept of the office as an administrative entity. Prior to 1349, mintmasters were the count's only fiscal officials not clearly subordinated to the general receiver; it would have been more remarkable if they had not eventually come under the control of the general receiver. The institution of a sovereign bailiff followed a similar pattern. The judicial duties of the general receiver formed a discrete body of responsibilities and capacities within the office itself; the connection between the receiver's essential financial mandate and his judicial obligations, although logical, was tenuous. Indeed, the loss of judicial responsibility may well have increased the general receiver's efficiency in the fiscal arena. Therefore, whatever changes Louis of Male wrought in the office, they did not affect its essential administrative nature. In effect, all Louis had done was first to extend and then to limit the general receiver's jurisdiction over judicial affairs.

The appointment charters act as *post hoc* acknowledgments of the functions, responsibilities, and procedures which had come to constitute the general receiver's routine. In the middle of the fourteenth century, as in the thirteenth, the general receiver's primary responsibility remained receiving and acknowledging all payments. In 1349, Louis mandated Andrew le Russe, for example, to receive, take, and levy all the count's rents and revenues (listed for the first time specifically),[91] duties also mentioned, albeit only in a general way, in the appointment charters of Thomas Fini and Nicholas Guiduche. But the charters of John Van der Delft (1351), John de la Fauchille (1359), Peter de la Fauchille (1361), and Gossuin le Wilde (1365) also make it clear that such power, although customary, was granted to the general receiver by the count: "We have given and do give power and authority to receive."[92] This does not mean that the receiver lost any of his authority. Rather, the count probably wanted to emphasize that the office existed at his wish, that its authority, even though by this time intrinsic in the routine execution of the functions that defined it, came from the count.

At the same time, Louis strengthened the general receiver's control over the count's fiscal officers. Although in Andrew le Russe's charter the count ordered fiscal officials simply to pay and deliver their revenues to the general receiver,[93] in that of John Van der Delft and subsequent receivers Louis ordered these officials to heed, respond, and obey the receiver and to deliver the money and profits of their receipt to him or to his particular deputy.[94] The latter charters thus empowered the general receiver to perform two functions: first, to receive profits and money from domainal and extra-domainal resources and, second, to command financial officials. The charter of John Van der Delft, for the first time, treats these two functions as separate, an explicit recognition of what had been implicit since the late thirteenth century. Furthermore, the wording used to empower the general receiver in this way was adopted in subsequent charters of appointment; by 1365, when the count appointed Gossuin le Wilde, the phrase had become formulaic.[95] Such a development suggests that the functions of the general receiver had reached a stage where they were conceived as being beyond customary; they had become and probably were immutable. As such, they needed no further definition or explanation. Therefore, although Louis further tinkered with the office after he had transferred its judicial responsibilities and capacities to the sovereign bailiff in 1372,[96] the office of general receiver which the Burgundians inherited at his death in 1384 was the same as that which had existed in 1372.

Notes

1. Nicholas, *Town and Countryside*, 177.

2. Pirenne, *Histoire de Belgique*, 2:134.

3. As Pirenne points out, Louis's solution for Flanders to the conflict between France and England was somewhat unorthodox: Although Louis himself did not recognize Edward III's claim to the French throne, he allowed his subjects to do so (*ibid.*, 2:187).

4. *Ibid.*, 2:203.

5. On 27 September 1354, for example, in the presence of John van der Delft and John of Zantford, Louis renewed his confirmation of the liberties and customs of Dendermonde that he had confirmed on 19 September 1348 in the process of securing his county (A. de Vlaminck, ed., *Inventaire des archives de la ville de Termonde* [Ghent, 1879], 1:67–68 #10).

6. Nicholas, *Town and Countryside*, 203.

7. This is not to say that the count no longer respected traditional urban judicial and economic privileges. What gradually disappeared was their influence over county-wide policy.

8. Nicholas, *Town and Countryside,* 203.

9. *Ibid.,* 90 and 205.

10. Andrew was specifically given the right to retain his status as a citizen of Ypres: "Item, lui ottroyons nous, que non contrestant que il soit nostre recheveur il puis tenir sa bourgoisie" (Limburg-Stirum, *Louis de Male,* 1:128 #126).

11. *Ibid.,* 16–17 #10.

12. "par le commun assent volenté et requeste de nos trois bonnes villes Gand, Bruges et Ypre" (Limburg-Stirum, *Louis de Male,* 1:127–131 #126).

13. "Item, que nous ne autres depar nous ne ferons assignement, quictance, ne don à heritage ne à vie sans le conseil et sceu dou dit Andrieu, et se par aventure le contraire en estoit fait il sera de nulle valeur"; "Item, que tout no bailliu soient commis et renouvelé par son conseil, et en samblable maniére tout eshievin de nos bonnes villes et pays"; "Item, tout autre officyer, vendere et petit bailli appertenant à estre renouvelé par le recheveur de Flandres, soient rapellé et renouvelé par ses lettrez toutes fois que mestiers sera." *Ibid.*

14. Limburg-Stirum, *Louis de Male,* 2:121–124 #848.

15. The appointment charter of John de la Fauchille (11 October 1359) reads: "Toutevoies est aussi nostre entent que nostre dit recheveur tenra a joura porra tenir a joir de sa bourgoisie de Gand contre toutes persones et en tout cas excepte tant seulement contre nous de chose touchans son office recheverie" (Nord, B1596 f. 100v #8146). That of Peter de la Fauchille (4 October 1362) reads: "Toutevoies est aussi nostre entent que nostre dit recheveur ne tenra ne joura ne porra tenir ne joir de sa bourgoisie de Gand contre nous en choses touchans son office" (*ibid.,* B1596 f. 107v #8705), while that of Gossuin le Wilde (5 July 1365) reads: "Toutevoies est aussi nostre entente que nostre dit recheveur ne tenra ne joura ne porra tenir ne joir de sa franchise dou franc ne de vrylaetscep contre nous en chose touchans son office" (*ibid.,* B1566 n. 252 f. 67 #9471).

16. Pol. chrs., #334, #392, #397, #408, #427.

17. "Item que toutes fois. . . . nous requerra de oïr ses comptes, nous les ferons oïr sans dylay" (Limburg-Stirum, *Louis de Male,* 1:130 #126).

18. Limburg-Stirum, *Louis de Male,* 2:121 #848. John obviously met with some success, for he remained receiver at least until 11 October 1359.

19. *Ibid.,* 2:414–415 #1333; F. Blockmans, 299.

20. Limburg-Stirum, *Louis de Male,* 2:420–421 #1340; F. Blockmans, 299.

21. Limburg-Stirum, *Louis de Male,* 2:421–422 #1341; St.-Genois, #1724; F. Blockmans, 299.

22. Limburg-Stirum, *Louis de Male,* 2:486–487 #1403; F. Blockmans, 299.

23. Nord, B1596 f. 166v #8009.

24. *Ibid.,* B1596 f. 162v #8640.

25. "et ou cas que nos dessus dis receveres nous requerra des ses compte hoir pour savoir nostre estat ou pour lui esclarchir et deschargier de nostre recepte" (Limburg-Stirum, *Louis de Male,* 2:123 #848).

26. The phrase "in order to clarify and to discharge our receipt" is deleted from two of them (Nord, B1569 f. 100–100v #8146; *ibid.,* B1596 f. 107v #8705; *ibid.,* B1566 n. 252 f. 66v–67 #9471). The charters of Peter de la Fauchille and Gossuin le Wilde even had the same spelling.

27. The *renenghe* was to be held annually and the accounts of the bailiffs were to be heard three times a year: "Item, volons nous et ordenons, que sans enfraindre, nos renenghes soient tenues chascun an une fois . . . et semblablement les comptes de nos baillis trois fois l'année" (Limburg-Stirum, *Louis de Male*, 2:121 #848; Nord, B1569 f. 100–100v #8146; *ibid.*, B1596 f. 107v #8705; *ibid.*, B1566 n. 252 f. 66v–67 #9471).

28. Monier, *Les institutions financières*, 66–67.

29. The only major change in the form of accounts in the second half of the fourteenth century was from the use of French to Flemish. (See RR, #8 to #2418). This was the second time the language of the accounts had changed. In the fourth quarter of the thirteenth century, a gradual change from Latin to French occurred. The change from French to Flemish in the fourteenth century affected all kinds of accounts. By 1370 all of the bailiffs' accounts were being written in Flemish. Unfortunately, because few of the bailiffs' accounts survive from the period 1336 to 1365, it is difficult to determine exactly when this linguistic switch occurred. The earliest extant account of a bailiff written in Flemish is that of the *rentes* at Saftinghen in 1350 (Baillis de Saftingen. Compte de l'année 1350 [environ], *ibid.*, #1605), but by 1355 almost all were in Flemish. The dates of the first records written in Flemish correspond roughly to the beginning of the reign of Louis of Male (Nowé, *Les baillis comtaux*, 184–185). The change might have been a political maneuver made to satisfy powerful Flemish-speaking factions. It also might have been a practical one; perhaps a large number of the count's bailiffs and domainal receivers were Flemish speakers. As Nowé points out, the count's chief administrators were French speakers. Thus although many of the accounts were written in Flemish, notations made by the major financial officials were usually in French (*ibid.*, 185). The chief financial official, of course, was the general receiver. The account of the receiver of the domains of Ninove, Haaltert, and Hocetem is in Flemish, but the notation that the deficit was paid to Gossuin le Wilde is in French: "paiet a messire Gossuin recheveur" (Domaines de Ninove, Haaltert et Hocetem. Compte du receveur Gautier de Dyn au 24 juin 1369 au 23 juin 1370, RR, #143). Gossuin, obviously, was a French speaker. The case of Peter de la Fauchille is similar. In 1364 it was noted in the account of the bailiff of Damme that he was "schuldich" (Flemish for "in debt") for 302 l. 17 s. 8 d., which he duly paid to Peter, but which was noted "payet a Pieter fils Jehan, recheveur," in French (Baillis de Damme, Houche et Monekerede. Compte du bailli, Jacques van Scatthille du 16 septembre 1364 au 12 janvier 1365, *ibid.*, #1105). A few of the domainal accounts continued to be written entirely in French, for instance, the accounts of the domains of Knesselaer (*ibid.*, #76–79), the accounts of the domain of Menin (*ibid.*, #121–137), and the accounts of the briefs of the Vier Ambachten and of Assenede (*ibid.*, #341–344). The accounts of the *rentes* at Sijsele are worth special note. Although the full account was written in Flemish (*ibid.*, #519, #520, #523), there exist abridged accounts in French (*ibid.*, #522, #524, #525; corrected copy of H. Nélis, *Chambres des comptes de Flandres et de Brabant. Inventaire des comptes en rouleaux* [Brussels, 1914], 36).

30. "Item que tout no baillis et autres officiers paieront ce quil auront recheu et exploitie au dit Nicolas comme recheveur non a autre" (Nord, B1565 n. 489 f. 76v).

31. The few entries which did not end that way prove to be those in which the income was paid directly to the count.

32. The charters of John and Peter de la Fauchille and Gossuin le Wilde read, "car nostre ententes nest mis anchois deffendons, que nulle autres lettres que les nostres propres ou les lettrez de nostre dit recheveur passent ou soient recheues par les maistres de nos comptes" (*ibid.*, B1596 f. 100 #8146; *ibid.*, B1596 f. 107v #8705; *ibid.*, B1562 n. 252 f. 67 #9471).

33. A document, issued by John Van der Delft on 10 June 1356, states: "Sacent tous que comme mes tres redoubte singneur et prince, monsieur le conte de Flandre, ait fait examiner . . . les comptes que je fis darrainement en presence de lui et pluseurs de mes singneurs de son conseil" (St.-Genois, #1724).

34. Limburg-Stirum, *Louis de Male*, 2:414–415 #1333; 2:420–421 #1340.

35. For Testard de Wastine, see J. Gilissen, "Les légistes en Flandre aux XIIIe et XIVe siècles," *Bulletin de la commission royale des anciennes lois et ordonnances de Belgique* 14 (1934), 154–159.

36. Siger de Beke, the count's chancellor, heard the account of 4 November 1354 to 17 May 1356 (Limburg-Stirum, *Louis de Male*, 2:421–422 #1341); John of Dareaux verified the account of 17 May 1356 to 26 March 1357 (*ibid.*, 2:486–487 #1403); whereas Thierry Montague verified the account of 26 March 1357 to 10 October 1358 (Nord, B1596 f. 166v #8009). John de la Fauchille's account was verified by Stephen de Wastine, John le Clerc, and Hugh de le Haye (*ibid.*, B1596 f. 162v #8640).

37. John le Clerc was a member of the council that approved John Van der Delft's account for this period (Limburg-Stirum, *Louis de Male*, 2:421–422 #1341).

38. *Ibid.*, 2:414–415 #1333; F. Blockmans, 299.

39. Limburg-Stirum, *Louis de Male*, 2:486–487 #1403.

40. Nord, B1596 f. 166v #8009. The document contains no explanation for the delay.

41. *Ibid.*, B1596 f. 100 #8146.

42. *Ibid.*, B1596 f. 107v #8705; *ibid.*, B1566 n. 252 f. 67 #9471.

43. This is implied in the charter of John Van der Delft ("et ce par restat de son compte final est trouvé que il ait plus avant finé pour nous que receu, nous lui devrons faire assennement souffissant diceli sourplus; de rechief volons nous et ottroions à nostre dit receveur, que si après son compte il estoit trouvé que il euist plus delivré et finé que receu, nous lui en ferons bon et soffissant paie ou assennement avant ce que nous le démettons de nostre office. Et ou case que après le dit compte il fuist trouvé que il euist aucune chose recheu dont il neuist point compté et fait recepte, nous lui ottroions que en paiant à nous y ce que trouvé seroit, comme dit est, il se puist acquiter sans malengien; et samblablement volons nous que se il avoit aucune chose oublié à mettre en date à son proffit il y puist adies revenir, en monstrant soffissament les parties, sauve en tous cas nostre héritage" [Limburg-Stirum, *Louis de Male*, 2:123 #848]). It is stated explicitly in the charters of John and Peter de la Fauchille and of Gossuin le Wilde ("Et ses dis comptes oys et examines de li donner après l'examination faite diceuls nos lettres de quittanche ou li monstrerer et dire comme raisonnable pour quoy nous ne li faisons" [Nord, B1596

f. 100 #8146; *ibid.,* 1596 f. 107v #8705; *ibid.,* B1566 n. 252 f. 67 #9471]). The charter of Andrew le Russe is illegible at this point. The phrase reads "nous le ferons sans dylay et yceux nos lettres de quittance" (Limburg-Stirum, *Louis de Male,* 1:130 #126).

44. In 1359 (Nord, B1596 f. 166v #8009).

45. Compte du receveur Gilles de le Walle du 28 septembre 1348 au 13 décembre 1348, RR, #6.

46. Nord, B1568 n. 174–175 f. 119 and 119v.

47. Limburg-Stirum, *Louis de Male,* 2:414–415 #1333; 2:420–421 #1340; 2:421–422 #1341; 2:486–487 #1403; Nord, B1596 f. 166 v #8009; B1596 f. 162 v #8640.

48. "Se . . . il estoit trouvé que il euist plus délivré et finé que receu, nous lui en ferons bon et soffissant paie ou assennement avant ce que nous le démettons de nostre office" (Limburg-Stirum, *Louis de Male,* 2:123 #848). The charters of John and Peter de la Fauchille and of Gossuin le Wilde include a similar provision (Nord, B1596 f. 100 #8146; *ibid.,* B1596 f. 107v #8705; *ibid.,* B1566 n. 252 f. 67 #9471).

49. *Ibid.,* B1565 n. 489 f. 76v.

50. "en son premier compte kil fist dou mis-quaresme lan 1305 kil entre en le recept de Flandre" (Comptes des arrérages de 1306 à 1309, RR, #3).

51. Limburg-Stirum, *Louis de Male,* 2:213 #848; Nord, B1596 f. 100 #8146; *ibid.,* B1596 f. 107v #8705; *ibid.,* B1566 n. 252 f. 67 #9471.

52. Charter of appointment of general receiver, 18 April 1306 (Gaillard, #574); grant of extension of powers of Thomas Fini, 7 November 1308 (*ibid.,* #588; *Codex,* 2:97 #238); charter of appointment of Nicholas Guiduche, 21 September 1335 (Nord, B1565 n. 489 f. 76v).

53. *Ibid.,* B1565 n. 799 f. 153.

54. RR, #788.

55. Since Nicholas Guiduche was receiver for most of the period covered by Perceval's account, his presence at this audit was only logical.

56. The illegible gap occurs just before the words "renneurs, receveurs de briefz, de renenghes, de rentes hors renenghe, censiers" (Limburg-Stirum, *Louis de Male,* 1:130 #126), which are also found in that order in John Van der Delft's charter. In John's charter, the words which precede them are "sergans, justichiers, officyers, mestre de nos monnoies, thonlieurs" (*ibid.,* 2:123 #848). The charters, however, are not identically worded. *Thonlieurs,* for example, preceded *renneurs* in John's charter, but succeeds *censiers* in Andrew's.

57. Monnaie de Gand. Compte des depenses de Parcheval du Porche du 24 novembre 1346 au 1 août 1350, RR, #794.

58. Nord, B1596 n. 100 #8146; *ibid.,* B1596 f. 107v #8705; *ibid.,* B1566 n. 252 f. 67 #9471.

59. Monnaie de Bruges. Compte de maitre Bernard Priem du 24 septembre 1352 au 6 septembre 1353, RR, #774.

60. Monnaie de Malines appartenant comte de Flandre. Compte de maître Pierre Platvoet du 29 janvier 1364 au 3 mars 1364, *ibid.,* #2138.

61. "Ensi doit Aldrighe de cest compte 8,300 l. par. paii a monsieur le re-

cheveur messire Gossuin le Wilde, chevalier, compte" (Monnaie de Gand. Compte des lyons d'or et argent d'Aldrighe Enterminelly de 28 juin 1365 au 18 octobre 1365, ibid., #805).

62. The mintmasters may have succeeded in resisting the count's attempts to bring all his resources under his financial administration because, for the most part, they were rich Italians. Not only were the counts of Flanders constantly in debt to the Italians, but Louis of Nevers also used them as a way of diminishing the powers of the hereditary nobility and powerful burgesses. He was, so to speak, doubly in debt to them, and may not have found it possible to subject them to the authority of the general receiver. His successor, Louis of Male, rejected his father's policy of relying on outsiders, and had few scruples about making all the receivers of his resources answerable to his general receiver. It is worth noting that despite the upheaval of the years 1343 to 1350, the work of the mintmaster of Ghent was not interrupted (Monnaie de Gand. Compte de Parcheval de Porche de 1343 à 1350, ibid., #792–794).

63. John le Clerc was present at the audit of the mint of Bruges in 1352 and 1353 (Monnaie de Bruges. Compte de maitre Bernard Priem du 24 septembre 1352 au 6 septembre 1353, ibid., #774; idem de Jean Parcheval de Lucques de 15 janvier 1352 au 4 septembre 1353, ibid., #775), the audit of the mints of Ghent in 1350, 1356, 1357, 1358, 1359, 1360, and 1361 (Monnaie de Gand, ibid., #794–796, #800, #801, #804), and the audit of the mint of Mechelen in 1360 (Monnaie de Malines appartenant au comte de Flandre, ibid., #2136, #2137). Testard de Wastine heard the account of the mints of Ghent in 1357, 1358, and 1360 (Monnaie de Gand, ibid., #796, #797, #801) and of Mechelen in 1358 and 1360 (Monnaie de Malines appartenant au comte de Flandre, ibid., #2135, #2137). The count was present at the audit of the mints of Ghent in 1356 and 1357 (Monnaie de Gand, ibid., #795, #796); the rest of the time, he appears to have left the responsibility to his commissioners.

64. On 24 May 1355, he approved the accounts of the mints of Bruges (Limburg-Stirum, Louis de Male, 2:419–420 #1339), in November 1355 and May 1356, the accounts of the mints of Ghent (ibid., 2:431 #1352; 2:433–434 #1354), and on 6 February 1365, he accepted the accounts of Peter Platvoet for the mints of Ghent and Mechelen (Nord, B1566 n. 504 f. 138 #9352). Granting quittance does not necessarily imply that the count was actually present at a particular audit. He may have quit a particular individual on the advice of his commissioners.

65. The first separate extant account of this revenue is dated 1369 and was handled by Gossuin le Wilde as general receiver (Compte messire Goossuin le Wilde, chevalier, recheveur de Flandre de tout que il rechuit des testes rachatees, bannissemens et calaenges, fourfaitures et explois de le recheveur de Flandre depuis le VIIème jour de may 1369 que le recheveur en compta à court jusques au XXème jour de septembre ensuivant fait à Bruges après les comptes des baillis, RR, #838). In June 1372 the count created the office of sovereign bailiff which took over the responsibility of the count's judicial system from the general receiver. Judicial revenues continue to appear in the accounts of the general receiver, but only in a summarized form.

66. For records of the *audientie,* see V. Gaillard, *Archives du Conseil de Flandre ou recueil des documents inédits relatifs à l'histoire politique, judiciare, artistique et littéraire* (Ghent, 1856), and N. de Pauw, *Bouc van der Audientie. Acten en sentencien van de Raad van Vlaanderen (1368–1378),* 2 vols. (Ghent, 1901–1907). The best discussion of the *audientie* and of its development and significance is J. Buntinx, *De Audientie van de Graven van Vlaanderen. Studie over het centraal grafelijke gerecht, c. 1330–1409* (Brussels, 1949).

67. General receivers had exercised this right informally during the reign of Louis of Nevers.

68. Nowé, "L'intervention," 86 and n. 1.

69. Nowé, "L'intervention," 81.

70. "et que en ce no dit bailli ne puissent allegier, ne proposer nulle costume anchienne en contraire" (Limburg-Stirum, *Louis de Male,* 1:128 #126; Nowé, "L'intervention," 89), which indicates that such development had met with resistance.

71. "vier manne die metter bailliu ghingen te Verleyenbeke, bi der langen Brugghe, bi bevelen van de ontfangher van vlaenderen, omme te verblendene den bailliu van Sinte-Baefs, dat hi gheene wet soude doen van den faite dat gheviel up mijns heren herstraete, tusschen den Everwins et hare partien, Zeghere de Zomers and sire partien" (Baillis de Gand. Compte du bailli du Pays de Waes et du bailli de Gand, Nicolas van den Clyte, chevalier, seigneur de Niewen Hove, du 23 janvier 1352 au 21 mai 1352, RR, #1362; Nowé, "L'intervention," 86 and n. 2).

72. "hebbent Pieter Folkier, Jan Stassins ende mester Jan Reubelin vorseid belooft ende ghezworen, in den name van der stede van Ypre, vor onse manne die up de vorseide zake ghemaent waren, ten beveilne van ons bi Janne vander Delft onsen ontfanghere" (Limburg-Stirum, *Louis de Male,* 1:448 #498; Nowé, "L'intervention," 86 and n. 4).

73. "onse ontfanghere van Vlaendren, Jan Van der Ziekele, ende onse bailljuw van Brugghe, Woutier Van der Brugghen, bi specialre commission die wij hem daerup gaven verbrunt hebben de husinghen ende de wonenghen van here Jan Tande ende van dudsen andren personen die clarelike benenden waren, dat zij ter doot brocht hadden, Piet Zoertard, onsen bailljuw van Ysendike en de . . . doen naer den laste date wij hemlieden derof gaven en presentien van den groten rade van onser stede van Brugghe" (Nord, B1596 f. 48v #8430).

74. "Item, voer de baeliu bi commiscien van den ontfangher te Werveke ende van danne te meenine met vier van mins heeren mannen om te bezoeken wie ballinghen gheuust of ghehoeft hadden, ende was ute 3 $^{1}/_{2}$ daghe" (Baillis de la châtellenie de Courtrai. Compte du bailli Baudouin fils de Jean, du 19 septembre 1364 au 12 janvier 1365, RR, #1055; Nowé, "L'intervention," 85 and n. 1).

75. "Item, quant le recheveur de Flandre me avoit commandé à tenir en fermité Monin de Gaent" (Baillis de Cassel. Compte du bailli, Jean de Vinc, du 4 fevrier 1367 au 3 mai 1367, RR, #1096; Nowé, "L'intervention," 85 and n. 2).

76. "Item, pour le justiche du dit Moenin, lequelle fu faite par le dit bailliu par le nobleiche de Madame et à le request du dit recheveur" (Baillis de Cassel. Compte du bailli, Jean de Vinc, du 4 fevrier 1367 au 3 mai 1367, RR, #1096; Nowé, "L'intervention," 85 and n. 4).

77. "Et après le doyen de la crestienté de IIII Mestiers requist au dit bailliu pour avoir restitution des dites persones. . . . Lequelle request le dit bailliu fist savoir au recheveur. Et sur ce, en obéissance de Sainte Eglise, le recheveur lis fist ramener de le prison de Gavre et les renvera arrière dedans le dit moustier" (Compte messire Gossuin le Wilde, chevalier, recheveur de Flandres de tout chou que il a rechuit des testes rachatees, bannissements, calenges, fourfaitures et explois de la recheverie de Flandres . . . RR, #840; Nowé, "L'intervention," 85 and n. 3).

78. Limburg-Stirum, *Louis de Male*, 1:519–522 #567.

79. Thierry de Limburg-Stirum, *Coutume de la ville et de la châtellenie de Courtrai* (Brussels, 1905), 171–172 #11bis.

80. A. Schouteet, ed., *Regesten op de oorkonden van het Stadsbestuur van Brugge* (Brussels, 1979), 2:207 #544.

81. At issue was the death of Hugh Saywin; Hugh's parents were accusing John Mulard (Limburg-Stirum, *Louis de Male*, 2:367 #1273; Thomas, *Textes,* 1:52–54 #30b). The decision was pronounced by the bailiff orally ("daden zeggen bi der mont van den bailliu van Eeclo"), which may be why this confirmation is the only surviving record of it (Limburg-Stirum, *Louis de Male*, 2:368 #1273).

82. That their judgment against Peter Colin for "many larcenies and horrible deeds" would stand even though he was apprehended at Merelbeek and not in Ghent (*ibid.*, 1:451 #502).

83. Siger of Bailleul was frequently chosen as an arbitrator on account of his prestige, which was based on personal standing and not on the functions he performed. He therefore was something of a free agent.

84. Nowé, "L'intervention," 86. There were fifteen sittings of the *audientie* from 19 February 1370 to 15 March 1372. The general receiver was present at thirteen of them and absent from two: on 21 October 1370, at Ghent, and on 1 September 1372, also at Ghent (de Pauw, *Audientie*, 1–267 #1–15; Gaillard, *Archives*, 70–71).

85. Buntinx, *Audientie*, 70–71.

86. RR, #838.

87. "quil puist . . . prendre et lever . . . fourfais . . . amendes. . . . Item, que nuls de nos baillius de nostre dicte conté ne puis quiter ne lessier appaisir à lui nulle amende de LX lib . . . Item, nous ne quitterons ne ferons accord d'amendes nulle à nous appertenans, ne renderons le pays, le teste ne le vie à personne nulle qui lait fourfaite sans le conseil dou dit Andrieu et par lui" (Limburg-Stirum, *Louis de Male,* 1:128 #126).

88. Nowé, "L'intervention," 89–90 and n. 5; Proost, 273. The constitution of this office was of enough significance to be noted in a chronicle: "Environs lan IIIIc LXIII apres les grandes commotions et rebellions, le conte Loys de Male, veuillant remettre son pays de Flandre en paix et justice, fist et institua ung souverain bailly de Flandre; il lui bailla pouvoir assez ample et premiers de punir tous cas surannez et de purges le pays de maulvaises gens" (P. Wieland, "Recueil des antiquités de Flandre," in *Recueil des croniques de Flandre*, J. J. de Smet, ed. [Brussels, 1865], 4:109. The date, 1463, is incorrect).

89. It must be recalled that burgesses and the clergy did not usually come under comital jurisdiction. Burgesses were subject to urban tribunals according to

the privileges granted to their communities and only exceptionally to the count's council. The clergy were under the jurisdiction of the Church.

90. As a member of the count's council he continued to settle cases. The line between the sovereign bailiff and the general receiver with regard to judicial matters was not immediately clear after June 1372. The general receivers (for the East and the West) continued to perform judicial functions for several years after the institution of the sovereign bailiff. Nonetheless, by the accession of Margaret of Flanders in 1384, the offices shared few or no functions.

91. "*rentes*, revenues, quitrents, forfeits, writs, fines, subsidies, gifts, dues, debts, arrears, aventures, flotsam, windfalls, revenues and lordships of our mints, and all other things that ought to be delivered and pertinent to us" (Limburg-Stirum, *Louis de Male*, 1:128 #126).

92. "nous avons donne et donnons pooir et autorite de recevoir" (*ibid.*, 2:122–126 #848; Nord, B1566 252 f. 100 #8146; *ibid.*, B1596 f. 107v #8705; *ibid.*, B1566 n. 252 f. 67 #9471).

93. The phrase before the words "et delivrent" is blank in Limburg-Stirum's published transcription of this document (Limburg-Stirum, *Louis de Male*, 1:128 #126). Nonetheless, a similar phrase is found in the charter of Thomas Fini and reads "paechent et delivrechent" (Gaillard, #574). This evidence strongly suggests that part of the illegible phrase is indeed "pay."

94. "entendent, respondent et obéissent . . . et à lui ou à son certain délégué seulement et à nul autre délivrent les deniers et proffis de leur receptes" (Limburg-Stirum, *Louis de Male*, 2:122–126 #848; Nord, B1596 f. 100 #8146; *ibid.*, B1596 f. 107v #8705; *ibid.*, B1566 n. 252 f. 67 #9471).

95. See Appendix C, 8–10.

96. At one point Louis divided the receivership into two—one receiver for the East and one for the West—but later reunited them into a single office.

8. Conclusion

THE ADMINISTRATIVE ACHIEVEMENTS of comital government in Flanders since the eleventh century testify to Flemish precocity, particularly in the sphere of fiscal management. Flemish counts of the thirteenth and fourteenth centuries were striving to realize two particular ambitions: to exploit the diversifying economy of their county in such a way as to make the resulting revenues most readily available and, at the same time, to consolidate their control over the Flemish communities—in the fourteenth century particularly over Ghent, Bruges, and Ypres. Both objectives were served by the construction of central financial institutions, particularly of the office of general receiver.

Though they may guide the general direction an evolving administration might take, intention and ambition are insufficient to sustain such evolution. Political and economic crises, as well as the day-to-day conditions that obtained in thirteenth and fourteenth century Flanders, posed problems which the count's fiscal administration had to be equipped not only to handle but also to exploit. Political, economic, and social exigencies in themselves may therefore provide the catalysts which trigger institutionalization, yet the way this occurs and the internal dynamic by which institutionalization is sustained is dependent upon agents, methods, and procedures already in place. The history of the office of general receiver demonstrates that it is routine, more than anything else, which provides an institution with the coherence and the stability indispensable for its continued existence. Routine was in turn the product of a process whereby *ad hoc* solutions, through repeated use, outgrew and transcended the contexts to which they had first been applied. In brief, the office of general receiver of Flanders emerged out of a process in which the *ad hoc* became routine. Correspondingly, the increasing complexity of the office was driven by an evolving dialectical relationship between, on the one hand, political and economic conditions and, on the other, the process by which the *ad hoc* measures taken by the counts to realize their ambitions turned into customary procedures.

As the systems which had developed in the course of the twelfth and early thirteenth century became entrenched, the strategy of going around or beyond them sometimes proved easier, and perhaps ultimately more efficient in meeting newly perceived needs, than trying to change their internal structure. Thus it was easier for Philip of Bourbourg in 1262 to assume responsibility for the various organizations already in place, such as the bailiffs and receivers, simply as part of an additional layer of administration, than it was to encharge an official—a particular bailiff or receiver, for example—already associated with a specific system with obligations that went beyond his routine competence. Once the assumption of such authority became customary, the inclusion of these heretofore semi-autonomous systems into a larger, more all-encompassing entity was accomplished. The essential feature of that entity was the general receiver. Although similar layering would occur in future centuries, this particular assumption of general competence marked the completion of the development of a county-wide fiscal hierarchy. It also provided the point of departure for the specialization and consequent separation of financial affairs from other comital business, which, under the guidance of the office of general receiver, would develop into a coherent department. Furthermore, the establishment of Philip of Bourbourg as head of all of Countess Margaret's fiscal matters was the critical step in the formulation of the concept of a central administrative official firmly attached to the count and his court, but having jurisdiction over the rest of the county in a specific administrative sphere.

The office's ever-increasing competence, and thus sophistication, resulted logically from routinization in the functions performed by the general receiver. The history of the general receivership was therefore marked throughout the thirteenth and fourteenth centuries by a progression of reasonable steps. The establishment of such an official provided for the permanent supervision of extraordinary revenues, an achievement attempted and realized by other northern European princes, and one which reflected the expansion of princely authority. Neither Philip of Bourbourg nor any other person or official had yet been made responsible for the count's expenses. It was a logical step in the reign of Guy of Dampierre for the general receiver to begin to take responsibility for the payment and accounting of expenses drawn from Guy's treasury. Another significant step taken during Guy's reign involved the supervision of bailiffs. Since the general receiver was already responsible for the income brought in by the comital bailiffs, his gradual assumption of authority over them was probably not perceived as anything out of the ordinary. Nevertheless, this assumption marked the first step toward the establishment of a central judicial office. Guy of Dampierre's continued use of his general receiver to meet other financial demands further expanded this official's competence, as the general receiver's right to contract and pay loans in the count's name testifies. In fact, the increasing number and complexity of the general receiver's obligations eventually reached the point where he could not handle his responsibilities alone; he began to gather around him a group of clerks and sergeants to whom he could entrust those functions which were already so routine as to be proof against any incompetence, or mistakes, or whose management did not require the personal prestige of the general receiver himself.

By the beginning of the fourteenth century the general receiver's purview comprised, with few exceptions, the management of all the revenues of Flanders. Furthermore, during the last half of the thirteenth century, the general receiver had gradually assumed responsibility for verifying and validating the accounts of financial officials such as bailiffs and receivers. He was not himself accountable, although during the last decade of the thirteenth century general receivers had drawn up accounts of the occasional revenues entrusted to them. It was not until the early fourteenth century that all of the count's varied revenues were first reckoned together into a single account. This development may be seen as a logical outgrowth of preceding ones, particularly as regarding supervision of the accounts of local financial officials, and its significance for the overall development of the count's financial system can hardly be overestimated. Nonetheless, this first appearance of a general account was in all probability an essentially *ad hoc* affair, the product of adventitious factors. In 1305, Robert of Béthune was reinvested by the French king with the county of Flanders. In early 1306, probably to fund the re-establishment of his authority and of his government in Flanders, Robert borrowed a large sum from the Italian banker, Thomas Fini. Not long after this, Robert made Thomas his general receiver. Robert's reinvestment with Flanders, his taking out of a loan from Fini, and his appointment of Fini as general receiver may well have provided the impetus for what was really only an *ad hoc* reckoning of all the count's revenues into a single account. As the count's chief financial officer, the general receiver was the logical choice to draw up such an account, and thus, implicitly, to take responsibility for it. The fact that the general receiver at the time was Thomas Fini, an Italian banker, experienced in financial matters in addition to being the count's creditor, made the construction of such an account even more logical. The form of the general account, however, was not without specifically Flemish antecedents. Thomas's tenancy may have provided the motive behind the establishment of a general account but the procedure for its audit and the construction of its form were clearly modeled on existing Flemish financial practices. Once the step was taken it set a precedent, and the drawing up of general accounts, although it never quite occurred on a routine basis, subsequently became integral to the office of general receiver. The general receiver's account was, in effect, one of the first of its kind in Europe.

The acquisition of a wage separate from the revenues of the office of general receiver followed a similar pattern. Comital bailiffs had received fixed wages since the early thirteenth century, but the concept of wages separate from revenues and paid at a specific time did not spread much beyond the level of local comital administration. Indeed, throughout most of the thirteenth century, individuals who held no regular office but who, as members of the count's household, performed administrative functions on his behalf were rewarded on a rather less definitive basis. The most common practice was for the count to contract with a person to perform certain tasks. Such "contracts" in fact often remained informal, and the relevant tasks were often not even fully specified. In return for a given undertaking on the part of one of his household members, the count would provide him with a source of income, a *gage*—a benefice if the person was a cleric, a receivership if the individual was a sergeant, or both. Livings nonetheless had the virtue of being paid at regular intervals, and thus a significant connection emerged between payment and performance. In the reign of Guy of Dampierre, the gap between a *gage* and a wage narrowed further. By the reign of Louis of Nevers, the *gage* had become a wage in the modern sense. Initially the general receiver's wage, unlike that of a bailiff, was calculated on a daily basis. This provides a clear indication that the general was being paid a wage and not a salary and that the functions that he performed were still perceived as separate functions, not necessarily as part of the implicit responsibilities of a bureaucratic office. The next step, then, was for the general receiver's wage to develop into a salary. In 1336, in a charter outlining Nicholas Guiduche's responsibilities as general receiver, Count Louis of Nevers mandated that the performance of these duties would merit the annual payment of 500 l. The subsequent pro-rating of Nicholas's salary in the account at the end of that year in no way contradicts the fact that in 1336 the general receiver's wage had indeed become a salary. Rather, the pro-rating of that salary simply reflects the weakness in the count's administration at this stage. There was as yet no notion nor any way of paying a fiscal officer at any time other than when his account was reckoned. Subsequent receivers would also be paid salaries, but no provision for regular payment was included in any of their appointment charters. When this step was finally taken, it was a logical consequence of the development of the notion of a salary—a notion essentially in place as early as 1336.

Finally, the splitting of the receiver's judicial functions from his fiscal ones, the essential act in the creation of the office of sovereign bailiff in 1372, came about as yet another logical consequence of the increasing complexity and specialization which marked the evolution of the general receivership. It was a step that would indeed have been revolutionary, not to say logistically impossible, fifty years earlier. Although heretofore merely a facet of the general receiver's office, the position of central judicial officer had fully developed by 1372. The office of count's bailiff had existed for a long time before it assumed its own distinctive form. In the same way, the concept of a general receiver had itself existed for more than a decade before receiving formal entitlement and even longer before it received formal recognition in an appointment charter. The concept of a sovereign bailiff, however, had not had a long history, and the creation of the post, unlike previous positions in the central comital administration, was not a *post hoc* acknowledgment of already existing circumstances. Once the count associated the new title "sovereign bailiff" with the receiver's judicial functions, he created a new position. The other alterations Louis of Male made in the general receivership at the time indicate that the office of sovereign bailiff resulted from a conscious reordering of the receivership. When the count created the office of sovereign bailiff, he did so on the model of the general receivership; that is, he constituted it as an office existing beyond the tenancy of its incumbent, and confided to its care specific functions whose performance implied the concept of a central, specialized administrative officer, responsible for a discrete department. Like the general receiver, the new official was to be accountable to the count through a yearly reckoning procedure; he was to be paid by a salary of a fixed amount; and he was to be included in the count's central general governance through the ascription to him of the right to sit on the count's council.

It becomes important at this point to ask what role the Italians might have played in the formation of the office of general receiver. Known for their commercial and financial skills, Italians found consistent employment in the financial administration of the Flemish counts, particularly during the reigns of Guy of Dampierre (1278–1305), Robert of Béthune (1299–1322), and Louis of Nevers (1322–1346). The preponderance of mintmasters, as well as general receivers, among Italian officeholders suggests that the Flemish counts were principally interested in Italians for their association with money. Italians were proven money-makers who had convenient access to networks capable of providing ready cash. It cannot be entirely coincidental that two of the Italian general receivers were appointed shortly after lending the count large sums of money. Indeed, Flemish counts probably hired Italians more on account of the chronic need for funds than because of any comital commitment to long-term fiscal reform.[1]

Significant though motives may be, it is the results that tell the tale. To be sure, it is possible that the Italians instituted reforms in the count's financial administration without specific comital mandate. The tenure of Gerard Lupichimi seems to be a case in point. But Gerard was the sole Italian to occupy the office during Guy of Dampierre's reign, and he held the office for only three years. In view of the fact that his successor, Jakemon of Deinze, held the office for at least eight years, it is nearly impossible to credit Gerard alone for the changes that took place in the count's financial administration in the last decade of Guy's reign. Instead, the splitting off of the general receivership from the count's household administration was foreshadowed not by Italian banking practices but by the organization of the count's local revenues already in place. Structural evidence demonstrates clear antecedents for this separation in the count's system of financial management on the local level.

Despite its strong antecedents in the local Flemish financial system, it is clear that the general receivership was something new. It differed from any other position in the comital government, such as bailiff, sergeant, or even the provost-chancellor of the eleventh through the early thirteenth centuries. The latter had official jurisdiction only over the count's domainal lands; he also held an ecclesiastical office in addition to his comital one. Unlike the loyalties of the receiver, therefore, those of the provost-chancellor were divided between count and Church. The office held by the general receiver was instead like that of bailiff insofar as its functions resulted from and participated in the exercise of the principle that comital interests surpassed local ones. In addition, by the first third of the fourteenth century, the general receiver, like the bailiff, had jurisdiction over a delineated area, an account of his activities, and a wage independent of the revenue he received. But bailiffs were local officials, whereas the general receiver acted from a central position. Furthermore, while bailiffs had a broad sphere of responsibility encompassing military, judicial, and feudal matters, the general receiver was a specialist, first in financial matters and later in both financial and judicial affairs. Fundamentally, then, bailiffs functioned primarily as territorial officials with jurisdiction over a variety of matters, whereas the general receiver, although also serving as a territorial official, had jurisdiction over some particular, functionally defined aspect of the count's government.

As a territorial official, the general receiver also differed from secretaries, sergeants, clerks, and even the traditional officers such as steward, chamberlain, butler, and constable, who had no jurisdiction beyond the household of the count. The general receiver was customarily referred to as the receiver of Flanders, while household officials remained the count's personal servants. The latter had no authority beyond that granted by the count for the performance of *ad hoc* tasks, while authority inhered in the general receivership. This authority had evolved through the development of the general receiver's responsibility for the performance of certain specified tasks whose routinization laid the basis first for the continued existence of the office and second for the increasing depersonalization of the office, leading to its evolution into a public position.

Central administrative offices such as that of the general receiver developed out of and, at the same time, were a constituent part of the transformation of the personal power of the prince into the impersonal authority of the state. Whether they evolved out of a department or functioned as the point of departure for the development of a bureau, the existence of central administrative offices in certain principalities throughout Europe provided princes with agents to whom they could entrust responsibility and its attendant power without ultimately diminishing their own authority. In fact the very routine which directed the actions of such officers, and which contributed so much to the impersonal nature of bureaus, went far to stabilize, sustain, and thus enhance the power of the prince.

The development of a department reflected the working of this internal dynamic and also encouraged it. Over the course of the thirteenth and fourteenth centuries, the ensemble of the general receiver's disparate responsibilities and diffuse authority gradually developed into a coherent sphere of activity. As this was achieved and as the office increased in complexity, a bureau developed. The count's fiscal department thus originated as a direct result of the confiding of a set of generic functions to the competence of a particular individual. It developed further out of the increasing complexity of the tasks with which the receiver was generally charged. Such a situation was uncommon in Northern Europe. Most departments evolved into coherent entities first before acquiring a specific head. In England, France, and elsewhere, functions associated with a specific sphere of activity, be it financial or judicial, usually came to be performed by certain officials who over time became associated with the performance of these tasks, without being formally charged with their execution. The union of functions and functionaries resulted in the evolution of a department; the position of department head did not usually develop first, as it did in Flanders.

The emergence of officials whose jurisdiction included the entire principality but whose functions were limited to a specific sphere of activity was thus not a peculiarly Flemish development. Other princes, such as the count of Artois, the duke of Brabant, and the duke of Lancaster in the fourteenth century, clearly profited by the Flemish example; by the late fourteenth century a general financial receiver was a significant member of these princes' councils. Nonetheless, the development of these offices in Artois and Brabant[2] owed at least as much to local currents and conditions as they did to borrowing from the Flemish. Economic and political conditions in Brabant and Artois were similar to those in Flanders, and administrative developments in this region show numerous logical similarities and parallels.

However, the presence of a general receiver in the train of John of Gaunt, duke of Lancaster, likely owed more to a direct borrowing of the Flemish model than to indigenous Lancastrian conditions.[3] The Lancastrian estates did not form a coherent geographical unit in England. Lands pertaining to John of Lancaster were scattered throughout England, and conditions in one area were not necessarily the determining characteristics of another. The office of general receiver was principally attached to a person, not to a department as in Flanders, Brabant, and Artois. Although it also was an office which could exist beyond the tenancy of any incumbent, the Lancastrian general receiver's existence depended less on administrative elements than on the enduring presence of the duke, who in his person centralized the management of his widely scattered lands in a manner more reminiscent of the French king in the thirteenth century than of the Flemish count in the fourteenth. Therefore, while the office of general receiver to the duke of Lancaster might have continued to exist despite the removal of its incumbent, the position to which it was attached, that of the duke of Lancaster, might not. And once this latter position was absorbed into that of king of England, as it was when Henry IV acceded to the English throne in 1399, the entity over which the Lancastrian general receiver had jurisdiction, the estates of Lancaster, ceased to have any real coherence or meaning.

That John borrowed the concept in its entirety is quite likely. His mother was an Hainalter, and the position had been in place in Hainaut since the late 1270s. Furthermore, John was no stranger to Flanders. Ghent, after all, was the city of his birth, and the exigencies of the Hundred Years War made it likely that the English prince's association with the county should be a close one. Finally, by the mid-fourteenth century, the office in Flanders had developed into an integral part of the Flemish count's government. The English duke's borrowing of the Flemish model probably testifies to a perception on his part that its efficiency would serve his needs better than any similar English model.

The phenomenon of impersonal centralization based on routine, as embodied in the evolution of the general receivership in Flanders, found expression in other European principalities, although elsewhere in Europe it did not necessarily manifest itself in the development of central financial institutions to the degree it did in Flanders. It is no accident that in Flanders centralization occurred in the realm of finance, and not, for example, in the realm of justice. Central judicial administration in Flanders lagged behind developments elsewhere in Europe, notably in England. This is doubtless attributable to the peculiar nature of the Flemish judicial system with its emphasis on negotiation instead of on judicial decision, so well analyzed by Van Caenegem, Nicholas, and others.[4] Such a state of affairs was a direct reflection of the influence and relative autonomy of various powerful groups, from nobles to urban patriciates, and the configuration of those groups gives Flemish medieval history its peculiar texture.

Equally, conditions specific to France, Aragon, England, and elsewhere influenced the direction a nascent cadre of administrative officials surrounding a particular prince might take. What the administrative developments throughout Europe had in common throughout the thirteenth and fourteenth centuries was the coalescence of special functions—either around an individual, such as the general receiver in Flanders, or a department, such as the Parlement in Paris—into discrete entities, entities that had territory-wide competence in the particular field in question, be it law, finance, diplomacy, or even the generating and collecting of letters, writs, and orders. Although the specific central government office and the form it took was directly tied to circumstances, economic or social, and although it was these circumstances which dictated that administrative developments would differ from area to area and from county to kingdom, the routine that stabilized and then sustained the performance of central government offices was not specific to any particular region or specialty. In the same way, while the likelihood of borrowing cannot be discounted, it can be more diverting than useful. Until such time as the notion is absorbed and integrated in a particular area—until that integration manifests itself in the establishment of a routine—the implementation of central administrative concepts remains, for all intents and purposes, *ad hoc.*

Notes

1. The appointment charter of Thomas Fini flatly states: "Et il nous doit permi ce pour les despens de no ostel fere chascune semaine delivrer chinc cents livres monnoie de Flandres" (Gaillard, #574).

2. See Delmaire for the general receivership of Artois and Martens and Uyttebrouck for the general receivers of Brabant.

3. For John of Gaunt and the Lancastrian estates, see Sydney Armitage-Smith, *John of Gaunt* (London, 1904).

4. R. C. Van Caenegem, *Geschiedenis van het strafrecht in Vlaanderen van de XIe tot de XIVe eeuw* (Brussels, 1954); *Geschiedenis van het strafprocesrecht in Vlaanderen van de XIe tot de XIVe eeuw* (Brussels, 1956); and *Judges, Legislators and Professors* (London, 1987); David Nicholas, "Crime and Punishment in Fourteenth Century Ghent," *RBPH* 48 n. 2 (1970), 289–334 and 48 n. 4 (1970), 1141–1176. See also J. Buntinx, *De audientie van de graven van Vlaanderen. Studie over het central grafelijk gerecht (c. 1330–c. 1409)* (Brussels, 1949); P. De Croos, *Histoire du droit criminal et pénal dans le comté de Flandres* (Brussels, 1878); A. Delcourt, *La vengeance de la commune. L'arsin et l'abbatis de maison en Flandre et en Hainaut* (Lille, 1930); F. L. Ganshof, "Etude sur le faussement de jugement dans le droit flamand des XIIe et XIIIe siècles," *Bulletin de la commission royale des anciennes lois et ordonnances de Belgique* 14 (Brussels, 1935), 115–140; and J. Gilissen, "Les légistes en Flandre aux XIIIe et XIVe siècles," *Bulletin de la commission royale des anciennes lois et ordonnances de Belgique* 14 (1934), 116–228, and *L'évolution de la plévine dans le droit flamand aux XIIIe et XIVe siècles* (Brussels, 1936).

Appendix A: Chronology of the Counts and Receivers of Flanders

5 December 1244 to
  29 December 1278
	COUNTESS MARGARET OF CONSTANTINOPLE
	  (abdicated in favor of son, Guy of Dampierre)
	  (d. 10 February 1280)

Philip of Bourbourg	1262(?)–1280

29 December 1278 to 1299	COUNT GUY OF DAMPIERRE
	  (abdicated in favor of son, Robert of Béthune
	    1299)
	  (d. 7 March 1305)

Lotin of Bruges	c. February 1280–*1282
Siger of Bailleul	*1282–*1283
Jeffrey of Ransières	*1283–*1285
Siger of Bailleul	*1285–*1289
Gerard Lupichimi	*1289–1292
Jakemon of Deinze	11 August 1292–c. 1300
1299 to 17 September 1322	COUNT ROBERT OF BÉTHUNE
Bonsignor de Bonsignori	1304–1306
Thomas Fini	18 April 1306–1309
Giles of Hertsberghe	1309–1311
Colard of Marchiennes	1311–1315
Guiduche Baldechon	1311–1317
Simon Vastin	1317–c. September 1322
17 September 1322 to 25 August 1346	COUNT LOUIS OF NEVERS
Conte Gualterotti	c. September 1322–1326
Donato Peruzzi	1326–1329
Simon Mirabello	1329
Jaquemard of Tournai	1329–1332
Vane Guy	1332–1333

*More than one individual bears the title "general receiver."

(13 May 1333 to 1 January 1334, Nicholas Guiduche informally exercised the office of general receiver.)

Ottelin Machet   1 January 1334–March 1334

(14 June 1334 to 1 October 1334, no general receiver.)

Nicholas Guiduche   21 September 1335–1337

Gerard de la Moor   1337–1338

(1338–1348, county in the hands of the Flemish towns. No general receiver.)

25 August 1346 to	COUNT LOUIS OF MALE
30 January 1384	
Gilles de le Walle	28 September 1348–December 1348
Bernard de Castre	6 March 1349
Andrew le Russe	6 August 1349–8 September 1350
Bernard de Castre	8 September 1350
John Van der Delft	25 May 1351–11 October 1359
John de la Fauchille	11 October 1359–4 October 1361
Peter de la Fauchille	4 October 1361–5 July 1365
Gossuin le Wilde	5 July 1365–June 1372

(June 1372, Gossuin le Wilde was appointed sovereign bailiff.)

Appendix B: The General Receivers (1262–1372): Class, Family, and Local Affiliations

Philip of Bourbourg (d. sometime before 3 December 1292)[1]

  Class: petty nobility; knighted, 1284.[2]

  Family: sister, Jeanne; spouse, Maria (noblewoman); son, Philip; possibly another son.[3]

  Area: Bourbourg?

Lotin of Bruges (disappears from records after 1294)[4]

  Class: burgher.[5]

  Family: possibly member of politically active Brugeois family.[6] Relatives unknown.

  Area: Bruges.

Siger of Bailleul (d. by 1301)[7]

  Class: noble; knight, Marshall of Flanders, 1282.[8]

  Family: married twice: Marie de Croix and Isabeau of Gistel; sister, Catherine, married into noble family of Haveskerk; two other sisters became nuns; three sons, John, Peter, and Siger; two daughters, Marie, and one known only as the wife of William van den Buch. Father, Baldwin of Bailleul, Marshall of Flanders.[9]

  Area: Bailleul area?

Jeffrey of Ransières (disappears from records from 1304)[10]

  Class: noble; knight.[11]

  Family: spouse, Margaret; son, John.[12]

  Area: unclear.

Gerard Lupichimi (disappears from records after 1296)[13]

  Class: Italian banker.[14]

  Family: nephew, John; brother, Francis Lupichimi.[15]

  Area: Florence.[16]

Jakemon (Gelert)[17] of Deinze (d. by 4 March 1304)[18]

  Class: cleric.[19]

  Family: two brothers, Enlars, Giles.[20]

  Area: Deinze.[21]

Bonsignor de Bonsignori (d. by 4 December 1315)[22]

  Class: Italian banker—member of the Bonsignori banking firm.[23]

  Family: spouse, Binda (of the Gallerani).[24]

  Area: Siena.

Thomas Fini (disappears from records after 1321)[25]

  Class: Italian banker: initially in business with brothers, joined Gallerani company sometime before 6 October 1303, two months after his brother Bartholomew had joined.[26]

Family: two brothers, Bartholomew and Mathew.[27]
Area: Siena.

Giles of Hertsberghe (disappears from records after 7 November 1336)[28]
Class: burgher.[29]
Family: spouse, Célie; children, Giles, Catherine, John; possible relative, Roger de Hertsberghe.[30]
Area: Bruges.[31]

Colard of Marchiennes (a.k.a. Nicolas of Marchiennes) (disappears from records after 27 August 1326)[32]
Class: cleric.[33]
Family: unknown.
Area: unknown.

Guiduche Baldechon (disappears from records after 1321)[34]
Class: banker?
Family: unknown.
Area: Siena.[35]

Simon Vastin (disappears from records after 1332)[36]
Class: unknown—may have been Italian or Flemish.
Family: possible relative, Monin Vastin.[37]
Area: unknown.

Conte Gualterotti (d. 1339)[38]
Class: burgher; banker.[39]
Family: spouse, Maria Rim, member of Rim family, connected with the powerful Borluut family of Ghent; six children, five girls, one boy, Sanders.[40]
Area: initially Florence, settled permanently in Ghent.[41]

Donato Peruzzi (disappears from records after 13 May 1331)[42]
Class: Italian banker.
Family: father, Pacino; brother, Philip; relatives, Guido and his son, Alexander.[43]
Area: Bruges of Florentine background.

Simon Mirabello (a.k.a. Simon van Halle) (assassinated 9 May 1346)[44]
Class: member of the urban patriciate of Ghent.
Family: Simon was illegitimate; father, John Mirabello; half-siblings, John, Frank, Elizabeth, and Clare; twice married, second spouse, Isabel (illegitimate sister of the count of Flanders); children, Katelijne, Lisbet, and perhaps Peter.[45]
Area: initially Florence, settled permanently in Ghent.

Jaquemard of Tournai (d. by 27 April 1333)[46]
Class: unknown.
Family: spouse, Katheline Christienne; son, John, and possibly Jacob.[47]
Area: Bruges?[48]

Vane Guy (d. by 1349)[49]
    Class: Italian banker.[50]
    Family: member of the Guidi family; father, Nicolas; brothers, Mouche
              (one of Philip VI of France's major officials) and Tote.[51]
    Area: Siena, with longtime association with the king of France.
Ottelin Machet (disappears from records after 1340)[52]
    Class: Italian, agent of the Peruzzi.[53]
    Family: Ottelin was illegitimate; father, Landuce; spouse, Natalie, daughter
              of Peter Bachterhalle; children, Louis, Johanna, Oddo, and an-
              other daughter.[54]
    Area: Florentine, eventually settled in Ghent.[55]
Nicholas Guiduche (a fugitive between 1343–1345, Nicholas disappears from the
    records after 1345)[56]
    Class: Italian, probably associated with banking.
    Family: sister, Sapience; relative, Jean.[57]
    Area: Siena.[58]
Gerard de la Moor (d. by 1346)[59]
    Class: noble; knight.[60]
    Family: son or grandson of Gerard le Moor; possible sons, Gerard and
              Gossuin.[61]
    Area: unknown.
Gilles de le Walle (disappears from records after 1356)[62]
    Class: burgher.[63]
    Family: father, Bartholomew; mother, Margaret; twice married, first to
              Catherine (last name unknown) and later to Margaret de Cou-
              debrouc; children, Giles, James, Bartholomew, John, Catherine,
              and Trude.[64]
    Area: Bruges.[65]
Bernard de Castre (disappears from records after 1351)[66]
    Class: cleric.
    Family: unknown.
    Area: unknown.
Andrew le Russe (disappears from records after 1371)[67]
    Class: wealthy burgher.
    Family: spouse, Marie Vierdincx; son, Oliver.[68]
    Area: Ypres.[69]
John Van der Delft (may have died soon after 9 July 1359)[70]
    Class: noble; knighted by 1356.[71]
    Family: son, William; possible father, Peter Van der Delft, possible son,
              Peter de le Delft; possible relative, Godevard Van der Delft.[72]
    Area: unknown.
John de la Fauchille (d. 26 September 1384 in a duel)[73]
    Class: burgher.[74]
    Family: father, Simon; sons, Peter and John.[75]
    Area: Ghent.

Peter de la Fauchille (may have sickened and died after 1 July 1366)[76]
    Class: burgher.
    Family: father, John; brother, John.
    Area: Ghent.
Gossuin le Wilde (last appears in records in 1392, after 52 years in comital ser-
    vice)[77]
    Class: noble; knight.[78]
    Family: spouse (name unknown); son, Marc.[79]
    Area: unknown.

Notes

1. He was alive in December 1291 (Nord, B1063 #3293). On 3 December 1292, however, a claim was brought against the residue of the estate of "feu Philippe de Bourbourg" (*ibid.*, B1544 #3418).

2. E. Warlop, *The Flemish Nobility to 1300* (Courtrai, 1975), 1:1:320. Warlop claims that Philip was never knighted (*ibid.*). It is probable that he confused Philip with his son, who had the same name. The Philip of Bourbourg whom Warlop describes as "the well known tax-collector of Flanders who was in the service of Countess Margaret" is indeed the Philip who was general receiver, but he does not appear to have been knighted until sometime between 14 January 1278 (at which time he is still referred to simply as the countess's faithful sergeant [Nord, B1564 n. 80 f. 24v #2437]) and 20 May 1284, when he is clearly called "chevalier" (G. des Marez, *La lettre de foire à Ypres au XIIIe siècle* [Brussels, 1901], 201 #110). On 15 June 1288, both he and his son, Philip, are described as knights (Coussemaker, *Bailleul*, 1:32 #30). As Warlop points out, Philip probably was not only never considered to be a member of the nobility but also purchased his son's knighthood, and perhaps even his own. For the best discussion of the development of the concept of nobility and the attitudes toward it in Flanders, see E. Warlop, *The Flemish Nobility to 1300*, 2 vols. (Courtrai, 1975).

3. RR, #270; Coussemaker, *Bailleul*, 1:32 #30; Warlop, *The Flemish Nobility*, 1:1:320.

4. Nord, B1561 n. 471 f. 128v #3574.

5. "recu par la main Lotin borgois de Bruges" (St.-Genois, #294).

6. Reiffenburg, 1:708–709.

7. He last appears alive in 1299 (De Smet and Wyffels, 770). Clearly, he had died by 1301 (Rennengue le roy, faite par Joffroi de Boi à Courtrai, 1301, RR, #257).

8. Nord, 10 H 231 n. 3697. He is called "knight" as early as 1265 (F. Bayley, *The Bailleuls of Flanders* [London, 1881], 33; Warlop, *The Flemish Nobility*, 2:1:644 #17bis). The title "Marshall of Flanders" was given to Baldwin and his heir in exchange for the "huisserie héréditaire," or hereditary bailiff (Nord, B1569 f. 13 #2404). Siger's sons do not bear the title, and it is likely that once Siger himself died it reverted to the count.

9. Gaillard, #208; Nord, B1561 n. 591 f. 162v #3465; Emile Gachet, "Le

couvent de l'abbiette à Lille. Sa fondation par la comtesse Marguerite et par Guy de Dampierre," *Messager des sciences* (1852), 50–51 #51, #52; Nord 130 H 5; Bayley, 41.

10. Nord, B449 #4437.

11. Nord, B449 #4181.

12. St.-Genois, #923; Codex, 1:303–304 #120.

13. Monier, *Les institutions financières,* 52.

14. D. E. Queller, "Diplomatic Personnel Employed by the Counts of Flanders in the Thirteenth Century," *Revue belge de philologie et d'histoire* 34 (1956), 395 and n. 2.

15. Nord, B4049 #3249; St.-Genois, #648.

16. "rechuit de mon signeur le conte de Flandre. . . . par le main Gerard Jehan de Florenche" (*ibid.,* #480).

17. "Jacobus Gelart dicitur de Donze, receptor flandrensis" (Gaillard, #528).

18. Nord, B449 #4437.

19. St.-Genois, #473.

20. Nord, B449 #4437.

21. "dicitur de Donze" (Gaillard, #528).

22. Bigwood, *Les livres des comptes des Gallerani,* 2:45.

23. Account of Eustace de le Spriete, bailiff of Nieuport, October 1304 to January 1305, RR, #1521.

24. Bigwood, *Les livres des comptes des Gallerani,* 2:44.

25. E. Boutaric, *Actes du Parlement de Paris* (Paris, 1867), 2:364 #6391, #6393).

26. Bigwood, *Le régime juridique,* 2:59–60.

27. *Ibid.*

28. Compte du receveur Nicolas Guiduche, du 7 septembre 1335 au 7 novembre 1336, RR, #5.

29. De Smet and Wyffels, 813.

30. Rennengue faite par Gilles de Hertsberghe à Bruges, 1311, RR, #272; Pol. chrs., #1306; A. Schouteet, *Regesten op de oorkonden,* 1:178–180 #472; bl. nr. #4748.

31. At one time Giles's family probably did come from Hertsberghe, but since Hertsberghe is only thirteen kilometers from Bruges, it is likely that they had moved to the larger town by the late thirteenth century. In 1292, "Johanne de Hertsbergh" was an alderman of Bruges (de Smet and Wyffels, 332), and Giles himself appears in the city accounts as early as 1290 (*ibid.,* 322). Unfortunately, it is not clear whether the two men were related. Giles did have a son, John, who may have been named after the alderman.

32. Vuylsteke, 1:501.

33. Nord, B1562 n. 422 f. 221–221v #5646.

34. Boutaric, 2:364 #6391, #6393; Chron. sup., #572.

35. St.-Genois, #1303; Vuylsteke, 1:15.

36. Nord, B7764 #157388.

37. Rennengue faite par Bartolemy Fin à Ypres, 1309, RR, #271; Rennengue faite par Gilles de Hertsberghe à Bruges, 1311 (*ibid.,* #272).

38. Rogghé, "de Gualterotti," 213 n. 7.

39. *Ibid.*, 200–202.

40. *Ibid.*, 213.

41. Vuylsteke, 1:82; see Rogghé, "de Gualterotti."

42. Pol. chrs., #358.

43. Bigwood, *Le régime juridique,* 1:184. For the Peruzzi in Flanders, see Raymond De Roover, *Money, Banking and Credit in Medieval Bruges* (Cambridge, 1948), 31–34.

44. N. de Pauw, "Les Mirabellos, dits van Halen," *Biographie Nationale* (Brussels, 1897), 14:875; Rogghé, "Simon de Mirabello," 46–49.

45. *Ibid.*, 7, 55; Schouteet, *Regesten op de oorkonden,* 2:193 #504; Nord, B1562 n. 422 f. 221–221v #5646; de Pauw, "Les Mirabellos," 872, 876.

46. Nord, B1565 n. 227 f. 38.

47. Compte du receveur Nicolas Guiduche, du 7 septembre 1335 au 7 novembre 1336, RR, #5; A. Desplanques, C. Dehaisnes, J. Finot, *Inventaire sommaire des archives départementales du Nord. Série B. Chambre des comptes de Lille, nr. 1561–3665* (Lille, 1872), 2:35; Bruges, Stadsarchief, Comptes erfelijke renten rentiers 1298–1395 (hereafter C.E.R.), Wezenboek, a. 1338 f. 8v.

48. He possessed a house in Bruges, located in front of King's Bridge (Nord, B1565 n. 277 f. 38).

49. Jules Viard, *Les journaux du trésor de Philippe VI* (Paris, 1940), #2614; Bigwood, *Le régime juridique,* 1:199–200.

50. Henri Pirenne, *Le soulèvement de la Flandre maritime de 1323–1328* (Brussels, 1900), xxvii n. 7.

51. Bigwood, *Le régime juridique,* 1:199–200.

52. From 26 March to 22 September 1340, he took part in the siege of Thun-l'Evêque as one of Louis de Nevers "ecuyers" (squires). Perhaps he died in this conflict (Jean Froissart, *Oeuvres,* M. le Baron Kervyn de Lettenhove, ed. [Brussels, 1868–1877], 21–215).

53. Bigwood, *Le régime juridique,* 1:59, 2:10–11; Van Duyse and de Busscher, #370, #379; Vuylsteke, 2:124–125.

54. Compte du receveur, Thomas Fin, du 25 décembre 1308 à juin 1309, RR, #1; Rogghé, "Machet," 190, 193; Pol. chrs., #1306 (328, 329).

55. For Ottelin and his family, see Paul Rogghé, "Het Florentijns geslacht Machet in Vlaanderen," *Appeltjes van het Meetjesland* 16 (1965), 188–196.

56. de Pauw and Vuylsteke, 2:272, 352, 457.

57. Rennengue faite par Jean de le Delft à Courtrai, 1351, RR #282; Nord, B1565 n. 253 f. 41.

58. Bigwood, *Le régime juridique,* 1:215.

59. Simon de Mirabello held lands of Gerard's widow (Rogghé, "Simon de Mirabello," 18–19), and Simon was assassinated on 9 May 1346. Gerard was one of Louis of Nevers's knights at the siege of Thun-l'Evêque in the early part of 1340 (Froissart, 21:220) and may have died then.

60. Pol. chrs., #442.

61. De Smet, "Corpus Cronicorum Flandriae," 162; *Annales Gandenses,* trans.

Hilda Johnston (New York, 1951), 76, 85, 89; Limburg-Stirum, *Louis de Male,* 1:221–222 #222.

62. Pol. chrs., #548.

63. On 18 May 1357, he is referred to as "lord" (bl. nr. #7276).

64. *Ibid.,* #4376; Pol. chrs., #249; #1320; Nord, B1596 f. 117 #8277; Schouteet, *Regesten op de oorkonden,* 2: #200, #471; C.E.R., Wezenboek, a. 1343 f. 22; a. 1344 f. 32; a. 1345 f. 1, 21; a. 1350 f. 8.

65. From at least 9 August 1329 (Pol. chrs., #334) to 18 June 1337 (*ibid.,* #427) he was one of the treasurers of the city of Bruges.

66. Limburg-Stirum, *Louis de Male,* 2:121–124 #848.

67. Nord, B1569 f. 60 #8804.

68. V. Gaillard, *Archives du conseil de Flandre* (Ghent, 1856), 129 #14.

69. Limburg-Stirum, *Louis de Male,* 1:127–131 #126.

70. Nord, B1596 f. 99v #8081.

71. Limburg-Stirum, *Louis de Male,* 2:147–148 #875.

72. Nowé, *Les baillis comtaux,* 374, 379, 402, 404; Gilliodts-Van Severen, *Coutume de Furnes,* 4:405; Nord, B1596 f. 147 #8402; B3232 #111716.

73. Froissart, 21:181.

74. *Ibid.,* 21:180; Nord, B1565 n. 217 f. 35v.

75. Froissart, 21:181–182; Nord, B1565 n. 217 f. 35v.

76. While his father continued in comital service for almost another twenty years, Peter disappears from the records after 1 July 1366 (Nord, B1566 n. 271 f. 71 #9797). It is possible that he was either too sick to continue or may have even died in office, or perhaps he simply left the comital administration.

77. Buntinx, *Audientie,* 77.

78. The first time Gossuin is called "knight" is on 29 October 1366 (Nord, B1567 f. 57 #9834). Up to this time he is listed as a squire (Froissart, 21:213; Buntinx, *Audientie,* 77).

79. Nord, B1567 n. 57 #9834.

Appendix C: The Commissions of the General Receivers of Flanders

1. Appointment of Jakemon of Deinze to be general receiver—11 August 1292 (Archives Départementales du Nord à Lille. Série B. 4050 #3382)

Nous Guis, cuens de Flandres et marchis de Namur, faisons savoir à tous ke nous nostre foiaule clerc, Jakemon de Donze, canone de Courtray, avons estauuli et estauulissons souvrain et général recheveur de toute nostre conté de Flandres et des appartenances jusques à nostre rapiel.

Si mandons et commandons à tous nos baillius, recheveurs et censisseurs de nos rentes et de nos censes de nostre devant dit contei et des appartenances ke au devantdit Jakemon il obéissent com à nostre recheveur, et à lui paicent et respondent de ce kil nous doient orendroit et deveront en après, tant ke li dis Jakemes sera nostra recheveures, et tout ce ke on paiera au devantdit Jakemon dont on ara ses lettres pendans, nous nos en tenrons à paiiet.

Par le tesmoing de ces lettres saielées de nostre saiel, ki furent faites et données en l'an de grace mil deus cens quatre vins et douze, le lundi après le jour Saint Lorent.

2. Appointment of Thomas Fini to be general receiver—18 April 1306 (Gaillard, #574)

Nous Robiers, coens de Flandres, faisons savoir à tous que nous avons mis et establi, mettons et establissons pour nous et en no lieu no chier et foiaule Thomas Fin, marcheant et compaignon dele compaignie des Gallerans de Siene, recheveur souverain et especiael de toutes nos rentes, revenues et issues de toute nostre conté de Flandres, de no terre d'Alost, de Geraumont, de Wayse, des Quatre Mestiers et de toutes les apendances pour prendre à lever, rechevoir et esploitier de toutes les revenues, les rentes, esplois et issues qui porront venir et iestre en quelconques manière que ce soit en no conté de Flandres et en nos terres dessus dites et apertenances comme dit est qui à nous apertienent.

Si mandons et commandons à tous ceaus à qui il apertient et puet apertenir rechevres d'espiers, des briefs, chenseurs, rentiers, baillius, serians, prevos, maieurs, eschevins, justices, et à toute autre manière de gens de quele condition que il soient, qui aucunes de nos chenses et de nos biens dessus dis ont ou oront entremains pour le tans passé et pour le tans avenir obbéissent, paechent et delivrechent à no devant dit recheveur ou à son certain command tout ce quil auront rechuit et rechevront et non à autre et obéissent à no dit recheveur comme à nous en son office faisant. Et lui avons donné et donnons plain pooir et mandement especiale. . . . auctorite de chensir de donner à chense toute manières de chose qui sont et seront à donner ou que on a acoustumé à fere en nostre terre dessus dite. Et avons rapelé et rapelons toute manière de recheveurs de quele condition que il soient les quel rapeler. . . . fors cheaus qui nos recheveurs i mettra et establira des ore en avant par ses lettres hors mis les hyretaules recheveurs.

Et tout ce que li devant dis recheveurs fera achensira et procurrera des choses dessus dites, nous le tenrons et ferons tenir ferm et establis jusques à nostre rapel et sauve nostre hyretage. Et ensur que tout à savoir est que nous ferons à nullui nul assenement se ce n'est par le dit Thomas no recheveur. Et il nous doit permi ce pour les despens de no ostel fere chascune semaine delivrer chinc cents livres monnoie de Flandres.

En tiesmoinage de la quel chose nous avons à ces presentes lettres fet mettre no séel pendant les queles furent faites et données à Male et de Bruges le lundi après le quinzaine de Pasques en l'an de grace mil trois cents et siis.

3. Extension of the authority of Thomas Fini as general receiver—7 November 1308 (Gaillard, #588; published in Codex, 2:97–98 #238)

Nous Robers, couens de Flandres, faisons savoir à tous, ke nous avons mis et establis, mettons et establisons, pour nous et ens nostre lui nostre amey, foiable Thumas Fin, nostre recheveur de Flandres, pour oster et pour mettre baillius, sous-baillius dans toute nostre conté et pooir de Flandres, en quelsconques villes, casteleries ou terroirs que ce soit appartenans à faire à nous, toutes les fois que il lui samblera (utile) pour nous et pour nostre pourfit, et ke il ou auchun d'eaus ne seroient obbéssant à lui et à ces commans pour nostre besoingnes, toutez les fois que il en seroit requis par lui; si mandons et commandons tant et si acertes que nous poons et savons à tous nostre baillis, sous baillis, serians, pour nostre dite conté et pooir de Flandres, quyconques le soit ou sera, à qui il poeut appartenir, que il à nostre dit recheveur et à ses commans obbéissent et soiient obbéissant, toutes les fois ke il leur en requerra pour nostre besoignes et nostre droit maintenir . . . comme il lui semblera le mieus et plus pourfitable pour nous et pour nostre dit pais; et ce que establit et ordeneit en sera par luy, si comme dit est . . . il ara délivrey ses lettres, nous le tenons et tenrons ferme et estable sauf nostre hieretage et jusques à nostre rapiel.

Encore lui donnons nous plain pooir, pour nous et en en luy de nous, de conter et de demander et faire compte final à tous eschevins, queries, burghemeestres, asseurs, ceulleur et recheveurs par tout nostre contey et pooir, de quel condition que il soiient, de toutes tailles faites par nostre dit paiis pour quelconques causse que elles aiient esteit faites (ou donneez) pour les deniers des neef des Zélandais, de sodoiiers, des florins de le court de Romme, de tous nostre dons ki nous ont esteit fait par nostre dit paiis pour nostre voiiages que nous avons fais en France par pluissieurs fois, et de tous arriérages de toutes tailles faites dariere, jusques au jour duy. . . . eaus constraindre et faire constraindre par le prisse de leurs cors et de leurs biens ki de auchune cosse seroient tenut pour les raisons des tailles desusdites. . . . conte fait de luy à eaus.

Si mandons et requerons à tous eschevins, queriers . . . pointeurs et recheveurs des dictes (tailles à) qui il poeut appartenir, que il à Thumas Fin, nostre dit recheveur de Flandres . . . final, et lui paicent et délivrecent sans aultre commandement atendre de nous, et tout cou dont il en seront tenut par le fin de leur compte. . . . ce ne laissent mie si chier comme il ont. . . . eur le paiis de nous, d'eaus et de nostre dit paiis, car ce que fait et ordenney en sera par luy. . . . à ses lettres pendans, nous le prometons fermement et loialement à tenir et à aemplir envers nous.

Par le tiesmoing de ces lettres séeléez de nostre grant séel, qui furent faites et donnéez à Yppre, l'an de grace mil trois cens et wit, le joesdi prochain après le jour le Toussains.

4. Commission to Nicolas Guiduche to receive the count's revenues—
20 November 1334 (Archives Départementales du Nord à Lille. Série B 1565 n.
513 f. 80v)

Nous, Loys, etc., faison savoir à tous que comme nos ames vallez Nicolas Guiduche se soit de nostre commant entremis de par nous de rechevoir par ce que nous naviens point de recheveur depuis le xiv jour de juing lan mille

CCC XXX IV jusques au premier jour d'octobre lan dessus dit, plusieurs de nos rentes, revenues, et autres manières de biens et esplois de nostre conté de Flandre. Sachent tout que nous pour le temps présent et avenir avons et aurons ferme et estable et aggréable tout ce que par no dit vallet et ses sousestablis a esté et sera fait recheu et quitié des choses dessus dites par le temps dessus dictes et avenir. Et dont il a donné et donra ses lettres sous son séel parmi tout que de ce quil a et aura receu et quité de par nous par le temps il nous doit et devra rendre bon compte.

5. Appointment of Nicolas Guiduche to be general receiver—21 September 1335 (Archives Départementales du Nord à Lille. Série B 1565 n. 489 f. 76v)

La commission baillie à Nicolas Guiduce pour estre
recheveur de la conté de Flandre

Nous Loys etc., faisons savoir à tous que nous nostre ame vallet Nicolas Guiduce avons fait et establi, faisons, mettons, et establissons recheveur de no contei de Flandres dessus dicte et des appartenances et appendances dicells. Et li avons donné et donnons plen pooir et auctorité avoeques mandement especial de recevoir et esploitier et fere recevoir et esploitier pour nous tout ce que d'en nous est et sera en nostre dicte conté de Flandres et ces appartenances et appendances dicelle dedens le terme quil sera nos recheveur de quiter et donner lettres de quitance de ce que il aura receu pour nous de acenser et donner à ferme et à chense nos thonlieus et autres chenses et fermes et de fere toutes autres choses que à office de bon et loyal recheveur appartient et sont acoustumées à fere en temps passé par les recheveurs de Flandres, ja fust ce que aucunes dicelles requissent mandement especial, promittans en bonne foy avoir ferme et estable tout ce que li dis Nicolas aura recheu, esploitié et quitté pour nous et dont il aura compté avons ou à nos gens pour nous et toutes autres choses quil pour cause del office dessus dit ara fait en nom de nous et pour nous durant le temps de son du office. De rechief nous avons promis et promettons au dit Nicolas affin quil puisse miex faire et exacter l'office de la dicte recheverie à fere et tenir les chose qui sensuit:

Cest assavoir que de toutes choses raisonnables que il par li et par ses sousestabliz aura fait et fait fere pour cause de son office tout il pourait aquirre en aucune manière la malucellance davoire fussent nobles ou nonoblez nous le devons et devrons garantir et porter et ses sousestabliz vers tous et contre tous.

Item, que nous ne trouvons ne ne devons trouvé nulles plaintes, ne informations, ou rapors que on nous feroit au valroit fere contre le dit Nicolas sans le appeller et oir devans celix que les dictes plaintes, rapors, ou informations deliverent fere.

Item, que tout no baillius et autres officyers le dit Nicolas estant nostre receveur seront fait mis et ostei quant li cas si offeront par son conseil selont ce que profitable li samblera estre pour nous.

Item, que nous orrons ou ferons oir ses comptes une fois chascun an sans faute.

Item, que nous ne autre de par nous ne le prefferons de finer autre son povoir.

Item, que pour fere le dit office nous li baillerons chascun an CCCCC par gros tournois pour 12 d. parisis par cause de gages.

Item, quil aura en nostre ostel et quant il ysera delivrance à chinc chevaus, VIII chandelles et autres choses si avant et en la manière que li recheveur de Flandres sont acoustumé anchienement à avoir en lostel des contes de Flandres.

Item, que tout ce que li dis Nicolas scellera, assenera et quittera par son scel ce quelque chose que ce soit pour cause de son dit office qui nous pourroit toucher sauve nostre heritage sera tenir et l'aurons ferme et estable sera tenu et l'aurons ferme et estable.

Item, que tout no baillius et autres officiers paieront ce quil auront recheu et esploitie au dit Nicolas comme recheveur non à autre.

Item, que nous ne ferons nul assenement sans li dit Nicolas li estant nostre recheveur.

Item, que nous aquitterons le dit Nicolas en ses lettres de tout ce que il sera trouvé par ses comptes que il ara receu et finé pour nous.

Mandons à tous nos baillius et autre iustices que le dit Nicolas en faisant les chose dessus dictes et tout ce qui sen depent diligent obéissant et entendent sauf en tous cas nostre heritage et le dit Nicolas durant au dit office iusques nostre rappel.

Par le tesmoing de ces lettres scellés de nostre scel. Donné à Bruges le XXI jour de septembre lan de grace mil CCCXXXV.

Par Monsieur le conte en son conseil en quel estoient li chastellan de Diquemue, li sire de Salise, messire Rogier Briseteste, messire Thierry Notage, vous, Rogier Thynis, Thierry de Belsele, Henri de Meetkerk et Ottenin Macet.

6. Appointment of Andrew le Russe to be general receiver—6 August 1349
(Limburg-Stirum, Louis de Male, 1:127–131 #126)

Commission Andrieu le Russe pour estre
recheveur de Flandres

Nous Loys, etc., faisons savoir a tous, que par nostre grand conseil ou quel il y avoit de ceux de nostre linage, chevaliers, clercs, escuyers et bourgoys, et par le commun volenté et requeste de nos trois bonnes villes Gand, Bruges et Ypre, pour le plus apparant et évidant proffit de nous et de nos bonnes gens, nous avons par bonne et meure délibération et avis, fait, ordené, commis, et establi, faisons, ordenons, commettons et establissons, par le teneur de ces présentes lettrez, nostre amé et feal vallet et conseillier, Andrieu le Russe, bourgoys de nostre ville dYppre, pour estre nostre recheveur souverain en nostre conté et pays de Flandres et ressors et appendances, en la fourme, manière et par les conditions qui s'esuient:

Premièrement, quil puist recevoir et faire recevoir, prendre et lever par ses députés toutes nos rentes, revenues, censses, fourfais, explois, ammendes, subventions, dons, redevances, debtes, arriérages, aventures, ges de mer, acques, revenues et seignourie de nos monnoies et toutes autres choses que à nous porront estre dehuwes et appertenir, comment que ce soit, et que on les appelle en quelconques manière ou par quelconques cause que che pourroit estre, sans ce que nous ne autres depar nous les puist rechevoir que il ou si députés tant seulement, et se autre personne queconque les recevoit, che seroit de nulle valeur.

Item, lui ottroyons nous, que non contrestant que il soit nostre recheveurs il puis tenir sa bourgoisie, bon compte faisant à nous de sa recepte.

Item, que nous ne autres depar nous ne ferons assignement, quictance, ne don à heritage ne à vie sans le conseil et sceu dou dit Andrieu, et se par aventure le contraire en estoit fait il sera de nulle valeur.

Item, nous volons que par son especial conseil et avis nos hostels soit ordenés de pouvéances de mesnies, de retenues, de congiemens de gens et de toutez autres choses.

Item, que tout no bailliu soient commis et renouvelé par son conseil, et en samblable maniére tout eschievin de nos bonnes villes et pays.

Item, tout autre officyer, vendere et petit bailli appertenant à estre renouvelé par le recheveur de Flandres, soient rapellé et renouvelé par ses lettrez toutes fois que mestiers sera.

Item, que nuls de nos baillius de nostre dicte conté ne puis quiter ne lessier appaisir à lui nulle amende de LX lib. ne deseure, et que en ce no dit bailli ne puissent allegier, ne proposer nulle costume anchienne en contraire.

Item, nous ne quitterons ne ferons accord d'amendes nulle à nous appertenans, ne renderons le pays, le teste ne le vie à personne nulle qui lait fourfaite sans le conseil dou dit Andrieu et par lui. Et samblablement nous ne quitterons ne soufferons quiter par personne nulle nul disime, denier et droiture à nous appertenans de vandages, alienations our esclichemens de fiefz quelconques, sans l'expres conseil et consent de nostre dit recheveur; et ou cas que nous par ignorance ou introduction en feriesmes le contraire, si volons nous quil soit et demeure de nulle valeur.

Item, volons nous quil puist baillier tous nos thonlieus, terres, polres, wagnages sur mer, acques, fourfaiturez et toutes autres assises et maletotes de nos bonnes villes et autres à cense et y mettre son ottroy à termes convenables, si comme milleur. . . . semblera.

Item, que se il estoit trouvé que nuls euist recheu en sa recepte aucune somme de deniers sans son sceu et cil qui recheu lauera le rendera et mettera. . . . avant che que nos dis recheveurs soit tenus de faire nulle délivrance en nostre hostel.

Item, se il avenoit que pour loccoison de nous il s'obligast en. . . . de deniers, ou fesist aucun markiet à meschief. Nous len porterons et warandirons de tous damages et len promettons à acquitter.

Item. . . . mie qu'il soit tenus, obligées ne constrains de payer aucunes sommes de deniers ou obligations dehuwes et faites devant la date de ces lettrez. . . . nous ou de par nous.

Item, lui donnons nous povoir et autorité de saisir, rataindre et remettre à nostre table et recepte tous biens fourcelés, fiefs. . . . meubles, heritages et fourfaitures à nous appertenans, comment que ce soit, sans estre calengnies ou repres daucun.

Item, volons nous et deffondons. . . . de nos officyers, receveurs, baillius ou censiers quelconques paient aucuns assignemens fais devant la date de ces lettrez sans le sceu et accourd dou. . . . Andrieu.

Item, lui promettons nous que toutes lettrez qu'il baillera de quittances, de rapiaus de bannis, conduis, testes rendues, assennemens et autrez. . . . appertenans à son office, nous les aurons pour fermes et agréablez.

Item, que toutes chose que le dit Andrieu et si deputé auront fait en l'occoison. . . . office nous les en porterons oultre et warandirons envers tous et contre tous, aussi bien après son compte et que nous l'auriemes delessié de nostre. . . . comme le dit office faisant. Et que son office durant, il ses familiers et deputés seront frans et paisivles tenus de toutes choses, rancunes et. . . . contre tous et envers tous, gentils et autres, sans che que il se melle nullement contre yceux ne euls encontre lui, hors mis de pais et accors. . . . et quiconques feroit au contraire sour lui ou sour ses familliers ou deputés, nous le crairiemes à nous estre fait comme sur nostre propre. . . . aucuns débas se meust entre parties dedens nostre conté, nobles ou nonnoblez, dou quel estat que il soient, si volons nous que le dit Andrieu ait. . . . les parties constraindre à faire trieuwes et pais, tout en la manière que bon li samblera et que nous meismes le porriens faire.

Item, que toutes fois. . . . nous requerra de oîr ses comptes, nous les ferons oîr sans dylay et yceux comptes oîs et examinés nous lui donrons dedens les. . . . nomination d'yceux nos lettrez de quittance; et se il avenoit que il euist aucune chose oubliée à compter sans fraude, en date ou en recepte. . . . la ou il appertenra, sans ce que pour celle cause il enchie en amende aucune envers nous, et ne desmetterons nullement le dit. . . . jusques à tant que plaine satisfaction lui soit faite de ce qu'il auroit plus paié et finé que recheu; de faire toutes les choses dessus dictez. . . . et toutes autres qui à bon et loyal recheveur appertienent affaire, nous avons donné et donnons à nostre dit recheveur povoir et. . . . expresses que non expresses as gages de mil livre de tournois de Flandres par an sans délivrance a court.

Si mandons et com. . . . renneurs, receveurs de briefz, de renenghes, de rentes hors renenghes, censiers, thonluiers, fermiers, à tous nos autres officiers. . . . les habitans, nobles et nonnobles, de nostre conté et pays de Flandres dessus dit et chascun à par lui, pour tant que à lui appertenra, que il et. . . . et délivrent à nostre dit recheveur toutes maniéres de rentes, revenues, dons, redevances, explois, amendes, fourfaistures, émolumens. . . . dehuwes à present et seront en temps à venir durant le terme de sa receverie, et avoeques ce il et chascuns dyaus obéissent. . . . de receverie dessus dit, et che que il y appertient en la maniére dessus dicte, si avant que il feroient à nous se présens y estiens, et toutes les. . . . aistime par lui volons nous estre fermes, estables et bien tenues, et les promettons loyaument tenir et remplir de point en point sans. . . . souffrir à faire al encontre par nous ne par autre comment que ce peuist estre, sauve en tous cas nostre héritage, ces lettrez durans en leur. . . . nostre volenté et rapiel.

Par le tesmoing de ces lettrez séellés de nostre séel. Donné à Gand, le VJ jour daoust lan XLIX.

Par le conte en son grand conseil ouquel furent messire dAinghien, mess. Loys de Namur, li signeur dAishove, de Praet, de Reninghsvliete, de Halewin. . . . Gossuin de le Moere, mess Henri Sporkin, vous, mestre

Jehan de Hertsberghe, mestre Testard de le Wastine, Gherard Leuward et
Henry le Pape.

7. Appointment of John Van der Delft to be general receiver—25 April 1351
(Limburg-Stirum, Louis de Male, 2:121–124 #848)

Commission de Jehan de le Delft estre
receveur de Flandres

Nos Loys, etc., que reguardans à nostre evidant proffit, voellans remettre en segur estat et bonne ordenance nos rentes, revenues, advenues,
fourfaitures et nobleches de nostre conté et pays de Flandres, qui par grant
temps ont esté démenée hors de riule de raison, tant par les guerres et
esmeutes passées, comme par mutations de receveurs et officyers renouveller en nostre dit pays de Flandres, en grant péril de nous et nos hoirs,
estre griefment deshéritez se de hastui remede ni eussiens pourveu; confians
de la loyauté et discrétion de nostre amé et feal vallet, Jehan de le Delft, nous
avons ycelui Jehan seul et pour le tout fait, mis, constitué et establi faisons,
mettons, constituons et establissons par le teneur de cez présentes lettrez
nostre receveur de nostre conté et pays de Flandres, des ressors et apperte-
nances dycelle; auquel Jehan nous avons donné et donnons pooir et auctorité de recevoir toutes nos rentes, revenues, proffis, advenues, fourfaitures, dons, courtoisies, tailles, gets de mer, debtes, arriarages, proffis de
nos monnoies, watergraveries de nostre mour et toutes autres choses quelconques appertenans à nous, comment que ce puist estre, dedens notre dite
conté de Flandres, sans riens excepter, en baillant en nom de nous à ferme et
à censse, à termes convenables, toutes censes et choses appertenans à office
de receveur, et recevant et faisans compositions á pais de toutes choses, tant
de rachat de tiestes de bannis comme dautres aventures, si comme il est de
costume, à nostre plus grant et apparant proffit; et volons que toutes fois,
que mestiers sera, il puist renouveler et constituer toutes manieres dofficyers dedens nostre dicte conté et pays de Flandres, ensi quil a esté
anchienement acostumé; avoeques ce volons nous que toutes fois que
aucunes amendes, fourfaitures ou droitures seront à nous acquises ou
engenrées, comment que ce soit, que il meismes les puist lever et recevoir et
donner en quittances à parties, non contrestans aucuns usages maintenus
par nos officiers en contraire dou temps passé, lesquels en celui cas nous
rappellons, et par espécial commandons et eniondons à nostre dit receveur,

que ou cas quil trouvera aucun de nos officyers quiconques il soit qui dedens son office quittera aucune chose ou lessera passer négligamment ou donra le nostre à censse ou excedera en son office, en damage de nous, il tantost et de fait mette nostre main à yceli, en souspendant et rappellant la chose dont le dit officyer auroit abusé, jusques à tant que par nous à nostre conseil le deffaute fuist adreché et le dit officier corrigié.

Item, volons nous que des maintenant il face préparacion de tous les membrez, grans et petis, quelconques qui dépendent ou ont dépendu et qui anciennement ont esté de nostre recept de Flandres, en esclarchissant yceux de toutes les charges dont il ont esté et sont chargiés, affin que li jimpeche-mens sur yceux fais et maintenus contre raison soient ostés, et li rachat qui diceulz se pevent et doivent faire soient fais hastiument par nous et nostre conseil, mesmement que plus convenable chose de deschargier nos propres rentes anchiennes que tendre à nouvielles acquerre et ycelles lessier; et avons promis et promettons à nostre dit receveur, que quelconques pais, accord ou quittances que nous ferons dedens notre dit pays, nous lui lairons joir des deniers qui en verront et escherront, ne ne ferons ne soufferons estre fait nul assennement dou jour de hui en avant dedens nostre dit pays, sur nos receptes sans le conseil de nostre dit receveur; et généralment et es-pécialment nous lui avons donné et donnons ou dit office faisant tout autel pooir comme nous meismes auriemes pour faire en yceli toutes choses qui à bon et loyal receveur pevent et doivent appertenir à faire; et pour le dit office faire et exercer par le dit Jehan, comme dit est, nous lui avons ottroiés et ottroions les gages de mil livres par. par an, et des maintenant nous avons pris et prendons le dit Jehan, ses valles, familliers et mesnies et biens quelconques en nostre sauve et espéciale garde et protection, et le promet-tons à garandir, censer et warder y tous jours mais enviers tous et contre tous de toutes choses quil auroit faites et exercées ou dit office, sans souffrir nullement que aucuns griefs ou rancunes lui en soient fais ou portés en aucun tempts.

Item, volons nous et ordenons, que sans enfraindre, nos renenghes soient tenues cascun an une fois, au terme acostumé, et semblablement les comptes de nos baillis trois fois l'année.

Si mandons et commandons estroitement à tous nos baillis, sousbaillis, sergans, justichiers, officyers, mestre de nos monnoies, thonluiers, reneurs, receveurs de briefs, en renenghes et de rentes hors renenghes, watergraves, receveurs de fourfaitures et tous autres quelconques il soient de nostre conté et pays dessus dit, à qui il touche, peut touchier, que à nostre dessus dit receveur en ceste office faisant, entendent, respondent et obéissent diligamment, sans contredit, et à lui ou à son certain délégué seulement et à nul autre délivrent les deniers et proffis de leurs receptes, car nostre entente nest mie ainchois deffendons que nulles autres lettrez que les nostrez propres les lettrez de nostre dit receveur passent ou soient receues par les maistres de nos comptes; et ou cas que nos dessus dis receveur nous requerra de ses comptes hoir pour savoir nostre estat ou pour lui esclarchir et deschargier de nostre recepte, nous serons tenus de y faire entendre, et ce par restat de son compte final est trouvé que il ait plus avant finé pour nous que receu, nous lui devrons faire assennement souffisant diceli sourplus; de rechief volons nous et ottroions à nostre dit receveur, que si après son compte il estoit trouvé que il euist plus délivré et finé que receu, nous lui en ferons bon et soffissant paie ou assennement avant ce que nous le démettons de nostre office. Et ou cas que aprés le dit compte il fuist trouvé que il euist aucune chose recheu dont il neuist point compté et fait recepte, nous lui ottroions que en paiant à nous y ce que trouvé seroit, comme dit est, il se puist acquiter sans malengien; et samblablement volons nous que se il avoit aucune chose oublié à mettre en date à son proffit il y puist adies revenir, en monstrant soffissament les parties, sauve en tous cas nostre héritage, et ces lettrez durans jusques à nostre rappiel.

Donné à Bapalme, le XXVe jour d'Avril lan chinquante et un.

Par monsieur le conte, present mons. de Renighersvliete et vous.

8. Appointment of John de la Fauchille to be general receiver—11 October 1359 (Archives Départementales du Nord à Lille. Série B. 1596 f. 100–100v #8146)

Commission à Jehan de le Faucille pour estre receveur de Flandrez

Nous Loys etc., faisons savoir à tous que nous confians en la loyauté, discretion et diligence de nostre amé et feal varlet Jehan de le Faucille, nous avons icelli Jehan seul et pour le tout fait, mis, constitué, et establi, faisons, mettons, constituons et establissons par le teneur de ces presentes lettres, nostre recheveur de nostre conté et pays de Flandres, des ressors et appartenances diceuli auquel Jehan nous avons donné et donnons pooir et auctorité de rechevoir toutes nos rentes, revenues, proffis, advenues, fourfaitures, dons, courtoisies, tailles, gets de mer, debtes. arrièrages, prouffit de nos monnoies, watergraveries de nostre mour et toutes autres choses quelconques appartenans à nous comment que ce puist estre dedens nostre dicte conté de Flandres sans riens excepter. En baillant en nom de nous à ferme et à cense à termes convenablez toutes chenses et choses appartenans à office de recheveur et rechevant et faisant compositions et pais de toutes choses tant de rachat de tiestes de bannis comme dautres aventures sicomme il est de acostumé ~~dedens nostre dicte conté et pays de Flandres ainsi quil est anchienement acoustumé par conseil~~ à nostre plus grant prouffit et plus apparant. Et volons que toutesfois que mestier sera il puist renouveller et constituer toutes manières dofficyers dedens nostre dicte conté et pays de Flandres ainsi quil est anchienement acoustumé par consent, conseil, et commandement de nous. Aveuques ce volons nous que toutes fois que aucunes amendes, foufaitures ou droitures seront à nous aquises ou engenrées comment que che soit que il mesmes les puist lever et rechevoir et donner en quitance à parties sans ce que aucuns de nos baillius de nostre dicte conté de Flandre puist quitier ou laissier apaisier à lui aucune amende de soissante livres ou deseure, non contrestans aucuns usaiges maintenus par nos officyers en contraire du temps passé les quels en chelli cas nous rappellons. Et par especial commandons et emoignons à nostre dit recheveur que ou cas quil trouvera aucuns de nos officiers quiconque il soit qui dedens son office quittera aucune chose ou laissera passer neggligaumment ou donra le nostre à cense ou excedera en son office en domaige de nous il tantost et de fait meche nostre main à ycelle en suspendant et rappellant la chose dont li dit officyer auroit abusé jusques à tant que par nous et nostre conseil la deffaute fuist adrechie et le dit officyer corrigié.

Item, volons nous que des maintenant il fache preparation de tous les membres, grans et petis, quelconques qui dependent ou ont dependu et qui anchienement ont esté de nostre recepte de Flandres, en esclarcissant yceulz de toutes les charges dont il ont esté et sont chargiés afin que li empechement sur yceulz fait et maintenus contre raison soient ostes et li rachat qui diceulx se pevent et doivent faire soient fais hastivement par nous et nostre conseil mesmement que plus convenable chose est de deschargier nos propres rentes anchienes que tendre à nouvelles acquerre et ycelles laissier. Et avons promis et promettons à nostre dit recheveur que quelconques pais, accort, ou quitance que nous ferons dedens nostre dit pais de Flandres nous lui laurons joir des deniers qui en venront et escherront. Et ne quitterons ne ne soufferrons quiter par personne nulle nul disime denier et droiture à nous appartenans de vendaiges, alienations, ou esclichemens de fiefs quelconques sans l'expres conseil de nostre dit recheveur. Ne ne ferons ne sufferons estre fait nul assenement dou jour dhuy en avant dedens nostre dit pays de Flandres sur nos receptes sans le conseil de nostre dit recheveur. Et se aucuns debas se meust entre parties dedens nostre conté et pays de Flandres, nobles ou non nobles de quelque estat quil soient, nous volons que nostre dit recheveur ait pooir de fere trieues entre les dictes parties et les apaisier et ad ce constraindre ycelles se faire ne le voloient par toutes manières raisonables sauve nostre droit. Et generalment et especialment nous lui avons donné et donnons ou dit office faisant tout au tel pooir comme nous mesmes auriemez pour fere en ycelle toutes choses qui a bon et loyal recheveur pevent et doivent appartenir à faire. Et pour le dit office faire et exercer par le dit Jehan comme dit est, nous lui avons ottroyet et ottroyons les gaiges de mil livres tournois par an. Et desmaintenant nous avons pris et prendons le dit Jehan, ses varles, familliers mesmes et biens quelconques en nostre sauve et especiale garde et protection et le promet- tons à warandir censer et warder à tous jours mais envers tous et contre tous de toutes chose quil auroit fers et exercées ou dit office sans souffrir nulle- ment que aucuns griefs ou rancuns lui en soient fais ou portés en aucun temps.

Item, volons nous et ordonons que sans enfraindre nos renenges soient tenues cascun an une fois au terme acoustumé et samblablement les comptes de nos baillius trois fois lannées.

Si mandons et commandons estroitement à tous nos baillis, sousbaillis, sergans, justichiers, officyers, maistres de nos monnoies, thonliers, reneurs, recheveurs de briefs en renenghes et de rentes hors renenghes, watergraves, recheveurs de fourfaitures, et tous autres quelconques il soient de nostre conté et pays dessus dit à qui il touche ou peut toucher que à nostre dit recheveur en cest office faisant, entendent, respondent et obéissent diligam- ment sans contredit et à lui ou à son certain deputé seulement et à nul autre delivrent les deniers et proffis de leur receptes car nostre entente nest mie auchois deffendons que nulles autres lettres que les nostres propres ou les lettres de nostre dit recheveur passent ou soient recheues par les maistre de nos comptes. Et ou cas que nos dis recheveres nous requerra de ses comptes oir pour savoir nostre estat ou pour lui esclarchir et deschargier de nostre recepte, nous serons tenus de y faire entendre. Et ses dis comptes oys et examinées de li donner dedens les XV jours après lexamination faite diceulz nos lettres de quitance ou li monstrer et dire comme raisonable pourquoy nous ne le faisons. Et se par le restat de sen compte final est trouvé que il ait plus avant finé pour nous que recheu nous lui devons faire assenement souffissent dicelli sourplus de rechief volons nous et ottroions à nostre dit recheveur que se après sen compte il estoit trouver quil euist plus delivré et finé que recheu nous lui en ferons bon et souffisant paie ou assenement avant che que nous le desmettrons de nostre office se nestoit à comme raisonable et convenable nous à ce mouvans sans malengien. Et ou cas que après le dit compte il fuist trouvé quil euist aucune chose recheu dont par neggligence il neuist point compté et fait recepte, nous lui ottroyons que en paient à nous ce que trouvé seroit comme dit est il se puist aquiter sans malengien se nestoit que nous fuissons soufissant infourmés du contraire de le dicte neggligence. Et samblablement volons nous que sil avoit aucune chose oublié à mettre en date à son proffit il y puist ades revenir en monstrant souffissant les parties. Et se nostre dit recheveur s'obligast pour l'ocoison de nous et de nostre especial commandement en aucunes sommes de deniers ou se fist aucun marchiet à meskief nous len promettons à acquiter souffissant et warandir de touz domaiges. Et ne volons mie que nostre dit recheveur soit tenue obligiés ne constranis à payer aucunes debtes ou obligations deues et faitez devant la date de ces lettres en nom de nous i depar nous. Toutevois est aussi nostre entent que nostre dit recheveur tenra à joira porra tenir et joir de sa bourgoisie de Gand contre toutes persones et en tous cas excepte tant seulement contre nous de choses touchans son office de recheverie et de conseil dont il devra respondre à nous sauf à lui en tous cas ses iustes et raisonnables despenses es quelles nous le promettons à oir et tenir en bonne foy sans fraude et malengien.

Ces lettres durans iusques à nostre rapiel sauf en tous cas nostre heritage.

Par le tesmoin de ces lettre scellés de nostre scel. Donné à Gand le XIe jour dottobre lan mil CCC cinquante et noef.

Par monsieur en son conseil ou quel estoit le seigneur de Praet, le seigneur de Maldigheem, vous et plusieurs autres.

9. *Appointment of Peter de la Fauchille to be general receiver—4 October 1362 (Archives Départementales du Nord à Lille. Série B. 1596 f. 107v #8705)*

Commission sur Pieter fil Jehan pour estre recheveur de Flandrez

Nous Loys etc., faisons savoir à tous que nous confians en la loyauté, discretion et diligence de nostre amé et feal varles Pieter fils Jehan, nous avons ycelli Pierre seul et pour le tout fait, mis, constitué, et establi, faisons, mettons, constituons et establissons par le teneur de ces presentes lettres, nostre recheveur de nostre conté et pays de Flandrez, des ressors et appartenances diceulz et aussi de nos villes, terres et appartenances de Malines et dAndwert. Au quel Pierre nous avons donné et donnons pooir et auctorité de rechevoir toutes nos rentes, revenuez, proffis, advenues, fourfaitures, dons, courtoisies, tailles, gets de mer, debtes, arrièrages, proffis de nos monnoyes, watergraveries de nostre mour et toutes autres choses quelconques appartenans à nous comment que se soit puist estre dedens nostre dicte conté de Flandrez et nos villes de Malines, dAndwers et des appartenances dessus dictez. En baillant en nom de nous à ferme et à chense à termes convenables toutes chenses et choses appartenans à office de recheveur ensi que anchienement à este acoustumé et rechevant et faisant compositions et pais de toutes choses tant de rachat de tiestes de bannis comme dautres aventures et calaignes sicomme il est de costumé et que che il fache à nostre plus grant prouffit et plus apparant. Et volons que toutesfois que mestiers sera il puist renouveller et constituer par consent, conseil, et commandement de nous toutes manières dofficyers dedens nostre dicte conté et pays de Flandres ainsi quil est anchiennement acoustumé. Aveoques ce volons nous que toutes fois que aucunez amendes, foufaitures ou droitures seront à nous acquises ou engenrées comment que ce soit que il mesmes les puist lever et rechevoir et donner en quittance à parties sanz che que aucuns de nos baillius de nostre dicte conté de Flandres puist quittier ou laissier apaisier à lui aucune amende de LX livres ou deseure non contrestans aucuns usaiges maintenus par nos officyers en contraire du temps passé les quels en celli cas nous rappellons. Et par especial commandons et emoignons à nostre dit recheveur que ou cas quil trouvera aucun de nos officyers quiconque il soit que dedens son office quittera aucune chose ou laissera passer neggligaument ou donra le nostre à chense ou excedera en son office ~~quittera aucun chose~~ en domiage de nous, il tantost et de fait meche nostre main à ycellui en suspendant et rappellant la chose dont li dit officyer auroit abusé et y fache autre officyer en son lieu iusques à tant que par nous et nostre conseil la deffaute seroit adrechie l'officyer corrigié ou autrement ordené.

Item, volons nous que desmaintenant il fache preparation de tous les membres, grans et petis, quelconques qui dependent ou ont dependu et qui anchiennement ont esté de nostre recepte de Flandrez, en esclarcissant yceuls de toutes les charges dont il ont esté et sont chargiés ad fin que li empechement sur yceuls fait et maintenu contre raison soient ostes et li rachat qui diceulz se pevent et doivent faire soient faiz hastivement par nous et nostre conseil mesmement que plus convenable chose est de deschargier noz propres rentes anchiennes que tendre à nouvelles acquerre et ycelles laissier. Et avons promis et promettons à nostre dit recheveur que quelconques pais, accort, ou quittance que nous ferons dedens nostre dit pays de Flandres nous li laurons joir des deniers qui en venront et escherront. Et ne quitterons ne ne soufferrons quitter par persone nulle nul disime, denier, et droiture à nous appartenans de vendaiges, alienations, ou esclichemens de fiefs quelconques sans le sceu de nostre dit recheveur. Ne ne ferons ne soufferrons estre fait nul assenement du jour dhuy en avant dedens nostre pays de Flandrez sur nos receptes sans le conseil de nostre dit recheveur. Et se aucun debat se meust entre parties dedens nostre conté et pays de Flandrez nobles ou nonnobles de quelque estat quil soient nous volons que nostre dit recheveur ait pooir de faire triewes entre les dictez parties et les apaisier et à che constraindre ycelles se faire ne voloient par toutes manières raisonables sauve che quil y garde bien nostre droit. Et generalment et especialment nous lui avons donné et donnons en dit office faisant tout autel pooir comme nous mesmes auriemes pour faire en ycelli toutes choses qui à bon et loyal recheveur pevent et doivent appartenir à faire et pour le dit office faire et exercer par le dit Pierre comme dit est, nous lui avons ottroyet et ottroyons de gaiges mil livres tournois par an. Et desmaintenant nous avons pris et prendons le dit Pierre, ses varles, familliers mesmes et biens quelconques en nostre sauve et especiale garde et protection et le promettons à warandir censer et warder à tous jours mais envers tous et contre tous de toutes choses quil auroit faites et exercées en dit office sans souffrir nullement que aucuns griefs ou rancune lui en soient fait ou portés en aucun temps.

Item, volons nous et emoignons à nostre dit recheveur que sans nulle faute nos renenghes soient tenues cascun an une fois au terme acoustumé et samblablement les comptes de nos baillius trois fois lannées.

Si mandons et commandons estroitement à tous nos baillis, sous-baillius, sergans, justichiers, officiers, maistres de nos monnoies, thonliers, reneurs, recheveurs de briefs en renenghes et de rentes hors renenghes, watergraves, recheveurs de fourfaitures, et tous autres quelconques il soient de nostre conté et pays dessus dit à qui il touche ou puet touchier que à nostre dit recheveur en cest office faisant, entendent, respondent et obéissent diligaument sans contredit et à lui ou à son certain deputé seulement et à nul autre delivrent les deniers et proffis de leur receptez car nostre entent nest mie anchois deffendons que nulles autres lettres que les nostres propres ou les lettrez de nostre dit recheveur passent ou soient recheues par les maistres de nos comptes. Et ou cas que nos dis recheveres nous requerra de ses comptes oir pour savoir nostre estat nous serons tenus de y faire entendre. Et ses dis comptez oys et examinées de li donner après lexamination faite diceuls nos lettres de quittanche ou li monstrer et dire comme raisonnable pourquoy nous ne le faisons. Et se par le restat de son compte final est trouvé que il ait plus avant finé pour nous que recheu nous lui devons faire assenement souffissent dicelli sourplus de rechief volons nous et ottroyons à nostre dit recheveur que se après son compte il estoit trouvé quil euist plus delivré et finé que recheu nous lui ferons bon et souffissant paie ou assenement avant che que nous le desmettons de nostre office se nestoit à comme raisonable et convenable nous à ce mouvans sans malengien. Et ou cas que après le dit compte il fuist trouvé quil euist aucune chose recheu dont par neggligence il neuist point compté et fait recepte nous lui ottroions que en paient à nous ce que trouvé seroit comme dit est il se puist acquiter sans malengien se nestoit que nous fuissons souffissant infourmés du contraire de le dicte neggligence. Et samblablement volons nous que sil avoit aucune chose oublyé à mettre en date à son proffit il y puist ades revenir en monstrant souffissant les parties. Et se nostre dit recheveur sobligast pour locoison de nous en aucunes sommes de deniers ou se fist aucun marchiet à meskief nous len promettons à acquitter souffissaument et warander de tous domaiges par ainsi quil le fait de nostre especial commandement. Toutevois est aussi nostre entent que nostre dit recheveur ne tenra ne joira ne porra tenir ne joir de sa bourgoisie de Gand contre nous en chose touchans son office.

Ces lettrez durans iusques à nostre rappel sauf en tous cas nostre heritage.

Par le tesmoing de ces lettres scellés de nostre scel. Donné à Gand le iii$_e$ jour dottobre lan mil CCC LXII.

Par Monsieur presens Loys de Namur, le seigneur de le Wastine et Jehan Blanchard.

10. Appointment of Gossuin le Wilde to be general receiver—5 July 1365 (Archives Départementales du Nord à Lille. Série B. 1566 n 252 f. 66v–67v #9471)

Commission sur messire Goessin le Wilde, chevalier,
pour estre recheveur de Flandre

Nous Loys etc., faisons savoir à tous que nous confians en la loyauté, discretion et diligence de nostre amé et feal chevalier, messire Goessin le

Wilde, nous avons ycelli messire Goessin, seul et pour le tout fait, mis, constitué, et establi, faisons, mettons, constituons et establissons par le teneur de ces presentes lettres nostre recheveur de nostre conté et pays de Flandres, des ressors et appartenances dyceulz et aussi de nos villes, terres et appartenances de Malines et dAndwert. Auquel messire Goessin nous avons donné et donnons pooir et auctorité de rechevoir toutes nos rentes, revenues, proffis, advenues, fourfaitures, dons, courtoisies, tailles, gets de mer, debtes, arrièrages, proffis de nos monnoies, watergraveries de nostre mour et toutes autres choses quelconques appartenans à nous comment que se soit puist estre dedens nostre conté de Flandres et nos villes de Malines, dAndwers et des appartenans dessus dictez. En baillant en nom de nous à ferme et à cense au termes de trois ans toutes chenses et choses appartenans à office de recheveur ensi que anchiennement à esté accoustumé sauve ce que à baillier les grans membres à cense al en prendre advis avoeques nostre conseil ainchois quil le faiche et rechevant et faisant compositions et pais de toutes choses tant de rachat de tiestes de bannis comme dautres aventures et calaignes sicomme il est de costumé et que ce il faiche à nostre plus grant proffit et plus apparant. Et volons que toutesfois que mestiers sera il puist oster tous sergans et vendres par toute nostre conté et seignorie qui nous sont proffitables en nostre service et constituer et mettre autres en leurs lieus ables et proffitables à ce sicomme bon luy samblera ainsi quil a est accoustumé. Aveoques ce volons nous que toutesfois que aucunes amendes, fourfaitures ou droitures seront à nous acquisez ou engenrées comment que ce soit que il meismes les puist lever et rechevoir et donner en quitance à parties sans ce que aucuns de nos baillius de nostre dicte conté de Flandres puist quittier ou laissier appaisier à luy aucune amende de LX livres ou deseure, non contrestans aucuns usages maintenus par nos officyers en contraire du temps passé les quels en ycelli cas nous rappellons. Et par especial commandons et emoignons à nostre dit recheveur que ou cas quil trouvera que aucun de nos officyers quiconque il soit qui dedens son office quittera aucune chose ou laissera passer neggligaument ou donra le nostre à chense ou excedera en son office en domiage de nous, il tantost et de fait meche nostre main à ycelli en souspendant et rappellant la chose dont li dit officyer auroit abusé et y faiche autre officyer en son lieu iusques à tant que par nous et nostre conseil la deffaute seroit adrechie lofficyer corrigié ou autrement ordené.

Item, volons nous que desmaintenant il faiche preparation de tous les membres, grans et petis, quelconques qui dependent ou ont dependu et qui anchiennement ont esté de nostre recepte de Flandres, en esclarcissant yceulz de toute les charges dont il ont esté et sont chargiés adfin que li empechement sur yceuls fait et maintenu contre raison soient ostés et li rachat qui dyceuls se peuvent et doivent faire soient fait hastivement par nous et nostre conseil mesmement comme plus convenable chose est de deschargier nos propres rentes anchiennes que tendre à nouvelles acquerre et ycelles laissier. Et avons promis et promettons à nostre dit recheveur que quelconques pais, accort, ou quittance que nous ferons dedens nostre dit pays de Flandres nous li laurons joir des deniers qui en venront et escherront. Et ne quitterons ne soufferons quittier par persone nulle nul disme, denier, et droiture à nous appartenans de vendaiges, alienations, ou esclichemens de fiefs quelconques sans le sceu de nostre dit recheveur. Et est nostre entention aussi que nostre dit recheveur ne se mellera point des commission des desheritances et esclichemens de nos fiefs et nen de nostre faire nul consentement à nostre doivent passer par nous mains bien volons quil en lieue ou nom de nous tous les proffis qui en peuvent venir et appartenir comme dit est. Ne ne ferons ne soufferons estre fait nul assenement dou jour dhuy en avant dedens nostre pays de Flandrez sur nos receptes sans le conseil de nostre dit recheveur. Et s'aucun debat meust entre parties dedens nostre conté et pays de Flandres nobles nonnobles de quelque estat quil soient nous volons que nostre dit recheveur ait pooir de faire triewes entre les dictez parties et les appaisier et que ce constraindre ycelles se faire ne voloient par toutes manières raisonnablez sauve ce quil y garde bien nostre droit. Et generalment et especialment nous li avons donné et donnons ou dit office faisant tout autel pooir comme nous meismes ariemes pour faire en ycelli toutes choses qui à bon et loial recheveur peuvent et doivent appartenir à faire et pour le dit office faire et exercer par le dit messire Goessin comme dit est nous luy avons ottroiet et ottroions de gaiges mil livres tournois par an. Et desmaintenant nous avons pris et prendons le dit messire Goessin, ses valles, familliers mesmes et biens quelconques en nostre sauve et especiale garde et protection et le promettons à warandir censer et warder à tous jours mais envers tous et contre tous de toutez choses quil auroit faites et exercées ou dit office sans souffrir nullement que aucuns griefs ou rancunez li en soient faite ou portés en aucun temps.

Item, volons nous et emoingnons à nostre dit recheveur que sans nulle faute nos renenghes soient tenues cascun an une fois au terme accoustumé et samblablement les comptes de nos baillius trois fois lannée.

Si mandons et commandons estroitement à tous nos baillius, sousbaillius, sergans, justichiers, officyers, maistres de nos monnoies, thonliers, reneurs, recheveurs de briefs en renenghez et de rentes hors renenghes, watergraves, recheveurz de fourfaitures, et tous autres quelconques il soient de nostre conté et pays dessus dit à qui il touche ou peut toucher que à nostre dit recheveur en cest office faisant, entendent, respondent et obéissent diligaument sans contredit et à luy ou à son certain deputé seulement et à nul autre delivrent les deniers et proffis de leur receptes car nostre entent nest mie ainchois deffendons que nulles autres lettres que les nostrez propres ou les lettres de nostre dit recheveur passent ou soient recheues par les maistre de nos comptes. Et ou cas que nos dis recheveres nous requerra de ses comptes oir pour savoir nostre estat nous serons tenus de y faire entendre. Et ses dis comptes oys et examinés de li donner après lexamination faite diceulz nos lettres de quittance ou li monstrer et dire comme raisonnable pour quoy nous ne le faisons. Et se par le restat de son compte final est trouvé que il ait plus avant finé pour nous que recheu nous li devons faire assennement souffissant dycelly sourplus de rechief volons nous et ottroions à nostre dit recheveur que se après son compte il estoit trouvé quil euist plus delivré et finé que recheu nous luy ferons bon et souffissant paie ou assennement avant ce que nous le desmettons de nostre office se nestoit à comme raisonnable et convenable nous à ce mouvans sans malengien. Et ou cas que après le dit compte il fust trouvé quil euist aucune chose recheu dont par neggligence il neuist point compté et fait recepte nous lui ~~promettons~~ ottroions que en paient à nous ce que trouvé seroit comme dit est il se puist acquiter sans malengien se nestoit que nous fuissons souffissant infourmé du contraire de le dicte neggligence. Et samblablement volons nous que sil avoit aucune chose oblyé à mettre en date à son proffit il y puist adies revenir en monstrant souffissant les parties. Et se nostre dit recheveur sobligast pour loccoison de nous en aucunez sommes de deniers ou se fist aucun marchiet à meskief nous len promettons à acquitter souffissant et warandir de tous domaiges par ainsi quil le fait de nostre especial commandement. Toutevois est aussi nostre entent que nostre dit recheveur ne tenra ne joira ne porra tenir ne joir de sa franchise dou franc ne de vrylaetscep contre nous au chose touchans son office.

Ches lettrez durans iusques à nostre rappel sauf en tous cas nostre heritage.

Par le tesmoing de ces lettrez scellés de nostre scel. Donné à Male le v_e jour juillet lan mil CCC LXVI.

Par Monsieur en son consel la estoient mons. de Ghistelle, mons. de Praet, mons. de Maldeghem, mons. de Dudsele, mons. Guillaume de Renighsvliet, vous, maistre Jehan dou Gardin et autres.

Bibliography

Archival Sources

Lille, Archives départementales du Nord
  Série B. Chambre des comptes du Comte de Flandres à Lille
  (Cfr. *Inventaire chronologique et détaillé de toutes les chartes qui se trouvent dans les archives des comtes de Flandres, déposées dans l'ancienne chambre des comptes du Roy à Lille* [Série B]. Ed. D. J. Godefroy, 1784–1786. 11 vols. In manuscript form at the departmental archives in Lille; the first two volumes have been published: *Inventaire analytique et chronologique des archives de la Chambre des comptes à Lille*. Ed. D. J. Godefroy. 2 vols. Paris and Lille, 1865; *Répertoire numérique de la série B. Chambre des comptes à Lille, nr. 1–1560*. Ed. Max Bruchet. 2 vols. Lille, 1899–1906; *Inventaire sommaire des archives départementales du Nord. Série B. Chambre des comptes de Lille, nr. 1561–3665*. Ed. A. Desplanques, C. Dehaisnes, and J. Finot. Vols. 2–8. Lille, 1872–1875.)
  Série H. Les ordres et établissements religieuses
  (Cfr. *Archives départementales du Nord. Répertoire numérique. Série H. (Fonds benedictines et cisterciens)*, I H à 25 H. Ed. Max Bruchet. 2 vols. Lille, 1928; *Archives départementales du Nord. Répertoire numérique. Série H, Vol. II (Ordres religieux divers. Ordres militaires. Hôpitaux et établissements de bienfaisance)*, 36 H à 214 H. Ed. P. and A.-M. Pietreson de Saint-Aubin. Avesnes-sur-Helpe, 1943.)
Lille, Archives municipales
  Stadscharters, Série AA
  (Cfr. *Inventaire sommaire des archives communales antérieures à 1790. Série AA.: cartons et régistres aux titres*. Ed. Max Bruchet. Lille, 1926.)
Ghent, Rijksarchief
  Fonds St.-Genois
  (Cfr. *Inventaire analytique des chartes des comtes de Flandre . . . autrefois déposées au château de Ruplemonde*. Ed. Jules de Saint-Genois. Ghent, 1843–1846.)
  Fonds Gaillard
  (Cfr. *Chartes des comtes de Flandre autrefois déposées au château de Ruplemonde et récemment retrouvées aux archives de l'ancien Conseil de Flandre à Gand*. Ed. Victor Gaillard. Brussels, 1854–1855.)
  Chronologisch supplement
  (Cfr. *Inventaris van de oorkonden der graven van Vlaanderen, chronologisch supplement*. Ed. Carlos Wyffels. Rijksarchief te Gent, undated.)

Bisdom St. Baafsabdij
Fonds Staten van Vlaanderen, #1349:
  Repertorium van Vane Guy, 1332–1336.
Chartes du prieuré de St. Bertin à Poperinghe
Ghent, Stadsarchief
Fonds Van Duyse and de Busscher
  (Cfr. *Inventaire analytique des chartes et documents appartenant aux archives de la
  ville de Gand*. Ed. Prudent Van Duyse and Edward de Busscher. Ghent,
  1867.)
Inventaire des archives de Gand. Ed. C. H. Diercx. Ghent, 1817.
Inventaire des archives de la ville de Gand. Ed. V. Van der Haeghen. Ghent,
  1896.
Bruges, Rijksarchief
Charters met blauwe nummers
Kerkarchief. Kapitalkerken. St. Donaas, 961–1779.
Bruges, Stadsarchief
Fonds Politiek Charters. Reeks 1
  (Cfr. *Regesten op de oorkonden, 1089–1300*. Ed. A. Schouteet. Bruges, 1973;
  Regesten op de oorkonden van het stadsbestuur van Brugge. Vol. 1: 1301–
  1339; vol. 2: 1339–1384. Ed. A. Schouteet. Brussels, 1978, 1979; *Inven-
  taire des Archives de la ville de Bruges [1228–1497]*. Ed. L. Gilliodts-Van
  Severen. Bruges, 1871–1878.)
Comptes rentiers, 1289–1395
H. Bloedkapel cartularium
Groot Seminarie, Ter Duinen-Ter Doest
  (Cfr. *Inventaire des chartes, bulles pontificales, privilèges et documents divers de la
  Bibliothèque du Seminaire épiscopal de Bruges*. Ed. Van de Putte. Bruges,
  1857.)
Archief Bisdom, Fonds Sint-Donaas, oorkonden dozen 12 (1296–1341) en
  19 (1294–1350).
Brussels, Algemeen Rijksarchief (ARA)
Rekenkamer
  (Cfr. *Inventaire des archives de chambre des comptes*. Ed. L. Gachard. Vol. 1.
  Brussels, 1837; vol. 5: Ed. A. Pinchart. Brussels, 1879; vol. 6: Ed. H. Nélis.
  Brussels, 1931.)
Rekenkamer, Rolrekeningen
  (Cfr. *Chambre des comptes de Flandre et de Brabant. Inventaire des comptes en
  rouleaux*. Ed. H. Nélis. Brussels, 1914.)

Published Documents

Adriaanse, J. "De Hulstersche stadsrekening van 1326," *Jaarboek van Oudheidkundige Kring 'De Vier Ambachten'* 6 (1934), 15–60.
Adriaanse, J., and L. M. Van Werveke. "Verzameling van akten der schepenen van

Hulst (1226–1499)," *Jaarboek van Oudheidkundige Kring 'De Vier Ambachten.'* Hulst, 1938.

Annales Gandenses. Translated by Hilda Johnston. New York, 1951.

Bautier, Robert-Henri, and Janine Sornay, with Françoise Muret. *Les sources de l'histoire économique et sociale du moyen âge: Les états de la maison de Bourgogne: Archives des principautés territoriales*, pt. 2: *Les principautés du Nord.* Paris, 1984.

Béthune, J. *Cartulaire du Béguinage de St. Elizabeth à Gand.* Bruges, 1883.

Bigwood, Georges. "Documents relatifs à une association de marchands Italiens," *HKCG* 78 (1909), 205–244.

———. *Les livres des comptes des Gallerani.* 2 vols. Brussels, 1961.

Blockmans, Frans. *1302. Vóór en na. Vlaanderen op een keerpunt van zijn geschiedenis.* Antwerp, 1943.

Borgnet, J. *Analyses des chartes namuroises qui se trouvent aux archives départementales du Nord, à Lille.* Brussels, 1863.

———, J. S. Bormans, and J. J. Brouwers. *Cartulaire de la commune de Namur (1118–1792).* 6 vols. Namur, 1876–1924.

Bormans, Stanislas, and Joseph Halbin. *Table chronologique des chartes et diplômes concernant l'histoire de la Belgique.* (Vol. 11 of Wauters, *Table.*) Brussels, 1907, 1912, and 1946.

Boutaric, Edgard. *Actes du Parlement de Paris. Première série de l'an 1254–1328.* 2 vols. Paris, 1863–1867.

Brouwers, D. D. *L'administration et les finances du comté de Namur de XIIIe au XVe siècle. Sources IV: chartes et règlements.* Namur, 1913–1914.

Bruyssel, E. Van. "Liste analytique des documents concernant l'histoire de la Belgique, qui sont conservés au *Record Office*," *HKCG* 3rd series 1 (1860), 95–118.

Buntinx, J. *Het Memoriaal van Jehan Makiel, klerk en ontvanger van Gwijde van Dampierre (1270–1275).* Brussels, 1944.

Bussche, Emile Vanden. *Inventaire des Archives de l'Etat à Bruges. Section première. Franc de Bruges, ancien quatrième membre de Flandre.* Vol. I. Bruges, 1881.

Caland, F. "Twee rekeningen der stad Hulst uit de eerste helft der XIVde eeuw," *Archief vroegere en latere mededelingen voornamelijk in betrekking tot Zeeland* 2 (1869), 149–196.

Callewaert, C. *Chartes anciennes de l'abbaye de Zonnebeke.* Bruges, 1928.

Chaplais, Pierre. *Diplomatic Documents Preserved in the P.R.O.* London, 1964.

Chronicon Hannoniense, quod dicitur Balduini Avennensis. Ed. J. Heller. *M.G.H. SS* 25:414–467.

Colens, J. *Le 1302 compte communal de la ville de Bruges, mai 1302 à février 1303 (n.s.).* Bruges, 1886.

Corpus cronicorum flandriae antiquissima genealogia forestariorum et comita flandriae (ex Libro Florido, monasterii Sancti Bavonis scripto circa annum MCXXI, a Lamberto Onulphi filio, canonico Audomarensi, f° 104 (Extat codex, anno MCXXI absolutus, in Bibliotheca Universitatis Gandavensis)) in *Collection des chroniques belges inédits: Recueil des chroniques de Flandre.* Ed. J. J. de Smet. Brussels, 1837.

Coussemaker, E. de. "Documents relatifs à la Flandre maritime," *Annales du Comité flamand de France* 5 (1859–1860), 297–383; 10 (1868–1869), 358–456.

Coussemaker, Ignace De. *Un cartulaire de l'abbaye de Notre-Dame de Bourbourg (1104–1793)*. 3 vols. Lille, 1882–1891.

———. *Documents inédits relatifs à la ville de Bailleul en Flandre*. 3 vols. Lille, 1877–1878.

Dehaisnes, C. *Documents et extraites divers concernant l'histoire de l'art dans la Flandre, l'Artois, et le Hainaut avant le XVe siècle*. Lille, 1877–1878.

Delepierre, Joseph O. *Précis analytique des documents que renferme le dépôt des archives de la Flandre occidentale à Bruges*. Bruges, 1840–1842.

Delmaire, Bernard. *Le compte général du receveur d'Artois pour 1303–1304. Edition précédée d'une introduction à l'étude des institutions financières de l'Artois aux XIIIe–XIVe siècles*. Brussels, 1977.

Demay, G. *Inventaire des Sceaux*. 2 vols. Paris, 1873.

Des Marez, G., and E. De Sagher. *Comptes de la ville d'Ypres (1267–1329)*. 2 vols. Brussels, 1909–1913.

De Smet, J. J., and Carlos Wyffels. *De rekeningen van de stad Brugge, 1280–1319*. 2 vols. Brussels, 1965.

Diegerick, I.L.A. *Inventaire analytique et chronologique des chartes et documents appartenant aux archives de la ville d'Ypres*. 7 vols. Bruges, 1853–1868.

———. *Inventaire analytique et chronologique des chartes et documents appartenant aux archives de l'ancienne abbaye de Messines*. Bruges, 1876.

Diericx, C. J. *Mémoires sur la ville de Gand*. 2 vols. Gand, 1814.

Dixmude, O. Van. *Merkwaerdige gebeurtenissen, vooral in Vlaenderen en Brabant en ook in de aangrenzende landstreken van 1377 to 1443*. Ed. J. J. Lambin. Ypres, 1835.

Duchet, T., and A. Giry. *Cartulaire de l'église de Térouanne*. St. Omer, 1881.

Espinas, Georges, and Henri Pirenne. *Recueil des documents relatifs à l'histoire de l'industrie drapière en Flandre*. 4 vols. Brussels, 1906–1924.

Espinas, Georges, Charles Verlinden, and J. Buntinx. *Privilèges et chartes de franchises de la Flandre*. 2 vols. Brussels, 1959.

Faider, Paul. *Catalogue des manuscrits de la bibliothèque publique de la ville de Courtrai*. Gembloux-Paris, 1936.

Feys, E., and A. Nélis. *Cartulaire de la prévôté de Saint-Martin à Ypres*. 2 vols. Bruges, 1880–1881.

Feys, E., and D. Van de Casteele. *Histoire d'Oudenbourg, accompagnée de pièces justificatives comprenant le cartulaire de la ville et de nombreux estraits des comptes communaux*. 2 vols. Bruges, 1873.

Foppens, J. *Compendium chronologicum episcoporum Brugensium, necnon praepositorum, decanorum et canonicorum, etc. ecclesiae cathedralis S. Donatianis Brugensis*. Bruges, 1731.

Froissart, Jean. *Oeuvres*. Ed. M. Le Baron Kervyn de Lettenhove. 26 vols. Brussels, 1868–1877.

Gachard, M. *La Bibliothèque Nationale, à Paris. Notes et extraits des manuscrits qui concernent l'histoire de Belgique*. 2 vols. Brussels, 1875–1877.

Gaillard, Victor. *Archives du conseil de Flandre ou recueil des documents inédits relatifs à l'histoire politique, judiciaire, artistique et littéraire, mis en ordre et accompagnés de notes d'éclaircissement*. Ghent, 1856.

Gilliodts-Van Severen, L. *Cartulaire de l'ancienne Estaple de Bruges*. 4 vols. Bruges, 1904–1906.
———. *Cartulaire de l'ancien Grand Tonlieu de Bruges*. 2 vols. Bruges, 1908–1909.
———. *Coutume de la prevôté de Bruges*. 2 vols. Brussels, 1887.
———. *Coutumes de la ville de Bruges*. 2 vols. Brussels, 1874–1875.
———. *Coutumes de la ville et châtellenie de Furnes*. 6 vols. Brussels, 1896–1902.
———. *Coutumes de Lombardside, Loo et Poperinghe*. Brussels, 1902.
———. *Coutumes des petites villes et seigneuries enclavées dans la Franc de Bruges*. 6 vols. Brussels, 1890–1893.
———. *Coutumes du Franc de Bruges*. Bruges, 1897.
———. *Sources et développement de la coutume d'Ypres*. 2 vols. Brussels, 1902.
Gueson, A. H. *Inventaire chronologique des chartes de la ville d'Arras*. Arras, 1862.
Gysseling, M., and A.C.F. Koch. *Diplomata Belgica ante annum Millesimum Centesimum Scripta*. Brussels, 1950.
Hautcoeur, l'Abbé E. *Cartulaire de l'abbaye de Flines*. 2 vols. Lille, 1873.
———. *Cartulaire de l'église collégiale de Saint-Pierre de Lille*. 2 vols. Lille and Paris, 1894.
———. *Documents liturgiques et necrologiques de l'église collégiale de Saint-Pierre de Lille*. Lille, 1895.
Herbomez, A. D'. *Chartes de l'abbaye de Saint Martin de Tournai (1094–1690)*. 2 vols. Brussels, 1898–1901.
Hoop, F.H.D'. *Recueil des chartes du prieuré de Saint-Bertin à Poperinghe et de ses dépendances à Bas-Warneton et à Coukelaere*. Bruges, 1870.
Johannes Longus de Ipra (Jan van Ieper). *Chronica monasterii Sancti Bertini*. Ed. H. Heller. *M.G.H. SS* 25:736–866.
Koch, A. "Een onderzoek naar de gedragingen van een lagen rechterlijken Ambtenaar in het graafscap Vlaanderen (1305)," *HKCG* 112 (1947), 127–142.
Laan, P.H.J. Van der. *Oorkondenboek van Amsterdam tot 1400*. Amsterdam, 1975.
Lacomblet, T. *Urkundenbuch für die Geschichte des Niederrheins*. 4 vols. Düsseldorf, 1840–1858.
Laenen, J. *Les archives de l'Etat à Vienne au point de vue de l'histoire de Belgique*. Brussels, 1924.
Lambert Ardensis. *Historia Comitum Ghisenensium*. Ed. Johannes Heller. *M.G.H. SS* 24, 550–642.
Laurent, H. *Actes et documents anciens intéressant la Belgique conservés aux Archives de l'Etat à Vienne. 1196–1356*. Brussels, 1933.
Limburg-Stirum, Thierry de. *Cartulaire de Louis de Male, 1348–1359*. 2 vols. Bruges, 1898–1901.
———. *Codex diplomaticus inde ab anno 1296 ad usque 1325* ou *Recueil de documents relatifs aux guerres et dissensions suscitées par Philippe-le-Bel, roi de France contre Gui de Dampierre, comte de Flandre*. 2 vols. Bruges, 1879, 1889.
———. *Coutume de la ville et de la châtellenie de Courtrai*. Brussels, 1905.
———. *Coutumes des deux villes et pays d'Alost (Alost et Grammont)*. Brussels, 1878.
———. *Coutumes de la ville d'Audenarde*. 2 vols. Brussels, 1886.
Lokeren, A. Van. *Chartes et documents de l'abbaye de Saint Pierre au Mont Blandin à Gand*. 2 vols. Ghent, 1868–1871.

Marechal, J. *Inventaris van het archief der Proosdij van St. Donaas te Brugge*. Brussels, 1960.

Mertens, J. *Inventaris van het archief van de kerkfabriek St. Gilliskerk te Brugge*. Brussels, 1967.

Mieris, F. Van. *Groot charterboek der graven van Holland en Zeeland en heeren van Vriesland*. 4 vols. Leiden, 1753–1756.

Mollat, Michel, with Robert Favreau. *Comptes généraux de l'Etat bourgogne entre 1416 et 1420. Première partie*. Paris, 1965.

Monier, Raymond. *Le livre Roisin*. Lille, Paris, 1932.

Muller, P. L. *Regesta Hannonesia*. 's Gravenhage, 1882.

Mussely, C. *Inventaire des archives de la ville de Courtrai*. 2 vols. Courtrai, 1854–1858.

———, and E. Molitor. *Cartulaire de l'ancienne église collégiale à Notre-Dame à Courtrai*. Ghent, 1880.

Nyhoff, I. S. *Gedenkwaardigheden uit de geschiedenis van Gelderland door onuitgegeven oorkonden opghelderd en bevestigd*. 7 vols. Arnhem, 1830–1864.

Oudegherst, P. d'. *Annales de Flandre*. Ed. M. Lesbroussart. 2 vols. Ghent, 1789.

Pauw, Napoleon de. *Bouc van der Audientie. Acten en sentencien van de Raad van Vlaanderen, 1368–1378*. 2 vols. Ghent, 1907.

———. "L'enquête de Bruges, après la bataille de Cassel, documents inédits publiés," *HKCG* 5th series 9 (1899), 665–704.

———. *Ypre jeghen Poperinghe angaende den verbonenen. Gedenkstuken der XIVde eeuw nopens het laken*. Ghent, 1899.

———, and J. Vuylsteke. *De rekeningen der stad Gent. Tijdvak van J. Artevelde (1336–1349)*. 3 vols. 1874–1885.

Pelsmaéker, Prosper de. *Registre aux sentences des échevins d'Ypres*. Brussels, 1914.

Perroy, Ed. "Anglo-French Negotiations at Bruges," in *The Camden Miscellany* 19 (Camden Third Series, 80). London, 1952.

Pilate-Prévost, H. *Table chronologique et analytique des archives de la mairie de Douai, depuis le onzième siècle jusqu'au dix-huitième d'après les travaux de feu M. Guilmot*. Douai, 1842.

Piot, C. *Cartulaire de l'abbaye de Eename*. Bruges, 1881.

Pirenne, Henri. *Le soulèvement de la Flandre maritime de 1323–1328*. Brussels, 1900.

Potter, F. de. *Petit cartulaire de Gand (1198–1753)*. Ghent, 1885.

———. *Second cartulaire de Gand*. Ghent, no date.

Potthast, A. *Regesta pontificum romanorum inde ab a post Christum MCXCVII ad a MCCCIV*. 2 vols. Berlin, 1874–1875.

Pruvost, A. *Chronique et cartulaire de l'abbaye de Bergues-Saint-Winnoc*. 2 vols. Bruges, 1875–1878.

Reiffenberg, M. le baron, J. J. De Smet, L. Devillers, A. Borgnet, E. Gachet, and H. Liebrecht. *Monuments pour servir à l'histoire des provinces de Namur, de Hainaut et de Luxembourg*. 10 vols. Brussels, 1844–1874.

Richerbé, A. "Compte de recettes de dépenses de la ville de Lille, 1301–1302," *Annales du Comité flamand de France* 21 (1893), 393–484.

Rymer, Thomas. *Feodera*. 10 vols. The Hague, 1739–1745.

Saige, G., and H. Lacaille. *Trésor des chartes du comté de Réthel.* 2 vols. Monaco, 1902–1904.

Saint-Genois, Joseph de. *Monuments anciens essentiellement utile à la France et aux provinces de Hainaut, Flandre, Brabant, Namur, Artois, Liège, Hollande, Zélande, Frise, Cologne, et autre pays limitrophes de l'Europe.* 2 vols. Lille and Brussels, 1806–1812.

Sammarthani, D. *Gallia christiana in provincias ecclesiasticas distributa.* 16 vols. Paris, 1715–1865.

Serrure, C. P. *Cartulaire de Saint-Bavon à Gand (655–1255).* Ghent, no date.

Thomas, Paul. *Textes historiques sur Lille et le Nord de la France.* 3 vols. Paris and Lille, 1930.

Valois, Noel. "Cartulaires de l'Abbaye de Notre-Dame des Près de Douai," *Cabinet Historique* n.s. 1 (1881), 40–82.

Van den Berghe, L. *Gedenkstukken tot opheldering der Nederlandsche geschiedenis.* 2 vols. Leiden, 1842–1847.

———. *Oorkondenboek van Holland en Zeeland.* 2 vols. Amsterdam, 1866–1873.

Van de Putte, F. *Cronica et cartularium monasterii de Dunis.* 3 vols. Bruges, 1864.

———, and C. Carton. *Chronicon et cartularium abbatiae Sanctae Nicholai Furnensis.* Bruges, 1862–1867.

Vanderhaeghen, V. *Het Klooster ten Walle en de Abjij den Groenen Briel. Stukken en Oorkonden.* Ghent, 1888.

Van Haeck, M. *Cartulaire de l'abbaye de Marquette.* Lille, 1937–1940.

Vercauteren, F. *Actes des comtes de Flandre (1071–1128).* Brussels, 1938.

———. "Documents pour servir à l'histoire des financières Lombards en Belgique (1309)," *Bulletin de l'institut historique belge de Rome* 26 (1950–1951), 43–67.

Verhulst, A., and M. Gysseling. *Le compte général de 1187, connu sour le nom de "Gros Brief," et les institutions financières du comté de Flandre au XIIe siècle.* Brussels, 1962.

Viard, Jules. *Le journaux du trésor de Philippe VI de Valois suivi de l'ordinarium Thesauri de 1338–1339.* Paris, 1940.

Vlaminck, A. De. *Inventaire des archives de la ville de Termonde.* Ghent, 1876.

Vuylsteke, Julius. *Gentsche stads- en baljuwsrekeningen 1280–1336.* Ghent, 1900.

Warnkönig, L. A. *Flandrische Staats- und Rechtsgeschichte bis zum jahr 1305.* 3 vols. Tübingen, 1835–1839.

———. *Histoire de Flandre et de ses institutions civiles et politiques jusqu'à l'année 1305.* Translated by A. E. Gheldolf. 5 vols. Brussels, 1835–1864.

Wauters, A. *Table chronologique des chartes et diplômes imprimés concernant l'histoire de la Belgique.* 13 vols. Brussels, 1866–1912.

Werveke, Alfons Van. *Gentse stads- en baljuwsrekeningen, 1351–1364.* Brussels, 1970.

Wielant, P. *Recueil des antiquités de Flandre.* Ed. J. J. De Smet, in *Corpus chronicon Flandriae* 4 (Brussels, 1865), 1–442.

Wyffels, Carlos. "De oudste rekening der stad Aardenburg (1309–1310) en de opstand van 1311," *Archief. Vroegere en latere mededelingen voornamelijk in betrekking tot Zeeland,* 1949–1950, 10–52.

Literature

Alberts, W. Japp, and H.P.H. Jansen. *Welvaart in wording. Sociaal-economische geschiedenis van Nederland van de vroegste tijden tot het einde van de Middeleeuwen.* The Hague, 1964.

Albrow, Martin. *Bureaucracy.* New York, 1970.

Altmeyer, J. J. "Notice historique sur la ville de Poperinghe," *Messager des sciences,* 1840, 22–57; 129–164.

Armitage-Smith, Sydney. *John of Gaunt.* London, 1904.

Auweele, D. Van den. "De Brugse gijzelaarslijsten van 1301, 1305 en 1328. Een komparatieve analyse," *Handelingen voor het genootschap voor geschiedenis "Société d'Emulation" te Brugge* 110 (1973), 105–167.

Bacha, E. *Le chancelier de Flandre.* Brussels, 1898.

Baldwin, John W. *The Government of Philip Augustus: Foundations of French Royal Power in the Middle Ages.* Berkeley, 1986.

Barbier, L'abbé Victor. *Histoire du monastère de Géronsart.* Namur, 1886.

Bayley, Francis. *The Bailleuls of Flanders.* London, 1881.

Beaucort de Noortvelde, P. *Description historique de l'église collégiale et paroissiale de Notre Dame à Bruges, avec une histoire chronologique de tous les prévôts, suivie d'un recueil des epitaphes anciennes et modernes de cette église.* Brussels, 1773.

Bendix, Reinhard. "Bureaucracy and the Problem of Power," in *Reader in Bureaucracy.* Ed. Robert King Merton. Glencoe, Illinois, 1952.

Berben, H. "Une guerre économique au moyen âge. L'embargo sur l'exportation des laines anglaises (1270–1274)," in *Etudes d'histoire dédiées à la memoire de Henri Pirenne.* Brussels, 1937, 1–17.

———. "Het verdrag van Montreuil 1274. De Engelsch-Vlaamsche handelspolitiek, 1266–1287," *RBPH* 23 (1944), 89–126.

Bigwood, Georges. "Les financières d'Arras," *RBPH* 3 (1924), 465–508; 769–819.

———. *Le régime juridique et économique du commerce de l'argent dans la Belgique du moyen âge.* 2 vols. Brussels, 1921–1922.

———. "Un relevé de recettes tenu par le personnel de Thomas Fini, receveur général de Flandre," in *Mélange d'histoire offert à H. Pirenne* 1 (Brussels, 1926), 31–42.

Blau, Peter M. *Bureaucracy in Modern Society.* New York, 1961.

Blockmans, F. "Le contrôle par le prince des comptes urbains en Flandre et en Brabant au moyen âge," in *Finances et comptabilité urbaines du XIII au XIVe siècle. Internationaal Colloquium Blankenberge 6–9 IX–1962. Acts.* Ghent, 1968, 287–330.

———. "Les lombards à Anvers du XIIIe à la fin du XIVe siècle," *Tablettes du Brabant* 1 (1956), 229–285.

Blockmans, W. "De ontwikkeling van een verstedelijkte samenleving," in *Geschiedenis van Vlaanderen.* Ed. E. Witte. Brussels, 1983, 45–103.

———. "The Social and Economic Effects of Plague in the Low Countries 1349–1500," *RBPH* 58 (1980), 833–863.

————, G. Pietiers, W. Prevenier, and R. van Schaik. "Tussen crisis en welvaart, social veranderingen 1300–1500," in *Algemene geschiedenis der Nederlanden* 4 (Haarlem, 1980), 42–60.

Blommaert, W. *Les châtelains de Flandre. Etude d'histoire constitutionelle.* Ghent, 1915.

Borrelli de Serrès. *Recherches sur divers services public du XIIIe au XVII siècle.* 3 vols. Paris, 1895–1909.

Boutaric, Edgard. *La France sous la règne de Philippe le Bel.* Geneva, 1975.

Bovesse, J. "Les baillies, receveurs et châtelaines comtaux namurois aux XIIIe et XIVe siècles," *Standen en Landen* 9 (1955), 115–119.

————. "Le comte de Namur Jean Ire et les événements du comté de Flandre en 1325–1326," *HKCG* 131 (1965), 385–454.

————. "Notes sur l'administration du comté de Namur aux XIIIe et XIVe siècles," *Revue du Nord* 37 (1955), 71.

————. "Le personnel administratif du comté de Namur au bas moyen âge. Aperçu général," *Revue de l'université de Bruxelles* 1970, 432–456.

Brown, Robert, Eugene Kamenka, Martin Krugur, Alec Erh, and Soon Tasy. *Bureaucracy: The Career of a Concept.* London, 1979.

Bruwier, M. "De centrale ambtenaren in de middeleeuwen," in *Flandria nostra.* Ed. J. L. Broeckx. 5 (Antwerp, 1960), 343–359.

Buntinx, J. *De audientie van de graven van Vlaanderen. Studie over het centraal grafelijk gerecht (c. 1330–1409).* Brussels, 1949.

————. "De instellingen van de vorstendommen. De dertiende eeuw," *Algemene geschiedenis der Nederlanden* 2 (Utrecht, 1950), 353–373.

————. "L'origine de l'audiènce des comtes de Flandre," *Revue du Nord* 30 (1948), 210–222.

————. "De XIVe eeuwse kanselarijregisters van het graafschap Vlaanderen," *HKCG* 63 (1948), 205–221.

Buntinx, Willy. "De enquête van Oudenburg. Hervorming van de repartitie van de beden in het graafschap Vlaanderen, 1408," *HKCG* 139 (1968), 75–137.

Cambridge Economic History, Volume II: Trade and Industry in the Middle Ages. Ed. Michael Postan and E. E. Rich. Cambridge, 1952.

Carus-Wilson, E. "The Woollen Industry," in the *Cambridge Economic History.* Ed. Michael Postan and E. E. Rich. Cambridge, 1952, 355–428.

Cazelles, R. *La société politique et la crise de la royauté sous Philippe de Valois.* Paris, 1958.

————. *Société politique, noblesse et couronne sous Jean le Bon et Charles V.* Geneva and Paris, 1982.

Chrimes, S. B. *An Introduction to the Administrative History of Medieval England.* Oxford, 1966.

Cockshaw, P. *Le personnel de la chancellerie de Bourgogne-Flandre sous les ducs de Bourgogne de la maison de Valois (1384–1477).* Courtrai-Heule, 1982.

Colinez, M. "Notice sur les renengues et les espiers en Flandre," *Messager des sciences* 1840, 289–306.

Constable, Giles. *Monastic Tithes.* Cambridge, 1964.

Croos, P. De. *Histoire du droit criminal et pénal dans la comté de Flandre*. Brussels, 1878.

Crozier, Michel. *The Bureaucratic Phenomenon*. Chicago, 1964.

Cuttino, G. P. *English Diplomatic Administration, 1259–1339*. Oxford, 1971.

Dehaisnes, C. *Histoire de l'art dans la Flandre, l'Artois et le Hainaut avant le XVe siècles*. 2 vols. Lille, 1886.

Delcourt, André. *La vengeance de la commune. L'arsin et l'abattis de maison en Flandre et en Hainaut*. Lille, 1930.

Demay, J. "Proeve tot raming van de bevolking en de weefgetouwen te Ieper van de XIIIe tot de XVIIe eeuw," in *Prisma van de geschiedenis van Ieper*. Ed. O. Mus. Ypres, 1974, 157–170.

Dept, Gaston G. *Les influences française et anglaise dans le comté de Flandre au début du XIIIe siècle*. Ghent and Paris, 1928.

Des Marez, G. *La lettre de foire à Ypres au XIIIe siècle*. Brussels, 1901.

Desplanques, Alexandre. *Nouvel essai sur l'histoire du chapitre Saint-Pierre de Lille*. Lille, 1863.

Dhondt, Jan. "Note sur les châtelains de Flandre," *Etudes historique de M. Rodière* 5 (1947), 43–52.

Dibben, L. B. "Secretaries in the Fourteenth and Fifteenth Centuries," *English Historical Review* 25 (1910), 430–444.

Donnet, F. "Les lombards dans les Pay-Bas," *Annales Cercle Archéalogique de Termonde* 2nd series 8 (1900), 126–161.

Downs, A. *Theory of Bureaucracy*. Santa Monica, California, 1964.

Dumont, G.-H. *Historie de la Belgique*. 1977.

Duviver, Charles. *Influences française et germanique en Belgique au XIIIe siècle: la querelle des Avesnes et des Dampierre. Volume 2: Preuves*. Brussels, 1894.

Eisenstadt, S. N. *The Political Systems of Empires*. New York, 1969.

Espinas, Georges. *Les finances de la commune de Douai des origines au XVe siècle*. 4 vols. Paris, 1913.

Essen, Leon Van der. *Les italiens en Flandre au XVIe siècle*. 1926.

Finot, J. *Etude historique sur les relations commerciales entre la France et la Flandre au moyen âge*. Paris, 1894.

Foucart, J. *Une institution baillivale en Flandre. La gouvernance du souverain-baillage de Lille, Douai, Orchies-Mortagne et Tournaisis*. Lille, 1937.

Fris, Victor. "La chronique des Pays-Bas, de France, d'Angleterre et de Tournai," *HKCG* 10 (1900), 65–82.

———. "Note sur Thomas Fin," *HKCG* 5th series 10 (1900), 8–14.

———. "Le testament olographe de Bartélémy Fin," *Bulletin de la société d'histoire et d'archéaologie de Gand* 15 (1907), 193–194.

Funck-Brentano, F. *Les origines de la guerre de cent ans. Philippe le Bel en Flandre*. Paris, 1897.

Gachard, M. *Notice historique et descriptive des archives de la ville de Gand*. Brussels, 1852.

Gachet, Emile. "Le couvent de l'Abbiette, à Lille. Sa foundation par la comtesse Marguerite et par Guy de Dampierre," *Messages des sciences* 1852, 12–57.

Gaillard, Victor. *Recherches sur les monnaies des comtes de Flandre depuis le temps les plus reculés jusqu'au règne de Robert de Béthune.* 2 vols. Ghent, 1852–1857.

———. *Recherches sur les monnaies des comtes de Flandre sous les règnes de Louis de Crécy et de Louis de Male.* Ghent, no date.

Ganshof, François Louis. "Etude sur le faussement de jugement dans le droit flamand des XIIe et XIIIe siècles," *Bulletin de la commission royale des anciennes lois et ordonnances de Belgique* 14 (1935), 115–140.

———. "La Flandre," in *Histoire des institutions françaises au moyen âge.* Ed. Ferdinand Lot and Robert Fawtier. *Volume I: Institutuion seigneuriales: Les droits du roi exercés par les grands vassaux.* Paris, 1957, 343–426.

———. *Geschiedenis van Vlaanderen,* vol. 2. Antwerp, 1936.

———. "Les transformations de l'organisation judicaire dans la comté de Flandre jusqu'à l'avènement de la maison de Bourgogne," *RBPH* 18 (1939), 43–61.

———. "De Vlaamsche instellingen in de XIIe, XIIIe, en XIVe eeuw.—Grongebied, vorst en standen-vertegenwoordiging," *Geschiedenis van Vlaanderen.* Ed. R. van Roosbroeck. Vol. 2. Antwerp, 1937, 109–130.

———, and Jan de Sturler. "De staatsinstellingen van Vlaanderen en Brabant," *Geschiedenis van Vlaanderen.* Ed. R. van Roosbroeck. Vol. 2. Antwerp, 1937, 107–188.

Gastout, Marguerite. *Béatrix de Brabant, landgravine de Thuringe, reine des Romains, comtesse de Flandre, dame de Courtrai, 1225?–1288.* Leuven, 1943.

Gilissen, Jean. *L'évolution de la plévine dans le droit flamand aux XIIIe et XIVe siècles.* Brussels, 1936.

———. "Les légistes en Flandre aux XIIIe et XIVe siècles," *Bulletin de la commission royale des anciennes lois et ordonnances de Belgique* 14 (1934), 116–228.

Giry, A. *Manuel de Diplomatique.* Paris, 1894.

Glay, E. Le. *Histoire des comtes de Flandre jusqu'à l'evénement de la maison des Bourgogne.* 2 vols. Brussels, 1843.

Gryse, L. M. de. "Some Observations on the Origins of the Flemish Bailiff: The Reign of Philip of Alsace," *Viator* 7 (1976), 245–294.

Guillois, A. *Recherches sur les maîtres des requêtes de l'hôtel des origines à 1350.* Paris, 1909.

Hallam, Elizabeth M. *Capetian France, 987–1238.* London and New York, 1980.

Hemptinne, T. de, and Maurice Vandermaesen. "De ambtenaren van de centrale administratie van het graafschap Vlaanderen van de XIIe tot de XIVe eeuw," *Tijdschrift voor Geschiedenis* 93 (1980), 177–209.

Henneman, J. B. *Royal Taxation in Fourteenth-Century France, 1322–1356.* Princeton, 1971.

———. *Royal Taxation in Fourteenth-Century France, 1356–1370.* Philadelphia, 1976.

Hill, Mary. *The King's Messengers, 1199–1377.* London, 1961.

Howard, Michael. *War in European History.* Oxford, 1976.

Jacoby, Henry. *The Bureaucratization of the World.* Translated by Eveline L. Kanes. Berkeley, 1973.

Joanne, Paul. *Dictionnaire géographique et administratif de la France.* Paris, no date.

Jordan, William C. *Louis IX and the Challenge of Crusade*. Princeton, 1979.

Jorden, E. "La faillite des Buonsignori," in *Mélanges Paul Fabre*. Paris, 1902, 416–435.

Kervyn de Lettenhove. "Beatrice de Courtrai," *Bulletin de l'Academie royal des lettres et des beaux-arts de Belgique* 21:403–15, 22:382–400.

———. *Etudes sur l'histoire du XIIIe siècle. Recherches sur la part que l'ordre de Cîteaux et le comte de Flandre prirent à la lutte de Boniface VIII et de Philippe le Bel*. Brussels, 1853.

Koch, A.C.F. "De rechtelijke organisatie van het graafschap Vlaanderen tot in de XIIIe eeuw," *Handelingen der Maatschappij voor Geschiedenis en Oudheidkunde te Gent*. New series 5 (1951), 1–214.

Limburg-Stirum, Thierry de. *Les bouteillers héréditaires de Flandre. Preuves*. Bruges, no date.

———. *La cour des comtes de Flandre. I. Le chambellan de Flandre et les sires de Ghistelles*. Ghent, 1868.

Linden, H. Van der. "Les relations politiques de la Flandre avec la France au XVIe siècle," *HKCG* 5th series 3 (1893), 469–542.

Lopez, Robert. *The Commercial Revolution of the Middle Ages, 950–1350*. Englewood Cliffs, New Jersey, 1971.

Lot, Ferdinand, and Robert Fawtier. *Histoire des institutions françaises au moyen âge*. Paris, 1957–1962.

———. *Le premier budget de la monarchie française*. 2 vols. Paris, 1932.

Lucas, H. *The Low Countries and the Hundred Years War, 1326–1347*. Ann Arbor, 1929.

Luchaire, Achille. *Histoire des institutions monarchiques de la France*. Paris, 1891.

———. *Manuel des institutions françaises: Période des capétiens directs*. Paris, 1892.

Lunt, William. *Papal Revenues in the Middle Ages*. New York, 1934.

Luykx, Theo. "Etude sur les chanceliers de Flandre pendant le règne de Jeanne de Constantinople (1205–1244)," *Revue du Nord* 112 (1946), 241–266.

———. *De grafelijke financiële bestuurinstellingen en het grafelijk patrimonium in Vlaanderen tijdens de regering van Margareta van Constantinopel (1244–1278)*. Brussels, 1961.

———. *Het grafelijke geslacht Dampierre en zijn strijd tegen Filips de Schone*. Leuven, 1952.

———. *Johanna van Constantinopel, gravin van Vlaanderen en Henegouwen. Haar leven (1199/1200–1244). Haar regering (1205–1244) vooral in Vlaanderen*. Antwerp, 1946.

———. "De lijst der Brugse baljuws gedurende de XIIIe eeuw," *Handelingen van het genootschap "Société d'Emulation" te Brugge* 88 (1951), 142–150.

Lyon, Bryce. "The *Fief-rente* in the Low Countries," *RBPH* 32 (1954), 161–179.

———. *From Fief to Indenture*. Cambridge, Massachusetts, 1957.

———. "The Money Fief under the English Kings," *English Historical Review* 66 (1951), 161–193.

———, and Adriaan Verhulst. *Medieval Finance: A Comparison of Financial Institutions in Northwestern Europe*. Providence, Rhode Island, 1967.

Macquet, L. *Historie de la ville de Damme, de ces institutions civiles et politiques et de ces monuments.* Bruges, 1856.

Maddens, N. "Bibliografie over de Kortrijkse Lievevrouwekerk, het kapittel en de gravenkapel," *De Leiegouw* 8 (1966), 37–54.

Maes, L. T. "Ambtenarij en bureaukratisering in regering en gewesten van de Zuidelijke Nederlanden de XIIIe–XVe eeuw," *Tijdschrift voor Geschiedenis* 90 (1977), 350–357.

Mannier, E. *Les Flamands à la bataille de Cassel.* Paris, 1863.

Marechal, J. *Bijdrage tot de geschiedenis van het Bankwezen te Brugge.* Bruges, 1955.

Martens, M. *L'administration du domaine ducal en Brabant au moyen âge (1250–1406).* Brussels, 1954.

Melis, Frederigo. *Storia della Ragioneria.* Bologna, 1950.

Mertens, J. "Les confiscation dans la châtellenie du Franc de Bruges après la bataille de Cassel (1329)," *HKCG* 134 (1968), 239–284.

Meulenaere, Pierre François de. *Documenta capituli Curtracensis.* 5 vols.

Monier, Raymond. *Les institutions centrales du comté de Flandre de la fin du IXe siècle.* Paris, 1944.

———. *Les institutions financières du comté de Flandre du XIe siècle à 1384.* Paris and Lille, 1948.

———. "Les relations entre les officiers du comte de Flandre et les bourgeois de Lille à la fin du XIIIe siècle," *Bulletin de la commission historique du département du Nord* 35 (1938), 302–308.

Morel, P. *Les lombards dans la Flandre française et le Hainaut.* Lille, 1908.

Murray, J. M., and Walter Prevenier. *Noteries Public in Medieval Flanders (1281–1450).* Forthcoming in the publications of the Commission Royale d'Histoire (Brussels).

Mus, O. *Prisma van de geschiedenis van Ieper.* Ypres, 1974.

Nicholas, David. "Crime and Punishment in Fourteenth Century Ghent," *RBPH* 48 n. 2 (1970), 289–334, and 48 n. 4 (1970), 1141–1176.

———. *Town and Countryside in Fourteenth-Century Flanders.* Bruges, 1971.

———. *The Van Arteveldes of Ghent: The Varieties of Vendetta and the Hero in History.* Ithaca, 1988.

Nowé, H. *Les baillis comtaux de Flandre des origines à la fin de XIVe siècle.* Brussels, 1929.

———. "Fonctionnaires flamands passès au service royal durant la guerre de Flandre (fin du XIIIe siècle)," *Revue du Nord* 10 (1924), 257–286.

———. "L'intervention du receveur de Flandre dans l'administration de la justice au XVIe siècle," *Handelingen der Maatschappij voor Geschiedenis en Oudheidkunde te Gent* 32 (1924), 78–93.

———. "Plaintes et enquêtes relative à la gestion des baillis comtaux de Flandre aux XIIIe et XIVe siècle," *RBPH* 3 (1924), 75–105.

———. "Les sénéchaux du comte de Flandre aux XIe et XIIe siècle," in *Mélanges Henri Pirenne* 1 (1936), 335–343.

Ozanam, Didier. "Les receveurs de Champagne," in *Recueil de travaux offert à Clovis Brunel* 2 (Paris, 1955), 335–348.

Pauw, Napoleon de. "Les Mirabello, dits van Halen," *Biographie Nationale* 14, Brussels, 1897, 870–882.

Perroy, Edouard. *The Hundred Years War*. Translated by B. Wells. New York, 1965.

Piot, Charles. "L'armement des côtes de Flandre," *HKCG* 4th series 11 (1883), 169–178.

Piquet, Jules. *Des banquiers au moyen âge. Les Templiers. Etude sur leurs opérations financières*. Paris, 1939.

Pirenne, Henri. *Bibliographie de l'histoire de Belgique*. Brussels, 1931.

————. "La chancellerie et les notaires des comtes de Flandre," in *Mélanges Havet*. Paris, 1895, 733–748.

————. "Documents relatifs à l'histoire de Flandre pendant la première moitié du XIV siècle," *HKCG* 5th series 7 (1897), 15–70.

————. "Dras d'Ypres à Novgorod au commencement du XIIe siècle," *RBPH* 9 (1930), 563–566. Reprinted in O. Mus, ed. *Prisma van de Geschiedenis van Ieper*. Ypres, 1974, 356–358.

————. *Histoire de Belgique*. 6 vols. Brussels, 1929.

Piton, Camille. *Les lombards en France et à Paris*. 2 vols. Paris, 1891–1892.

Pollack, F., and F. W. Maitland. *History of English Law*. 2 vols. Cambridge, 1895.

Poston, Michael. "The Trade of Medieval Europe: The North," in the *Cambridge Economic History*. ed. Michael Postan and E. E. Rich. Cambridge, 1952, 119–256.

Prevenier, Walter. "La chancellerie des comtes de Flandre dans le cadre européen à la fin du XII siècle," *Bibliothèque de l'Ecole des Chartes* 125 (1967), 34–39 (also reprinted in *Studia Historica Gandensia* 76).

————. Financiële geschiedenis en geschiedenis der boekhouding in de middeleeuwen en de nieuwe tijd. Unpublished manuscript. Ghent, 1971.

————. "En marge de l'assistance aux pauvres. L'aumônerie des comtes de Flandre et des ducs de Bourgogne," *Recht en instellingen in de oude Nederlanden tijdens de middeleeuwen en de nieuwe tijd. Liber amicorum Jan Buntinx*. Leuven, 1981.

————. "Officials in Town and Countryside in the Low Countries: Social and Professional Developments from the Fourteenth to the Sixteenth Century," *Acta Historiae Neerlandicae* 7 (1974), 1–17.

————, and W. Blockmans. *The Burgundian Netherlands*. Translated by Peter King and Yvette Mead. Cambridge, 1986.

Proost, J. J. "Recherches historiques sur le souverain bailliage de Flandre," *Messager des sciences* 1876, 259–311.

Queller, Donald E. "Diplomatic Personnel Employed by the Counts of Flanders in the Thirteenth Century," *RBPH* 34 (1956), 69–98, 385–422.

————. *The Office of the Ambassador in the Middle Ages*. Princeton, 1976.

————, and Ellen E. Kittell. "Jakemon of Deinze, General Receiver of Flanders, 1292–1300," *RBPH* 61 (1983), 286–321.

Reader in Bureaucracy. Ed. Robert King Merton. Glencoe, Illinois, 1952.

Richerbé, R. *Essai sur le régime financier de la Flandre avant l'institution de la chambre des comptes de Lille*. Paris, 1889.

Rogghé, Paul. "Het Florentijnse geslacht Machet in Vlaanderen," *Appeltjes van het Meetjesland* 16 (1965), 188–196.

———. "Italianen te Gent in the XIVe eeuw. Een merkwaardig Florentijnsche hostellier- en makelaarsgeslacht: de Gualterotti," *Bijdragen voor de Geschiedenis der Nederlanden* 1 (1946), 197–225.

———. "Simon de Mirabello in Vlaanderen," *Appeltjes van het Meetjesland* 9 (1958), 5–55.

Roover, Raymond De. "The Development of Accounting prior to Luca Pacioli According to the Account Books of Medieval Merchants," in *Business, Banking, and Economic Thought in Late Medieval and Early Modern Europe: Selected Studies of Raymond De Roover.* Ed. Julius Kirshner. Chicago, 1974, 119–180.

———. *Money, Banking and Credit in Medieval Bruges.* Cambridge, Massachusetts, 1948.

Sagher, Emile De. *Notice sur les archives communales d'Ypres et documents pour servir à l'histoire de Flandre du XIIIe au XVIe siècle.* Ypres, 1898.

Schepper, Hugo de. *Bronnen voor de geschiedenis van de instellingen in België. Sources de l'histoire des institutions de la Belgique. Handelingen van het colloquium te Brussel. Actes du colloque de Bruxelles. 15–18 4 1975.* Brussels, 1977.

Seyn, Eugene. *Dictionnaire de l'histoire de Belgique.* Liège, no date.

———. *Dictionnaire historique et géographique des communes belges.* 2 vols. Brussels, 1933–1934.

Sivéry, Gérard. *L'économie du royaume de France au siècle de Saint Louis.* Lille, 1983.

Spufford, Peter. *Money and Its Use in Medieval Europe.* London, 1988.

Stengers, J. *Les juifs dans les Pays-Bas au moyen âge.* Brussels, 1950.

Stockman, L. "De brieven van Aalter," *Appeltjes van het Meetjesland* (1969), 96–156.

Strayer, Joseph. *The Administration of Normandy under St. Louis.* Cambridge, Massachusetts, 1932.

———. "Italian Bankers and Philip the Fair," in *Medieval Statecraft and the Perspectives of History.* Ed. Joseph Strayer. Princeton, 1971, 239–247.

———. *The Reign of Philip the Fair.* Princeton, 1980.

Strubbe, E. *Egidius van Breedene (11..–1270).* Bruges, 1942.

———. "De oorkonden uit het vlaamsch gravelijke archief op het S. Donaasfonds te Brugge," *Handelingen van het gennotschap "Société d'Emulation" te Brugge* 77 (Bruges, 1934), 96–112.

Thomas, Paul. "Une commission de bailli sous Guy de Dampierre (1280)," *Bulletin de la commission historique du département du Nord* 34 (1933), 23–25.

———. "Le 9ème cartulaire de Flandre aux Archives du Nord," *Bulletin de la commission historique du département du Nord* 32 (1925), 45–47.

———. "Lacunes des gros briefs de Flandre aux XII et XIII siècles, reconstitutions possibles des gros brief de 1187, 1239, et 1295," *Revue du Nord* 19 (1933), 222–224.

———. "Le pouvoir du comte de Flandre d'après une définition officielle (1318–1324)," *Revue du Nord* 21 (1935), 216–218, 222–228.

———. "La renenghelle de Flandre au XIIIe et XIVe siècle," *Bulletin de la commission historique du département du Nord* 33 (1930), 168–170.

———. "Une source nouvelle pour l'histoire administrative de la Flandre. Le registre de Guillaume d'Auxonne, chancelier de Louis de Nevers, comte de Flandre," *Revue du Nord* 10 (1924), 5–38.

Tihon, C. "Coup d'oeil sur l'établissement des Lombards dans les Pays-Bas aux XIIIe et XIVe siècles," *RBPH* 39 (1961), 334–364.

Tout, F. L. *Chapters in the Administrative History of Medieval England* 6 vols. Manchester, 1920.

Uyttebrouck, A. *Le gouvernement du duché de Brabant au bas moyen âge (1355–1430)*. Brussels, 1975.

Van Caenegem, R. C. *Judges, Legislators, and Professors*. London, 1987.

———. *Geschiedenis van het strafprocesrecht in Vlaanderen van de XIe tot de XIVe eeuw*. Brussels, 1956.

———. *Geschiedenis van het strafrecht in Vlaanderen van de XIe tot de XIVe eeuw*. Brussels, 1954.

———. *Over koningen et bureaucraten*. Amsterdam and Brussels, 1977.

———, and F. L. Ganshof. *Encyclopedie van de geschiedenis der middeleeuwen. Inleiding tot de geschreven bronnen van de geschiedenis der westerse middeleeuwen*. Ghent, 1962.

———. *Kurze Quellenkunde des westeuropäischen Mittelalters. Eine typologische, historische, und bibliographische Einführung*. Gottingen, 1964.

Vandepeerboom, A. *Ypriana. Notices, études, et documents sur Ypres* 7 vols. Bruges, 1878–1883.

Vandermaesen, M. *De besluitvorming in het graafschap Vlaanderen tijdens de XIVde eeuw. Bijdrage tot een politieke sociologie van de Raad en van de raadsheren achter de figuur van Lodewijk II van Nevers (1322–1346)*. Unpublished dissertation, Rijksuniversiteit te Gent, 1977.

———. "Raadsheren en invloeden achter de grafelijke politiek in Vlaanderen in de XVIde eeuw," *Handelingen XLI Congres van de Federahe voor geschiedenis en Oudheidkunde van België* 2, Mechelen, 1971, 212–220.

Van Uyten, R. "Vorst, adel en steden: en driehoeksverhouding in Brabant van de twaalfde tot de zestiende eeuw," *Bijdragen tot de Geschiedenis* 59 (1976), 93–122.

Van Werveke, Hans. "Avesnes en Dampierre. Vlaanderens Vrijheidsoorlog 1244–1305," in *Algemene Geschiedenis der Nederlanden*. Vol. II. Antwerp, 1950, 306–337.

———. "Les clauses financières issues du traité d'Athis (1305)," *Revue du Nord* 32 (1950), 81–93, 126–127.

———. *De gentsche stadsfinanciën in de Middeleeuwen*. Brussels, 1934.

———. "Lodewijk van Male en de eerste Bourgondiërs," in *Algemene geschiedenis der Nederlanden*. Vol. III. Antwerp, 1951, 190–225.

———. *De muntslag in Vlaanderen onder Lodewijk van Male*. Brussels, 1949.

———. "De Nederlanden tegenover Frankrijk, 1305–1346," in *Algemene geschiedenis der Nederlanden*. Vol. III. Antwerp, 1951, 16–62.

———. "Vlaanderen en Brabant, 1305–1346. De sociaal-economische achtergrond," in *Algemene geschiedenis der Nederlanden*. Vol. III. Antwerp, 1951, 1–15.

Varenbergh, E. *Histoire des relations diplomatiques entre le comte de Flandre et l'Angleterre au moyen âge*. Brussels, 1874.

Verhulst, Adriaan. "L'organisation financière du comté de Flandre, du duché de Normandie et du domain royale français du XIe au XIIIe siècle. Des finances domaniales aux finances d'état," in *L'impôt dans le cadre de la ville et de l'état. De belasting in het raam van stad en staat. Colloque Internationaal. Spa 6–9 9 1964. Actes*. Ghent, 1966.

Verwijs, E., and J. Verdam. *Middelnederlandsche Woordenboek*. 11 vols. The Hague, 1907.

Violett, P. *Histoire des institutions politiques et administratives de la France*. Paris, 1890–1903.

Voet, L. "De graven van Vlaanderen en hun domein (864–1191)," *Wetenschappelijke Tijdingen* 8 (1942), 25–32.

Warlop, E. "De baljuws van graven van Vlaanderen en hun domein," *Wetenschappelijke Tijdingen* 8 (1942).

———. "De baljuws van Brugge tot 1300," in *Album Albert Schouteet*. Bruges, 1973, 221–234.

———. *The Flemish Nobility*. 2 vols. Courtrai, 1975.

Weber, Max. "Essentials of Bureaucratic Organization: An Ideal-Type Construction," in *Reader in Bureaucracy*. Ed. Robert King Merton. Glencoe, Illinois, 1952, 18–27.

———. *From Max Weber: Essays in Sociology*. New York, 1958.

———. "Presuppositions and Causes of Bureaucracy," in *Reader in Bureaucracy*. Ed. Robert King Merton. Glencoe, Illinois, 1952, 60–68.

———. *The Theory of Social and Economic Organization*. New York, 1968.

Willard, J. F., and William Morris. *The English Government at Work*. 3 vols. Cambridge, Massachusetts, 1940.

Wood, Charles T. *The French Appanages and the Capetian Monarchy, 1224–1328*. Cambridge, Massachusetts, 1966.

Wyffels, Carlos. "Nieuwe gegevens betreffende een XIIIde eeuwse 'democratische' stedelijke opstand: de Brugse 'Moerlemaye,'" *HKCG* 132 (1966), 37–142.

Ziegler, J. E. "Edward III and Low Countries Finances: 1338–1340, with Particular Emphasis on the Dominant Position of Brabant," *RBPH* 61 (1983), 802–817.

Index

Aalst, 183, 185
  bailiff of, 57 n.41, 74, 135–136 n.56
  and Transport of Flanders, 114, 116,
    152, 155
Aardenburg, 70, 90
  and Transport of Flanders, 114, 116,
    152, 155
Aarschot, 114, 116, 152, 155
Ability, administrative, 157
Account, general, 30, 32, 56 n.20, 85, 86,
    119–125, 146, 163–164 n.27,
    172–176, 186, 198
  audit of, 119, 120, 122, 141, 143–145,
    146, 172–175
    as annual event, 120, 121, 141, 144,
      172–173
    commissioners of, 122, 123, 140,
      144–145, 174
  deficits, 126, 175, 190–191 n.43
  form of, 121–122, 123, 124, 140, 145–
    146, 165 n.34, 174
  genesis of, 110, 119, 122–125
  of Gilles de le Walle, 146, 172, 177
  of Nicholas Guiduche, 141–146, 150,
    162 n.11, 178
  of Ottelin Machet, 141–144, 146, 162
    n.12
  procedure of, 174–176
  surpluses, 126, 175–176, 190–191 n.43
  of Thomas Fini, 119–120, 122–125,
    145
  verification of, 174–175
Accounts, 7, 23, 29, 63, 81–86, 172–176,
    198
  ad hoc, 85, 120, 133 n.36, 198
  of almoners, 28–29
  of bailiffs, 27, 44, 93, 142, 144, 147
  conservation of, 45, 83, 84, 90, 122,
    174, 177
  of farmers, 28–29
  form of, 174, 177
  gros brief, 14 n.11, 39 n.62, 86, 103 n.99
  increase in numbers of, 61, 82, 96
  of judicial revenues, 178, 192 n.65
  language of, 134 n.46

  as management, 134 n.36
  of mintmasters, 177
  of receivers, 28–29, 144
  separate individual, 83–84, 104 n.102,
    177–178
  sophistication of, 134 n.46
  of towns, 60, 63, 165 n.40, 173
  See also Account, general; Audit; Rec-
    ords, financial
Ackre, William, 134 n.37
Administration, 2–3, 4, 8, 9, 10, 11, 13,
    17, 20, 24, 27, 30, 52, 90, 129,
    130, 137 n.76, 157, 170–171, 172,
    176, 186, 196–197, 199, 203
  central, 1, 3, 4, 6, 7, 11, 12, 15, 43, 54
    n.1, 62, 80, 93, 94, 177, 180, 197,
    200, 202, 205
  costs of, 25
  development of, 2, 11, 33, 151, 197,
    203–204
  districts, 18
  efficiency of, 65, 103 n.9, 140, 150, 173,
    197
  experience in, 145, 159, 166 n.39
  financial, 13 n.6, 15–16, 24–25, 30, 33–
    34, 35 n.12, 48, 62, 80, 124, 128,
    130, 146, 150, 151, 156, 158, 161,
    165–166 n.39, 173, 178, 181, 192,
    196, 200–201
  household, 1, 7, 24, 54, 109, 161, 201
  independence of, 10, 11
  judicial, 8, 9, 172, 178–179, 181, 204
  local, 7, 16–20, 85, 86, 199
  officials, 1, 3–4, 7, 8, 9, 10, 11, 13, 17,
    29, 30, 40, 50, 53, 65, 129, 144,
    148–149, 157, 189 n.29, 200, 202,
    204
  personal, 1, 5, 6–8, 10, 11, 14 n.17, 14
    n.23, 15, 40, 42, 59 n.57, 61, 65,
    70, 80, 81, 97, 129, 144, 149, 202
  public, 7–8, 10, 61, 65, 149, 180
Aenaegen, 182
Aksel, 82, 170
Alin, Henry, 183
Alms, 29

UNIVERSITY OF PENNSYLVANIA PRESS
Middle Ages Series
Edward Peters, General Editor

Edward Peters, ed. *Christian Society and the Crusades, 1198–1229.* Sources in Translation, including The Capture of Damietta by Oliver of Paderborn. 1971

Edward Peters, ed. *The First Crusade: The Chronicle of Fulcher of Chartres and Other Source Materials.* 1971

Katherine Fischer Drew, trans. *The Burgundian Code: The Book of Constitutions or Law of Gundobad and Additional Enactments.* 1972

G. G. Coulton. *From St. Francis to Dante: Translations from the Chronicle of the Franciscan Salimbene (1221–1288).* 1972

Alan C. Kors and Edward Peters, eds. *Witchcraft in Europe, 1110–1700: A Documentary History.* 1972

Richard C. Dales. *The Scientific Achievement of the Middle Ages.* 1973

Katherine Fischer Drew, trans. *The Lombard Laws.* 1973

Edward Peters, ed. *Monks, Bishops, and Pagans: Christian Culture in Gaul and Italy, 500–700.* 1975

Jeanne Krochalis and Edward Peters, ed. and trans. *The World of Piers Plowman.* 1975

Julius Goebel, Jr. *Felony and Misdemeanor: A Study in the History of Criminal Law.* 1976

Susan Mosher Stuard, ed. *Women in Medieval Society.* 1976

Clifford Peterson. *Saint Erkenwald.* 1977

Robert Somerville and Kenneth Pennington, eds. *Law, Church, and Society: Essays in Honor of Stephan Kuttner.* 1977

Donald E. Queller. *The Fourth Crusade: The Conquest of Constantinople, 1201–1204.* 1977

Pierre Riché (Jo Ann McNamara, trans.). *Daily Life in the World of Charlemagne.* 1978

Edward Peters, ed. *Heresy and Authority in Medieval Europe.* 1980

Suzanne Fonay Wemple. *Women in Frankish Society: Marriage and the Cloister, 500–900.* 1981

Edward Peters. *The Magician, the Witch, and the Law.* 1982

Barbara H. Rosenwein. *Rhinoceros Bound: Cluny in the Tenth Century.* 1982

Steven D. Sargent, ed. and trans. *On the Threshold of Exact Science: Selected Writings of Anneliese Maier on Late Medieval Natural Philosophy.* 1982

Benedicta Ward. *Miracles and the Medieval Mind: Theory, Record, and Event, 1000–1215.* 1982

Harry Turtledove, trans. *The Chronicle of Theophanes: An English Translation of* anni mundi *6095–6305 (A.D. 602–813).* 1982

Leonard Cantor, ed. *The English Medieval Landscape.* 1982

Charles T. Davis. *Dante's Italy and Other Essays.* 1984

George T. Dennis, trans. *Maurice's Strategikon: Handbook of Byzantine Military Strategy.* 1984

Thomas F. X. Noble. *The Republic of St. Peter: The Birth of the Papal State, 680–825.* 1984

Kenneth Pennington. *Pope and Bishops: The Papal Monarchy in the Twelfth and Thirteenth Centuries.* 1984

Patrick J. Geary. *Aristocracy in Provence: The Rhône Basin at the Dawn of the Carolingian Age.* 1985

C. Stephen Jaeger. *The Origins of Courtliness: Civilizing Trends and the Formation of Courtly Ideals, 939–1210.* 1985

J. N. Hillgarth, ed. *Christianity and Paganism, 350–750: The Conversion of Western Europe.* 1986

William Chester Jordan. *From Servitude to Freedom: Manumission in the Sénonais in the Thirteenth Century.* 1986

James William Brodman. *Ransoming Captives in Crusader Spain: The Order of Merced on the Christian-Islamic Frontier.* 1986

Frank Tobin. *Meister Eckhart: Thought and Language.* 1986

Daniel Bornstein, trans. *Dino Compagni's Chronicle of Florence.* 1986

James M. Powell. *Anatomy of a Crusade, 1213–1221.* 1986

Jonathan Riley-Smith. *The First Crusade and the Idea of Crusading.* 1986

Susan Mosher Stuard, ed. *Women in Medieval History and Historiography.* 1987

Avril Henry, ed. *The Mirour of Mans Saluacioune.* 1987

María Rosa Menocal. *The Arabic Role in Medieval Literary History.* 1987

Margaret J. Ehrhart. *The Judgment of the Trojan Prince Paris in Medieval Literature.* 1987

Betsy Bowden. *Chaucer Aloud: The Varieties of Textual Interpretation.* 1987

Michael Resler, trans. *EREC by Hartmann von Aue.* 1987

A. J. Minnis. *Medieval Theory of Authorship.* 1988

Uta-Renate Blumenthal. *The Investiture Controversy: Church and Monarchy from the Ninth to the Twelfth Century.* 1988

Robert Hollander. *Boccaccio's Last Fiction: "Il Corbaccio."* 1988

Ralph Turner. *Men Raised from the Dust: Administrative Service and Upward Mobility in Angevin England.* 1988

David Anderson. *Before the Knight's Tale: Imitation of Classical Epic in Boccaccio's* Teseida. 1988

Charlotte A. Newman. *The Anglo-Norman Nobility in the Reign of Henry I: The Second Generation.* 1988

Joseph F. O'Callaghan. *The Cortes of Castile-León, 1188–1350.* 1989

William D. Paden, ed. *The Voice of the Trobairitz: Essays on the Women Troubadors.* 1989

William Chester Jordan. *The French Monarchy and the Jews: From Philip Augustus to the Last Capetians.* 1989

Edward B. Irving, Jr. *Rereading* Beowulf. 1989

David Burr. *Olivi and Franciscan Poverty: The Origins of the* Usus Pauper *Controversy.* 1989

Willene B. Clark and Meradith T. McMunn, eds. *Beasts and Birds of the Middle Ages: The Bestiary and Its Legacy.* 1989

Richard C. Hoffmann. *Land, Liberties, and Lordship in a Late Medieval Countryside: Agrarian Structures and Change in the Duchy of Wrocław.* 1990

J. M. W. Bean. *From Lord to Patron: Lordship in Late Medieval England.* 1990

Mary F. Wack. *Lovesickness in the Middle Ages: The* Viaticum *and Its Commentaries.* 1990

Robert I. Burns, S.J., ed. *Emperor of Culture: Alfonso X the Learned of Castile and His Thirteenth-Century Renaissance.* 1990

E. Ann Matter. *The Voice of My Beloved: The Song of Songs in Western Medieval Christianity.* 1990

Patricia Terry, trans. *Poems of the Elder Edda.* 1990

Ronald E. Surtz. *The Guitar of God: Gender, Power, and Authority in the Visionary World of Mother Juana de la Cruz (1481–1534).* 1990

Nancy Edwards. *The Archaeology of Early Medieval Ireland.* 1990

Lawrence Nees. *A Tainted Mantle: Hercules and the Classical Tradition at the Carolingian Court.* 1991

Anthony K. Cassell and Victoria Kirkham, eds. and trans. *Diana's Hunt. Caccia di Diana. Boccaccio's First Fiction.* 1991

Ellen E. Kittell. *From* Ad Hoc *to Routine: A Case Study in Medieval Bureaucracy.* 1991

Katherine Fischer Drew, trans. *Laws of the Salian Franks.* 1991

Thomas M. Cable. *The English Alliterative Tradition.* 1991

This book has been set in Linotron Galliard. Galliard was designed for Merganthaler in 1978 by Matthew Carter. Galliard retains many of the features of a sixteenth century typeface cut by Robert Granjon but has some modifications which give it a more contemporary look.

Printed on acid-free paper.